Program
Development
in Special
Education

McGraw-Hill Series in Special Education

Robert M. Smith, *Consulting Editor*

Program Development In Special Education

Designing Individualized Education Programs

Paul Wehman, Ph.D
Programs in Mental Retardation
School of Education
Virginia Commonwealth University

Phillip J. McLaughlin, Ed.D
Division for Education of Exceptional Children
College of Education
University of Georgia

With contributions by
Ferol Menzel, Ph.D.
C. Milton Blue, Ph.D.

McGraw-Hill Book Company
New York   St. Louis   San Francisco   Auckland   Bogotá   Hamburg
Johannesburg   London   Madrid   Mexico   Montreal   New Delhi   Panama
Paris   São Paulo   Singapore   Sydney   Tokyo   Toronto

This book was set in Times Roman by Black Dot, Inc. The editors were Phillip A. Butcher and David Dunham; the cover was designed by Jane Moorman; the production supervisor was John Mancia. The drawings were done by VIS.
R. R. Donnelley & Sons Company was printer and binder.

See Acknowledgments on pages 440-443. Copyrights included on this page by reference.

PROGRAM DEVELOPMENT IN SPECIAL EDUCATION

Library of Congress Cataloging in Publication Data

Wehman, Paul.

    Program development in special education.
    (McGraw-Hill series in special education)
    Includes bibliographies and index.
    1. Handicapped children—Education—United States. 2. Individualized instruction.
I. McLaughlin, Phillip J., joint author.
II. Title.
LC4031.W43   371.9'043   79-22846
ISBN 0-07-068991-1

Contents

2

CURRICULUM DEVELOPMENT

Preface

Special education is currently going through a steady period of growth and introspection. New developments in the past decade are being viewed as major breakthroughs for handicapped individuals. Parent advocacy, legal decisions, important legislative mandates, new Department of Education priorities toward in-service, and continued upgrading of personnel preparation programs in special education are major forces in offering new or expanded services for handicapped children. For the first time, we are witnessing handicapped children receiving appropriate educational services alongside their nonhandicapped peers. Significantly, many regular education administrators and teachers are becoming aware of the rights of handicapped individuals.

During the dramatic sequence of events which occurred between 1970 and 1980, a continual stream of special education literature became available. Certainly many of the new materials and texts filled important gaps in our knowledge; regrettably, many did not. We have undertaken a review of the better texts in the field, especially those which address teaching methods, and have tried in developing *Program Development in Special Education* not to repeat similar efforts. Our work has spanned approximately three years and integrates the major tenets of Public Law 94–142 with critical program development principles. We have relied heavily on learning theory and other empirically verifiable practices to guide our suggestions and recommendations for program planning and implementation.

This text is for undergraduate and graduate special education courses in methods and/or curriculum. Part One, "Program Development," presents an orderly plan for teaching handicapped individuals. This systematic instruction process involves assessment, setting objectives, task analysis, instructional strategies, and program evaluation. Three chapters emphasize translating learning principles into practical instructional strategies. Part Two, "Curriculum Development," presents detailed information on a range of content areas. Chapters on self-care, motor development, language and speech, functional academics, vocational education and placement, and recreation provide content relevant to teaching handicapped students. Each curriculum chapter contains sample lesson plans based on the learning principles described in Part One.

It is our hope that *Program Development in Special Education* will help preservice and in-service teachers understand how to teach relevant curriculum through systematic instruction. In writing the text, we have tried to follow the instructional strategies we prescribe for teachers.

ACKNOWLEDGMENTS

There are a number of individuals we want to thank for their help in preparing this book. First, thanks go to our colleagues Ferol Menzel and C. Milton Blue for contributing Chapters 9 and 10, respectively. These two chapters are the best two curriculum chapters in the book. Second, thanks go to Kathryn Blake for allowing us to use so much of her material. Chapters 4 and 5 are based on her trailblazing work in translating learning theory research into instructional methods. Third, thanks go to Ronald Eaves for his help in structuring the assessment chapter (2). This chapter is based on his systems approach to assessment. We are also grateful to Sheila Myers and Libby Fouche for their extraordinary typing skills.

Paul Wehman originated the idea to write this book. Therefore, his name appears first. However, we both contributed equally in the actual writing of the text.

Paul Wehman
Phillip J. McLaughlin

Part One

Program Development

Chapter 1

Implementing Public Law 94-142

This chapter presents information to help teachers implement Public Law (P.L.) 94-142, Education for All Handicapped Children Act. The principle features of the law are highlighted, and the component parts and steps in developing and implementing individualized education programs are reviewed.

Learning Goals

You should be able to answer the following questions when you finish this chapter:

- What is the purpose of P.L. 94-142? Explain if all states are required to provide a free appropriate public education to all handicapped children from age 3 to 21.
- How does the definition of education for P.L. 94-142 differ from traditional definitions?
- What are the due process procedures guaranteed by P.L. 94-142?
- What is the difference between placement and the delivery of services? Why is it important to know the difference?

- How and when is a child's placement determined? Explain the concept of a continuum of alternative placements.
- What is an individualized education program (IEP)? Briefly describe the required content and steps in developing an IEP.
- What is the primary question to ask when you specify the goals for a handicapped child?
- How does P.L. 94-142 define special education and related services?
- Does a handicapped child have to be integrated into regular educational programs? Explain your answer.
- What are the steps in the program-development process? Explain how the steps are related.

Within the past decade, dramatic changes have occured in the field of special education. Severely and multihandicapped children have begun to receive public school education for the first time. In all states, it is mandatory that all school-age handicapped children receive a free appropriate public education. School systems can no longer exclude or postpone the education of handicapped children on the grounds that they cannot learn, their handicap is too severe, programs do not exist, or for any other reason. Furthermore, handicapped children must be educated with nonhandicapped children as much as possible. For many mildly handicapped children this may mean partial or full placement into a regular education classroom.

These events represent significant milestones in the development of educational services for handicapped individuals. Through the combined forces of parent advocacy, the courts, and landmark legislation, special education has evolved to a point where it can begin to provide all handicapped students with an equal opportunity for an education. It is through Public Law 94-142 that the legislative mandate for education of handicapped children is provided.

Public Law 94-142 requires that a written individualized education program, known as the IEP, be developed for every handicapped child who requires special education and related services. The IEP is the keystone to effectively complying with P.L. 94-142. As such, the IEP is the central building block to providing a free appropriate public education for each handicapped child. This book has been written to provide information relevant to designing and implementing IEPs.

The plan of this chapter is to highlight the principle features of Public Law 94-142 by summarizing its major aspects. The latter half of the chapter is a review of the components involved in designing individualized education programs. A sample IEP is also included in this chapter.

HIGHLIGHTS OF PUBLIC LAW 94-142

Right to Education

Before 1970 public schools were not required to serve the more-severely handicapped child. What this usually meant was that parents with children who were not toilet-trained, who exhibited severe behavior problems, who had serious medical problems, or who were nonverbal could not get their child accepted into a special education class (Sontag, Burke, & York, 1973). These children were typically excluded and were either kept at home, institutionalized, or in some communities attended day care centers. Public Law 94-142 now requires, however, that all school-age handicapped children be provided a free and appropriate education by the local public school division. School age is defined in P.L. 94-142 as ranging from age 3 to 21 except in states where the education of 3 to 5 and 18 to 21 age ranges would be inconsistent with state law or practice or any court decree.

The impetus for this positive development came about as a result of two precedent-setting right-to-education lawsuits. The first lawsuit was *Pennsylvania Association for Retarded Children (PARC) v. Commonwealth of Pennsylvania* (1972). Among other things, this suit asked that all school-age retarded children, regardless of severity of handicap, be provided a free public education. The court agreed with most of the issues raised in the suit and appointed two court masters to oversee the progress which Pennsylvania made in (1) identifying retarded children and (2) making an appropriate classroom placement for each child. For details about specific issues in the PARC case, consult Burt's (1975) in-depth discussion. Kuriloff, True, Kirp, and Buss (1974) noted that the Pennsylvania agreement has been only partially effective in its implementation. However, these authors point out that the vast majority of Pennsylvania's retarded children are now in some form of program and that many school districts have developed new programs to meet the needs of the severely handicapped students.

Following the PARC consent agreement, another similar case, *Mills v. Board of Education of the District of Columbia* (1972), was brought on behalf of all out-of-school handicapped children. The outcome of the Mills decision was a court order providing for public education for the complete spectrum of handicapped children.

In order to gain perspective on the rapid developments in special education in the past decade, it is important to understand the critical role of the right-to-education litigation. These cases have had a major impact on the development of new specialized teaching training programs (Stainback, Stainback, & Maurer, 1976; Brown & York, 1974) and specialized therapy services in classrooms, e.g., occupational therapy. These results have also met serious resistance in some states. There are a number of administrators and teachers in regular and special education who do not feel that education of severely and multihandicapped children justifies the large expenditure of money in times when financial resources are tight (Burton, Burton, & Hirshoren, 1977a, 1977b; Ross, 1977).

Public Law 94-142, however, is quite clear on the right-to-education issue. The purpose of the law is stated as follows:

> It is the purpose of this Act to assure that all handicapped children have available to them, within the time periods specified, a free appropriate public education which emphasizes special education and related services designed to meet their unique needs. (Public Law 94-142, 1975, Sec. 3, c)

Closely related to this statement of purpose is the definition of education. In discussing P.L. 94-142, Abeson and Zettel (1977) stated that "education cannot be defined traditionally but rather must be considered as a continuous process by which individuals learn to cope and function within their environment" (p. 122). This definition emerged from the PARC litigation in 1972. Translated to curriculum planning, it means that self-care skills for the severely handicapped or vocational training for the mildly handicapped is no different from teaching reading or math to nonhandicapped children.

Due Process Procedures for Children and Parents

The law requires certain procedural safeguards against violating the pupil's rights as the assessment team and the IEP committee go about locating, evaluating, planning, and providing education for the pupil. The intent of due process is to allow for fair consideration of the interests of all who are involved in the education of the pupil, including the parents. These due process procedures are also rooted in case law. Both the PARC and Mills cases required specific due process procedures to be established.

Public Law 94-142 ensures that all the rights created by the law are guaranteed to handicapped children, their families, and the public schools. Abeson and Zettel (1977) have specified the required elements of due process in P.L. 94-142 as follows:

1 Written notification before evaluation. In addition, the right to an interpreter/translator if the family's native language is not English (unless it is clearly not feasible to do so).
2 Written notification when initiating or refusing to initiate a change in educational placement.
3 Opportunity to present complaints regarding the identification, evaluation, placement, or the provision of a free appropriate education.
4 Opportunity to obtain an independent educational evaluation of the child.
5 Access to all relevant records.
6 Opportunity for an impartial due process hearing including the right to:
   a Receive timely and specific notice of the hearing.
   b Be accompanied and advised by counsel and by individuals with special knowledge or training with respect to the problems of children with handicaps.
   c Confront, cross examine, and compel the attendance of witnesses.
   d Present evidence:
      1 Written or electronic verbatim record of the hearing.
      2 Written findings of fact and decisions.
7 The right to appeal the findings and decisions of the hearing. (pp. 125–126)

Right to Nondiscriminatory Testing and Evaluation

Court cases such as the PARC and Mills were characterized by getting children, who were previously excluded, into school. However, there have also been court cases which pertain to placement of handicapped children. The placement cases usually reflect unfair placement of a child into a special education class. Unfair or biased testing has been a frequently cited reason for labeling children retarded; this has been particularly true with black children who may be economically disadvantaged (Dunn, 1968).

MacMillan (1977) has done an excellent job of summarizing several of the more common criticisms of placement procedures:

1 "Tests used are biased and inappropriate" (p. 290). Since many of the intelligence tests which are used for placement of pupils are heavily weighted with verbal items that tap a child's familiarity with the English language, the true learning abilities of children from racial and cultural minorities may be marked.

2 "Test administration is often performed incompetently" (p. 291). The ability of the examiner to administer the test fairly and therefore in a reliable fashion is critical to an accurate assessment of the child's learning ability. The importance of reliability in evaluation is discussed in more depth in Chapter 7.

3 "Parents are not involved" (p. 291). Participation of the parents in the assessment process is a helpful, and maybe critical, factor in determining the child's true learning capacity. The public law mandates parental involvement in the development of individual education programs.

4 "Special education programs are inadequate" (p. 291). Many feel that special education and vocational education programs are not effective. If this is so, then it follows that many handicapped students will never leave the special class.

5 "Placement is stigmatizing" (p. 291). Labeling a child mentally retarded or learning-disabled is viewed by some as causing irreparable damage to social adjustment and the self-concept. It is argued that once a child is labeled handicapped, it is very difficult to remove the label.

A number of court decisions have paved the way for the nondiscriminatory testing and evaluation component of Public Law 94-142. In *Hobson v. Hansen* (1967) it was ruled that children could not be placed into different ability tracks on the basis of test performance. This was further supported in California by black students who challenged whether group tests of intelligence were a valid basis for educational placement [*Spangler v. Board of Education* (1970)]. It was ruled that this was a faulty means of placing pupils Since then other court cases have challenged placement of black children [*Larry P. v. Riles* (1972)], Mexican-Americans [*Diana v. State Board of Education* (1970)], and Indian children [*Guadalupe v. Tempe Elementary School District* (1971)] in special classrooms for educable mentally retarded (EMR) students. As might be expected, these court cases have had a significant impact on testing and evaluation practices addressed in P.L. 94-142.

Because of the relevance of nondiscriminatory testing and evaluation to the assessment process in designing an individualized education program, this area as well as the specific federal regulations in P.L. 94-142 concerning nondiscriminatory testing, are discussed in depth in Chapter 2. In brief, P.L. 94-142 requires that all evaluation materials and procedures used to assess handicapped children be nondiscriminatory.

Placement and the Requirement of Least-Restrictive Environment

The child's placement is where he or she is assigned to receive instruction. There is a distinction between placement and the delivery of services. Placement is the child's location for services to be delivered. Instructional services are the activities designed to help the child meet the goals and objectives of his or her program. Placement and services are not synonyms. Placement alone does not guarantee that the child will receive appropriate educational services.

The child's placement is determined by the committee writing the individualized education program. The placement decision is one of the last decisions the committee makes. Public Law 94-142 is specific about this point. The child's placement is determined by the services he or she needs to meet the goals and objectives of the educational program. The child's goals and objectives are specified before, not after, placement.

There are many options for locating children for the delivery of educational services. Usually these options include regular-class placement, resource-room placement, self-contained special-class placement, separate day school placement, home or hospital placement, and residential placement. Public Law 94-142 requires that children be placed in the least-restrictive environment in which they can get along. This means that handicapped children must not be separated from nonhandicapped children any more than is necessary to fit instruction to their special needs.

According to P.L. 94-142, each state education agency must ensure that in local school divisions:

> **1** To the maximum extent appropriate, handicapped children, including children in public or private institutions or other care facilities, are educated with children who are not handicapped; and
>
> **2** Special classes, separate schooling or other removal of handicapped children from the regular educational environment occurs only when the nature or severity of the handicap is such that education in regular classes with the use of supplementary aids and services cannot be achieved satisfactorily. (Federal Register, 1977, 121.550)

Placement represents a difficult problem. The committee must decide how specialized, i.e., restrictive, the placement should be. Since the studies to determine how much specialization is actually necessary to fit instruction to special needs have not been completed (Blake, 1976), the committee's decision is difficult.

The idea of a continuum of alternative placement from the least restrictive to the most restrictive will help the committee decide on the most-appropriate placement. Deno (1970) first illustrated this idea as a cascade of options ranging from the least-restrictive (regular classroom) to the most-restrictive placement (residential school). Figure 1-1 depicts a cascade of placement options. The pyramid arrangement of the cascade indicates the proportionate number of

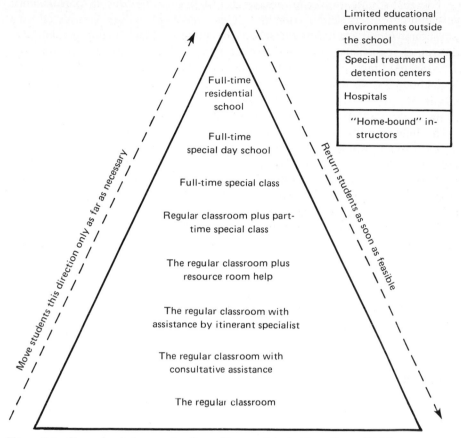

Limited educational
environments outside
the school

| Special treatment and detention centers |
| Hospitals |
| "Home-bound" instructors |

Full-time
residential
school

Full-time
special day school

Full-time special class

Regular classroom plus part-
time special class

The regular classroom plus
resource room help

The regular classroom with
assistance by itinerant specialist

The regular classroom with
consultative assistance

The regular classroom

Move students this direction only as far as necessary

Return students as soon as feasible

Figure 1-1   Cascade of placement options. (Source: Adapted from Deno, 1970.)

handicapped children served in each setting; that is, more handicapped children
will be served in the less-restrictive environments.

The Individualized Education Program

Public Law 94-142 requires that all handicapped children have an individualized
education program (IEP) developed and implemented. The IEP, in many ways,
represents an educational blueprint of the child's program. It should be a
dynamic plan which is sensitive to the changes and progress of the child. It
should not be a piece of paper which is rapidly completed and then shifted into
one corner of the teacher's desk. The IEP is developed in a meeting by a
representative of the local education agency (LEA), who shall be qualified to
provide, or supervise the production of, specially designed instruction to meet
the pupil's unique needs; the teacher; the pupil's parents or guardians; and
whenever appropriate, the pupil. The LEA representative should be able to
guarantee implementation of the IEP.

The IEP should reflect an assessment of the child's present performance levels in different curriculum domains. This assessment will be conducted by a team of individuals, including the school psychologist, teacher, parents, and any educational specialists who may provide specific information relevant to the child's needs. Once these data are collected, the IEP committee reviews the information. From this review, annual goals and short-term instructional objectives must be written, a statement of special services detailed, and a method of program evaluation described. Specific dates as to when the IEP is to be implemented must also be provided. If it is the decision of the IEP committee to place the child in a special class but provide for partial involvement in either a regular class, a physical education class with nonhandicapped peers, or recess, this should be stated. In sum, the IEP committee must complete essentially two major tasks: (1) review the child's data and formulate a viable IEP and (2) make an appropriate placement which is in accordance with the child's needs.

Public Law 94-142 requires the following content be included in all IEPs:

1   A statement of the child's present levels of performance;

2   A statement of annual goals, including short-term instructional objectives;

3   A statement of the specific special education and related services to be provided to the child, and the extent to which the child will be able to participate in regular educational programs;

4   The projected dates for initiation of services and the anticipated duration of services;

5   Appropriate objective criteria and evaluation procedures and schedules for determining, on at least, an annual basis, whether the short-term instructional objectives are being achieved. (Federal Register, 1977, 121a.346)

The first half of this book addresses how to develop an IEP. Each area of the IEP is discussed in depth. Although the IEP does not require a detailed description of instructional sequences and teaching procedures, it is necessary for the teacher to have this information regardless of the category of handicapped children in the class. Therefore, several chapters are presented which will provide teachers with a greater understanding of instructional strategies required to actually implement the IEP.

COMPONENTS OF THE IEP

Developing an IEP is a difficult task. Blake (in press) has made the job easier by specifying a systematic approach to its development. First, Blake took the content requirements of P.L. 94-142 and organized them into component parts. She then specified a step-by-step approach to developing the IEP. Figure 1-2 depicts the relationship among components and the 17 steps in developing an IEP. Table 1-1 presents the steps in more detail. Following is a brief description of the major components of the IEP.

DEVELOPERS

1. Choose/identify the developers of the IEP.

TIME PROJECTIONS

2. Specify the time projections for beginning,
evaluating, and revising
the IEP.

PRESENT PERFORMANCE
LEVELS

3. Collect evidence about the
pupil's present performance
levels.
4. Organize evidence.
5. Specify principles for individualizing instruction.

GOALS: OBJECTIVES
AND RATES

6. Specify the pupil's instructional objectives.
7. Specify the pupil's rates of
instruction.

SPECIAL EDUCATION
SERVICES

8. Select the pupil's in-
structional materials
and strategies.

RELATED SERVICES

9. Select the pupil's therapeutic services.
10. Select the pupil's equipment.
11. Select the pupil's transportation.

SERVICE DELIVERY
ARRANGEMENTS

12. Select the pupil's placement option.
13. Check facilities.
14. Identify the pupil's
extracurricular activ-
ities.

EVALUATION

15. Specify the objective
criteria and evaluation
procedures for each
objective.
16. Monitor the pupil's
progress.
17. Make recommendations.

Figure 1-2 Relationships among components and steps in the individualized education program
(IEP). (Source: Blake, in press.)

Table 1-1   Steps in Doing an Individual Education Program

Components	Steps
Developers	1 Choose/identify the developer of the individual education program.
Time projections	2 Specify time projections for beginning, evaluating, and revising the pupil's individual education program.

Present performance levels	3 Collect evidence about the pupil's present performance levels.
	  a Get evidence about the pupil's present performance levels.
	  b Observe due process for evaluation.
	  c Assure protection in evaluation.
	4 Organize evidence about the pupil's present performance levels.
	  a Use techniques for synthesizing evidence about the pupil's present performance levels.
	  b Observe confidentiality requirements.
	5 Specify principles for individualizing instruction on the basis of the pupil's present performance levels.

Goals: objectives and rates	6 Specify the pupil's instructional objectives.
	7 Specify the pupil's rates of instruction.
	  a Do a time schedule for each domain.
	  b Do a time schedule across domains.

Instructional services	8 Select the pupil's instructional materials and strategies.

Related services	9 Select the pupil's therapeutic services.
	  a Summarize needed therapy.
	  b Describe therapeutic services.
	10 Select the pupil's equipment.
	11 Select the pupil's transportation.

Service-delivery arrangements	12 Select the pupil's placement option.
	  a Specify school location(s).
	  b Observe due process in placement.
	  c Make personnel arrangements.
	13 Check facilities.
	14 Identify the pupil's extracurricular activities.

Evaluation	15 Specify the objective criteria and evaluation procedures for each objective. 16 Monitor the pupil's progress. 17 Make recommendations.

Source: Blake (in press).

Summary of Present Levels of Performance

The only way in which accurate statements can be made about current levels of performance is to have functional up-to-date assessment information. In fact, the entire IEP is completely dependent on accurate assessment information and the appropriate analysis of these data. The current levels of performance for handicapped children may include data on gross motor skills, communication skills, social skills, self-help skills, cognitive and academic skills, specific health concerns (medication, seizures, allergies, illness, etc.), and physical involvement (positioning).

Annual Goals

Annual goals, including short-term instructional objectives, must be written for the special education and related services needed by the handicapped child. The goals need to be related to the statement of present levels of performance. The primary question to ask at this point is, What do we want the child to be able to do at the end of the year? In reality, this question should have also been addressed during the assessment phase. Basically, this idea has to do with the careful consideration of attainable goals and the subsequent programming needed to reach these goals. Specific short-term objectives need to be developed that will lead to the accomplishment of each yearly goal. These objectives should be stated in terms of observable child behavior with specific criteria for success. Each specific instructional objective and each instructional activity must relate to some future functional behavior. The careful selection of meaningful, pertinent yearly goals is the major safeguard that prevents inappropriate instruction.

Specific Educational Services Provided

This component requires the committee to list all special services that are needed to meet the child's specific needs. These services include special education and necessary related services. Public Law 94-142 defines these services precisely. Special education means the following:

> 1   Special education means specially designed instruction, at no cost to the parent, to meet the unique needs of a handicapped child, including classroom instruction, instruction in physical education, home instruction, and instruction in hospitals and institutions.
> 2   The term includes speech pathology, or any other related service, if the service consists of specially designed instruction, at no cost to the parents, to meet the unique needs of a handicapped child, and is considered "special education" rather than a "related service" under State standards.
> 3   The term also includes vocational education if it consists of specially designed instruction, at no cost to the parents, to meet the unique needs of a handicapped child. (Federal Register, 1977, 121a.14)

Related services mean the following:

Transportation and such developmental, corrective, and other supportive services as are required to assist a handicapped child to benefit from special education, and includes speech pathology and audiology, psychological services, physical and occupational therapy, recreation, early identification and assessment of disabilities in children, counseling services, and medical services for diagnostic or evaluation purposes. The term also includes school health services, social work services in schools, and parent counseling and training. (Federal Register, 1977, 121a.13)

Service-Delivery Arrangements

This component requires the IEP committee to specify the arrangements for delivering the special education and related services. The issues of concern are placement in the least-restrictive environment, personnel and facilities, and extracurricular activities. The committee must include a statement describing the extent to which the handicapped student will be integrated into regular educational programs. In some cases, integration might not be appropriate. Each committee, however, must ask the question, Can this child profit from interaction with the nonhandicapped? If the answer is affirmative, provisions for such interaction must be specified.

Evaluation Criteria and Dates of Services

The projected beginning date and duration of services for each objective must be recorded on the IEP. The precise method and criteria for evaluating each objective must also be specified. Good behavioral objectives, by definition, give this information. Each objective should include exactly what the *child* will do, to what observable criteria, and under which specific circumstances. Schedules for determining, at least on a yearly basis, whether the goals and objectives are being achieved must be included in the IEP.

In Table 1-2 a sample IEP is provided for a young handicapped child. Although there are a variety of IEP formats which may be used, this plan reflects all major components of an IEP.

THE PROGRAM-DEVELOPMENT PROCESS

The program-development process is a *systematic* approach to developing and implementing an IEP. The program-development process set forth in this book is an orderly plan for teaching handicapped children. The steps in this process are assessment, setting goals and instructional objectives, task analysis, instructional strategies, and program evaluation. The relationship of these steps is shown in Figure 1-3. The steps in the program-development process are described below. The remainder of the book presents information on how to implement this systematic approach to teaching handicapped children.

Assessment

An important initial step in writing the IEP is to collect information relevant to the child's true performance level. This requires interviewing parents and

Table 1-2   Sample Program Form for Susan: Individualized Education Program

Child's Name: ___Susan_____   School: ___Morrison_____

Date of Birth: ___9-1-71_____   Age: __9_____

Placement Recommendation and Justification: ___Self-contained special class:_____

This program provides the least-restrictive educational opportunity for Susan in which

she can adequately function._____

Date of Reevaluation: ___February 1983_____

Summary of Present Levels of Performance:

(Specific data should be appended to this report.)
   Gross Motor. Susan can jump, run, climb, and ride a tricycle.
   Self-Help. She can dress and undress, toilet, and feed herself.
   Communication. She says her own name, cookie, juice, and momma, and uses these
   appropriately.
   Social. Susan plays in isolation but seeks out adults.
   Preacademic. She can match simple objects.
   Psychological. Susan is severely retarded intellectually.

Yearly Goals:

1   Susan will throw a ball (6-in. diameter) a distance of 10 ft to a peer.
2   Susan will follow the rules at lunch time without 1:1 teacher supervision.
3   Susan will initiate appropriate greetings to the teacher each morning.
4   Susan will learn the function use of 3 objects (spoon, cup, hairbrush).
5   Susan will engage in parallel play with 1 or 2 peers 25% of the time.
6   Susan will match 3 words (toilet, eat, drink) to appropriate pictures.

Regularly Planned Activities with Nonhandicapped Children:

Susan will have lunch with nonhandicapped peers. The lunchroom aide will encourage interaction between Susan and the other children.

Committee Recommendations for Specific Special Education Services (Include physical education plan, special media or materials.):

1   The language therapist will help teacher to establish the greetings program and other
    spontaneous speech programs.
2   School nurse will consult with the home concerning mealtime manners.
3   Physical education teacher will consult with the teacher to develop a program for ball
    throwing and bicycle riding.

Medical Concerns (Drugs, Seizures, etc.):

Medication for seizures (no seizures in past 2 years) administered by teacher at lunch (1 pill,
10 mg Dilantin). No restrictions on physical activity.

Proven Reinforcers:

Susan consistently works for all types of sugar-coated cereal and orange juice. Social praise
is becoming reinforcing, but acquisition tasks should be pursued with edibles. Music, especially country, has shown promise during gross motor activities.

Table 1-2 (Continued)

Precautions:

1   In the past, Susan has been known to have violent temper tantrums. The most effective technique to handle these is to remove Susan from the room and ignore her. She has not run, destroyed property, or harmed herself once removed from the class.

2   Seizures have been controlled for the past 2 years. However, Susan has had grand mal seizures in the past. If she has a seizure, use standard procedures and inform the parents. Her physician is monitoring her medications, and the exact time of the seizure as well as the duration should be noted.

Physical Assessment:

Susan has no major physical problems. Her left hand, however, is somewhat nonfunctional, so all fine motor activities should be directed toward her right hand. Physical therapy has been discontinued for her left hand under recommendation from her physician.

Dates of Committee Meetings:

September 5, 1980

Child's Name: ___Susan___

Long-Term-Goal Statement: Susan will throw a 6-in. diameter ball to a peer at a distance of 10 ft.

Short-term objectives (include evaluation criteria)	Specific educa-tional and/or support services	Persons responsible for imple-mentation	Beginning, end date	Review date
a Susan will throw ball, with teacher assis-tance, on 5 of 5 trials, 2 consecutive days.	Physical education teacher/consult	Teacher/ aide	9/80 10/1/80 change criteria.	10/1/80
b Susan will throw ball toward teacher, with-out assistance, on 5 of 5 trials, 2 consecutive days.	Physical education teacher	Teacher/ aide	10/1/80 11/1/80	11/1/80
c Susan will throw ball to teacher and another child for a distance of 2 ft on 5 of 5 trials, 2 consecutive days.	Physical education teacher	Teacher/ aide	11/1/80 12/15/80	12/15/80
d Susan will throw ball to teacher and child for a distance of 5 ft on 5 of 5 trials, 2 con-secutive days.	Physical education teacher	Teacher/ aide	1/4/81 3/1/81	3/1/81
e Susan will throw ball to child a distance of 10 ft on 5 of 5 trials, 2 consecutive days.	Physical education teacher	Teacher/ aide	3/5/81 5/15/81	5/15/81

Table 1-2 (Continued)

Child's Name: ___Susan___

Long-Term-Goal Statement: Susan will follow the rules at lunchtime without

1:1 teacher supervision.

(Rules are: no disturbing others; stay in lunchroom)

Short-term objectives (include evaluation criteria)	Specific educational and/or support services	Persons responsible for implementation	Beginning, end date	Review date
a Susan will stay in lunchroom with teacher attention.		Teacher	9/80 10/80	10/1/80
b Susan will stay in lunchroom without teacher attention.		Teacher	10/1/80 12/1/80	12/1/80
c Susan will not disturb other children, with teacher attention.		Teacher	1/4/81 3/1/81	3/1/81
d Susan will not disturb other children, without teacher attention.		Teacher	3/1/81 5/30/81	5/30/81

Child's Name: ___Susan___

Long-Term-Goal Statement: Susan will initiate appropriate greetings to the

teacher each morning.

Short-term objectives (include evaluation criteria)	Specific educational and/or support services	Persons responsible for implementation	Beginning, end date	Review date
a Susan will imitate teacher's saying "hello" 5 of 5 trials.	Language therapist	Teacher	9/80 10/1/80	10/1/80
b Susan will imitate teacher's saying "hello" in morning on 3 consecutive days.	Language therapist	Teacher	10/1/81 1/1/81	1/1/81
c Susan will imitate content with teacher and imitate "hello" on 3 consecutive mornings.	Language therapist	Teacher	11/1/80 1/15/81	1/15/81
d Susan will imitate content and say "hello" to teacher.	Language therapist	Teacher	1/15/81 4/15/81	4/15/81

Child's Name: ___Susan___

Long-Term-Goal Statement: Susan will identify function of 3 objects (spoon,

cup, hairbrush).

Table 1-2 (Continued)

Short-term objectives (include evaluation criteria)	Specific educational and/or support services	Persons responsible for implementation	Beginning, end date	Review date
a Susan will imitate teacher and say "spoon," with no distractors; 5 of 5 trials on 2 consecutive days (repeat for cup and hairbrush).	Language therapist	Teacher	9/80 11/15/80	11/15/80
b Susan will say "spoon" (cup, hairbrush) upon presentation; with no distractors, 5 of 5 trials on 2 consecutive days.	Language therapist	Teacher	11/15/80 2/30/81	2/30/81
c Susan will say "spoon" (cup, hairbrush), with one distractor, 5 of 5 trials on 2 consecutive days.	Language therapist	Teacher	2/30/81 4/15/81	4/15/81
d Susan will demonstrate function of cup, spoon, and hairbrush, 5 of 5 trials on 2 consecutive days.	Language therapist	Teacher	4/15/81 5/30/81	5/30/81

Child's Name: ___Susan___

Long-Term-Goal Statement: Susan will match 3 words (toilet, eat, drink)

to appropriate pictures.

Short-term objectives (include evaluation criteria)	Specific educational and/or support services	Persons responsible for implementation	Beginning, end date	Review date
a Susan will match the word *toilet,* with 1 distractor, 5 of 5 trials on 3 consecutive days.		Teacher	9/80 11/15/80	11/15/80
b Susan will match the word *eat* with 1 distractor, 5 of 5 trials on 3 consecutive days.		Teacher	11/15/80 1/30/81	1/30/81
c Susan will match the word *drink,* with 1 distractor, 5 of 5 trials on 3 consecutive days.		Teacher	1/30/81 3/15/81	3/15/81

Table 1-2 (Continued)

Child's Name: ___Susan___

Long-Term-Goal Statement: Susan will engage in parallel play with 1 or 2

children 25% of time during free-play activity.

Short-term objectives (include evaluation criteria)	Specific educational and/or support services	Persons responsible for implementation	Beginning, end date	Review date
a Susan will engage in play activity with teacher assistance		Classroom staff	9/10/80 10/10/80 change criteria (CC): compliant 4 successive days	10/10/80
b Susan will engage in play activity when verbally cued by teacher			10/10/80 11/10/80 CC = 75% for 4 successive days	11/10/80
c Susan will play with teacher beside another child			1/10/81 CC = 75% for 4 successive days	
d Susan will play with another child in vicinity of teacher			1/10/81 1/30/81	
e Susan will play 3 ft from other child without teacher present.			2/1/81 2/15/81	
f Susan will play beside other child.			2/16/81	2/16/81

teachers, using screening devices and behavior checklist formats, giving standardized and nonstandardized tests, and directly observing the child. Data collected from these instruments will help the IEP committee develop a program which is in line with the student's needs and present level of functioning.

Effective assessment techniques will provide reliable data that are not culturally biased or unfair. Assessment should be completed in all curriculum areas which are deemed appropriate for the child's educational program. It may also be necessary to gather initial assessment data on level of physical skill, sensory acuity, or other nonacademic areas. This type of information will be important in deciding specific special services which may be required to augment the child's program.

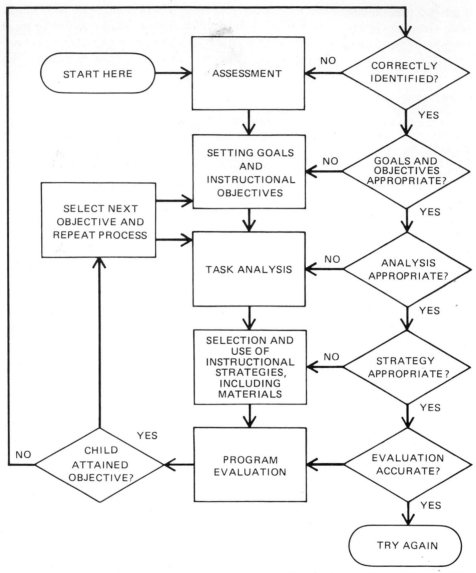

Figure 1-3 Steps in the program development process. (Source: McLaughlin and Eaves, 1976, p. 5.)

Setting Goals and Instructional Objectives

Once the assessment data are gathered, the next step is to identify in each curriculum area annual goals that the IEP committee feels are realistic and attainable for the child. Selection of these goals should be governed by the relevance of the skills to the child in adapting to the community and future placements.

From the annual goals, short-term instructional objectives must be generated. These are specific statements of terminal behaviors which the child must attain. A sequence of objectives within each curriculum area should be arranged in a priority of most important to least important. Once criterion is reached, the teacher can then begin instruction on the next skill.

Task Analysis

Task analysis involves the breaking down of skills into small steps and ordering the steps into a logical sequence. The order in which material is presented will influence how quickly students learn skills. By sequencing content from easy to hard, it will be easier to individualize instruction for children at different levels of functioning. It will also facilitate pinpoint assessment and objective evaluation.

Task analysis is a competency which all special education teachers should have. Although the amount of detail in the skill breakdown will vary depending on the skill selected for instruction and the child's level of functioning, a basic understanding of the rationale for skill sequencing and ability to task-analyze skills is necessary.

Instructional Strategies

While task analysis involves *what* is taught, instructional strategies reflect *how* to teach. Instructional procedures are the behaviors which the teacher emits in order to elicit designated target skills from students. Teaching procedures may include verbal instructions, demonstrations, practice, feedback, reinforcement, or even manual guidance.

There is an abundance of information available about how humans learn. From the psychology of learning, special educators can profit by translating much of the technical information into practical teaching guidelines. An excellent example of how this has been done is in an article by Mercer and Algozzine (1977). These authors have reviewed observational learning research with mildly, moderately, and severely retarded individuals. From their review, specific guidelines were delineated for the classroom teacher.

Instructional strategies involve either presentation of material or some form of feedback or consequence once the child responds (or fails to respond). Learning variables which influence how effective a lesson will be are described in depth in Chapters 4 to 6. By understanding the conditions of learning and reinforcement, the teacher has the ability to systematically manipulate instructional variables which can have an effect on the child's performance.

Program Evaluation

When the program has been fully implemented, it is necessary to verify the progress the child is making. If the child is not meeting an objective after a reasonable amount of time, then the program must be reviewed. It may be that the material selected was too difficult or not broken down into small-enough steps. On the other hand, the instructional strategies may be ineffective. For example, instructions may not be given clearly or reinforcers may not be used consistently.

Regular program evaluation will facilitate communication with parents and administrators. It will be helpful to clarify for parents how the child's progress is being evaluated and also how frequently they will receive progress reports. Objective and unambiguous evaluation devices will be useful in providing a frame of reference as to where the child was, where the child is now, and where the child should be going.

SUMMARY

Public Law 94-142 provides the legislative mandate for the education of handicapped children. The purpose of this law is to ensure a free appropriate public education for all school-age handicapped children. School age is defined as ranging from age 3 to 21 unless state law specifies otherwise.

School systems can no longer exclude or postpone the education of handicapped children on the grounds that they cannot learn, their handicap is too severe, programs do not exist, or for any other reason. Education for handicapped children must be considered as a continuous process by which individuals learn to cope and function within their environment. As much as possible, handicapped children must be educated with nonhandicapped children.

Public Law 94-142 guarantees due process procedures for children and parents. The intent of due process is to allow for fair consideration of the interests of all who are involved in the education of the pupil. Public Law 94-142 also requires the right to nondiscriminatory testing and evaluation. Testing must not be culture-biased.

The handicapped child must not be separated from nonhandicapped children any more than is necessary to fit instruction to his or her special needs. The child's placement is determined by the committee writing his or her individualized education program. This placement decision is made after the goals and objectives for the child have been specified, not before. The placement options usually include regular class (the least restrictive), resource room, self-contained special class, separate day school, home or hospital, and residential (the most restrictive).

Along with the proper placement, educational services must also be delivered. These services are special education and related services designed to help the child meet the goals and objectives of his or her program. Placement alone does not guarantee that the child will receive appropriate services.

All handicapped children must have an individualized education program (IEP) developed and implemented. The IEP is the keystone to providing a free appropriate public education. After evaluation data are collected the IEP is developed by a representative of the local education agency (LEA), who can guarantee specially designed instruction to meet the child's needs; the teacher; the child's parents or guardians; and whenever appropriate, the child.

An IEP must include the child's present levels of performance; annual goals, including short-term instructional objectives; specific special education and related services to be provided to the child, and the extent to which the child will be able to participate in regular educational programs; projected dates for initiation of services and the anticipated duration of services; and schedule for determining, at least annually, whether objectives are being achieved. Figure 1-2 and Table 1-1 present the component parts and the steps in developing an IEP.

An IEP does not require a detailed description of instructional sequences or teaching procedures. However, this information is necessary for its effective implementation. The program-development process set forth in this book is a systematic approach to developing and implementing an IEP. In sum, the program-development process is an orderly plan for teaching handicapped children. The steps in this process are assessment, setting goals and instructional objectives, task analysis, instructional strategies, and program evaluation. Figure 1-3 presents the relationship between the steps in the program-development process. The remainder of this book provides information on implementing this systematic approach to teaching handicapped children.

REFERENCES

Abeson, A., & Zettel, J. The end of the quiet revolution: The Education for All Handicapped Children Act of 1975. *Exceptional Children*, 1977, *44*(5), 114–128.

Blake, K. A. *The Mentally Retarded: An Educational Psychology*, Englewood Cliffs, N.J.: Prentice-Hall, 1976.

Blake, K. A. *Educating Exceptional Pupils: An Introduction to Contemporary Practices*. Reading, Mass.: Addison-Wesley, in press.

Brown, L., & York, R. Developing programs for severely handicapped students: Teacher training and classroom instruction. *Focus on Exceptional Children*, 1974, *6*.

Burt, R. A. Judicial action to aid the retarded. In N. Hobbs (ed.), *Issues in the classification of children* (Vol. 2, pp. 293 318). San Francisco: Jossey-Bass, 1975.

Burton, T. A., Burton, S. F., & Hirshoren, A. For sale: The state of Alabama. *The Journal of Special Education*, 1977, *11*, 59–64. (a)

Burton, T. A., Burton, S. F., & Hirshoren, A. Rhetoric versus reality *The Journal of Special Education*, 1977, *11*, 69–72. (b)

Deno, E. Special education as developmental capital. *Exceptional Children*, 1970, *37*, 229–237.

Diana v. State Board of Education. C-70-37 (R.F.P. Dist. N. Calif. 1970).

Dunn, L. M., Special Education in the mildly retarded—Is much of it justifiable? *Exceptional Children*, 1968, *35*, 5-22.

Federal Register, 1977, *42*, 163.

Guadolupe v. Tempe Elementary School District. Civil Action 71-435 (D. Ariz. 1971).

Hobson v. Hansen. 269 F. Supp. 401 (D.D.C. 1967).

Kuriloff, P., True, R., Kirp, D., & Buss, W. Legal reform and educational change: The Pennsylvania case. *Exceptional Children*, 1974, *41*, 35–42.

Larry, P. v. Riles. VSLW 2033 (U.S. June 21, 1972).

Macmillan, D. L. *Mental retardation in school and society*. Boston: Little, Brown, 1977.

McLaughlin, P. J., & Eaves, R. *Evaluations: Interactions in the special education classroom*. Paper presented at the annual international meeting of the Council for Exceptional Children, Chicago, April 1976.

Mercer, C., & Algozzine, R. Observational learning and the retarded: Teaching implications. *Education and Training of the Mentally Retarded*, 1977, *12*(4), 345–353.

Mills v. Board of Education of the District of Columbia, 348 F. Supp. 866 (D.D.C. 1972).

Pennsylvania Association for Retarded Children v. Commonwealth of Pennsylvania, F. Supp. 279 (E.D. Pa. 1972).

Public Law 94-142, *Education for All Handicapped Children Act*, November 29, 1975.

Roos, P. The U.S. constitution: Is it for sale? *The Journal of Speical Education*, 1977, *11*, 65–68.

Sontag, E., Burke, P., & York, R. Considerations for serving the severely handicapped in the public schools. *Education and Training of the Mentally Retarded*, 1973, *8*, 20–26.

Spangler v. Board of Education. 311 F. Supp. 501 (Calif. 1970).

Stainback, S., Stainback, W., & Maurer, S. Training teachers for the severely and profoundly handicapped: A new frontier. *Exceptional Children*, 1976, *42*(4), 203–210.

Chapter 2

Assessment of Present Performance Levels

This chapter presents information on a systematic approach to educational assessment. The procedural safeguards for protection in evaluation, due process, and confidentiality covered in P.L. 94-142 are also presented. The purpose of the chapter is to supply knowledge on how to assess an individual's present performance levels, i.e., how to find out what an individual can and cannot do.

Learning Goals

You should be able to answer the following questions when you finish this chapter:

- What is the relationship of assessment to the individualized education program and P.L. 94-142?
- What is required by the public law's safeguards for protection-in-evaluation procedures?
- How do you meet P.L. 94-142's requirements of due process for evaluation?

- What is the rationale for making assessment decisions? Specify the three variables which must be considered in relation to this rationale.
- What is a domain? Describe the relationship between broad skills and specific skills within a domain.
- What are the six general assessment methods? Describe their usefulness and sample instruments for each method.
- What are the three steps to systematic assessment? Describe each step. Include in your description the purpose, the quality of evidence, the assessment methods used, the level of information acquired, and the resulting outcome of each step.
- Which assessment step provides information that becomes part of the IEP? How is this information used?

Assessment methods are the means for collecting evidence about an individual's performance. After a student has been referred, assessment of present performance levels is the first step in developing the individualized education program. The assessment results are used to make decisions at every step in the development of the program. It is a complex task to accurately collect and organize assessment data and move to the subsequent steps of specifying annual goals, instructional objectives, special educational services, related services, and evaluation procedures. Wrong decisions will probably be made if the assessment of the individual's present performance levels is incorrect.

RELATIONSHIP OF ASSESSMENT TO PUBLIC LAW 94-142

Excerpted below from the final regulations of the Public Law (Federal Register, 1977) are the procedural safeguards requiring protection-in-evaluation procedures. These regulations are the rules which must be followed when assessing a student's present level of performance.

> *General.*   Testing and evaluation materials and procedures used for the purposes of evaluation and placement of handicapped children must be selected and administered so as not to be racially or culturally discriminatory (121a.530).

> *Replacement evaluation.*   Before any action is taken with respect to the initial placement of a handicapped child in a special education program, a full and individual evaluation of the child's educational needs must be conducted. . . . (121a.531).

> *Evaluation procedures.*   State and local educational agencies shall insure at a minimum, that:
> a   Tests and other evaluation materials:
>   1   Are provided and administered in the child's native language or other mode of communication, unless it is clearly not feasible to do so;
>   2   Have been validated for the specific purpose for which they are used; and
>   3   Are administered by trained personnel in conformance with the instructions provided by their producer;
> b   Tests and other evaluation materials include those tailored to assess specific

areas of educational need and not merely those which are designed to provide a single general intelligence quotient;

c   Tests are selected and administered so as best to ensure that when a test is administered to a child with impaired sensory, manual, or speaking skills, the test results accurately reflect the child's aptitude or achievement level or whatever other factors the test purports to measure, rather than reflecting the child's impaired sensory, manual, or speaking skills (except where those skills are the factors which the test purports to measure);

d   No single procedure is used as the sole criterion for determining an appropriate educational program for a child; and

e   The evaluation is made by a multidisciplinary team or group of persons, including at least one teacher or other specialist with knowledge in the area of suspected disability;

f   The child is assessed in all areas related to the suspected disability, including, where appropriate, health, vision, hearing, social and emotional status, general intelligence, academic performance, communicative status, and motor abilities (121a.532).

Reevaluation.   Each state and local educational agency shall insure: That an evaluation of the child, based on procedures which meet the requirements under 121a.532 is conducted every three years or more frequently if conditions warrant or if the child's parent or teacher requests an evaluation (121a.534).

The public law also requires that due process procedures for parents and children and confidentiality of information be observed at the time the evaluation is conducted. Procedures for observing due process in evaluation assure that the child's parents understand what is happening and have ways to contest evaluation procedures and decisions. Meeting the requirements of due process for evaluation involves these activities:

1   Obtaining the parent's permission to assess the child
2   Sharing all assessment results with the parents
3   Informing the parents about their right to obtain an independent educational evaluation of their child (at public expense under certain conditions)
4   Making available appeal procedures if the parents object to procedures or results

The confidentiality of all personally identifiable information at collection, storage, disclosure, and destruction stages must also be protected. All persons who have access to data must be named publicly and trained in confidentiality procedures.

MEETING THE ASSESSMENT REQUIREMENTS OF PUBLIC LAW 94-142

From the information presented above it should be apparent that meeting the assessment requirements of P.L. 94-142 is a difficult job. The assessment team, which includes a teacher, is responsible for using assessment methods and materials that assure protection in evaluation. This requirement includes technical soundness, nondiscriminatory testing, validity, and reliability (Blake, in press). The assessment team is also responsible for observing due process for parents and children and confidentiality of information.

The knowledge which is required to make these judgments extends beyond the scope of this book. The *Standards for Educational and Psychological Tests* and *Use of Tests in Schools*, both published by the American Psychological Association, should be consulted when making these assessment decisions. Blake (1976, in press) has also considered the procedures necessary to meet the evaluation requirements of P.L. 94-142.

Monitoring Assessment Requirements

Blake (in press) has prepared useful checklists for monitoring due process procedures, protection in evaluation, and confidentiality of information. These checklists are briefly described below and presented in Tables 2-1, 2-2, and 2-3,

Table 2-1   Monitoring Observation of Due Process in Evaluation

Pupil _____   Date _____

1   Advocate
   a   Is the pupil old enough and competent to participate? (Explain.)
   b   Are the parents/guardians competent and willing to participate? (Explain.)
   c   If parents refuse to participate, document reasons and procedures used to satisfy their objections or other reasons.
   d   Is a surrogate necessary? If so, what is his/her name?
   e   What is the advocate's native language?
   f   Does the advocate have a hearing or sensory impairment?
   g   If one is needed, who is the translator/communicator?

2   Information about procedures and rights
   a   Was information about the individual educational plan, the assessment process, and due process communicated to the advocate orally and in writing and in terms appropriate to his/her apparent level of understanding?
   b   Is there evidence that the advocate apparently understands the procedures and the pupil's rights?

3   Permission
   Has the advocate's permission been obtained for each procedure used?

4   Information about results
   Has the advocate been given information about the results of the evaluations?

5   Independent assessments
   Has the advocate been informed about the right to obtain independent assessments?

6   Appeal
   a   Does the advocate have objections to the assessment procedure or the results?
   b   Have appeal procedures been established and followed?

Source: Blake (in press).

Table 2-2   Monitoring Protection-in-Evaluation

Pupil _____   Date _____

The pupil's characteristics

1 Native language
   a What language is predominantly spoken in the pupil's home?
   b Does the pupil need a translator?

2 Speech
   a Is the pupil's speech intelligible?
   b If not, how does he communicate his responses?

3 Hearing
   a Does the pupil have a hearing impairment sufficient to interfere with his understanding of the test directions?
   b If so, what means of communication can be used?

4 How mature is the pupil's understanding and use of language (i.e., syntactical functions and vocabulary meanings)?

5 Vision
   a Does the pupil have a visual impairment sufficient to interfere with his grasping the test directions and responding to the test materials?
   b If so, what adjustments need to be made?

6 Hand use
   a Does the pupil have sufficient control of his hands to manipulate test items which must be moved?
   b If not, what adjustments need to be made?

7 Head and postural control
   a Is the pupil able to maintain a reasonably upright sitting/body position and head position?
   b If not, what adjustments need to be made?

8 Socio-cultural and experience background
   Has the pupil been in an environment where he may not have had experience with activities like those used in the test items?

The requirements

Consider the following requirements *for each instrument used.*

Requirement #1: Technical Soundness

1 Administrator
2 Qualifications

Requirement #2: Non-Discriminating
Supply the following information *for each instrument used.*

1 Test Name:
2 Test Producer:
3 Is the test norm-referenced or criterion-referenced?
4 Norm-Referenced Tests

Table 2-2 (Continued)

   a If the test is norm-referenced, what information does the test producer furnish about the characteristics of the norm group?

   b Are the norms appropriate standards to use in judging the pupil's performance.

      1 Consider the pupil's characteristics—his native language, speech, hearing, language, vision, hand use, head and postural control, and socio-cultural and experiential background. Are the pupil's characteristics so different from the characteristics of the pupils in the norm group that the pupil's performance cannot be judged in relation to the norm group's performance? If yes, restate reasons.

      2 Consider the adjustments which must be made for problems the pupil may have with his native language, speech, hearing, language, vision, hand use, and head and postural control. Did these adjustments cause the way the pupil was tested to be so different from the way the pupils in the norm group were tested that the pupil's performance cannot be judged in relation to the norm group's performance? If yes, restate reasons.

5 Criterion-Referenced Tests

   a If the test is criterion-referenced, what information does the test producer furnish about what behavior is sampled, the conditions under which that behavior is sampled, and the criterion for mastery?

   b Consider the pupil's characteristics and adjustments which must be made for problems he has. Do these characteristics and adjustments make the conditions of testing so different from the conditions of testing specified in the instructional objective that the pupil's performance cannot be judged against the criterion? If yes, restate reasons.

Requirement #3: Validity
Answer these questions *separately for each score being used.*

Test 1—

1 What is the pupil characteristic to be sampled and what is the purpose for sampling it?

2 What evidence does the test producer give to indicate that the test samples the behavior appropriately?

3 For scores on ability tests, what evidence does the test producer give to indicate that the score is related to (predicts) the pupil's behavior on educational tests and other educational situations?

4 Is the test valid for the purpose it is to be used? If no, describe.

Requirement #4: Reliability
Answer these questions *separately for each score being used.*

Test 1—

1 What is the reliability coefficient and standard error of measurement for the score?

2 Is the margin of error small enough for the decision to be made?

Source: Blake (in press).

respectively. The completed checklists become part of the written evidence for meeting the assessment requirements of P.L. 94-142.

    Due Process Checklist   This checklist asks questions about who represents the pupil, understanding procedures and rights, obtaining permission to test, obtaining independent assessments, and appeal procedures.

Table 2-3 Monitoring Observation of Confidentiality Requirements

Pupil _____   Date _____

Name of information maintained

1 Notice
   a Has notice been given for all activities—data collection, data use, etc.?
   b Were the notices published in the native language of the groups involved?

2 Access rights
   a Are parents, and when appropriate the pupil, given access to the data?
   b Have they been informed of the right of access?

3 Hearing rights
   a Are parents, and when appropriate the pupil, given a hearing about any change which they request?
   b Is the hearing scheduled at a reasonable time?
   c Is this hearing in the parents' native language or, if needed is an interpreter present?
   d If their request is denied, is their rebuttal filed in the pupil's records?

4 Consent
   Is the parents' consent or, if appropriate the pupil's consent, requested for wider disclosure of data?

5 Safeguards
   a Who is responsible for insuring confidentiality of data?
   b What employees have access to the data?
   c Have these employees' names been published?
   d Have these employees been given proper training in procedures for protecting confidentiality?

6 Destruction
   a Does the agency have procedures for destroying data?
   b Are parents, and when appropriate pupils, informed of their rights to copies of data before they are destroyed?

Source: Blake (in press)

Protection-in-Evaluation Checklist   This checklist specifies pertinent questions about the pupil's characteristics. The pupil's characteristics help decide the assessment methods and materials. For each assessment instrument used, this checklist requires information about its technical soundness, nondiscriminating nature, validity, and reliability.

Confidentiality Checklist   This checklist asks questions about notice, access rights, hearing rights, consent, safeguards, and destruction of information.

A RATIONALE FOR ASSESSMENT DECISION MAKING

Assessment is the process of determining and understanding the performance of students in their current environment. Assessment involves considerably more than the administration of a test. In assessing handicapped students, it is necessary to look at the way they perform on a variety of tasks in a variety of settings, the meaning of their performances in terms of the total functioning of the individual, and the explanations for those performances (Salvia & Ysseldyke, 1978).

Testing is a part of assessment. However, much assessment takes place apart from formal testing. There are several different methods for gathering evidence about a child's performance level. For example, is the pupil toilet-trained? Can the pupil work independently for 10 minutes? Can the pupil apply the CVC + e vowel pronunciation principle? This evidence can be gathered using several different assessment methods, e.g., a structured interview, a norm-referenced or criterion-referenced test, or a behavioral observation (Eaves & McLaughlin, 1977). How does a teacher decide which specific assessment methods or methods to use? In sum, what is the rationale for making assessment decisions?

First, as described in the preceding section, the assessment method must meet the requirements of P.L. 94-142. Ideally, the method of choice should also be the method that provides the best estimate of the child's current performance. However, the ideal is seldom the context within which assessment is conducted. In a real situation, there are many restraints which can keep the teacher from using the method that provides the best estimate. Therefore, on what criteria, besides the requirements of P.L. 94-142, is the decision made?

The answers to three highly related questions enter into this decision: (1) How important is it that the individual being assessed show competence on the variable to be estimated? (2) How accurate must the estimate be in order to be considered accurate enough? (3) How much time, expense, and effort can be devoted to gathering data for the estimate?

Importance of the Variable

While all assessment questions should be directed to important variables, it is true that some important variables are even more crucial than others. For instance, one reason why handwriting skill is frequently shunted into a secondary role in the general classroom scheme is probably because most educators simply do not consider the skill as crucial as basic arithmetic or reading skills. That minimal legibility is usually accepted can easily be shown by randomly examining the handwriting of practicing professionals in most areas of study. Whether or not one agrees with the example, most professionals probably can construct a hierarchy of skills based on their presumed importance to the child and his future functioning in the real world. Because of this, assessment of some variables takes precedence over others; that is, the more important the variable, the more accurate the estimate must be, and the more time, expense, and effort we are likely to devote in gathering the data for the estimate.

Accuracy of the Estimate

Depending on the breadth of the assessment question, teachers are more or less able to provide accurate estimates. For example, consider the question, "Can the child write the correct answer when visually presented with the addition problem, $6 + 3 = $ ____?" By repeatedly sampling a youngster's behavior, a teacher can estimate his usual response to this stimulus with reasonable accuracy. However, when attempting to measure the child's typical behavior with respect to the domain called arithmetic, the teacher will probably achieve a less-accurate estimate. Theoretically, a teacher could individually assess every broad and specific skill in the domain of arithmetic, but the time, expense, and effort required would make this unrealistic during initial assessment. Consequently, although the estimate sought is a very important one, when broad-based questions are asked, teachers are usually limited to relatively small (less-than-ideal) samples of the child's behavior. Of course, such a limitation neither invalidates the requirement that the teacher select the most accurate method available (other factors being equal) nor neutralizes the advantages of collecting long-term, formative assessment data.

Time, Expense, and Effort

The rationale for considering how this variable fits into the selection of assessment methods has been explicitly discussed in the two previous sections. One additional point should be made, however. Too frequently, the time, expense, and effort required by various assessment methods becomes the overriding factor in determining the method of choice. With recognition that there are absolute limits on the time, expense, and effort that can be spent in assessment, under most conditions, this variable should be the least decisive of the three. If the question being asked is a crucial one, it is usually worth the extra time, expense, and effort it takes to get a more-accurate estimate.

VARIABLES OF IMPORTANCE IN THE ASSESSMENT PROCESS

The assessment team must be very knowledgeable about three variables that form the foundation for assessment decisions: (1) the domains or characteristics of the child and his environment that are relevant to his future well-being, (2) the available resources which can be used during the assessment process, and (3) the assessment methods which can be used to help investigate the attributes of the child and his environment.

Relevant Domains

A domain is a set of content and behavior elements which potentially can be taught to pupils. A synonym for domain is curriculum area. Depending on circumstances (e.g., age, sex, prior experiences of the child), the particular cluster of relevant domains may vary somewhat, but generally, teachers are interested in the domains of arithmetic, language, motor, reading, recreation, self-help, social skills, and vocation.

Further, the teacher must have a very clear understanding of what the domains, reading, mathematics, and so on, include. This understanding should be in the form of a sequence of skills for each domain. This is also referred to as *scope and sequence information.* Scope and sequence charts are diagrams of a domain. Scope refers to what is taught—both the broad and the specific skills. Sequence refers to the order in which the skills are taught. Skill sequences may be adopted from the work of others or may be a synthesis of all the teacher has learned from readings and experience. Table 2-4 is a partial skill sequence for the domain of arithmetic.

While it is true that no existing scope and sequence of skills for all domains has been accepted by all, unless the teacher has some hierarchy in mind as the child is assessed, little more than a conglomeration of estimates will be collected.

Detailed scope and sequence information for each domain is necessary to formulate goals and objectives. This information is a vital thread that connects assessment and the specification of objectives. Part Two of this book focuses on the domains you will most likely be assessing and teaching. The skills within each domain presented in Part Two have been sequenced to aid in assessment and objective formulation.

Available Resources

There are at least five types of resources the assessment team can use in gathering data. They are (1) individuals in the school, (2) individuals in or near the home, (3) community agencies, (4) independent professionals, and (5) literary resources. A list of specific examples within each type of resource is shown in Table 2-5. In some cases the resource can actually gather data for the assessment team (e.g., school psychologist); in other instances the resource contributes the data (e.g., sibling); finally, some resources provide information which leads to better decisions concerning the assessment strategy (e.g., reference books).

Assessment Methods

There are six general methods used to collect information about a child and his environment. They are:

1 Informal consultations
2 Structured interviews
3 Screening devices
4 Norm-referenced tests
5 Criterion-referenced tests
6 Observations

These methods can be classified according to the time the information is

Table 2-4   Partial Arithmetic Skill Sequence

Skill	Mental age	
	5–6 years	7 years
Number		
Cardinals	1–5	6–9
Ordinals	—	1st fifth
Numerator/Denominator	—	—
Rationals	½ of object	¼ of object
Relations		
Equality/inequality	One-to-one correspondence	Equality symbol
	As many as, less, and more than	
Location	Inside, outside	—
Ratio	—	—
Numeration		
Number words	—	1–10
Arabic numerals	—	0–99
Roman numerals	—	—
Decimals/fractions	—	Write ½
		Write ¼
Place value	—	1s
		10s
Operations with whole numbers		
Counting	—	0–99
		By 1s, 10s to 100
		By 5s to 100
		By 2s to 40
Addition	—	Sums to 5 or less
		Vertical, 3 addends
		2 digits + 1 digit
		Sums to 12
Subtraction	—	Differences to 5
		2 digits
		Differences to 12
Multiplication	—	—
Division	—	—
Measurement		
Liquid	Full and empty	Recognizes cup, tablespoon
		Recognizes teaspoon
Weight	Light and heavy	Nearest pound
Linear	Long and short	Nearest inch
Time	—	Hour
		Half-hour
		Days of week
Money	Recognizes penny	Value of penny
	Recognizes nickel	Value of nickel
		Value of dime
		Value of set with above coins
Temperature	—	—

Table 2-5 Assessment Resources

Individuals in the school	Individuals in or near the home	Community agencies	Independent professionals	Literary resources
Former teachers	Parents	Mental health	Physicians	Textbooks
Current teachers	Siblings	clinics	Neurologists	Journals
Psychologists	Other relatives	Counseling	Psychiatrists	Magazines
Counselors	Child himself	services	Otologists	Reference
Nurses	Friends	Church	Dentists	books
Social workers	Friends' parents	Easter Seal		
Administrators		Society		
Lunchroom workers		Associations for		
Peers		the handicapped		
		Advocacy groups		

collected (current or historical) and how the information is collected (direct observation, tests, or judgments). Each general method usually contains many specific instruments. Table 2-6 shows this classification of the different assessment methods.

Within each method, the assessment team must select an appropriate available instrument or construct an instrument to use. Following are descriptions of the methods and some comments regarding their usefulness. If appropriate, representative and commonly used instruments are presented. The reader should note that some instruments fit more than one method. The key is how the instrument is actually used. Buros' *Mental Measurement Yearbooks* and Salvia and Ysseldyke's *Assessment in Special and Remedial Education* are two reference books to consult for information about specific assessment instruments. Below is a further description of assessment methods.

1   *Informal consultations* may be used with knowledgeable resources who can make judgments about the child that the assessor cannot. Although information gained from informal consultation is not usually obtained with a clear-cut guideline in mind, consultations may still yield valuable results (e.g., clues for further assessment). The method requires little time, but the accuracy of the information must be held suspect without additional support. By definition there are no instruments for this method. The assessor simply takes notes on information that seems significant.

2   *Structured interviews* may be used for either specific or generic purposes. Advance planning with respect to the purpose and guidelines of the interview is the main key to the effective use of the method. Two common purposes include gathering information about the child's areas of difficulty and determining what resources have previously collected information. Structured interviews require relatively little time, but the data obtained are only as good as the assessor's ability to ask the right questions and the resource's ability to provide helpful answers. The Preschool Attainment Record and the Vineland Social Maturity Scale are two examples of commercial structured interviews.

3   *Screening devices*, in the form of questionnaires, rating scales, check-

Table 2-6   Methods of Assessment, Classified by Type of Information and Time of Information Collection

Type of information	Time at which information is collected	
	Current	Historical
Judgments	Informal consultations, structured interviews, and screening devices	Informal consultations, structured interviews, and screening devices
	For example: rating scales completed by teachers, etc. teacher's reason for referral parents' opinion of how child gets along at home	For example: previous report cards parents' recall of developmental history previous medical report
Tests	Norm-referenced and criterion-referenced	Norm-referenced and criterion-referenced
	For example: results of an intelligence test administered during the assessment results of this week's arithmetic test	For example: results of a standardized achievement-test battery given at the end of last year
Observations	Systematic observation and nonsystematic observation	Systematic observation and nonsystematic observation
	For example: frequency counts of occurrence of a particular behavior antecedents of behavior critical incidents	For example: anecdotal records observations by last year's teachers contained in the record folder

Source: Adapted from Salvia and Ysseldyke (1978, p. 7).

lists, and inventories, comprise the last of the "quick and dirty" assessment methods (i.e., methods that gather data in a hurry, almost invariably through report). As with the previous methods, screening devices are efficient instruments, but the accuracy of the estimate may vary widely depending on the respondent's skill in making judgments as well as the reliability and validity of the device itself. Some examples of screening devices include the Myklebust Pupil Rating Scale, and the Peterson-Quay Problem Behavior Checklist.

   4 *Norm-referenced tests* compare the individual's performance to the performance of peers. The emphasis is on an individual's relative standing in the reference group rather than on absolute mastery of content. All norm-referenced tests are objective, i.e., they have predetermined answers and standards for scoring a response. All norm-referenced tests have the advantage of an estimate which is the direct result of the behavior of the child and not someone's judgment about the behavior. This is the first assessment method so far that requires face to face interaction with the individual being assessed. Another advantage of norm-referenced tests is that they offer suggestions for more-specific assessment, in spite of the fact that they seldom say much about functional behavior in settings within the natural environment (e.g., classroom, home, community). Table 2-7 lists some sample norm-referenced tests. These tests have been divided into group or individually administered tests and single-skill (e.g., reading) or multiple-skills (e.g., general achievement) tests.

   5   *Criterion-referenced tests* compare the individual's performance against the content to be learned. Other pupils' achievements are immaterial. For example, given twenty synonyms, the pupil's performance is judged on the basis of how many he learns. He may learn 100 percent, 50 percent, etc. The emphasis in criterion-referenced testing is on assessing specific and relevant behaviors that have been mastered. Items on criterion-referenced tests are often linked directly to instructional objectives. Table 2-8 lists some criterion-referenced tests. These tests have been divided into group or individually administered tests and single-skill or multiple-skills tests. As noted earlier, some tests, e.g., Key Math, may be both norm-referenced and criterion-referenced.

   6   *Observations* refers to the collection of assessment data as the behavior to be measured spontaneously occurs in the natural environment, usually the classroom. This method can provide highly accurate, detailed, verifiable information about the skill being assessed and the contexts in which the observations are being made. There are two types of observations: systematic and nonsystematic. In nonsystematic observation, the assessor simply watches an individual in his environment and takes notes of the behaviors and interactions that seem important. In systematic observation, the assessor

Table 2-7   Norm-Referenced Tests

Group-administered		Individually administered	
Single-skill	**Multiple-skills**	**Single-skill**	**Multiple-skills**
Gates-MacGinitie Reading Test	California Achievement Test	Gray Oral Reading Test	Peabody Individual Achievement Test
Stanford Diagnostic Reading Test	Iowa Tests of Basic Skills	Durrell Analysis of Reading Difficulty	Wide Range Achievement Test
Silent Reading Diagnostic Test	Metropolitan Achievement Test	Diagnostic Reading Scales	
	Stanford Achievement Test	Gates-McKillop Reading Diagnostic Tests	
		Gilmore Oral Reading Test	
		Woodcock Reading Mastery Tests	
		Key Math Diagnostic Arithmetic Test	

Source: Adapted from Salvia and Yssledyke (1978, p. 126).

Table 2-8 Criterion-Referenced Tests

Group-administered		Individually administered	
Single-skill	Multiple-skills	Single-skill	Multiple-skills
None	Stanford Achieve-ment Test	Key Math Diag-nostic Arithmetic Test	None
		Fountain Valley Reading Test	
		Stanford Diagnostic Reading Test	

Source: Adapted from Salvia and Yssledyke (1978, p. 127).

observes one or more specific behaviors. The assessor defines the behaviors to be observed beforehand and then counts or otherwise measures the frequency, duration, magnitude, or latency of the behaviors, such as the number of times a child is out of his seat or the type of addition errors when adding facts 6 to 9.

Behavioral observation and recording is very time-consuming but it plays an integral role in the total assessment process. Systematic observational assessment is also a key element in task-analytic teaching. This specific type of systematic observational assessment will be explained in detail in Chapter 3.

A SYSTEM FOR EDUCATIONAL ASSESSMENT

The rationale for and the important variables of the assessment process have been presented. This part of the chapter translates that information into a systematic approach to assessment. The goal is to collect and analyze the assessment information necessary to develop an IEP. To summarize, the major obstacle in assessment is that the teacher cannot realistically assess all of the content in every domain. How does the teacher, or the assessment team, overcome this obstacle?

The answer is that during the initial step of assessment the teacher must be willing to accept evidence of relatively low quality, which at the same time is collected efficiently. This would include using historical information and current judgmental methods, e.g., informal consultations, structured interviews, and screening devices. As assessment progresses, less-efficient (time-consuming), yet higher-quality methods can be used.

Figure 2-1 illustrates a scheme for estimating the quality of evidence gathered during assessment of the child and his environment (Eaves & McLaughlin, 1977). In the figure, the quality levels of evidence can be defined as follows:

1 Mush—evidence that may be rather inaccurate, is usually general in nature, and allows only tentative conclusions at the domain level.

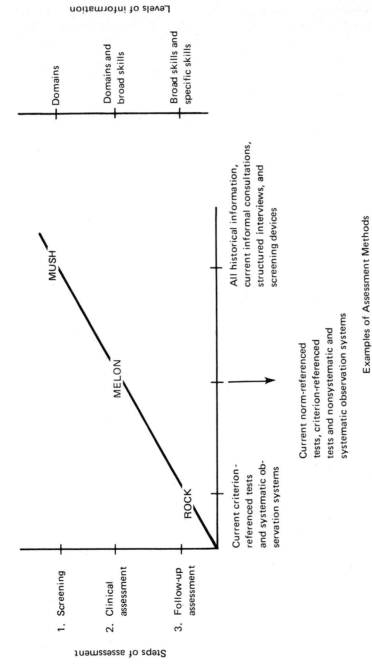

Figure 2-1 A scheme for determining the absolute quality of evidence gathered during the assessment of the child and his or her environment. (Source: Adapted from Yarger, 1975.)

2   Melon—evidence that is moderately accurate, usually either general or somewhat specific, and allows fairly definite conclusions concerning domains (e.g., arithmetic) and broad skills (e.g., operation with whole numbers, addition, subtraction, etc.).

3   Rock—evidence that is highly accurate, very specific, and allows rather precise conclusions regarding specific skills (e.g., addition facts 0 to 5, 6 to 9, 0 to 9, etc.).

The quality levels of evidence cut across the three steps of assessment. These steps are screening, clinical assessment, and follow-up assessment. They provide a systematic approach to gathering and analyzing the information necessary to develop an IEP. The three steps are described and illustrated below.

Step 1: Screening (Mush)

Screening is the first step of assessment. It happens immediately after a child has been referred for special education.

Evidence collected during screening is farther removed from the specification of goals and instructional objectives than any other data collected during assessment. Its main purpose is to uncover the views of those who have prior knowledge of the child and his work and to gather some preliminary evidence which will guide later assessment decisions. The basic question to ask during screening is, What domains are considered strengths and what domains are considered weaknesses for the child? Screening evidence is characterized by: (1) its use of opinions and historical information as a data base; (2) its broad scope, which includes all the curriculum domains; (3) its use of informal consultation, structured interviews, and screening devices as assessment methods; (4) the efficiency with which data are collected; and (5) the opportunity provided for the collection of environmental information (e.g., attitudes, expectations, prior instructional strategies).

Although screening evidence is often mushy with respect to resulting instructional decisions, it does possess two advantages which justify its use. First, it provides the teacher with a picture of those resource people who have had the most contact with the child in the past. Thus, the realism with which parents view their child's successes or failures can be observed, the skill with which the child's former teacher selected materials can be determined, peers' attitudes toward the child may be polled, and so on. Second, screening helps to generate hypotheses about those domains of the child which are most in need of improvement, as well as ruling in or out domains as candidates for intensive remedial help.

Screening should result in a summary profile, rating the domains considered to be strengths and those considered to be weaknesses. Of course, many of the designations are necessarily tentative at this step and require clinical assessment to support or deny them. A sample screening summary profile is shown in Figure 2-2. This summary profile was completed by an assessment team at the

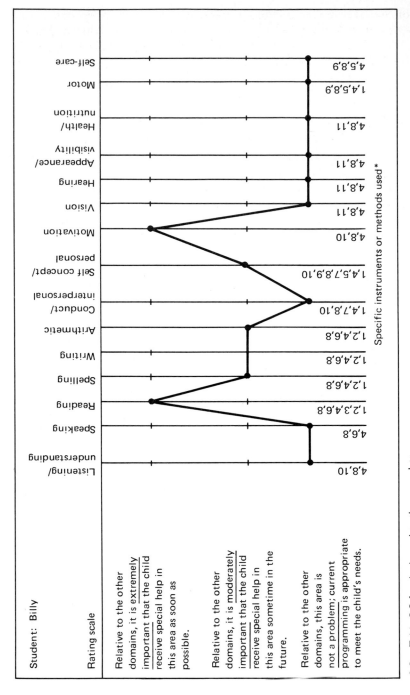

Student: Billy

Rating scale

Relative to the other domains, it is extremely important that the child receive special help in this area as soon as possible.

Relative to the other domains, it is moderately important that the child receive special help in this area sometime in the future.

Relative to the other domains, this area is not a problem; current programming is appropriate to meet the child's needs.

Self-care — 4,5,8,9
Motor — 1,4,5,8,9
Health/ nutrition —
Health/ — 4,8,11
Appearance/ visibility — 4,8,11
Hearing — 4,8,11
Vision — 4,8,11
Motivation — 4,8,10
Self concept/ personal —
Self concept/ — 1,4,5,7,8,9,10
Conduct/ interpersonal —
Conduct/ — 1,4,7,8,10
Arithmetic — 1,2,4,6,8
Writing — 1,2,4,6,8
Spelling — 1,2,4,6,8
Reading — 1,2,3,4,6,8
Speaking — 4,6,8
Listening/ understanding — 4,8,10

Specific instruments or methods used *

* See Table 2-9 for the legend to these numbers.

Figure 2-2 Step 1: Screening. Overall summary profile.

conclusion of Step 1: Screening. Before completing this summary profile the assessment team had reviewed all available historical information, conducted several informal consultations and structured interviews, and used two screening devices. Table 2-9 lists the resources and assessment methods and instruments used during Step 1: Screening.

Step 2: Clinical Assessment (Melon)

The main function of clinical assessment is to measure the broad skills in the domains that were tentatively identified as strengths and weaknesses during screening. Clinical assessment is characterized by: (1) direct assessment of the child as opposed to the historical and judgmental evidence of screening; (2) use of relatively broad-based norm-referenced tests, criterion-referenced tests, and nonsystematic and systematic observations as the assessment methods; (3) a "telescopic" narrowing down of possible strengths and weaknesses; and (4) use of clinical environments, not the classroom, as the primary setting for data collection.

Clinical assessment fills an intermediate position between the three assessment steps. Although the data are generally of equal or better caliber than that collected during screening, they are seldom as instructionally worthwhile as follow-up assessment, hence the term *melon*. The results of clinical assessment are not viewed in isolation but are interpreted in an acturial process which takes into account all currently available data (including those gathered during

Table 2-9   Resources, Methods, and Instruments Used in Step 1: Screening
Student: Billy

Resource	Method		Instrument	
Historical				
Cumulative file	1	Observation	1	Report cards for last 2 years
Cumulative file	2	Norm-referenced test	2	Wide Range Achievement Test administered 3 years ago
Cumulative file	3	Criterion-referenced Test	3	Standard Diagnostic Reading Test administered 2 years ago
Current				
Classroom teacher	4	Informal consultation	4	NA
Classroom teacher	5	Structured interview	5	Vineland Social Maturity Scale
Classroom teacher	6	Screening device	6	Myklebust Pupil Rating Scale
Classroom teacher	7	Screening device	7	Devereux Elementary School Behavior Rating Scale
Parents	8	Informal consultation	8	NA
Parents	9	Structured interview	9	Vineland Social Maturity Scale
School psychologist	10	Informal consultation	10	NA
School nurse	11	Informal consultation	11	NA

screening). Therefore, as evidence is accumulated, mush may turn into melon and melon into rock.

Clinical assessment should result in several profiles and narrative statements. A profile and a narrative statement rating the broad skills in each domain assessed should be developed. This information should then be summarized into an overall profile rating the domains considered to be strengths and weaknesses. Such evidence leads the assessment team to still more specific hypotheses about particular skills to be tested during follow-up assessment. Figures 2-3 and 2-4 show two of the clinical assessment profiles developed for Billy, our sample case. Table 2-10 shows the narrative statement developed to accompany the Key Math profile presented in Figure 2-4. Figure 2-5 shows the summary profile developed by the assessment team at the conclusion of Step 2: Clinical Assessment. Note that as a result of the information gathered during this step, arithmetic was added to the rating of extremely important domains. Table 2-11 lists all the resources and their assessment methods used during Step 2: Clinical Assessment.

Step 3: Follow-up Assessment (Rock)

The major purpose of this step is to estimate the current status of the specific skills identified as potential strengths and weaknesses at the end of clinical assessment. It is important that the child's specific level of functioning be determined so that instruction will begin on an appropriate specific skill. These are the main characteristics of follow-up assessment: (1) exclusive use of direct behavioral evidence; (2) documentation of the need for instruction in specific

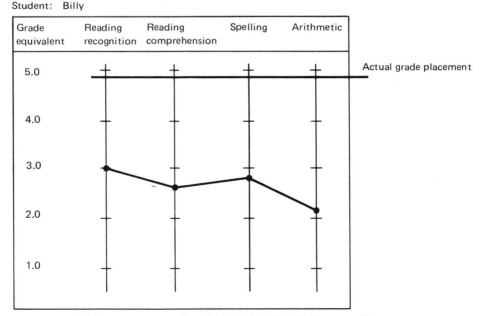

Figure 2-3   Clinic assessment profile—Peabody Individual Achievement Test.

Student: Billy

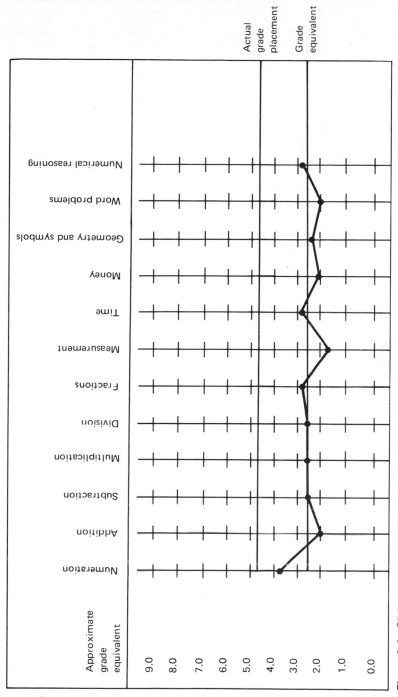

Figure 2-4 Clinic assessment profile—Key Math Diagnostic Arithmetic Test.

Table 2-10 Key Math Diagnostic Arithmetic Test Summary Statement

The major outcome of the administration of the Key Math test is that Billy is significantly behind his current grade placement in arithmetic skills. His current grade placement is about 4.9 while his grade equivalent was about 2.6 ± 0.15 (2 standard errors of measurement). With approximately 2 years to make up in this area, considerable time should be spent here. This statement can be made with some confidence because Billy consistently worked hard, trying to do his best throughout the testing.

Although Billy's profile on this test seems to indicate a couple of potential strengths and weaknesses, little can be said with any certainty about broad skills. For example, while *numeration* appears as a relative strength, taking the standard error of the measurement into account, Billy's true score could be as low as 2.8 or about equal to his overall grade equivalent.

In summary, Billy's math skills (as a result of the Key Math test administration) present a fairly flat profile. This is not consistent with screening information received from the teacher and the historical data from the cumulative file that was inspected earlier. It seems doubtful that specific skill deficits are preventing Billy from progressing at an average rate. If the results of the Key Math test are representative, Billy's abilities in all of the broad skills of arithmetic will have to be increased. However, follow-up assessment will be completed before firm statements can be made.

skills; (3) use of only precise, single-skill criterion-referenced tests and systematic observation as assessment methods; (4) relative inefficiency in terms of time, effort, and expense; and (5) collection of assessment data solely within the child's natural environment, usually the classroom.

From a behavioral point of view, data collected during follow-up assessment are the most valid. This is because behavior is assessed so frequently and in such small "bits" that there can be little doubt that it represents the construct or specific skill in question (Bersoff, 1973; DeCecco & Crawford, 1974). Consequently, such evidence can usually be considered as "rock hard" in Yarger's (1975) term.

The most important outcome of the follow-up assessment is a profile of present levels of performance for each important domain. For our sample case,

Table 2-11 Resources, Methods, and Instruments Used in Step 2: Clinical Assessment
(Student: Billy)

Resource	Method	Instrument
School psychologist	Norm-referenced test	Wechsler Intelligence Scale for Children—Revised (WISC—R)
School psychologist	Norm-referenced test	Peabody Individual Achievement Test (PIAT)
Reading specialists	Criterion-referenced test	Fountain Valley Reading Test
Classroom teacher	Norm-referenced test	Key Math Diagnostic Arithmetic Test
Classroom teacher	Nonsystematic observation	NA

Student: Billy

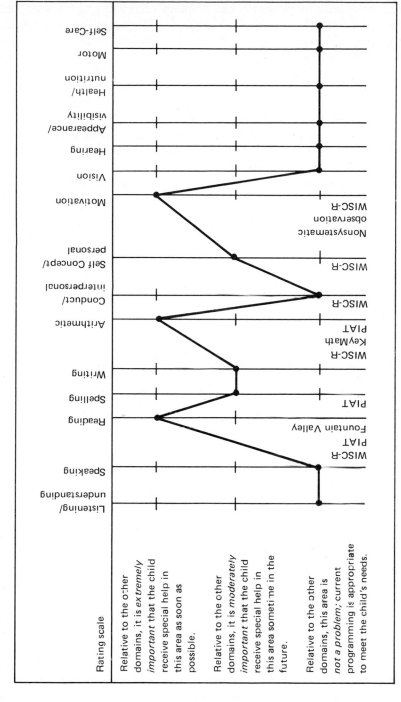

Figure 2-5 Step 2: Clinical assessment. Overall summary profile.

Billy, this would mean developing three profiles. Billy's current classroom performance on specific skills within the domains of reading, arithmetic, and motivation must be developed. Table 2-12 shows Billy's present performance levels in arithmetic. Notice that information is included about broad skills and, where Billy's proficiency and rate of correct answers is low, about specific skills within the broad skill (e.g., information on specific addition skills). The follow-up assessment information must be viewed within the context of the sequence of skills in the domain and the assessment instrument used. For example, to accurately analyze the information presented in Table 2-12, it will be helpful to be familiar with Science Research Associates' series of math probes and their scope and sequence of math skills. Table 2-13 lists all the resources and assessment methods and instruments used during Step 3: Follow-up Assessment.

The information from follow-up assessment becomes part of the child's IEP. These data are then used along with skill sequence charts to develop appropriate annual goals and short-term instructional objectives. Follow-up assessment data also serves a valuable function during program evaluation. These data become the baseline used for comparison with data collected during instruction. Used this way, data for evaluating instructional strategies become rock-type data instead of melon or mush.

Objectives for Teachers

The point in going through the three steps of assessment is that the teacher cannot individually assess all of the broad and specific skills in every domain. The time, expense, and effort involved in using increasingly narrow instruments in all situations makes it impossible, except in theory. The system proposed herein allows the teacher to telescope down to the critical specific skills. Refer back to Figure 2-1 to review the relationship between the three steps of assessment, the three levels of information collected, and the assessment methods used.

A teacher needs many skills to be able to effectively assess an individual's present performance levels. Below are the broad objectives teachers must perform in conducting each of the three steps of systematic assessment (McLaughlin & Eaves, 1977).

1 Given several questions about an actual child and his environment, *select the assessment methods and instruments* that can best answer the questions.

2 Given several questions about an actual child and his environment, *construct assessment methods and instruments* that can best answer the questions (assuming that appropriate instruments are unavailable).

3 Given the methods and instruments for assessment, *collect the assessment data* according to the instructions suggested by the producers of the instruments and incorporate appropriate means to record the raw data.

4 Given raw assessment data, *summarize the data* in a relevant and meaningful way in order to help answer assessment questions.

5 Given summaries and interpretations of assessment data derived from a variety of assessment methods and resources and covering a variety of attributes,

Table 2-12 Classroom Follow-up Assessment Profile: Rate of Correctly Solving Arithmetic Problems and Date Achieved

Student: Billy; Instrument: Science Research Associates Diagnosis Math Classroom Probes

Broad and specific skills	Proficiency levels									
	0–10%	11–20%	21–30%	31–40%	41–50%	51–60%	61–70%	71–80%	81–90%	91–100%
Sets and set theory										9/1/79 19 per min
Numbers and numeral										9/1/79 20 per min
Addition					9/3/79 8 per min					
Addition facts— 0–5			9/3/79 11 per min							
Addition facts— 6–9		10/-/79 7 per min								
Formal operations— 2-digit, 2-row, no regrouping					10/2/79 9 per min					
Formal operations— 3-row, regrouping				10/2/79 6 per min						
Formal operations— 2-digit, 2-row, regrouping			10/4/79 4 per min							
Formal operations— 3-digit, 3-row, regrouping		1C/4/79 2 per min								

Table 2-13   Resources, Methods, and Instruments Used in Step 3: Follow-up Assessment
(Student: Billy)

Resource	Method	Instrument
Classroom teacher	Criterion-referenced test	Science Research Associates, Inc. (SRA) Math Probes: sets (L-5), cardinal number (L-6), order (L-7), and place value (L-8)
Classroom teacher	Criterion-referenced test	Fountain Valley Reading Test: phonetic analysis, instructional analysis, vocabulary development, comprehension, and study skills
Classroom teacher and school psychologist	Systematic observation	Frequency count of specific off-task behavior: inappropriate talking and out-of-seat

determine the attributes most in need of improvement and *state estimates of the child's entry proficiency levels* for each broad skill *and* the enabling skills which undergird each broad skill.

   6 *Given accurate, relevant, and meaningful summaries of assessment data, interpret* the summaries and discuss their implications with regard to the assessment questions.

The information in this chapter provides the initial step in acquiring these skills and meeting the assessment requirements of P.L. 94-142.

SUMMARY

The assessment of an individual's present performance levels is the first step in developing the individualized education program. The assessment results are then used to make decisions at every subsequent step in developing the individual's program. If the assessment is incorrect, wrong decisions about the individual will be made.

   The final regulations for P.L. 94-142 specify the rules which must be followed when assessing an individual's present levels of performance. These rules require protection-in-evaluation procedures, due process procedures for parents and children, and confidentiality of information.

   The assessment team, which includes a teacher, is responsible for using assessment methods and materials that assure protection-in-evaluation. This requires the methods and materials be technically sound, nondiscriminatory, valid, and reliable.

   To help the assessment team monitor the requirements of P.L. 94-142, checklists for protection-in-evaluation, due process, and confidentiality have been supplied. These checklists require the assessment team to provide information pertinent to the required assurances. The completed checklists become part of the written evidence to meeting the assessment requirements of P.L. 94-142.

Assessment decisions must reflect criteria besides the requirements of P.L. 94-142. These criteria emerge from the restraints involved in assessing an individual's performance in real rather than theoretical or textbook situations. The importance of the variable, the accuracy of the estimates, and the time, expense, and effort involved are all factors which must be considered.

The chapter answers three questions about these factors for the decision-making rationale:

1 How important is it that the individual being assessed show competence on the variable to be estimated?

2 How accurate must the estimate be in order to be accurate enough?

3 How much time, expense, and effort can be devoted in gathering data for the estimate?

Three important variables must be considered in relation to the decision-making rationale. These variables are as follows:

1 The domains, i.e., curriculum areas such as reading, self-care, etc., that are relevant to the individual's future well-being. The assessment team must have a very clear understanding of the skills in each domain. This understanding should be in the form of a sequence of skills for each domain.

2 The resources that are available which can be used as aids during the assessment process. These resources include individuals in the school, individuals in or near the home, community agencies, independent professionals, and literary resources.

3 The various assessment methods which can be used to collect information about a child and his environmental circumstances. The methods include informal consultations, structured interviews, screening devices, norm-referenced tests, criterion-referenced tests, and behavioral observations.

Screening, clinical assessment, and follow-up assessment form a systematic approach to assessment. These three steps translate the decision-making rationale and the important assessment variables into an assessment plan that works.

Screening. The purposes of screening are to uncover the views of those who have prior knowledge of the child and his work and to gather preliminary evidence. Screening evidence is characterized by its broad scope, i.e., general information about domains. Screening results contain a list of domains considered strengths and a list of domains considered weaknesses.

Clinical assessment. The main function of clinical assessment is to estimate the current status of domains that were tentatively identified as strengths and weaknesses during screening. Clinical assessment is characterized by assessing the broad skills of the relevant domains. The evidence is still general or somewhat specific and allows for conclusions concerning domains and broad skills. Such evidence leads to hypothesis about specific skills which make up the broad skills.

Follow-up assessment. Identifying the lowest functional level of each pertinent specific skill is the major purpose of follow-up assessment. Follow-up assessment uses only precise criterion-referenced tests and direct systematic observation as assessment methods. It is relatively inefficient in terms of time, effort, and expense. The outcome of the follow-up assessment is a profile of present performance levels, i.e., exact behavioral strengths and weaknesses of the child and his or her environment. This profile is then used to specify annual goals and short-term objectives in the IEP.

REFERENCES

Bersoff, D. N. Behavioral approaches to assessment and observation in the school. In J. F. Magary (ed.), *Handbook for school psychology services.* St. Louis: Mosby, 1973.

Blake, K. A. *The mentally retarded: An educational psychology.* Englewood Cliffs, N.J.: Prentice-Hall, 1976.

Blake, K. A. *Educating exceptional pupils:: An introduction to contemporary practice.* Reading, Mass.: Addison-Wesley, in press.

Buros, O. K. (ed.), *The seventh mental measurements yearbook.* Highland Park, N.J.: Gryphon, 1972.

Committee on Test Standards (APA, AERA, NCME). *Standards for educational and psychological tests and manuals.* Washington, D.C.: American Psychological Association, 1974.

Committee on Test Use (APA, CEC, NASP). *Use of tests in schools.* Washington, D.C.: American Psychological Association, in press.

DeCecco, J. P., & Crawford, W. R. *The psychology of learning and instruction.* Englewood Cliffs, N.J.: Prentice-Hall, 1974.

Eaves, R., & McLaughlin, P. J. A systems approach for the assessment of the child and his environment: Getting back to basics. *Journal of Special Education,* 1977, *11*(1), 97–111.

Federal Register, 1977, *42*,163.

McLaughlin, P. J., & Eaves, R. *Teacher competency journal: Assessment and selection of instructional strategies.* Paper presented at annual international convention of the Council for Exceptional Children, Atlanta, 1977 (ERIC Document Reproduction Service No. ED 139 171).

Salvia, J., & Ysseldyke, J. *Assessment in special and remedial education,* Boston: Houghton Mifflin, 1978.

Yarger, S. J. From rock through melon to mush: The place of the teaching center in research and evaluation. In G. F. Dickson (ed.), *Research and evaluation in operationally competency-based teacher education programs.* Toledo: University of Toledo, 1975.

Setting Objectives and Task Analysis for Teaching

In the previous chapter, a model for assessing the child was presented. This assessment process allows for the crucial task of identifying the child's present performance levels. With the assessment data, the individualized education program (IEP) committee will then formulate annual goals and short-term instructional objectives for each relevant domain.

Learning Goals

The questions below should key your reading of Chapter 3:

- How do annual goals relate to the development of an individualized education program?
- What criteria should be used in selection of goals?
- Provide an example of a short-term instructional objective which reflects conditions, criteria, and an observable behavior.
- What is task analysis?
- What are four reasons why special education teachers should have task-analysis skills?

- How does task analysis relate to pinpoint assessment? Describe how a task-analytic approach facilitates ongoing evaluation.
- What resources are available to teachers seeking task analyses? In what way can developmental norms and child-development texts be helpful in delineating task analysis?
- How does task analysis relate to the process of curriculum development?

The selection of objectives is an important program decision, which must be made in the initial stages of program development. Careful choice of what to teach will play a major factor in whether the child will learn the skill, and also how quickly the skill will be acquired. Program objectives which are irrelevant, too difficult, or too easy will result in needless failure and may lead to inappropriate classroom behavior.

It is also important that instructional objectives be logically sequenced. Handicapped students learn more quickly when material is presented in a logical progression of easy to hard. Lack of sequencing, or faulty sequencing, is, unfortunately, a frequent limitation of many instructional programs for handicapped students. The inability to present objectives in a carefully developed skill sequence reduces the speed with which the objective will be attained as well as diminishes the effectiveness of instructional procedures.

The purpose of the present chapter is to discuss how to develop annual goals and set short-term instructional objectives which are relevant to a child's educational program. A second aspect of the chapter is to describe the role of task analysis and skill sequencing in developing instructional programs.

RELATIONSHIP OF ANNUAL GOALS AND INSTRUCTIONAL OBJECTIVES TO THE INDIVIDUALIZED EDUCATION PROGRAM

At the completion of assessing the child's present levels of performance the IEP committee will have a profile of strengths and weaknesses. This profile includes the follow-up assessment data stating entry proficiency levels for each broad skill and the specific skills which make up each broad skill for every relevant domain. This information must now be translated into annual goals and instructional objectives. Public Law 94-142 requires that the individualized education program for each child must include (1) a statement of annual goals, including short term instructional objectives and (2) appropriate objective criteria and evaluation procedures and schedules for determining, on at least an annual basis, whether the short-term instructional objectives are being achieved.

ANNUAL GOALS

Goals are statements about broad skills within relevant domains. They describe what broad skills a pupil should attain and at what rates, i.e., in what particular time periods. Below are two annual goals from the domain of arithmetic. These goals were formulated using the follow-up assessment profile in Table 2-12.

1   Billy will add the 100 basic addition facts involving the digits 0 through 9.
2   Billy will add 3-digit, 3-row problems involving no regrouping and regrouping.

The Criteria of Ultimate Functioning

Annual goals must be determined carefully by assessing each child and then ordering individual needs into priorities. Because most handicapped children exhibit numerous skill deficits, the IEP committee must attempt to make judicious decisions concerning which skills should receive the highest priority.

Arrival at a decision of the most-appropriate goals for instruction should be influenced by what Brown has termed the "criterion of ultimate functioning":

> The criterion of ultimate functioning refers to the ever changing, expanding, localized, and personalized cluster of factors that each person must possess in order to function as productively and independently as possible in socially, vocationally, and domestically integrated adult community environments. (Brown, Nietupski, & Hamre-Nietupski, 1976, p. 8)

It will be necessary to make some attempts at predicting what curriculum content will influence the child's adult functioning. Although this is not an easy decision, it is essential that longitudinal planning be exercised for each child. As parents become more involved in the planning process, they will inquire more frequently as to the relevance of skills which are being taught. Educators must be prepared to defend and justify skill priorities in the educational curriculum for each child.

Identifying Annual Goals

What are relevant goals for handicapped students? More specifically, what issues should be taken into consideration when selecting skill areas for instruction? At a minimum, special educators must answer the following questions in selecting appropriate curricula for students:

1   Why should the skill(s) be taught?
2   Is the skill(s) necessary to prepare students to ultimately function in complex heterogenous community settings?
3   Could students function as adults if they did not acquire the skill(s)?
4   Are there other important skills which might be taught more quickly and efficiently?

If selection of appropriate goals cannot be justified, then educators may be teaching handicapped students skills which are not critical to a long-range plan for the child. As an illustration, consider teaching phonics skills to a secondary-level class of trainable retarded students. The purpose of these daily lessons would be to develop reading abilities in students. In all likelihood, these reading goals would not be wise since 16-, 17-, 18- and 19-year-old moderately and severely handicapped students spend a very limited amount of time in public school (until age 21), and phonics training can be a lengthy means of attaining reading skills. An alternative set of reading skills which could be more desirable would involve basic sight-word recognition and comprehension skills. These skills might facilitate prevocational training and community-living preparation.

A second example describes the critical aspects of goal selection in further detail. With the current proliferation of early intervention programs for developmentally delayed children, preschool programs are increasingly serving toddlers with a wide range of disabilities. Assume that a given preschool program has a preponderance of multiply handicapped infants with severe physical disabilities and that a major portion of the curricula for the class calls for learning shape-, size-, and color discriminations, as well as other preacademic "readiness" activities. Unfortunately, a very limited amount of time is left for potty training, physical therapy, language training through use of communication boards, etc. Clearly, this is an illustration of selection of goals which are not as relevant or appropriate as they could be.

Although these examples may appear remote and somewhat exaggerated, they, unfortunately, are not. In many special education classes, students are not taught skills which are important for them. Goals which are selected for instruction are usually (1) those with which the teacher is familiar, that is, has either taught before or has been trained in, (2) those which the teacher believes erroneously are the most critical for the student's successful work or community placement upon completion of school.

Setting Goals

Setting goals requires that broad skills be specified for students. Rates at which the child are expected to learn to accomplish those skills must also be projected. This is the point where broad skills of instruction, as well as rates of instruction, are adjusted to the child's present levels of performance. Consequently, this is a critical juncture in individualizing instruction.

In order to formulate relevant annual goals the following information is required:

1 Specification of the individual's present levels of performance. This must include data stating the individual's proficiency level for each broad skill and the underlying specific skills for each relevant domain. These data are available from the follow-up assessment profile.

2 Specification of the individual's rate of learning for each relevant broad skill. This information should also be available from the follow-up assessment data.

3 A chart that describes a logical sequence of broad skills in each relevant domain.

In Table 3-1 are some annual goals from the domains reading, arithmetic, and self-care. Specific short-term instructional objectives are also presented.

Table 3-1 Examples of Annual Goals and Short-Term Instructional Objectives

		Reading
Annual goal	**A**	Julie will be able to apply the 4 structural-analysis skills presented in her 3d-year reader.
Short-term objectives	**A1**	Given compound words on her reading level, Julie can identify the root words with 100% accuracy.
	A2	Given words to which suffixes have been added, Julie can identify the roots and suffixes with 100% accuracy.
	A3	Given words to which prefixes have been added, Julie can identify the roots and prefixes with 100% accuracy.
	A4	Given words to which more than one affix has been added, Julie can identify each prefix, root, and suffix with 100% accuracy.

		Arithmetic
Annual goal:	**A**	Billy will add the basic addition facts involving the digits 0–9.
Short-term objectives:	**A1**	Given the 60 basic addition problems involving the digits 0–5, Billy will correctly answer all of the problems at the rate of 15 correct per min.
	A2	Given the 40 basic addition problems involving the digits 6–9, Billy will correctly answer all of the problems at the rate of 15 per min.

		Self-Care
Annual goal:	**A**	Beth will dress independently on a minimum of 4 dressing skills.
Short-term objectives:	**A1**	Given the verbal cue, "Put your underpants on," Beth will do so correctly, within 2 min on 3 consecutive days.
	A2	Given the verbal cue, "Put your socks on," Beth will do so correctly within 2 min on 3 consecutive days.
	A3	Given the verbal cue, "Put your pants on," Beth will do so correctly within 2 min on 3 consecutive days.
	A4	Given the verbal cue, "Put your shirt on," Beth will do so correctly within 2 min on 3 consecutive days.

INSTRUCTIONAL OBJECTIVES

Instructional objectives are statements about the specific skills a student must master in order to meet annual goals. They describe the specific skills which make up the broad skills. The relationship is as follows:

   1 A domain is made up of broad skills in a given area, such as reading, arithmetic, motor, or self-care.
   2 Each broad skill within a domain is made up of several specific skills.
   3 Annual goals are stated in terms of broad skills which need to be taught.

4 Instructional objectives are stated in terms of sequenced specific skills which the pupil must master in order to learn the broad skill.

5 The decisions about which domains, broad skills, and specific skills need to be taught are based on the assessment data and the appropriate skill sequence chart.

Table 3-1 presents sequenced short-term instructional objectives for three annual goals. Notice the relationship between the annual goals and the short-term instructional objectives.

Sequenced instructional objectives become the cornerstone of the individualized education program. They are the target end products and have two basic purposes:

1 They serve as the basis for selecting instructional procedures. That is, the instructional procedures should be designed to lead to the behavior specified in the instructional objective.

2 They serve as the basis for selecting evaluation procedures. Evaluation procedures should be designed to enable the pupil to demonstrate whether the behavior specified in the instructional objective has been attained.

Criteria for Instructional Objectives

As teachers develop and select instructional objectives, they should be guided by five criteria. These criteria pertain to sources, comprehensiveness, specificity, explicitness, and completeness (Blake, 1974). Blake states these criteria as follows:

1 The instructional objectives should be relevant to the society, appropriate for the learner, and suitably placed within the structure of the content discipline. . . .

2 The instructional objectives should be stated. All material in instructional programs should be keyed to particular objectives. If not, the material should not be there. The instructional program should have material for each objective. . . .

3 The instructional objectives should be neither too precise nor too broad. They should be at the generality level which the teacher and pupils can deal with. . . .

4 The instructional objectives should be unambiguous. Everyone who reads them should be able to agree about what instructional and evaluation methods are appropriate, and when the objective has been attained. . . .

5 The instructional objective should be complete. It should contain the three components—the content elements, the behavior elements, and the required level of mastery. (p. 174–177)

Procedures for Specifying Instructional Objectives

A behaviorally stated instructional objective involves anchoring the objective in the specific skill and the pupil's behavior. According to Mager (1962), this involves three components: a statement of given conditions under which the desired performance should occur, a description of the desired performance, and a listing of the criterion for adequate performance.

Specifying Performance Conditions   The performance conditions specify the testing conditions, i.e., what the learner will be given or allowed to use during the testing situation. Such statements are usually introduced by the words *Given* . . . or *Using* . . . or *Referring to* . . . , and the entire phrase generally precedes the terminal behavior. For example,

> Given words in which the spelling conforms to the final *e* principle, the pupil can supply the correct spelling, with 95-percent accuracy.

Specifying Desired Performance   When decisions are made about the desired performance, the specific skills are selected in order to achieve the broad skill specified in the annual goals. As stated earlier, it will be necessary to consult a skill sequence chart for the relevant domain and the follow-up assessment profile. Judgments should be based on what specific skills the student has mastered and what specific skills remain to be mastered before the broad skill is learned.

It is difficult to be explicit about the specific skills the pupil must learn. The key element is the verbs which are used. These verbs must be concrete; that is, they must refer unequivocally to behavior that is clearly observable. Usually action verbs provide the most effectively descriptions.

Specifying Criterion of Adequate Performance   When the performance criterion is established, it is necessary to specify the *how well* part of the instructional objective. This is the achievement level that a teacher considers sufficient for the student to begin work on the next highest specific skill. To specify the ahcievement level, it is necessary to decide about reference standards and cutting points.

Blake (1974) describes two types of reference standards: absolute mastery and relative mastery. Absolute mastery means criterion referenced. Each pupil's performance is judged against how much content is learned. The achievements of other pupils' are immaterial. Relative mastery is norm-referenced. Each pupil's performance is judged against how much is learned in relation to how much other pupils learn.

After a reference standard is selected, the next decision is about cutting points. The question is, How much should the student be expected to attain in relation to the content or group? The following rationale undergirds setting cut-off points (Blake, 1974): Specific skills are taught in order to ultimately achieve broad skills. Therefore, it is necessary to teach for a maximum of retention and positive transfer. Conditions which facilitate retention and transfer are discussed in Chapter 4.

TASK ANALYSIS AND SKILL SEQUENCING

Once annual goals have been identified and instructional objectives written, then the specific skills of the instructional objectives must be sequenced and broken down into small steps for teaching. The relationship of goals, objectives, and task analysis is shown in Figure 3-1.

Task analysis is the breaking down of specific skills into smaller steps which may be easier for the child to learn. It is a process which involves a logical sequencing of material from easier to more complex. A task analysis of a specific skill provides a precise description of the child behaviors which are expected in a given instructional situation. For example, in most classroom programs, the teacher will ask a question or make a request of the child in order to elicit specific answers about an assignment or task. The child will in turn respond either correctly or incorrectly. Correct child responses may be considered as target behaviors in a task analysis. Careful sequencing of the desired child responses will ensure continuity within the program as well as facilitate learning for the student.

Skill sequencing may also be considered as a logical progression of instructional objectives within a given domain. Williams and Gotts (1977) define skill sequences: "A skill sequence is delineated to provide a framework of tasks or objectives within which many types of instructional programs may be organized. A sequence is not a statement of how to teach but rather a statement of what is to be taught and in what order" (p. 221).

The continual development and field testing of reliable and valid task-analyzed skill sequences which are effective with handicapped students is an important task which faces special educators. There are unquestionably alternatives to the sequence provided above; these alternatives might be tried out and evaluated by teachers in an effort to find the most-effective sequence.

What must be recognized, however, is that careful sequencing of specific skills is a critical aspect of the instructional situation between the teacher and child. Expensive materials, favorable staff ratios, and the most innovative of teaching activities are not being efficiently used when material is not presented in a logical sequence, or worse, when no sequence is provided at all.

The arbitrary selection of isolated skills for handicapped students is an inadequate means of providing optimal educational services. In order for the child's educational program to flow logically and consistently over the approximately 18 years in school, skills must be selected from relevant domains that are clearly tied to the child's longitudinal or long-range educational plan.

WHY A TEACHER SHOULD HAVE TASK-ANALYSIS COMPETENCIES

A task-analysis approach to presenting information is optimal because it provides an instructional sequence and allows for the presentation of material in small chunks. By analyzing objectives and teaching the material in small steps which are logically sequenced, the teacher will help the child more quickly grasp

Curriculum Domain
↓
Annual Goals Written for Broad Skills

Broad skill	Broad skill	Broad skill
A	B	C

↓

Short-term Instruction Objectives Written for the
Specific Skills Making up Each Broad Skill

Broad skill	Broad skill	Broad skill
A	B	C
Sequenced specific skills	Sequenced specific skills	Sequenced specific skills
A1, A2, A3, and A4	B1, B2, and B3	C1, C2, and C3

↓

Each Specific Skill Is Task-Analyzed into Small
Steps for Teaching

Specific skills				Specific skills			Specific skills		
A1	A2	A3	A4	B1	B2	B3	C1	C2	C3
Step 1	Step 1	Step 1	Step 1	Step 1	Step 1	Step 1	Step 1	Step 1	Step 1
Step 2	Step 2	Step 2	Step 2	Step 2	Step 2	Step 2	Step 2	Step 2	Step 2
Step 3	Step 3	Step 3	Step 3	Step 3	Step 3	Step 3	Step 3	Step 3	Step 3
Step 4	Step 4	Step 4	Step 4	Step 4	Step 4	Step 4	Step 4	Step 4	Step 4
	Step 5	Step 5	Step 5	Step 5	Step 5	Step 5		Step 5	Step 5
	Step 6	Step 6	Step 6	Step 6	Step 6	Step 6		Step 6	Step 6
	Step 7	Step 7	Step 7	Step 7	Step 7	Step 7		Step 7	Step 7
	Step 8	Step 8	Step 8	Step 8	Step 8	Step 8		Step 8	Step 8
	Step 9	Step 9	Step 9	Step 9	Step 9	Step 9			Step 9
	Step 10	Step 10	Step 10		Step 10	Step 10			Step 10
		Step 11	Step 11			Step 11			
		Step 12				Step 12			
		Step 13				Step 13			
		Step 14				Step 14			
		Step 15				Step 15			
						Step 16			
						Step 17			
						Step 18			
						Step 19			
						Step 20			
						Step 21			
						Step 22			
						Step 23			
						Step 24			
						Step 25			

Figure 3-1 Relationship of goals, objectives, and task analysis.

the information. Special educators must be able to effectively employ task analyses and skill sequences in classroom programming and should thoroughly understand the multiple advantages of this approach.

Recent research (Edgar, Maser, Smith, & Haring, 1977) clearly supports the efficacy of teaching in small steps with more severely handicapped learners. With mildly handicapped students, the findings also indicate that in most cases the amount of material presented is directly related to the accuracy of the child's response (Blake, 1976).

Individualizing Instruction

Another major advantage of a task-analysis approach is that instruction for students with different levels of functioning may be individualized. Although some students can perform the majority of steps in a skill sequence, others will be unable to complete even one-third or one-fourth of the task. With task analysis, a child's instructional program can be tailored to the appropriate level of functioning. Furthermore, children can move through the sequence at their own speed.

Homogeneous grouping within the class, and according to skill level, will also be facilitated for each curriculum area. Because it is not usually realistic or practical to provide one to one instruction for each child in the class, it may be advantageous to place students in small groups with regard to their performance in a skill sequence.

Facilitates Teaching

In conducting precision assessments of the child's given skill level in a given domain, it is helpful to pinpoint the entry-level target behavior at which the child is presently functioning. With a task analysis it will be possible to decide exactly on what level the student requires instruction (Knapczyk, 1975). Reliable observational assessment will indicate the student's strengths and weaknesses in a given specific skill, thereby providing objective evidence that the child needs a program prescribed to remediate those weaknesses. This specific assessment is done by the teacher, usually independent of the IEP committee, as the child's program is implemented.

Consider the following illustration of how an entry-level step in the motor domain might be assessed for a severely involved deaf-blind child. The specific skill of concern is standing up from a sitting position independently. For a deaf and blind child, sense of balance and equilibrium is grossly underdeveloped and requires training. Table 3-2 is a task analysis for standing up independently. Each plus indicates that the step was performed with no assistance; minuses reveal that the child was unable to complete that part of the skill without physical assistance. It should be noted that this is only one possible task analysis of standing-up behavior.

When this task-analytic assessment is performed over a period of several days, it becomes apparent that there is a consistent breakdown in learning between Steps 3 and 4. This suggests that the entry level to begin instruction is at

Table 3-2 Task Analysis for Standing Up
(Instructional objective: Given the verbal cue, "Stand up," the child will do so independently within 1 min on 3 consecutive days)

Steps in task	Performs independently	Needs assistance
1 Child sits on floor in 4-point stance.	+	
2 Child puts right foot flat on floor.	+	
3 Child reaches for support table with right hand.	+	
4 Child puts left foot on floor.		−
5 Child straightens back and lifts head up.		−
6 Child pulls self ½-way up to standing position.		−
7 Child pulls self ¾-way up to standing position.		−
8 Child stands up completely with support table.		
9 Child completes Steps 4–8 without support table.		−

Step 4. Finding behavioral pinpoints within well-developed instructional sequences facilitates learning by handicapped students and promotes more efficient instruction. Children who receive instruction at a level in which they are already proficient will become bored; on the other hand, students who are taught steps at too high a level are more likely to fail.

Pinpointing entry-level behaviors through observational assessment can also be conducted with less-handicapped students. Assume that you have a secondary-level class of educable retarded students. One of the relevant curriculum areas should be community preparation skills, since these students will eventually have to go to work and function in the community. One broad skill within this domain which will probably be required is the use of public transportation. Being able to ride a bus could be the basis for one short-term instructional objective. Certo, Schwartz, and Brown (1976) here validated an excellent instructional task analysis for riding a bus, and this analysis is presented in an abbreviated form in Table 3-3.

Careful observational assessment of the student's steps on this sequence would probably reveal that each student could perform at slightly different levels. The behavioral pinpointing of specific strengths and weaknesses within this sequence for riding a bus allows the teacher to focus on the precise area to begin instruction.

Objective Means of Evaluation

In order to evaluate progress which handicapped children make in instructional programs, it is advantageous to objectively record the performance gains which

Table 3-3   Skill Sequence for Riding a Public Bus

Instructional Objective: Given a task requiring the student to ride a bus, the student will be able to ride the appropriate bus with 100% accuracy.

Task Analysis of Objective
  Phases:
  I   Teaching Ss to ride a simulated city bus in the classroom.
  II Teaching Ss selected places in the city of Madison, Wis., where food, clothing, opportunities for recreation, and other services could be obtained, and to determine what bus to take in order to reach those places from Capitol Park.
  III Teaching Ss to ride an actual city bus to and from Capitol Park to obtain the food, clothing, recreation opportunities, or other services listed on the bus route cards.
  IV Teaching Ss to determine what buses to take to places that do not appear on bus route cards.

Phase I: Teaching Ss to ride a simulated city bus in the classroom.
  Step 1—S tells *T* the differences between a school bus and a city bus and what is meant by the term *destination.*

  Step 2—S labels the various parts of a Madison Metro bus, recognizes a bus stop, and demonstrates knowledge of the student fare.

  Step 3—S emits the following behaviors in sequence after *T*'s cues have been faded, using a simulated Madison Metro bus:

  a *S* says where he/she wants to go.
  b *S* walks to a bus stop.
  c *S* waves bus to a stop.
  d *S* reads the destination sign on the front of the bus.
  e *S* enters the bus by the front door.
  f *S* hands the driver the bus route card and says, "Let me off near _____."
  g *S* pays the fare.
  h *S* sits or stands (varies).
  i *S* rings the buzzer and goes to a door on cue from the driver.
  j *S* gets off.

Phase II: Teaching *S* selected places in the city of Madison, where food, clothing, opportunities for recreation, and other services could be obtained and what bus to take to reach the destination from Capitol Park.

  Step 1—S demonstrates the ability to label 9 "sight words" individually presented. (These are words which will appear on individual bus route cards. Each bus route card should be considered a set of 8 words.)

  Step 2—S points to the 8 words appearing on the bus route card learned in Step 1 on cue from *T.*

  Step 3—S tells *T* the name of the bus route that would appear on the bus destination sign when traveling between 2 points listed on the bus route card.

  Step 4—T asks *S* to view a videotape of a bus route and names a destination where *S* should get off. *S* responds by throwing a switch which lights a bulb when the appropriate stop flashes on the monitor.

Phase III: Teaching Ss to ride an actual city bus to and from Capitol Park to obtain the food, clothing, recreational opportunities, or other services listed on the bus route cards.

Table 3-3 (Continued)

Step 1—Ss choose one of the bus routes they have learned. *T* chooses the last stop on this route as *Ss'* destination. Using their bus route cards, *Ss* determine the name of the route leaving and returning to Capitol Park from the destination chosen. *Ss* verbally rehearse the stops along this route. They find the proper bus stop at Capitol Square.

Step 2—Ss, starting at Capitol Park, take the appropriate bus to the destination chosen in Step 1 and return. They travel in a small group with *T*.

Step 3—Same as Step 2, except *Ss* travel without *T* in a small group.

Step 4—Same as Step 2, except *Ss* travel alone.

Step 5—Ss perform in the classroom the prerequisite skills necessary to transfer buses.

Step 6—Using their bus route cards in the classroom, *Ss* gain experience at finding the buses they need to take when transferring.

Step 7—Ss ride a city bus, traveling in a small group with *T*, choose two destinations, and transfer to reach them.

Step 8—Same as Step 7, except *Ss* travel in small group without *T*.

Step 9—Same as Step 7, except *Ss* travel alone.

Step 10—Ss perform in the classroom the prerequisite skills for taking a city bus from their houses to Capitol Park and returning home.

Step 11—S chooses a destination, takes a city bus from his/her home, traveling with *T* to Capitol Park, transfers to the destination, and returns home.

Step 12—Same as Step 11, except *S* rides alone.

Phase IV: Teaching *Ss* how to determine what bus to take to places that do not appear on bus route cards.

Step 1—Teaching *Ss* to label cards with the names of major streets in the city of Madison. (This is done to facilitate labeling addresses in later stages of this phase.)

Step 2—S looks up one of the streets acquired in Step 1 of this phase in the *Street Index* on the back of a map of Madison. He/she then labels the coordinates listed next to the name of the street located.

Step 3—S gains experience at finding streets on a map of Madison.

Step 4—Teaching *Ss* how to use the Madison telephone directory to find addresses and phone numbers of places they would like to go to. *S* also writes down the address and phone number that he/she finds.

Step 5—S calls Directory Assistance to find out the phone number of a place he/she has been unable to locate in the phone book. *S* then calls the number to find the address.

Step 6—S uses an actual phone to call Directory Assistance to find a phone number. *S* calls this number and writes down the address.

Step 7—S finds an exact location on a map of Madison using the numerical component of the address.

Step 8—S gains experience at finding exact locations on the map.

Step 9—S is taught the names of various bus routes listed on the map.

Table 3-3 (Continued)

Step 10—S gains experience finding bus routes on the map.

Step 11—S learns how to find the closest route to a particular street address he/she has located on the front of the map.

Step 12—S gains experience at finding the appropriate bus route for various addresses using a map of Madison.

Step 13—S looks up an address in the phone book, locates the closest bus route, and rides the bus to the destination with T and a small group of Ss.

Step 14—Same as Step 13, except Ss travel in a small group without T.

Step 15—Same as Step 13, except S travels alone.

Source: Certo, Schwartz, & Brown (1976, pp. 444–456)

are observed by the teacher. Evaluating progress demonstrated on a task-analyzed skill sequence is a logical extension of the assessment process described above. Use of task-analysis sequences is one means of evaluation which will minimize teacher bias of the child's progress.

As an illustration, consider the bus-riding sequence which is described in Table 3-3. Assume that this sequence was initiated at the beginning of the school year; the first 3 months have now passed and it is time to prepare an evaluation of each student's progress in this program. If the teacher decides to provide an objective behavioral evaluation, the following process may be undertaken. The number of steps in the sequence which each student has performed consistently, through instruction, may be tabulated. This will indicate which students were making progress and whether the reference standard within the instructional objective was met. Written anecdotal descriptions which accompany this evaluation will be helpful and further illuminate the progress of the child in this skill sequence. However, written descriptions alone are susceptible to personal biases of the teacher, who may be unable to completely objectify the student's performance.

Another aspect of this form of evaluation is that it can provide reinforcing feedback to parents and teachers who are working with severely handicapped children. Students who exhibit gross language and motor handicaps usually progress very slowly. A task-analysis sequence which is subdivided into minute behavioral increments will more precisely reflect the child's progress. Although the steps achieved may be very small, it is still positive to see the gains which can be made.

Such small gains often cannot be discerned unless they are recorded and evaluated on a chart (Mira, 1977). Hanson (1976) has done an excellent job of demonstrating how progress in physically handicapped infants can be evaluated. The vertical axes in Figure 3-2 indicate percentage of steps which were aquired in the task analyses for (1) localizing to sound, (2) reaching and grasping, and (3) rolling—back to side. The roman numerals on the graph indicate lesser degrees

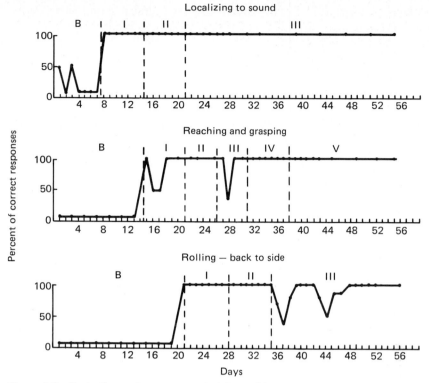

Figure 3-2 Evaluating motor responses in infants. (Hanson, 1976, p. 46.)

of teacher support and assistance as the infants become more proficient at the motor skill.

Replicability

Another positive feature of a task-analysis approach is that it facilitates replicability of the instructional program by other classroom staff. If a skill sequence is implemented for a child, there will be a logical order in which the child's behavior should develop; there should also be a sequence to the behaviors which are required by the teacher in order to make the responses in the skill sequence occur.

In order for teaching associates, practicum students, student teachers or other paraprofessional staff to effectively help the teacher carry through a program there must be consistency. When the order of instructional behaviors is clearly specified, then, with minimal instruction, other staff may be able to also implement the program. For substitute teachers who must fill in for extended periods of time, skill sequences will be helpful.

It will also be beneficial if other teachers can obtain similar results with instructional-program sequences. If a certain task analysis facilitates learning for one class of handicapped students, it may be successful with another class. This might reduce the amount of time which educators must spend in selecting appropriately sequenced and analyzed task analyses. Increasing success with selected task analyses will also suggest the empirical validity of such a sequence.

METHODS OF GENERATING TASK ANALYSES

To this point, discussion has centered around why teachers should select relevant goals and objectives, and why task analysis is an important instructional competency. The purpose of this section is to identify and describe how to develop task analyses. Several specific methods of generating task analyses and locating resources which facilitate the development of instructional sequences are presented.

Reviewing Existing Resources

Once relevant domains for instruction have been selected for the child, it is necessary to do a careful review of the available commercial materials. In recent years, more and more publishers have been providing texts which offer already completed and field-tested skill sequences. Through use of these books the teacher can save valuable curriculum-development time by modifying, adapting, or replicating relevant instructional sequences.

A good example of one such resource is the text developed by Anderson, Hodson and Jones (1974), which is entitled *Instructional Programming for the Handicapped Students*. Within this compendium are well over 100 task-analysis sequences representing a number of curriculum areas, among them, writing, arithmetic, motor development, self-help and vocational training. Similar texts have been published by Bender and Valletutti (1976), Myers, Sinco, and Stalma (1973), Wehman (1979), and Wehman and McLaughlin (1980).

The value of texts such as these is that replicable instructional sequences are provided which may facilitate task analytic assessment, learning in small parts, and objective evaluation. Furthermore, they usually span a large number of curricular areas across a wide range of disability categories. Clearly, the use of such commercial resources can be a savings on teacher time.

On the other hand, a caution should be noted. The wise teacher will not take every printed word as gospel; it may be that some of the skill sequences which are published are inadequate or unacceptable. Simply because the work is published does not indicate that it shows the only way, or even the right way. In selecting skill sequences from commercial resources, it is usually a good practice to confer with several other teachers involved in programming with a similar population of students.

Modifying Developmental Sequences

Skill sequences may also be generated through careful perusal of textbooks which provide sequences of normal child development. These may be found in child-development texts, adaptive physical education books, or occupational and physical therapy textbooks. Much of the cognitive-developmental theory generated by Jean Piaget (1962) may be helpful to the teacher in verifying whether curriculum content and sequence is relevant for students. Another excellent source in the sequencing of cognitive development of infants is the work of Uzgiris and Hunt (1975).

Since most handicapped children are developmentally young in one or more curriculum areas, the application of child-development norms to sequencing instructional content may be quite fruitful. Although developmental milestones are usually too broad for teachers to use as specific skills, they provide a general developmental structure. This is particularly true in cases for which little work has been published.

A good illustration of this would be fine motor sequencing for physically handicapped children, developmentally delayed toddlers, or severely retarded individuals. Presently, there are few valid skill sequences which exist for fine motor curriculum. Since the skills involved in this domain (reaching, grasping, transfer, bilateral reach, etc.) are critical to development, a sequence in this area is necessary. A logical means of accomplishing this goal is to carefully scan and review occupational therapy, physical therapy, and motor-learning textbooks. From these books, a number of different sequences in fine motor development will be available. These can be modified into one tentative sequence which must then be field-tested with the class. This will allow the teacher to conclude whether the sequence is viable for future use.

Adapting Curriculum Guides

Another means of identifying skill sequences which may be potentially useful is through careful inspection of curriculum guides which have relevant information. These may include workbooks, detailed guides for a similar population of handicapped students, or "homemade" activity books developed by other teachers.

In many ways, educational materials and resources which are already available, although not exactly suitable for a given class, are an ideal source for teachers to review for skill sequences. They fulfill the criteria of having been field-tested by other teachers. Frequently, such materials can be located quickly and inexpensively through the public school system or possibly a nearby university.

What is critical is that teachers know how to modify educational materials and curriculum guides for the purpose of implementing a logical skill sequence. A good example of the pitfalls which may occur from not doing this is reflected in the extensive reliance of many teachers on commercial workbooks. Large numbers of special education classes rely solely on the content, and sequence of that content, for reading, arithmetic, and other domains. This is regrettable since these workbooks may:

    1   Be inadequate in terms of relevant content
    2   Be "culturally-biased," and, therefore, unfair to inner-city black children and other minority groups

3 Fail to provide necessary breakdown of material which is being presented

4 Fail to provide a logical sequence of material

If curriculum guides and workbooks are used as modifiable resources which provide only the initial curriculum-content outline for instruction, then they become an invaluable means of developing individualized skill sequences which are relevant to each child's own educational needs. Before curriculum guides can be employed effectively, however, an education plan must be established for the child, in terms of what skills will be taught. Secondly, the teacher should have the basic skill of knowing *how* to generate a task-analyzed skill sequence without the use of any other materials. This competency will facilitate developing instructional sequences through each of the previous three methods that have been discussed above. It is this competency in breaking down skills and logically sequencing objectives that will now be discussed.

Breaking Down Skills Into Small Steps[1]

In developing skill sequences, there are seven steps which must be carried through. These are listed below and will be explained in detail.

1 Write the instructional objective for the specific skill.

2 Review instructional relevant resources for the task analysis breakdown of the specific skill.

3 Derive the basic steps of the objective.

4 Sequence the basic steps.

5 Eliminate unnecessary steps.

6 Eliminate redundant steps.

7 Determine prerequisite skills. (Williams, 1975, p. 34)

Since writing an instructional objective was discussed in depth earlier in this chapter, it will not be necessary to discuss this process. It should be apparent, however, that the instructional objective is the destination which the teacher is trying to help the child reach. Following the skill sequence will hopefully move the child closer to that objective.

As has been noted above, it is most efficient to review any possible resources which might be considered relevant to the task of generating a sequence. However, if this search proves fruitless, as it well may, particularly with the more-severely involved student, then the basic steps of the task analysis may be derived through several processes (Williams, 1975). Initially, it may be of value to list all the steps of a given skill which have been identified, although not sequenced, in other resources, such as curriculum guides and developmental scales. These steps can then be arranged in an order which the teacher feels is a logical progression from easy to hard.

[1]Much of this section was developed from a paper written by Wes Williams (1975), assistant professor at the University of Vermont's Center on Special Education.

Another means of generating the basic steps for a task is to observe students and simply ask the question: "To master this objective, what steps must be performed?"

A third process can also be effective. By slowly performing the target objective or watching others complete the objective, one is able to record the steps which are necessary. Whether imagining the requisite steps, or actually performing them, the teacher is sequentially taken through the steps which lead to the target objective. It is this precise type of task analysis which is necessary before goals of pinpoint assessment and evaluation, and learning in small steps can be accomplished.

Once the basic steps of the target objective are identified through task analysis, they must be arranged in the logical order required for completion. As an illustration, consider the self-care task of combing one's hair. There may be as many as twenty-three steps of this skill derived from the processes described on the next page; these steps are generated in a somewhat random order in the first part of Table 3-4. In order to be a viable task-analysis sequence, those steps need to be arranged into a logical and orderly progression. This is done in the second part of the table.

Field Testing

At this point it may be advantageous to review the sequence and determine whether there are any steps which are either not necessary or repetitious. Furthermore, it is necessary to "trial-run" the sequence before fully implementing it with a whole class of children. In may be that what seemed logical in the analysis stages is very clumsy for actual instructional purposes. The hair-combing task analysis provides one example of this. This task could be subdivided into the child combing hair in sections of eighths instead of fourths; however, it would probably make instructional activities and teaching procedures very awkward to implement effectively.

In the final stage of development, prerequisite skills which are necessary to realistically perform the steps of the task must be identified. These skills can also be considered entry-level skills or responses. Prerequisite skills are important because they indicate to the teacher at what level different students must perform before they can be reasonably expected to acquire the target objective. For example, in order to teach a deaf child to use sign language, a logical prerequisite skill would be motor imitation. A prerequisite skill to independent toileting might be proficiency in pulling down and pulling up pants before and after going to the toilet. Entry-level skills for counting or addition would involve, at a minimum, knowing the concept of set and number. There is frequently more than one entry-level skill which precedes the target objective.

Developing Curriculum from Skill Sequences

In many domains there has been little curriculum development or inadequate and limited curriculum. When this is a problem, it may be advantageous to

Table 3-4   Task Analysis for Combing Hair

Part 1: Identifying component steps in the task

---

 1   Child locates comb.
 2   Child picks up comb in one hand.
20   Child places comb back in its proper place.
19   Child brings teeth of comb completely through rear portion of hair.
 3   Child raises comb to center of the head.
18   Child combs rear portion of hair by bringing teeth of comb ¾ of the way through hair from top rear to bottom rear of hair.
 6   Child combs hair in the center of the head forward by bringing teeth of comb ¾ of the way through hair from center of head towards front of head.
 5   Child combs hair in the center of the head forward by bringing teeth of comb ½ of the way through hair from center of head towards front of head.
17   Child combs rear portion of hair by bringing teeth of comb ½ of the way through hair from top rear to bottom rear of head.
 4   Child combs hair in the center of the head forward by bringing teeth of comb ¼ of the way through hair from center of head towards front of head.
 7   Child brings teeth of comb completely through hair in the center of the head using many strokes from center of head towards front of head.
12   Child combs hair on the opposite side of head by bringing teeth of comb ¼ of the way through hair from top side to bottom of 1 side.
 8   Child combs hair on 1 side of head by bringing teeth of comb ¼ of the way through hair from top side to bottom of 1 side.
11   Child brings teeth of comb completely through hair.
 9   Child combs hair on 1 side of head by bringing teeth of comb ½ of the way through hair from top side to bottom of 1 side.
10   Child combs hair on 1 side of head by bringing teeth of comb ¾ of the way through hair from top side to bottom of 1 side.
13   Child combs hair on opposite side of the head by bringing teeth of comb ½ of the way through hair from top side to bottom of 1 side.
16   Child combs rear portion of hair by bringing teeth of comb ¼ of the way through hair from top rear of head to bottom rear of head.
14   Child combs hair on opposite side of the head by bringing teeth of comb ¾ of the way through hair from top side to bottom of 1 side.
15   Child brings teeth of comb completely through hair.

---

consider building a curriculum from skill sequences which have been previously acquired or developed. In this way, there will be a steady accrual of sequenced content within a given cluster of skills.

An example of one domain which requires greater attention by teachers is community skill training. There is little doubt that if handicapped students of all categories are to be mainstreamed into the flow of society, then community-adjustment skills must be a priority. Unfortunately, there have been a limited number of community skill sequences which have been developed and validated with handicapped students. What is required is a gradual accumulation of the skill sequences which have been generated. These sequences can then be placed together logically in a horizontal as well as vertical fashion. An illustration of this

Table 3-4 (Continued)

Part II: Logical sequencing of components in the task

1 Child locates comb.
2 Child picks up comb in 1 hand.
3 Child raises comb to center of the head.
4 Child combs hair in the center of the head forward by bringing teeth of comb ¼ of the way through hair from center of head towards front of head.
5 Child combs hair in the center of the head forward by bringing teeth of comb ½ of the way through hair from center of head towards front of head.
6 Child combs hair in the center of the head forward by bringing teeth of comb ¾ of the way through hair from center of head towards front of head.
7 Child brings teeth of comb completely through hair in the center of the head using many strokes from center of head towards front of head.
8 Child combs hair on 1 side of head by bringing teeth of comb ¼ of the way through hair from top side to bottom of 1 side.
9 Child combs hair on 1 side of head by bringing teeth of comb ½ of the way through hair from top side to bottom of 1 side.
10 Child combs hair on 1 side of head by bringing teeth of comb ¾ of the way through hair from top side to bottom of 1 side.
11 Child brings teeth of comb completely through hair.
12 Child combs hair on the opposite side of head by bringing teeth of comb ¼ of the way through hair from top side to bottom of 1 side.
13 Child combs hair on opposite side of the head by bringing teeth of comb ½ of the way through hair from top side to bottom of 1 side.
14 Child combs hair on opposite side of the head by bringing teeth of comb ¾ of the way through hair from top side to bottom of 1 side.
15 Child brings teeth of comb completely through hair.
16 Child combs rear portion of hair by bringing teeth of comb ¼ of the way through hair from top rear to bottom rear of head.
17 Child combs rear portion of hair by bringing teeth of comb ½ of the way through hair from top rear to bottom rear of head.
18 Child combs rear portion of hair by bringing teeth of comb ¾ of the way through hair from top rear to bottom rear of hair.
19 Child brings teeth of comb completely through rear portion of hair.
20 Child places comb back in its proper place.

is the functional use of money. Making change is a necessary skill required for (1) supermarket shopping, (2) going to the post office, (3) riding a public bus, and (4) going to the movie theater. Of course, the list of skills is endless and depends on the type of community setting (i.e., rural, urban) in which the student lives.

Brown, Certo, and their colleagues have begun to generate exemplary skill sequences for handicapped students in the area of community skill programming. These include riding a public bus (Certo, Schwartz, & Brown, 1976), which was outlined earlier in the chapter, functional money use in community settings (Certo & Swetlik, 1976), and how to write a shopping list and make purchases in a supermarket (Nietupski, Certo, Pumpian, & Belmore, 1976).

Through acquisition of these skill sequences, as well as the initial work published in commercial resources, the scope and sequence of a community-living-skills curriculum may be effectively established. Clearly, this is a long and painstaking process, and one that would probably not be engaged in by one or two teachers, but instead by groups of teachers in task-force arrangements.

SUMMARY

The purpose of the chapter is to describe how to select annual goals and instructional objectives for handicapped students. The importance of selecting relevant objectives is emphasized; those objectives are described. Task analysis and skill sequencing in the context of assessment, instruction, and evaluation of instructional programs and the advantages of skill sequencing are discussed in detail. Finally, methods of generating skill sequences are also reviewed with several illustrations provided.

The selection of relevant annual goals is discussed as being critical in the development of the individualized education program (IEP). Goals are statements about broad skills within a given domain. The goals selected for instruction should reflect criteria such as *why* the skill should be taught, is the skill *necessary* for the child to function in the community, and are there other skills on which it might be more *efficient* to concentrate.

Short-term objectives should be derived from the annual goals. They should reflect a specific statement of the learning conditions, the observable behavior to be attained, and a performance criteria. The criteria is necessary for determining when the child has mastered the skill and is ready to move to the next skill.

Once objectives have been determined, a task analysis of the skill must be completed. A task analysis is the systematic breakdown of a behavior into smaller steps. Task analysis is an important skill for teachers to have because it (1) facilitates replicability of instruction, (2) helps determine the child's specific skill level (assessment), (3) is valuable for evaluating progress in children who make gains slowly, and (4) provides a sequence for children to learn material.

Task analysis is especially valuable in determining the progress a severely handicapped student makes. By assessing the number of steps in the task analysis which the child performs independent of assistance, the teacher is able to provide a criterion-referenced means of evaluation.

Task analysis can be obtained from curriculum guides and commercial resources. Task-analyzed skill sequences also can be derived from developmental norms and child-development texts. In many cases, however, teachers must be able to generate task analyses without this assistance. This requires a logical breakdown of the skill and continual field testing of the effectiveness of the analysis with students. When a series of task analyses have been cumulatively established, this may lead to the development of a curriculum. The most effective curricula are those which have come through a rigorous field-testing process.

REFERENCES

Anderson, D., Hodson, G., & Jones, W. *Instructional programming for the handicapped student.* Springfield, Ill.: Charles C. Thomas, 1974.

Blake, K. A. *Teaching the retarded.* Englewood Cliffs, N.J.: Prentice-Hall, 1974.

Blake, K. A. *The mentally retarded: An educational psychology.* Englewood Cliffs, N.J.: Prentice-Hall, 1976.

Bender, M., & Valletutti, P. *Teaching the moderately and severely handicapped* (Vol. II). Baltimore: University Park Press, 1976.

Brown, L., Nietupski, J., & Hamre-Nietupski, S. The criterion of ultimate functioning and public school services for severely handicapped students. In *Hey don't forget about me, education's investment in the severely, profoundly, and multiply handicapped.* Reston, Va.: Council on Exceptional Children, 1977.

Certo, N., & Swetlik, B. Making pruchases: A functional money use program for severely handicapped students. In L. Brown, N. Certo, K. Belmore, & T. Crowner (eds.), *Papers and programs related to public school services for secondary age severely handicapped students* (Vol. VI). Madison, Wis.: Madison Public Schools, 1976.

Certo, N., Schwartz, R., & Brown, L. Teaching severely handicapped students to ride a public bus. In N. Haring & L. Brown (eds.), *Teaching the severely handicapped* (Vol. II). New York: Grune & Stratton, 1976.

Edgar, E., Maser, J., Smith, D., & Haring, N. Developing an instructional sequence for teaching a self-help skill. *Education and Training of the Mentally Retarded,* 1977, *12*(1), 42–51.

Hanson, M. Evaluation of training procedures used in a parent-implemented intervention program for Down's Syndrome infants. *American Association for the Education of Severely/Profoundly Handicapped Review,* 1976, *1*(4), 36–55.

Knapczyk, D. Task analytic assessment for severe learning problems. *Education and Training of the Mentally Retarded,* 1975, *10*, 24–27.

Mager, R. *Preparing instructional objectives* (2d Ed.), Belmont, Calif.: Fearon, 1976.

Mira, M. Tracking the motor development of multihandicapped infants. *Mental Retardation,* 1977, *15*(3), 32–37.

Myers, D., Sinco, R., & Stalma, M. *The right-to-education child.* Springfield, Ill.: Charles C. Thomas, 1973.

Nietupski, J., Certo, N., Pumplan, I., & Belmore, K. Supermarket shopping: Teaching severely handicapped students to generate shopping lists and make purchases functionally linked to meal preparation. In L. Brown, N. Certo, K. Belmore, & T. Crowner (eds.), *Papers and programs related to public school services for secondary age severely handicapped students* (Vol. VI). Madison, Wis.: Madison Public Schools, 1976.

Piaget, J. *Play, dreams, and imitation.* New York: Norton, 1962.

Uzgiris, I., & Hunt, J. McV. *Instrument for assessing infant psychological development.* Urbana, Ill.: University of Illinois Press, 1975.

Wehman, P. *Curriculum design for severely and profoundly handicapped students.* New York: Human Sciences Press, 1979.

Wehman, P., & McLaughlin, P. J. *Vocational curriculum for developmentally disabled persons.* Baltimore: University Park Press, 1980.

Williams, W. W. Procedures of task analysis as related to developing instructional programs for severely handicapped students. In L. Brown, T. Crowner, W. Williams, & R. York (eds.), *Madison's alternative for zero exclusion* (Vol. V.). Madison, Wis.: Madison Public Schools, 1975.

Williams, W. W., & Gotts, E. Selected considerations in developing curriculum for severely handicapped students. In *Educational programming for the severely and profoundly handicapped.* Reston, Va.: Council on Exceptional Children, 1977.

Chapter 4

Instructional Strategies: General Principles of Learning

As a teacher, you will make decisions about instructional strategies. Your task is to use the most practicable and effective strategies. The next three chapters are designed to supply information to help you make sound decisions. Chapters 4 and 5 present information on antecedent principles, i.e., how to present new information to ensure learning. Chapter 6 presents information on consequent principles, i.e., how to reinforce correct responses.

Learning Goals

You should be able to answer the following questions when you finish this chapter:

- What is acquisition? What are the two critical tasks when teaching for acquisition?
- Define the ten general principles of learning that influence acquisition. How does each principle apply to developing instructional strategies? Give an example of how to use each principle.

- Define retention. What is the relationship between teaching for acquisition and teaching for retention?
- Define the four general principles of learning that influence retention. How does each principle apply to developing instructional strategies? Give an example of how to use each principle.
- Define transfer. What is the relationship between teaching for acquisition and teaching for transfer?
- Define the three general principles of learning that influence transfer. How does each principle apply to developing instructional strategies? Give an example of how to use each principle.
- Describe the lesson-plan format presented in this chapter. What parts relate to acquisition teaching? What part relates to retention and transfer teaching?

The term *instructional strategies* is a label which includes the various methods, materials, and time allocations used in teaching. Instructional strategies are the tools teachers use to help their students achieve instructional objectives. There are a large number of learning principles that teachers should use when they develop instructional strategies.

Individuals such as Blake (1976b, in press), Bugelski (1971), DeCecco and Crawford (1974), and Gagné (1970) have specified many of these principles by applying research on the psychology of learning and motivation to teaching practice. These principles are not new. For example, the literature on distribution of practice and knowledge of results extends back into the 1930s. Nevertheless, some teachers wait for days to let the student know how he or she has performed. Some teachers fail to let the students know what they did wrong or how to correct their mistakes. Some teachers also refuse to use drill techniques even when the objective specifies speed and rote memory as the terminal performance, as, for example, with multiplication facts. Contrarily, other teachers use drill regardless of the type of learning involved.

BASIC TEACHING MODEL

Teaching involves an interaction between the teacher and the student. Effective teachers structure the teaching situation to ensure student learning. This structure is provided by the selection and use of appropriate instructional strategies. The basic teaching model presented herein provides a frame of reference for selecting appropriate instructional strategies.

Structuring the teaching situation so the student will learn is difficult. It involves careful manipulation of the variables that influence learning. Our basic teaching model specifies a number of general principles that influence all types of learning in the same way. These include principles acquisition and retention and transfer, and they pertain to all the skills in the domains described in Part Two. You should apply these general principles of learning as you develop your instructional strategies. They are described and illustrated below.

ACQUISITION

Acquisition refers to original learning. It is teaching a new skill to a student. The teacher has two critical tasks when teaching for acquisition. First, the teacher must present the new information so the student will be able to perform the required task. Second, the teacher must provide appropriate practice so the student's performance will improve over time. The teacher should use the following ten general principles to develop instructional strategies for acquisition.

Instructions and Intent

Instructions and intent refer to intentional learning, i.e., learning with awareness in response to instruction. With intentional learning the student consciously undertakes learning the task. The student knows when he or she has learned the task. The opposite of intentional learning is incidental learning. In incidental learning the student does not consciously undertake to learn a skill. For example (Blake, 1976b), most college students can recite the numerals 1 to 100 with no difficulty. They have received instruction, practiced appropriately, and had ample experience. However, most college students cannot recite the letters and numerals on each respective button on the telephone. Although they have had ample experience with a telephone, they have not received instruction in the letter-digit combinations or practiced them purposefully.

Incidental learning does occur. However, much more is learned purposely when intent is present and instruction is given. Intent and instruction affect task persistence and orientation and attention to relevant materials. Your instructional strategies should include procedures to enhance intention and awareness. That is, students should know what they are doing, what they are supposed to do, how they are supposed to do it, and how they will be evaluated (Blake, 1974).

The following is a basic sequence of teaching procedures to increase instructions and intent (Wehman and McLaughlin, 1980):

1 Get the student's attention.
2 Give verbal instructions to perform the task.
3 Help the student make the correct response by promoting and modeling, and give the instructions again.
4 If the student still does not perform the task, the teacher must physically guide the student through it.
5 Appropriately fade prompts, models, and physical help.
6 Steps 1 to 5 are always accompanied by reinforcement for correct responding.

Get the Student's Attention   Prior to giving the verbal instructions to perform the task, it is necessary for the student to be paying attention to the teacher. Otherwise the instructions will be wasted. Eye contact is a good indicator that a student is attending. Effective teachers use methods to gain and hold the student's attention.

An effective way of getting a student's attention is to introduce the instructions with his or her name. An effective way of holding the student's attention and improving the quality of the verbal instruction is to emphasize the important words during instruction. For example, for a severely retarded child there may be little difference between the words, "Tom, take off your shoes," and "Tom, put on your shoes." For this reason it is beneficial to emphasize the action words *off* and *on.* Poor teachers often make the mistake of putting the student's name after the instruction. In this case the instruction is wasted since it may have been completed before the student was listening. Poor teachers also tend to speak in a mechanical manner, not emphasizing any words in particular.

Verbal Instructions   Instructions should be appropriate for the student's language maturity. Verbal instructions should be given with an enthusiastic or dramatic flair. As a general rule teachers should use simple kernel sentences in their instructions (Schelly, 1975). They should avoid using questions (as part of instructions), negative, passive, or negative-passive transformations of kernel sentences (Semmel & Dolley, 1971). For example, a good teacher will say, "Billy, write your name on your paper." An example of a poor instruction would be, "Why don't you write your name on your paper, Billy?"

Prompting and Modeling   Frequently, handicapped students either do not comprehend or do not respond to verbal instructions. This is particularly characteristic of more severely handicapped students. When this occurs during a teaching situation, the teacher must use prompts or models to evoke the desired behavior. This is a key point in teaching for acquisition. The teacher must present the new information so the student will be able to perform the required task.

Prompts are cues used to initiate the correct response (Kazdin, 1975). A gesture is a form of prompt. Verbal or written cues like "remember to dot your *i*'s" are also prompts. Modeling is the demonstration of the correct response. Modeling can be done by the teacher or other students. Prompts and models can be on bulletin boards or wall charts. The use of prompting and modeling is a valuable means of increasing instructions and intent (Wehman, 1976; York, Williams, & Brown, 1976). Prompts and models should be used simultaneously with verbal instructions.

Physical Guidance   When verbal instructions and prompting and modeling have not worked, it may be necessary to physically guide the student through the task. For example, to teach a severely developmentally delayed student to put on a shirt, the teacher may have to manually guide the child through the task.

Skills in some domains, e.g., language, cannot be physically guided. If verbal instructions and prompting and modeling have not worked for these skills, then the student probably does not have the prerequisite skills to learn the new skill.

Fading   Fading refers to the gradual removal of prompts, models, or physical guidance. For example, initially it may be necessary to put both arms on the student's shoulders to prompt him to sit down, then maybe one arm. Later it may be enough to put your arm on his shoulder to get the student to sit.

Knowing when to fade is critically important. Removal of a prompt, model, or physical guidance too early will result in the loss of the response. On the other hand, failure to fade often leads to dependence on the teacher. It then becomes increasingly difficult to encourage independent, self-initiated behavior (Kazdin, 1975).

Reinforcement during Steps 1 to 5   Positive reinforcement is a critical component of any instructional program. Chapter 6 discusses reinforcement in depth. In brief, all correct responses should be reinforced when teaching for acquisition. This includes responses which result from verbal instructions, prompts and models, and physical guidance.

Whole and Parts Methods

Whole and parts procedures refer to the way the total task is divided for teaching. With the whole method the task is not divided. The student practices the entire task to be learned in one chunk. With the parts method, the task is divided into parts. The student concentrates on learning each part separately. Shaping and backward chaining are two types of parts methods.

Shaping   Behavior shaping is one way to implement a task-analytic approach to teaching. In shaping, the behavioral objective is taught by reinforcing small steps or approximations of the final desired response. By reinforcing successive approximations of the final desired response, the behavioral objective is gradually achieved (Kazdin, 1975). For example, consider teaching a student to talk. Shaping is an effective method. The teacher starts out by reinforcing babbling, then verbal imitation of sounds associated with toys (e.g., car: m-m-m), then verbal imitation of consonant/vowels (e.g., buh-muh-nuh), and so on until the final objective is achieved. As the initial response becomes consistent, reinforcement is given only for a new response which more closely resembles the final desired behavior.

Backward Chaining   Backward chaining is another way to implement a task-analytic approach to teaching. Most behavioral objectives consist of a sequence of several responses. A sequence of responses is referred to as a chain. The order of the responses is fixed in the sense that earlier responses must precede later ones. For example, consider the task analysis for spoon feeding presented in Table 4-1. Before a student can put a filled spoon in the mouth

Table 4-1   Spoon Feeding Task Analysis

The student:

1   Reaches toward the spoon
2   Touches the spoon
3   Grasps the spoon
4   Picks up the spoon
5   Approaches the plate with the spoon
6   Touches the plate with the spoon
7   Scoops some food on the spoon
8   Lifts filled spoon away from plate
9   Lifts the spoon above the plate
10   Lifts the spoon halfway to mouth
11   Lifts the spoon 3 in from mouth
12   Lifts the spoon 1 in from mouth
13   Gets filled spoon to mouth without spilling
14   Puts filled spoon in mouth without spilling
15   Puts spoon back on plate
16   Will continue all steps until the meal is eaten

(Step 14), he or she must have completed the previous steps in the task analysis. With backward chaining, the last step in the response chain is taught first. The student is guided through all the steps and drilled on the last step repetitively until he or she has learned it. After the student has learned the last step, the teacher then guides up to the next-to-last step, drills the next-to-last step, and allows the student to carry through the last step alone. This procedure continues until all the steps are learned.

Whole versus Parts Methods   A combination of whole and parts methods is generally superior to either method alone (Blake, 1976b). The whole method is superior to the parts method when the task is not too long and the objective relates to grasping organization, underlying themes, etc. The parts methods are conducive to students' focusing on smaller amounts of information. Shaping is usually used to develop a terminal response. The behaviors along the way to the goal usually are not evident when the shaping is completed. Backward chaining is normally used to develop a specific sequence of behaviors. In backward chaining, behaviors developed early in the training are still evident when the training is completed. For many objectives either shaping or backward chaining may be used (Kazdin, 1975).

As an illustration of a way to combine whole and parts methods, consider the task of teaching handwriting. The parts of the task are the separate letters, and the whole is words or sentences. A good teaching approach would be a parts-whole-parts arrangement. For example, students need to learn to make basic letters. This could be done by using a shaping procedure. Then, early on, the students should start writing words and brief sentences. Next, they should work on learning more letters, as they continue to work on accuracy and speed in writing words and sentences (Blake, 1974).

Distribution of Practice

Massed and distributed practice are two ways to arrange study time. For example, suppose a student has 2 hours to study. With massed practice, he or she might work for one 2-hour long period. With distributed practice, he or she might divide his time into shorter sessions, such as four ½-hour sessions with rest periods or other activities in between sessions.

Which is the best way to distribute study time? When total time is held constant, massed and distributed practice have about the same effect. Relative value depends on task and student characteristics. For example, some students have shorter attention spans and greater needs for variety. They do well with distributed practice. Other students have longer attention spans and get confused by trying to deal with too many things at one time. Massed practice is best for them. On some tasks massed practice gives students time to get warmed up and to focus on the tasks; on the other hand, they may get tired, bored, and confused. With distributed practice, the students are not so likely to get tired, bored, and confused; yet they may be penalized for insufficient warm-up and focus.

In sum, teachers have to make decisions about massed and distributed practice in relation to specific characteristics of the tasks and students (Blake, 1976a; Sperber, Greenfield, & House, 1973). However, as a rule of thumb, the more severely handicapped the student, the shorter the attention span, and thus, the need for distributed practice. Teachers should try to determine the optimal length of study or practice sessions for each of their students for every task they teach.

Amount of Material

Amount of material refers to task size, i.e., the number of items to be learned. Task size strongly influences learning. When material is added, the task gets disproportionately harder (Blake, 1975a). For example, learning fifteen new sight vocabulary words is more than twice as hard as learning ten new words.

In most instances, the teacher controls the size of the task. She should adjust the task size to the capability of the student. Not all students in one class are capable of learning the same amount of information in a specified period of time. Some students will be able to work only six arithmetic problems in the same amount of time that other students work twelve problems. In sum, the more severely handicapped the student, the shorter the task size should be.

Recitation

Once a student has received instruction on a new task, he or she needs recitation to learn the skill. Recitation is practicing the new task in the absence of the material used to present it (e.g., reading, lecture, etc.). In other words, reading about how to do a task or being lectured about it is not sufficient to actually learn the task.

Students learn more efficiently when they use recitation. Blake (1975c) and Blake and Williams (1961) have studied mildly retarded students' responses to recitation. They found that about a 1:4 ratio of reading to recitation was most effective. Generally, students need enough information presentation and reception to help them avoid too many errors during recitation; and they need enough recitation to keep active, to get feedback, and to get practice with the materials in the form in which they will use them. The amount of recitation necessary for severely handicapped students to learn a new task has not been specifically studied. Although there is no generalized ratio, it is clear that severely handicapped students need a tremendous amount of recitation to learn a new task.

Blake (1975c) also studied what type of recitation was most effective. She found oral and written recitation similarly effective. However, combined oral and written recitation is much more effective than either type alone.

As an illustration of how to implement this principle, consider the task of learning to spell five new words. Study takes the form of analyzing the words, discussing the order of the letters, etc. Recitation involves actual practice in spelling the words. This recitation should involve both written and oral practice. The amount of time spent on recitation should be at least four times the amount spent on information presentation and study.

Knowledge of Results

Knowledge of results is corrective feedback to the student about the adequacy of his or her performance. This feedback should give the students information about what they have mastered and what they are doing wrong, including how to correct their errors. Knowledge of results facilitates learning and may influence students' motivation (Blake, 1974). The key to implementing this principle is to go beyond brief indications of right or wrong and include the entire correct answer and appropriate information about why it is correct. The effects of timing and frequency of feedback vary with the task.

The principle of knowledge of results is crucial to learning. Although giving corrective feedback is difficult and time-consuming, teachers must be able to do it. To implement this principle teachers must have a working knowledge of the subject matter they are teaching. For example, consider teaching the following spelling concept—the principle for changing a root when adding a suffix beginning with a vowel. Suppose we limit the material to verb roots and the *ing* inflectional suffix. The three necessary parts of the rule pertain to:

Words where roots are not changed (e.g., *do* to *doing*)
Words ending in *-e* (e.g., *give* to *giving*)
Words ending in a single vowel followed by a single consonant (e.g., *get* to *getting*)

To start with, the teacher must know when to double the last consonant and when to drop the last -*e*. Then, when the students make errors, e.g., changing *run* to *runing* or *have* to *haveing*, the teacher must be able to explain how to correct the mistakes. To be effective the explanation must be more than just a restatement of the rule. Effective teachers will base their corrective feedback on other principles of learning. For example, they could use prompts, models, and consider reducing the amount of material.

Amount of Practice

Amount of practice is the total number of practice sessions or the time students spend to learn a task. One trial is not enough practice for students to master the task. Handicapped students usually need many practice sessions to reach the mastery criterion. For some tasks, the student's improvement is rapid in early stages and then levels off, while in other tasks, the reverse is true. In still other tasks, there is rapid early learning, followed by a plateau, and then another period of improvement (Blake, 1975b; Tucker, 1976).

The teacher's instructional strategies should provide for the student's continuing to practice the task until he or she reaches mastery. Time allowances and practice materials should be adjusted to the characteristics of the tasks and the students. The same materials and activities should not be used over and over; this bores the student as well as the teacher. It is the teacher's responsibility to use varied materials and activities designed to teach the required skill.

Oral and Visual Presentations

Teachers can present information orally through lectures, audio tapes, etc. They can also present information visually through printed material and pictures. Sometimes information is presented both orally and visually through TV, sound films, and tape and printed material combinations. After reviewing the literature, Blake (1976b) concluded that there is no decisive evidence that one medium is superior to any other.

The instructional strategies should involve oral presentations or visual presentations or combined oral-visual presentations, as convenient and appropriate for the task. For example, in handwriting, the teacher should use both oral and visual strategies. The teacher should describe how the letters are made and show models.

Orientation and Attention

Orientation means surveying information and getting ready to respond to it. Attention is the selective scanning of information to focus on particular instances. Orientation and attention strategies help students respond to relevant stimuli and thus facilitate learning. This principle leads to the von Resteroff effect, i.e., students more efficiently learn isolated material and adjacent material.

Orientation and attention are central to good instructional strategies. Teachers should use coding techniques like underlining, color coding, preview questions, etc., to help students' orientation and attention to critical elements of the task. The preview questions at the beginning of each chapter in this book are an example of the orientation and attention principle. These questions are bulleted and introduced by a head to set them off from the rest of the text.

The key to implementing this principle is to make the task as easy as possible for the student to learn. For example, a reading lesson usually starts out by introducing the new words in the story. This is a form of orientation. These new words could also be color-coded or underlined in the story's text. This form of attention focusing helps the students recognize the new words. As the students' performance improves, these methods may be faded from the lesson.

Structure

Structure refers to how the task is organized. It includes the arrangement and interrelation of the parts of the whole task. The structure of knowledge for a given task refers to the components—specified elements, associations, concepts, etc.—and the way these components relate to one another. A student's cognitive structure refers to his or her grasp of the structure of knowledge for a given task.

Cognitive structure helps acquisition. It enables the student to get the meaning of the task, i.e., to see the relevance of the new task to previously learned tasks. Cognitive structure helps the student understand the components of the task to be learned—its parts and how they fit together in learning the task.

Teachers should use advance organizers to enhance the student's cognitive structure (Ausubel, 1978). Advance organizers deliberately use existing information in the student's cognitive structure to bridge the gap between what the student already knows and what he needs to know in order to learn the new task. Traditional advance organizers include introductory statements, teaching rules, preview outlines, and overviews.

For example, consider the introductory lesson in teaching the sound-change of the letter c when it is followed by the vowels e, i, or y. The teacher could start the lesson by asking her students what sound a cat makes when it is mad. Most students will know it says, Sss. The teacher can then explain that the ss sound is the sound the letter c has when it is followed by the vowels e, i, or y. This introduction would help link the new task, i.e., the phonics principle, with some information presently in the student's cognitive structure, i.e., the sound of a mad cat.

Sometimes the teacher can organize the new task to help the student's cognitive structure. For example, Blake (1974) suggests for teaching handwriting grouping the letters on the basis of their formation. Figure 4-1 shows how she grouped the letters. The teacher could then point out the patterns in each group of letters, which should make the letters easier for the students to remember and make.

a c e o

b d

f h

g p q y

i j

k l t

m n r s u   **Figure 4-1** Letters grouped by the way
they are made. (Source: Blake, 1974, p.
v w x z   253.)

APPLICATION OF GENERAL PRINCIPLES INFLUENCING ACQUISITION

To recap, ten general principles that influence acquisition have been described and illustrated. These principles should be followed as you develop instructional strategies to teach new skills. Below is an illustration of how to integrate these principles into a lesson plan.

Sample Lesson Plan for Spelling

This lesson plan is designed to teach the spelling principle for changing a root when adding a suffix beginning with a vowel. The learning principles used are identified in the left margin.

Parts method	*Scope:* This lesson plan is limited to verb roots and the *ing* inflectional suffix. This lesson plan has three parts: **A** Initial Presentation **B** Instruction and Practice **C** Evaluation *Objective:* Given a list of thirty verbs, the student will be able to correctly add the *ing* inflectional suffix in 5 minutes, with 100 percent accuracy for 3 consecutive days. **A** *Initial presentation*

Instructions and intent
  Verbal instructions
  Modeling
  Reinforcement
Instructions and intent
Oral and visual presentations
Structure
	Get the students' attention by using a prearranged signal, e.g., ringing a bell or writing the objective on the board. Enthusiastically tell them it is time to work on spelling. Tell the students to get out their spelling notebooks. Take out your spelling notebook at the same time. Reinforce appropriate behavior with verbal praise, e.g., "Bill's ready to work on spelling."
	Read and explain the objective, including the mastery criteria, to the students. Have the students copy the objective in their notebooks. Emphasize that they are going to learn how to add *ing* to verbs.
	State the three parts of the rule pertaining to: words where roots are not changed, words ending in *-e,* and words ending in a

Table 4-2   Sample Overhead of Spelling Rule

	ing verb endings	
Add *ing* to most verbs.	If a verb ends with *e*, drop the *e* before adding *ing*.	If a verb ends with a single vowel followed by a single consonant, double the last consonant and add *ing*.
do ⟶ doing	come ⟶ coming	get ⟶ getting
call ⟶ calling	give ⟶ giving	run ⟶ running
find ⟶ finding	have ⟶ having	shop ⟶ shopping

Oral and visual
presentations

Amount of
practice

Structure
Orientation and
attention

single vowel followed by a single consonant. Show an overhead of these three parts of the rule (see Table 4-2). Review the examples on the overhead. Call attention to the spelling of *do-ing, coming,* and *getting.* Ask *several* students to explain the three ways you can spell *ing* ending on words. Have the students copy the overhead, including the examples, for future reference. Call the students' attention to the teaching chart displayed in the room (see Figure 4-2). Describe how this chart illustrates the use of the three parts of the rule. Point out that the *e* in the verbs ending in *e* is red. Also point out that in verbs

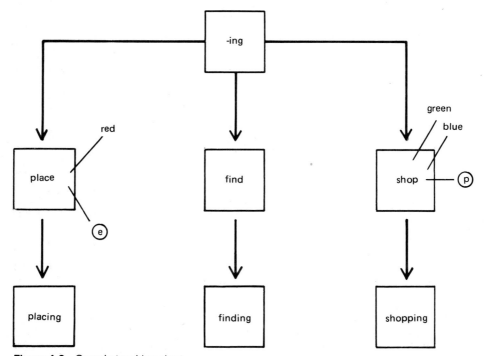

Figure 4-2   Sample teaching chart.

ending with a single vowel followed by a single consonant, the vowel is green and the consonant is blue. Ask *several* students to explain how to use this chart. Reinforce the students' responses and attending behavior.

B *Instruction and Practice*

Parts method
Distribution of practice
Amount of material
Orientation and attention
Knowledge of results
Instructions and intent
  Prompting and modeling

Provide a separate 2-minute practice session for each of the three parts of the rule. Have a separate worksheet of ten examples for each part. The examples should be color-coded in the same way as the worksheet. While the students are completing each worksheet, walk around the room providing corrective feedback. After the students complete each 2-minute practice session, review the correct answers. Have students tell why certain answers are correct or incorrect. Let the students use the information copied in their notebooks or the information on the teaching chart to help obtain the correct answer during these initial practice sessions.

Amount of practice
Amount of material
Orientation and attention
Knowledge of results
Instructions and intent
Orientation and attention-
Recitation

Provide a 5-minute practice session for all three parts of the rule at the same time. Have a worksheet with thirty examples. The worksheet should be color-coded as before. Feedback procedures should be given as described previously. Provide two more practice sessions like those described above, but gradually fade the prompts and models (i.e., the use of the teaching chart and information in the notebooks) and the color-coded examples. Review and illustrate the rule before each practice session. Continue to provide appropriate knowledge of results and reinforcement.

Oral and written recitation activities must be incorporated into instruction and practice. The activities should include worksheets, oral questions, and games. Students should be asked to write and say the three parts of the rule and practice using the rule to spell verbs ending in *ing*. A spelling bee on verbs ending in *ing* could be held. No prompts or models can be used during recitation. Approximately twelve different recitation activities should be used. Continue to provide corrective feedback and reinforcement during recitation.

Knowledge of results

C *Evaluation*

The initial presentation and instruction and practice activities described above will probably take 4 to 5 days (20 minutes per day) to complete. When the students are completing the recitation activities without any errors, you should begin to evaluate your objective. Your evaluation will take 5 minutes a day for 3 consecutive days. See Table 4-3 for a sample evaluation sheet.

RETENTION

Given the total amount of material learned during acquisition, retention refers to what the student remembers over an extended time period. Blake (1976b) specified two kinds of questions about principles of learning affecting retention.

1 Are there principles of learning that pertain especially to retention?
2 Do principles that influence acquisition also influence retention in the same way? That is, in addition to their effect on original learning, do they have a *further* effect on retention? (p. 377)

Table 4-3   Sample Evaluation Sheet

1	love	_____	16	vote	_____
2	swim	_____	17	print	_____
3	go	_____	18	hit	_____
4	like	_____	19	skate	_____
5	quit	_____	20	spell	_____
6	help	_____	21	rise	_____
7	live	_____	22	hug	_____
8	trap	_____	23	shoot	_____
9	have	_____	24	use	_____
10	hold	_____	25	rub	_____
11	give	_____	26	smoke	_____
12	plan	_____	27	sell	_____
13	jump	_____	28	shake	_____
14	face	_____	29	shut	_____
15'	trip	_____	30	pick	_____

The answer to the first question is yes. There are four principles which pertain especially to retention. These are overlearning, type of retention measure, instructions to recall, and reminiscence.

The second set of questions is difficult to answer. For these questions to be studied, the students' learning on the first task must be equal under all principles of original learning. It is hard to achieve this condition. Students who learn different amounts on the original task are certainly going to remember different amounts. Therefore, if you are going to study the effects of principles on retention beyond their effects on acquisition, you have to be sure that students start at the same place on the retention task. Blake (1976b) states that when first-task learning is thus held constant, most principles affecting original learning do not have much further effect on retention.

The principles of learning influencing retention of all types of skills are described and illustrated below. The teacher should use there four principles to develop instructional strategies for retention. Remember, the student must first acquire the skill before learning to retain it; in other words, you must teach for acquisition before you teach for retention.

Overlearning

Overlearning refers to practice beyond the point of acquisition. For example, suppose the students' objective was to be able to correctly add the *ing* inflectional suffix to a list of thirty verbs in 5 minutes, with 100 percent accuracy for 3 consecutive days. To master this objective it took the students ten 20-minute practice sessions. To get overlearning, the students would continue to practice.

How much overlearning is necessary for retention? Blake (1974) stated that 50 percent overlearning beyond mastery greatly facilitates retention. To achieve

50 percent overlearning the students would need to practice half again as long as it took to reach mastery. In the above example, the students would need to continue practicing for five additional 20-minute practice sessions. As the teacher conducts these continued practice sessions, she needs to use a variety of activities and materials.

Overlearning is the most critical principle influencing retention. However, implementing overlearning is not easy. In many situations by the time acquisition is achieved, both the students and the teacher are tired of the task. It is difficult for the teacher to design interesting new activities and materials for the additional practice sessions. For example, some severely handicapped students might take fifty 200-trial-practice sessions to learn a task. For 50 percent overlearning the teacher would need to design new activities for twenty-five additional 200-trial-practice sessions.

Type of Retention Measure

Recognition, structured recall, and relearning are measures of retention. They are defined below.

> *Recognition* is the selection of previously learned items from unlearned or false items, for example, a multiple-choice test.
> *Structured recall* is supplying items within a specific context, for example, essay tests and items starting with the verbs, *name, list,* etc.
> *Relearning* is the time or effort required to relearn previously learned material. (Blake, 1974, p. 254)

These different retention measures, used with the same materials, produce different results. Recognition is easiest and structured recall is the hardest. More teaching and practice time should be provided when using the harder measures of retention. When teaching for retention, the instructional strategies should include the type of retention measure which is appropriate for the objective. The students should also be given practice with the type of measure used. For example, structured recall is the appropriate measure for spelling. Students should practice spelling as they use rules, look at models, and receive verbal instructions. Their practice should require structured recall. You would not want to give them practice with just recognition items (e.g., circling the correct spelling—*securety, security, securoty*) and then test for retention with a structured recall item (e.g., asking the student to write the word *security*).

Instructions to Recall

Instructions to recall refers to directing the student to learn with the specific idea of recalling the material at a later time. Students can be given specific instructions about what to remember. For example, sometimes teachers assign students a chapter to read and then supply no further information. When exam time comes, they select certain bits of information to be tested. In such situations, the students' job is to learn everything he has read. Other teachers may give additional information about material to be learned and tested. Instructions to recall specific information facilitates retention.

The instructional strategies should provide explicit instructions about retaining the material taught. For example, students should be told what they need to remember for later use; they should be given sample evaluation items and practice in recalling the material in the form it will be used for testing. Students given such information will retain more of the material.

Reminiscence

Reminiscence is an increase in performance after resting which comes after a relatively long, massed practice session. That is, a student practices a task, rests, and then remembers more than he did when he stopped practice. The rest allows fatigue, confusion, etc., to disappear and the true level of learning to show up. This retention phenomenon is true for both handicapped and nonhandicapped students (Ellis, Bryer, & Barnett, 1960; Wright & Willis, 1969).

Instructional strategies should allow for a rest period after long periods of study and practice in order for reminiscence to occur. For example, in handwriting the teacher should not give tests for mastery at the end of a long practice period. Instead, the teacher should schedule tests early in the session after the students have had time to warm up but before fatigue has set in.

APPLICATION OF GENERAL PRINCIPLES INFLUENCING RETENTION

In sum, four general principles that influence retention have been described and illustrated. These principles should be followed as you develop instructional strategies for retention. Remember, however, you cannot teach for retention until the students have acquired the new skill.

Earlier in this chapter a sample lesson plan was presented. This lesson plan was designed to teach a spelling principle for acquisition. It had three parts: *Initial Presentation, Instruction and Practice, and Evaluation*. A fourth part to this lesson plan is presented below. This part, called *Generalization*, integrates the retention principles into the overall instructional plan. This part of the plan is implemented after the evaluation procedures show that the students have met the specified objective.

Sample Lesson Plan for Spelling

This lesson plan is designed to teach the spelling principle for changing a root when adding a suffix beginning with a vowel. The learning principles used are identified in the left margin.

Scope: This lesson plan is limited to verb roots and the *ing* inflectional suffix. This lesson plan has four parts:

A Initial Presentation
B Instruction and Practice

C   Evaluation
D   Generalization
Objective: Given a list of thirty verbs, the student will be able to correctly add the *ing* inflectional suffix in 5 minutes, with 100 percent accuracy for 3 consecutive days.
A   *Initial Presentation*
See pages 87 to 89 and Table 4-2 and Figure 4-2.
B   *Instruction and Practice*
See page 89.
C   *Evaluation*
See page 89 and Table 4-3.
D   *Generalization*

Instructions to recall

Type of retention measure

Overlearning

Reinforce the students for achieving the objective. Review the three parts of the rule pertaining to words where roots are not changed, words ending in -*e,* and words ending in a single vowel followed by a single consonant. Show the overhead of these three parts of the rule (see Table 4-2). Tell the students they will be tested on these rules again in another week. Specify that you want them to be able to (1) write the three parts of the rule and (2) use the rule on the list of thirty verbs. Review the criterion of 100 percent accuracy in a 5-minute test period. Tell the students they will be given extra time on the test to write the three parts of the rule. Give the students a practice test. Plan five additional 20-minute practice sessions. (It took ten 20-minute practice sessions for original learning.) The materials and activities should be different from the activities used for acquisition. Possible activities include:

1   Table games in which the students must use the parts of the rule (i.e., the student must use the rule to add *ing* to a verb before moving his man in checkers).
2   Challenge matches where two students try to stump each other.
3   Timed worksheet drills to improve rate of response.
4   Structured recall worksheets in the same form as the retention test.

Reminiscence

Evaluate for retention after the fifth additional 20-minute practice session. Give the students a 10-minute break before administering the test.

TRANSFER

Transfer refers to learning in one situation that influences learning in a second situation. Positive transfer happens when learning in the first situation helps learning in the second. For example, in self-care skills, toilet training to a schedule at school should facilitate toilet training at home. Negative transfer occurs when the first learning hinders the second. For example, learning the CVC rule for short vowel sounds could interfere with learning the CVC + *e* rule for long vowel sounds. Drew and Espeseth (1968), Kaufman and Prehn (1966), and Wehman, Abramson, and Norman (1977) have reviewed research on handicapped students' transfer.

Transfer varies according to the type of material being transferred. The two main varieties of transfer are specific and general transfer. These are described below.

1   *Specific transfer* is transfer of particular motor skills, discriminations, verbal associations, concepts, and problem solutions (Blake, 1976b).
2   *General transfer* is transfer of sets, a readiness to respond to a situation. Sets which transfer include cognitive sets, performance sets, and learning sets (Blake, 1976b).
    a   *Cognitive set* is when the student's previous experience and language patterns cause him to perceive new situations in a given way.
    b   *Performance sets* are attentional and emotional predispositions to respond to particular situations. These include a readiness to respond to the requirements of the new learning situation.
    c   *Learning set* is learning how to learn particular kinds of tasks. There are discrimination learning sets, concept learning sets, etc.

As with retention, there are two kinds of questions about principles of learning affecting transfer (Blake, 1976b).

1   Do principles influencing acquisition have an additional influence on transfer?
2   Are there principles of learning that pertain especially to transfer?

The first question is difficult to answer since first there must be equal learning on the acquisition task. However, when such learning is held constant, the principles influencing original learning do not have much further effect on transfer (Blake, 1976b). Second, there are three general principles of learning that influence transfer. They are intertask similarity, specific instructions to transfer, and overlearning.

The principles of learning influencing transfer of all types of skills are described and illustrated below. These principles should be used to develop instructional strategies for transfer. Remember, in order to teach for transfer the students must first learn the skill. In other words, you must teach for acquisition before transfer.

Intertask Similarity

Intertask similarity refers to the relationship between the stimuli and the responses in the original learning task and the transfer task. Transfer occurs when there is similarity, or overlap, between the original learning task and the transfer task. The kind and degree of transfer depends on the kind and degree of similarity between the stimuli in the two tasks and the responses in the two tasks. Positive transfer happens when the required responses and stimuli in the two tasks are similar. Negative transfer happens when the required responses in the two tasks change while the stimuli remain similar. Blake (1974) specified the following relationship influencing transfer.

Similarity between Stimuli   Consider old and new tasks where the responses remain about the same and the stimuli vary. You get maximum positive transfer when the stimuli in the two situations are the same or highly similar. For example, the original task was teaching a handicapped student to take a rest or bathroom break only between classes at school. The new task is to teach the student to take a rest or bathroom break only at the assigned time on an assembyline job. To get maximum positive transfer the teacher should arrange the classroom stimuli to approximate the stimuli found on the assembly line job. One way to do this is to extend the class periods to the same length of time as the job work periods.

Similarity between Responses   Consider old and new tasks where the stimuli remain about the same and the responses vary. You get less negative transfer when the responses are less different and more similar. You get maximum negative transfer when the responses are crucially different. For example, students have negative transfer when they move from manuscript to cursive writing. That is, they are required to make different responses (cursive letters rather than manuscript letters) to the same stimuli (teacher's command to write the alphabet). This negative transfer could be reduced by using the transitional teaching structures shown in Figure 4-3. These structures reduce the negative transfer by grouping letters that are made similarly in manuscript and cursive writing.

In sum, the instructional strategies should deal specifically with intertask similarity and its implications for transfer. Specific instructions should stress the stimuli in the old and new tasks that are the same or similar and the responses to

Figure 4-3   Transitional structures: Manuscript and cursive letters. (Source: Blake, 1974, p. 98.)

the old task that are appropriate to the new task. In other words, the strategies should be designed to stress the possibility of positive transfer and should also deal specifically with difficult situations involving negative transfer by providing extra help for the students.

Instructions to Transfer

Instructions to transfer refers to teaching students to see the connection between the acquisition (old) and transfer (new) tasks. Instructions can be used to point out links and the applicability of transfer from one task to another.

The instructional strategies should contain specific instructions to increase positive transfer and reduce negative transfer. These instructions should be specifically designed to help students judge that the learning in the old task can or cannot be appropriately applied to the new task. For example, tell the students exactly what to expect. Describe the intertask similarity. Help the students deal with the applicability of the first task to the second.

Overlearning

Overlearning refers to practice beyond the point of acquisition. Earlier in this chapter overlearning was presented as a principle influencing retention. Fifty percent overlearning beyond mastery was specified for retention instructional strategies. Overlearning also affects transfer.

Positive transfer increases with overlearning. Negative transfer levels off with high amounts of overlearning. Therefore, transfer instructional strategies should require 50 to 100 percent overlearning beyond acquisition (Blake, 1974). For example, suppose it took the students ten 20-minute practice sessions to reach acquisition. To teach for transfer, instructional strategies would need to provide ten additional 20-minute practice sessions.

As with retention, implementing the principle of overlearning is not easy. It is a difficult task to design interesting new activities and materials for the additional practice sessions.

APPLICATION OF GENERAL PRINCIPLES INFLUENCING TRANSFER

To recap, three general principles influencing transfer have been described and illustrated. These principles should be followed as you develop instructional strategies for transfer. Remember, just as for retention, you cannot teach for transfer until the students have acquired the new skill.

Earlier in this chapter a sample four-part lesson plan on spelling was presented. The first three parts of the lesson plan, *i.e.*, *Initial Presentation*, *Instruction and Practice, and Evaluation*, addressed acquisition teaching. The fourth part of the plan is called *Generalization*. This part contains instructional strategies for retention *and* transfer. Below is an illustration of how to integrate the transfer principles into the *Generalization* part of the sample spelling lesson plan.

Sample Lesson Plan for Spelling

This lesson plan is designed to teach the spelling principle for changing a root when adding a suffix beginning with a vowel. The learning principles are identified in the left margin.

Scope: This lesson plan is limited to verb roots and the *ing* inflectional suffix. This lesson plan has four parts:

A Initial Presentation
B Instruction and Practice
C Evaluation
D Generalization

Objective: Given a list of thirty verbs, the student will be able to correctly add the *ing* inflectional suffix in 5 minutes, with 100 percent accuracy for 3 consecutive days.

A *Initial Presentation*
  See pages 87 to 89 and Table 4-2 and Figure 4-2.
B *Instruction and Practice*
  See page 89.
C *Evaluation*
  See page 89 and Table 4-3.
D *Generalization*
  Retention. See page 93.
  Transfer. The objective and scope of this spelling lesson plan

General transfer concept-learning set
Specific transfer Intertask similarity

Instructions to transfer

has two transfer tasks. First, students should be able to apply the rule to verbs not listed on the original study list. Second, students should be able to apply the rule in their day to day spelling activities. Provide students with a list of thirty new verbs. Construct practice activities and materials like those used for acquisition teaching. This makes the required responses and stimuli very similar and creates a maximum positive transfer situation. Tell the students about this overlap. Point out how the students can use the three parts of the rule they have learned with these new verbs. Give some examples. Help them sort the new list of verbs into three groups (one group for each part of the rule).

Overlearning

Plan at least five additional 20-minute practice sessions for these new verbs. Continue to apply the criterion of 100 percent accuracy in a 5-minute time period.

Overlearning

Plan from five to ten practice activities that will require the students to use the rule in day to day activities. Possible activities include: writing experience stories or short letters home, writing answers to questions about their reading lesson, filling out

Intertask similarity
Instructions to transfer

job applications, etc. Design these activities to have high positive transfer. As before, describe the overlap between the old and new tasks. Stress the need to learn how to use the rule in new situations.

SUMMARY

Effective teachers structure the learning situation to ensure student learning. This structure is achieved through the selection and use of appropriate instructional strategies. The teaching model presented in this chapter specifies a number of general principles that influence all types of learning in the same way. They include principles influencing acquisition and principles influencing retention and transfer. These principles can be applied in developing instructional strategies to teach all the skills in the domains described in Part Two of this book.

Acquisition

Acquisition is mastery of new material. The teacher has two critical tasks when teaching for acquisition. First, the teacher must present the new information so the student will be able to perform the required task. Second, the teacher must provide appropriate practice so the student's performance will improve over time. The following principles should be used to develop acquisition instructional strategies.

Instructions and intent. Students should know what they are doing, what they are supposed to do, how they are supposed to do it, and how they will be evaluated. The following is the teaching sequence to increase instructions and intent: attention, verbal instructions, prompting and modeling, physical guidance, fading, and reinforcement.

Whole and parts methods. A combination of whole and parts is generally superior to either method alone. Shaping and backward chaining are two types of parts methods. In shaping, the behavioral objective is taught by reinforcing small steps or approximations of the final desired response. With backward chaining, a sequence of responses is taught from the last step back to the first.

Distribution of practice. The relative value of massed or distributed practice depends on task and student characteristics. However, as a rule of thumb, more severely handicapped students need distributed practice.

Amount of material. The longer the size of the task, the more difficult it is. The teacher should adjust task size to the capability of her students.

Recitation. The amount of time spent on recitation should be at least four times the amount spent on information presentation and study. This recitation should involve both written and oral practice.

Knowledge of results. Students must receive corrective feedback about the adequacy of their performance. This feedback should give students information about what they have mastered and about what they are doing wrong, including how to correct their errors.

Amount of practice. One trial is not enough practice for students to master a task. Multiple-practice activities, with different materials, must be used to ensure student learning.

Oral and visual presentations. As a general rule, both oral and visual presentations of new information should be used.

Orientation and attention. Teachers should use coding techniques like underlining, color coding, preview questions, etc., to help students select and respond to the critical elements of the task.

Structure. The teacher should organize the new task so the students will see its relevance to previously learned tasks. Advance organizers should be used to help the students understand the new task.

Retention

Retention is the amount of material remembered over an extended period of time. Retention must be taught; it does not come automatically. However, a teacher must teach for acquisition before teaching for retention. The following principles should be used to develop retention instructional strategies.

Overlearning. Fifty percent overlearning beyond mastery greatly facilitates retention. To achieve 50 percent overlearning the students need to practice half again as long as it took to reach mastery. New material and activities, i.e., different from the ones used during acquisition teaching, should be used for the additional practice sessions.

Type of retention measure. The instructional strategies should use the type of retention measure appropriate for the objective. The students should be told and given practice with the type of measure used.

Instructions to recall. Students should be given explicit instructions about retaining the material taught. They should be told what they need to remember and be given practice in recalling the material in the form used for testing.

Reminiscence. The instructional strategies should provide a rest period after long periods of study and practice in order for reminiscence to occur. The rest periods allows fatigue and confusion to disappear and the true level of learning to show up.

Transfer

Transfer refers to learning in one situation influencing learning in a second situation. Positive transfer happens when learning in the first situation helps learning in the second. Negative transfer occurs when the original learning hinders the second. As with retention, acquisition must be taught before transfer. The following principles should guide the development of instructional strategies.

Intertask similarity. Specific instructions should stress when stimuli in the old and new tasks are similar and the responses to the old task are appropriate to the new task. Activities and materials should be designed to provide this type of positive transfer.

Instructions to transfer. Instructions should be used to point out the connection between the acquisition and transfer tasks. Students should be told exactly what to expect in the new situations.

Overlearning. Transfer instructional strategies should require 50 to 100 percent overlearning beyond acquisition.

REFERENCES

Ausubel, D. P. In defense of advance organizers; A reply to critics. *Review of Educational Research*, 1978, *48*, 215–258.

Blake, K. A. *Teaching the retarded.* Englewood Cliffs, N.J.: Prentice-Hall, 1974.

Blake, K. A. Amount of material and retarded and normal pupils' learning. *Journal of Research and Development in Education*, 1975, *8*, 128–136. (a)

Blake, K. A. Amount of practice and retarded and normal pupils' learning. *Journal of Research and Development in Education*, 1975, *8*, 128–136. (b)

Blake, K. A. Type of recitation and retarded and normal pupils' learning sentence material. *Journal of Research and Development in Education*, 1975, *8*, 79–80. (c)

Blake, K. A. Massed and distributed practice and retarded and normal pupils' learning sight vocabulary. *Journal of Research and Development in Education*, 1976, *9*, 12–14. (a)

Blake, K. A. *The mentally retarded: An educational psychology.* Englewood Cliffs, N.J.: Prentice-Hall, 1976. (b)

Blake, K. A. *Educating exceptional pupils: An introduction to contemporary practice.* Reading, Mass.: Addison-Wesley, in press.

Blake, K. A., & Williams, C. L. *Studies of the effects of systematic variations of certain conditions related to learning II, Conditions of practice.* Washington, D.C.: U.S. Office of Education, Cooperative Research Program, 1961.

Bugelski, B. *The psychology of learning applied to teaching* (2d ed.). New York: Bobbs-Merrill, 1971.

DeCecco, J. P., & Crawford, W. R. *The psychology of learning and instruction.* Englewood, Cliffs, N.J.: Prentice-Hall, 1974.

Drew, C. J., & Espeseth, V. K. Transfer of training in the mentally retarded: A review. *Exceptional Children*, 1968, *35*, 129–131.

Ellis, N. R., Pryer, M. W., & Barnett, C. D. Motor learning and retention in normals and defectives. *Perceptual and Motor Skills*, 1960, *10*, 83–91.

Gagné, R. M. *The conditions of learning* (2d ed.). New York: Holt, 1970.

Kaufman, M. E., & Prehm, H. J. A review of research on learning sets and transfer of training in mental defectives. In N. R. Ellis (ed.), *International review of research in mental retardation* (Vol 2). New York: Academic Press, 1966, 123–147.

Kazdin, A. *Behavior modification in applied settings.* Homewood, Ill.: Dorsey Press, 1975.

Schelly, J. Instructional procedures and comprehension of sentence transformations. *Journal of Research and Development in Education*, 1975, *8*, 71–72. (Monograph Supplement)

Semmel, M. I., & Dolley, D. G. Comprehension and imitation of sentences by Down's Syndrome children as a function of transformational complexity. *American Journal of Mental Deficiency*, 1971, *75*, 739–745.

Sperber, R. D., Greenfield, D. B., & House, B. J. A nonmonotonic effect of distribution of trials in retardate learning and memory. *Journal of Experimental Psychology*, 1973, *99*, 186–198.

Tucker, J. Amount of training and retarded and normal pupils' learning new words and transformations. *Journal of Research and Development in Education*, 1976, *9*, 11–12.

Wehman, P. Imitation as a facilitator of treatment of the mentally retarded. *Rehabilitation Literature*, 1976, *37*, 41–48.

Wehman, P., Abramson, ., & Norman, C. Transfer of training in behavior modification programs: An evaluative review. *The Journal of Special Education*, 1977, *11*, 217–231.

Wehman, P., & McLaughlin, P. J. *Vocational curriculum for developmentally disabled persons.* Baltimore, Md.: University Park Press, 1980.

Wright, L., & Willis, C. Reminiscence in normals and defectives. *American Journal of Mental Deficiency*, 1969, *73*, 700–702.

York, R., Williams, W., & Brown, L. Teacher modeling and student imitation: An instructional procedure for teacher competency. *American Association for the Education of Severely/Profoundly Handicapped Review*, 1976, *1*, 11–15.

Chapter 5

Instructional Strategies: Specific Principles of Learning

This chapter continues the description of antecedent principles affecting learning. It contains information on how to present specific types of new information to ensure learning.

Learning Goals

When you finish this chapter you should be able to answer the following questions:

- What is the relationship between general and specific principles of learning? How does the teacher decide which specific principles of learning apply to a given instructional objective?
- What is concept learning? List the teaching topics which involve concept learning. Describe the seven specific principles which affect students' acquisition of concepts. Give an original example of how to use each principle.
- What is verbal learning? List the teaching topics which involve verbal learning. Describe the four specific principles which influence verbal learning. Give an original example of how to use each principle.

- What is discrimination learning? List the teaching topics which involve discrimination learning. Describe the four specific principles which affect discrimination learning. Give an original example of how to use each principle.
- What is meant by learning connected discourse? List the teaching topics which involve connected discourse. Describe the three principles which influence learning connected discourse. Give an original example of each principle.

The preceding chapter presented a basic teaching model. It described the general learning principles used to develop instructional strategies for acquisition, retention, and transfer teaching. These general learning principles apply to all types of learning and pertain to all the skills in the domains described in Part Two of this book.

The instructional strategies should also be appropriate for the type of behavior specified in the instructional objective. The behavior specified in the instructional objective involves various types of learning. Researchers such as Blake (1974), Bugelski (1971), DeCecco and Crawford (1974), and Gagné (1970) have identified learning principles which are specific to four types of learning: concept learning, verbal learning, discrimination learning, and learning connected discourse. Your instructional strategies should be based on the appropriate specific learning principles as well as the general principles of learning.

For example, consider the instructional objective for the sample spelling lesson plan presented in Chapter 4. The objective stated: Given a list of thirty verbs, the student will be able to correctly add the *ing* inflectional suffix in 5 minutes, with 100 percent accuracy for 3 consecutive days. This objective requires the students to learn an abstract rule (see Table 4-2 for the three parts of the rule). Rule learning is one type of concept learning. Therefore, the teacher should use the specific principles of learning which influence concept learning *and* the general learning principles to develop effective instructional strategies.

We have identified the type of learning involved for many of the topics you will be teaching. For topics not listed in this chapter, Blake (1974) outlined a five-step process used to decide what aspects of learning are involved in an instructional objective.

1 Examine the behavior required by the instructional objective.
2 Compare the required behavior to the nature of the various types of learning.
3 Identify the type(s) of learning involved in the instructional objective.
4 Identify the principles which facilitate the specific type(s) of learning.
5 Be sure that the instructional strategies are based on the appropriate specific and general principles of learning.

The specific principles of learning that influence concept learning, verbal learning, discrimination learning, and learning connected discourse are described and illustrated below.

CONCEPT LEARNING

A concept is a set of stimuli which are related in some way. Synonyms for concept include set, class, group, and category. Concept learning is frequently described as the type of learning which makes it possible for an individual to put objects, events, or persons into a class and respond to the class as a whole (Gagné, 1970). The acquisition of concepts transforms the student's surroundings into an understandable and organized environment (DeCecco & Crawford, 1974). Students are more often called upon to use concept learning than any other type of learning.

There are two basic types of concepts: concrete and abstract. Concrete concepts can be observed (Gagné, 1970). Vegetables, automobiles, birds, books, cats, numbers, and vowels are examples of concrete concepts. The student can learn concrete concepts by direct observation. For example, a young preschool student might learn the concept *cat* by observing several small four-legged animals identified for him as *cats* or *not cats* by his parents.

The second type of concept is called a defined, or abstract, concept. Defined concepts must be learned by definition; they do not refer to observables. Instead, they refer to rules relating simpler concepts (Blake, 1974). For example, place value in numeration, work functions (nouns, verbs, etc.), and syllabication principles are defined concepts. Learning defined concepts requires the student to learn a rule. As mentioned earlier, the sample spelling lesson in Chapter 4 is based on learning an abstract rule.

Blake (1974, 1976b) has been the trailblazer in applying information about concept learning to teaching. Table 5-1 shows the domains and teaching topics she has identified as involving concept learning. Table 5-2 shows the domains and topics involving concept learning that McLaughlin, Eaves, and Fallen identified as appropriate to teach preschool handicapped students.

Listed below are some illustrations of instructional objectives involving concept learning.

> Given the CVC + *e* rule for pronouncing vowels, the student can apply the rule, with 90-percent accuracy.
> Given sets of four numbers, the student can add the numbers in the set, with 100-percent accuracy at a rate of twenty sets per minute.
> Given the names of people, the student can identify classmates, with 100-percent accuracy.

Seven specific principles of learning affect students' acquisition of concepts. Three of the seven pertain to the nature of the material: nature of rules, relevant and irrelevant dimensions, and taxonomic level. Four pertain to the methods of presenting the concepts to be learned: contiguity of instances, positive and negative instances, simultaneous and successive exposure, and expository and discovery methods. These seven principles are described and illustrated below. Table 5-3 lists the pertinent points for each principle.

Table 5-1 Topics Involving Concept Learning

Domains	Topics
Oral language: listening and speech	Prefixes, suffixes, concepts—labels and instances, figurative language, word functions—nouns, verbs, adjectives, adverbs, connectives, and dictionary use
Reading	Consonant grapheme-phoneme correspondences, consonant pronunciation principles, vowel grapheme-phoneme correspondences, vowel pronunciation principles, syllabication principles, principles of accent, prefixes, suffixes, rules for spelling changes, and dictionary use
Written language: spelling, handwriting usage, and genre	Consonant phoneme-grapheme correspondences, consonant spelling patterns, vowel phoneme-grapheme correspondences, vowel spelling patterns, syllabication, accent, principles for forming plurals, dictionary use, and correct usage-punctuation and parts of speech
Arithmetic	All subtopics in number, relations, measurement, operations with whole numbers, and operations with rational numbers; place value in numeration
Personal social skills	All concepts, e.g., community helpers, family, personal liability and property damage, credit, income tax, games, safety hazards in the home, cleanliness, and so on

Source: Blake (1974, p. 205).

Table 5-2 Topics Involving Concept Learning Appropriate to Teach Preschool Handicapped Students

Domains	Topics
Gross motor	People: participant player positions in many games (e.g., being "it", "chaser," "little Indians").
	Objects: types of games and manipulative toys, their names, and parts (e.g., tricycle, pedal). Body parts (e.g., arm, shoulder, legs, hands, fingers, toes).
	Events: moving, crawling, walking, running, balancing, holding, carrying, hopping, skipping, jumping, hammering, catching, throwing, being strong, weak, tired.
Fine motor	People: participant player positions in many fine motor games (e.g., imitating majorette in a band, guitarist, pianist, seamstress).
	Objects: shapes, forms, names, and types of manipulative utensils and their parts (e.g., pencil, book, scissors, page).
	Events: drawing, copying, tracing, picking up, cutting, turning (on, off), coloring, touching, feeling.

Table 5-2 (Continued)

Domains	Topics
	People: mother, father, sister, brother, self, family, friend, neighbor, enemy, boy, girl, leader, follower, helper, bully, community workers (e.g., police officer, doctor, pastor, teacher).
	Objects: all concepts concerning home (e.g., rooms, toys, car), school (e.g., books, games, personal and community property), community (e.g., stores, offices, street lights).
	Events: attending, approving, helping, requesting, accepting, offering, smiling, sharing, allowing, cooperating, insulting, disapproving, blaming, demanding, attacking, teasing, grabbing, refusing, rejecting, ignoring, interfering, frowning, yelling, whispering. Being afraid, honest, neat, happy, sad, "good."
Self-help	People: self.
	Objects: bathroom appliances and implements, kitchen utensils and appliances, clothing and its parts, food, body parts.
	Events: toileting, washing, wiping, drying, dressing, eating, brushing, lacing, cutting, buttoning, zipping, cleaning (up), pouring, spreading, drinking.
Arithmetic	People: teacher, all concepts and concept labels (e.g., people in the home, school, and community) already mentioned which involve sets, numbers, and numerals.
	Objects: all concepts and concept labels (e.g., objects in the home, school, and community) already mentioned which involve sets, numbers, and numerals.
	Events: counting, grouping, writing, sequencing, naming.
Oral language: listening and speech	People: all concepts and concept labels (e.g., people in the home, school, and community) already mentioned.
	Objects: all concepts and concept labels (e.g., objects in the home, school, and community) already mentioned.
	Events: all concepts and concept labels (e.g., events in the home, school, and community) already mentioned. Identifying and supplying nouns (people, places, things), verbs (action, existence), modifiers, connectives, pronouns, possessives.
Written language: reading and writing	People: correspondence between a few words and real people (e.g., self, mom, dad, etc.).
	Objects: correspondence between a few grapheme combinations and real objects (e.g., dog, cat, etc.), letters.
	Events: Writing and reading.

Source: McLaughlin, Eaves, & Fallen (1978, pp. 198–199).

Nature of Rules

Rules define concepts by specifying how attributes are related or how they function. McLaughlin (1976c) has described three conceptual rules and some sample corresponding phonics principles.

Table 5-3 Specific Principles Influencing Concept Learning

Nature of rules

The instructional procedures should vary the amount of teaching and practice according to the difficulty of the rule. More teaching and practice should be provided for disjunction rules than for simple affirmation rules. (p. 207)

Relevant and irrelevant dimensions

The number of relevant dimensions should be reduced to the minimum needed to define the concept, and the number of irrelevant dimensions should be reduced as much as possible. In addition, instructional procedures should be used to emphasize the differences between relevant and irrelevant dimensions. For example, instructional procedures should be used to stress the relevant features and minimize the irrelevant features and to vary the degree of difference in the relevant and irrelevant features from instance to instance. They also should include forms of instances with fewer irrelevant features (e.g., schematic diagrams versus concrete objects). More teaching and practice time should be provided when dimensions cannot be manipulated. (p. 208)

Taxonomic level

The instructional procedures should vary the amount of teaching and practice according to the hierarchical level of the concept, i.e., the number of lower-order concepts it subsumes. In addition, instructional procedures should be used to identify the key relevant dimensions going through the hierarchy to define the higher-order concepts. (pp. 216–217)

Contiguity of instances

When there are several concepts to be learned, the instructional procedures should include an unmixed presentation. Each concept should be learned separately rather than several concepts learned concomitantly. The instructional procedures should provide overlearning, verbal meditation, and similar methods to facilitate reversal shifts and learning set. (pp. 217–218)

Positive and negative instances

The instructional procedures should include simultaneous exposure. After the pupil responds to a set of instances and gets feedback, the set of instances should be kept in view, and he or she should be told not to try to rely on memory, but rather to refer back to it as often as necessary, to see what the positive instances were. As the pupil has more instances to refer to, the instructional procedures should allow more time for study. (p. 220)

Simultaneous and successive exposure

The instructional procedures should include simultaneous exposure. After the pupil responds to a set of instances and gets feedback, the set of instances should be kept in view, and he or she should be told not to try to rely on memory, but rather to refer back to it as often as necessary to see what the positive instances were. As the pupil has more instances to refer to, the instructional procedures should allow more time for study. (p. 220)

Expository and discovery methods

When the goal is to teach a specific concept, instructional procedures should include an expository method. Pupils should be given information about rules, relevant and irrelevant dimensions, etc., and practice applying that information. When the goal is to give pupils practice trying out strategies and to teach pupils to tolerate frustration in dealing with concepts, instructional procedures should include a discovery method. (p. 222)

Source: Blake (1974).

Conjunction involves the joint presence of multiple attributes. For example, when *y* is the last vowel pronounced in a one-syllable word, it is sounded as long *i.*

Inclusive disjunction involves the presence of either one or another attribute or both. For example, when *c* is followed by *a, o,* or *u,* or when it comes at the end of the word, or when it comes before the other consonants in consonant blends, it is called hard and sounded as *k.*

Exclusion involves the presence of one attribute and the absence of another. For example, when *g* is followed by letters other than *e, i,* or *y,* it is called hard and sounded as *g.*

Conceptual rules vary in difficulty. The difficulty depends on the complexity, length, and familiarity of the rule (Blake & Williams, 1963; Bourne, 1970; McLaughlin, 1976a, 1976b, 1976c). For example, it is easier for a student to learn a phonics principle based on a conjunction rule than one based on an exclusion rule.

As an additional illustration consider the following example. The rule for the concept *number* is a simple affirmation rule. Elements are members of the concept (1, 2, 3, and so on) or they are not. The concept *big* involves comparisons in terms of size or amount; therefore, it involves a relations rule. For instance, an object is big only in relation to some other object. The latter concept is the more complex, and the teacher should spend more time presenting this concept and should allow the students more time to practice for acquisition.

Relevant and Irrelevant Dimensions

Relevant dimensions define the concept; they help make the instances of the concept alike. Irrelevant dimensions are present but they do not define the concept; they help make the instances of the concept different. Consider the concept of automobile repairman. Relevant dimensions include such things as what he works on and the nature of his work. Irrelevant dimensions include such things as wages and the hours that he works.

When the number of relevant and/or irrelevant dimensions are increased, concept learning becomes harder. Increases in either dimension affect the amount and type of information the child has to consider (May, 1973). These negative effects can be reduced by decreasing the number of dimensions. If that is impossible, they can be reduced by making the relevant dimensions more obvious than the irrelevant dimensions or by using a form of instances which shows fewer irrelevant features, e.g., verbal statements or schematic illustrations in contrast to concrete objects (Blake, 1974).

The following example illustrates this principle. For the concept *square* there is only one relevant dimension, form. All other dimensions vary with particular instances, but they are irrelevant. Such irrelevant dimensions are size, color, and orientation. Irrelevant dimensions should be held constant within each stimulus presentation, or confusion might result. Verbal comments can help to avoid confusion in the learner too. Consider the presentations in Figure 5-1 in which size and orientation are varied in addition to form.

Now look at the three presentations in Figure 5-2. They maintain constancy for size and orientation within each presentation, but vary *across* presentations in order to introduce a variety of contexts. Confusion is reduced through verbal clues which help the learner distinguish between relevant and irrelevant dimensions.

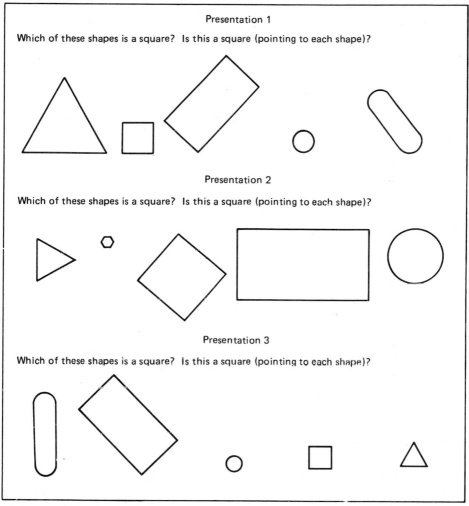

Figure 5-1 Uncontrolled relevant and irrelevant dimensions. (Source: McLaughlin, Eaves, and Fallen, 1978, p. 201.)

Presentation 1

Instructions. A square is the shape that has four sides, all the same size. The four corners are like the corners of a page in a book. A square looks like this: (show a positive instance of a square as a model). Which of these shapes is a square?

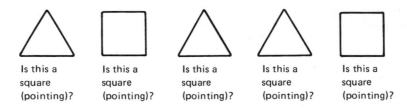

| Is this a square (pointing)? | Is this a square (pointing)? | Is this a square (pointing)? | Is this a square (pointing)? | Is this a square (pointing)? |

Presentation 2

Instructions. Remember that a square has four sides all the same size and its four courners are like the corners of a page of a book. Now, see if you can find a square when you look at these shapes that have been turned.

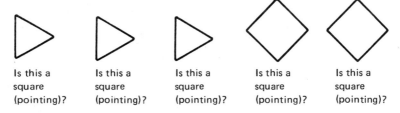

| Is this a square (pointing)? | Is this a square (pointing)? | Is this a square (pointing)? | Is this a square (pointing)? | Is this a square (pointing)? |

Now you can see that a square is the same whether it stands up straight or it is turned. It is still a square.

Presentation 3

Instructions. You've found a square when it stands up straight and when it is turned. A square is always the same. It doesn't even matter if it is big or little; it is still a square. The special thing about a square is that it has four sides that are all the same size and its corners are like the pages of a book. See if you can find the square when the shapes are little.

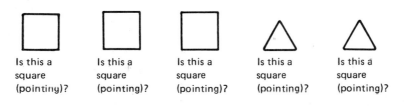

| Is this a square (pointing)? | Is this a square (pointing)? | Is this a square (pointing)? | Is this a square (pointing)? | Is this a square (pointing)? |

Figure 5-2 Controlled relevant and irrelevant dimensions. (Source: McLaughlin, Eaves, and Fallen, 1978, p. 202.)

Taxonomic Level

A taxonomy is a hierarchical classification system. Taxonomic level refers to how many other concepts a concept includes. For example, the concept of threeness is at a low taxonomic level. In contrast, the concept of odd numbers is at a higher taxonomic level.

Higher-order concepts are harder to learn because they are further removed from concrete objects and events. They include a large number of disparate instances which show subtle defining characteristics and differ on a large number of irrelevant attributes (Blake & Williams, 1968b). For example, it is easier for a child to learn the concept *threeness* than it is for him to learn the concept *odd number*.

This principle is further illustrated by the following examples. The concepts *dog, pet,* and *animal* are all members of the same hierarchy. Dog is the lowest-order concept, pet is second, and animal is the highest-order concept. In this example and all others like it, the lowest-order concept has the greatest number of relevant dimensions. As the concept progresses to higher orders, previously relevant dimensions become irrelevant and, therefore, the concept becomes harder to learn. For example, relevant dimensions of a dog are barking, wagging tail, sniffing. Because these dimensions are not true of all pets, they become irrelevant to the concept of pet. The dimensions of all pets become relevant. For the concept *animal* (the highest-order concept in the example), one relevant dimension is locomotion. Animals move their bodies; nonanimals are stationary unless someone else moves them. This relevant dimension maintains throughout the hierarchy.

The teacher must continuously identify the dimensions that are relevant at the highest order, or confusion results. When teaching concepts, the teacher considers the number of lower-order concepts they subsume and varies the amount of time and practice accordingly.

Contiguity of Instances

Contiguity is how closely together instances of a given concept are presented when several concepts are being learned concurrently (Blake, 1974). When the instances for only one concept are presented until the concept is learned, there is high contiguity. This is an unmixed presentation and the instances are close together or highly contiguous. There is low contiguity in a mixed presentation when instances of several concepts are presented together. As an example, if the concepts *fruit, vegetables,* and *meat* were taught, in an unmixed presentation, instances of each concept would be presented separately until each was mastered. The types of fruit would be presented first, types of vegetables next, and types of meats last. In a mixed presentation, the concepts would be presented concurrently. Peaches, steak, carrots, beans, chicken, pears, pork chops, and apples would be presented at the same time until the three concepts—*fruit, vegetable,* and *meat*—were mastered.

The unmixed presentation with higher contiguity is easier. The mixed presentation, and thus lower contiguity, puts more of a strain on the child's

Twoness

Twoness is the group represented by this set (1, 2). Find groups which have the characteristics of this set. Count the objects in a group and compare it to the set (1, 2). Then, look at the groups of two and at all the other groups and see how they are alike and different.

| Presentation 1 | Presentation 2 | Presentation 3 |

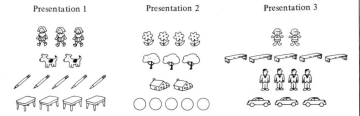

Such presentations would continue until the students master the concept.

Threeness

Threeness is the group represented by this set (1, 2, 3). Find groups which have the characteristics of this set. Be careful not to get confused. You've already learned about twoness (1, 2). You are not working on twoness now. You are working on three, so when you see two don't mark it because it is not right for this problem. However, you use the same methods. You count the objects in a group and compare them to the set. You look at the groups of three and at all the other groups and see how they are alike and different.

| Presentation 1 | Presentation 2 | Presentation 3 |

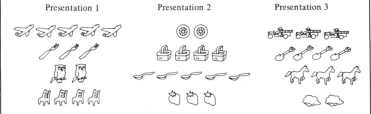

Such presentations also would continue until pupils master the concept.

Fourness

Fourness is the group represented by the set (1, 2, 3, 4). Find groups which have the characteristics of this set. Be careful not to get confused. You've already learned about twoness (1, 2) and threeness (1, 2, 3). They are not what you are working on now. So when you see two and three, don't mark them because they are not right for this problem.

However, use the same methods. Count the objects in a group and compare it to the set (1, 2, 3, 4). Then, look at the group of four and all the other groups and see how they are alike and different.

| Presentation 1 | Presentation 2 | Presentation 3 |

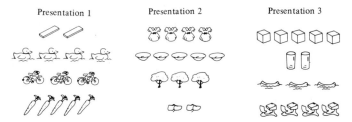

Such presentations would continue until the pupils master the concept.

Figure 5-3 High contiguity. (Source: Blake, 1974, pp. 218-219.)

Three concepts concomitantly

Here are the sets for twoness, threeness, and fourness:

Twoness   (1, 2)
Threeness   (1, 2, 3)
Fourness   (1, 2, 3, 4)

Here are several groups; count the objects in each group. Write 2 for set (1, 2). Write 3 for set (1, 2, 3). Write 4 for set (1, 2, 3, 4). Then look and see how the groups for two, three, and four are different.

Presentation 1   Presentation 2   Presentation 3

Such presentations would continue until the pupils master all the concepts.

Figure 5-4   Low contiguity. (Source: Blake, 1974, pp. 219-220.)

memory since instances of any one concept are farther apart in time (Bourne & Jennings, 1963; Hurley, 1975a).

Consider the following teaching situation. The teacher must teach the concepts of several numbers; those for one, two, three, four, and so on. Based on the principle of contiguity of instances the most effective strategy is to teach one number concept at a time. That is, teach the concept *one*, then the concept *two*, then the concept *three*, and so on. It is much more difficult for the student to learn all the number sets concomitantly. As an example, examine Blake's (1974) arrangements for teaching twoness, threeness, and fourness. Figure 5-3 presents her layouts for teaching each concept separately. Figure 5-4 presents her layout for teaching the three concepts at the same time.

Positive and Negative Instances

Positive instances are examples of the concept. Negative instances are not. For example, for the concept *fruit*, positive instances are apples, oranges, pears, grapes, and negative instances are chairs, pens, shirts, dogs, hamburgers.

Positive instances help concept learning by showing what characteristics define the concept. Negative instances help by showing what characteristics do not define the concept. The child can learn in situations where there are only positive instances or only negative instances. However, a mixed sequence of positive and negative instances is best. The best mix is more positive than negative instances (Hurley, 1973, 1975b). The positive and negative instances

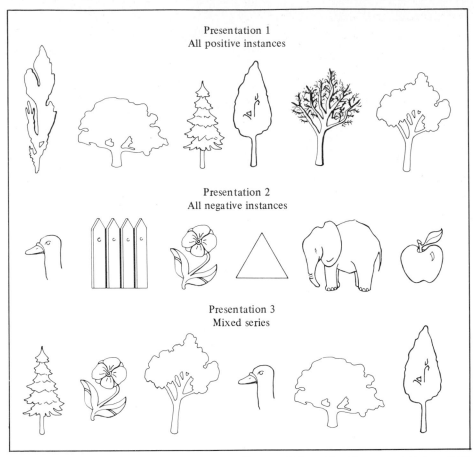

Figure 5-5 Positive and negative instances. (Source: McLaughlin, Eaves, and Fallen, 1978, p. 208.)

should be of the same form; that is, either all verbal or all concrete rather than some of both.

For example, although the concept *tree* can be taught in three ways (i.e., all positive instances, all negative instances, and a mixed series), a mixed presentation of both positive and negative instances is best. Figure 5-5 shows layouts of the three possibilities.

The third presentation and others like it would help the child define the limits of the concept *tree* more quickly than the other presentations, because the instances are mixed and with more positive instances than negative. Verbal aids which expose the student to the relevant dimensions of trees also help. For students who have difficulty with the abstractness of line drawings, photographs of the positive and negative instances would facilitate learning. Even more concrete presentations of the instances could be used during walks outside the classroom.

Simultaneous and Successive Exposure

In successive exposure, the student sees only one instance at a time. After he responds and gets feedback, the instance is removed. In simultaneous exposure, the instances are kept in view after the pupil responds and gets feedback. Simultaneous exposure permits the child to look back at earlier instances.

Simultaneous exposure simplifies concept learning. It reduces memory load and increases ease of making inferences. As the amount of information the child is exposed to is increased, the time available for him to deal with it also needs to be increased (Bourne, Goldstein, & Link, 1964; McLaughlin, 1976d).

The following example illustrates this principle. If the concept *number* were being taught, exposure of positive and negative instances of the concept could be made successively or simultaneously. In concept learning, simultaneous presentations are best. Figure 5-6 shows a layout using successive exposures and 3 × 5 inch cards as stimuli.

A child can learn the concept *number* using the successive presentation approach, but he will learn the concept more quickly if he is allowed to refer back to previous examples to which he has been exposed. Figure 5-7 illustrates a layout for teaching *number* as a concept using a simultaneous presentation. Again, 3 × 5 inch cards provide the stimuli. In this case, all prior instances to which the pupil has responded are left in full view so that he may use them as aids when necessary. In concept learning, the child will reach mastery more quickly if simultaneous presentation is used.

Expository and Discovery Methods

When the expository method is used, the students are given information about the concept—the relevant and irrelevant dimensions, attributes, rules, and other information. With a discovery method, they are given a question and allowed to discover the dimensions, attributes, rules, and other information. These methods have often been called deductive and inductive methods, respectively.

Concept learning is faster with expository methods. The students have more information, make fewer errors, and experience less failure and frustration (Blake & Williams, 1968a). However, with discovery methods, the students have to be more active, and this activity may lead to more attention.

As an illustration, refer to the section on relevant and irrelevant dimensions. For the three presentations in Figure 5-1 (in which irrelevant dimensions were allowed to vary within each presentation), the pupil is told nothing about the concept (*square*). No information is given about rules, relevant dimensions, irrelevant dimensions, and no model is presented. It is left up to the child to *discover* this information on his own.

With reference to the second three presentations shown in Figure 5-2, the pupil is told about the important dimension concerning the concept *square*. He is told the rules: "A square has four sides, all the same size. The four corners are like the pages in a book." He is presented with a model square. He is given

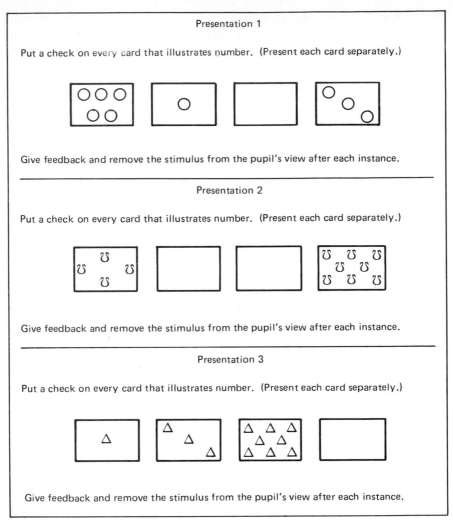

Figure 5-6 Successive exposure of the concept of number. (Source: McLaughlin, Eaves, and Fallen, 1978, p. 209.)

pertinent information about the irrelevant dimensions (orientation, size). In short, an expository method is used. In concept learning, expository methods lead to more efficient mastery.

VERBAL LEARNING

There are three types of verbal learning: paired-associates learning, free-recall learning, and serial learning. *Paired-associates learning* requires the student to pair, or learn the relations, between particular stimuli and responses. For example, supplying the Arabic numerals that correspond to the names of

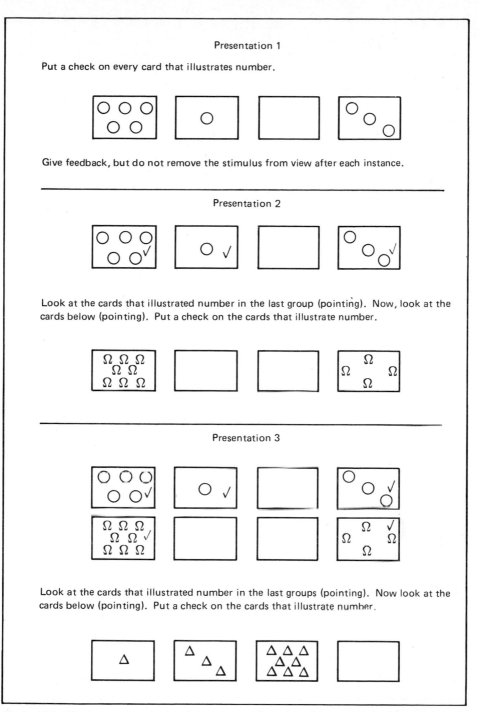

Figure 5-7 Simultaneous exposure of the concept of number. (Source: McLaughlin, Eaves, and Fallen, 1978, p. 210.)

the numbers requires paired-associates learning. Learning sight vocabulary words also requires paired-associates learning. *Free-recall learning* requires the student to learn the items in a set or list and recall them in any order. Learning the names of classmates is an example of free-recall learning. Learning the jobs in an occupational cluster is another example. *Serial learning* requires the students to learn the items in a set or list in a particular sequence. Serial learning is required in spelling, in learning travel routes, and in learning the steps in a task analysis.

Table 5-4 shows the domains and teaching topics Blake identified as involving verbal learning. Listed below are some illustrations of instructional objectives involving verbal learning.

> Given five vocabulary words, the student can supply their synonyms, with 100-percent accuracy in 1 minute.
>
> Given the verbal cue, "Name six jobs in the food service area," the student will name any six jobs listed in the food service unit, with 100-percent accuracy in 1 minute.
>
> Given the verbal cue, "Tell me your phone number," the student will be able to do so, with 100-percent accuracy in 15 seconds.

Four specific learning principles influence verbal learning. Three of the four relate to the nature of the material: meaningfulness, intratask similarity, and serial position. Organizational devices, the fourth principle, pertains to the method of presenting the information to the students. These four principles are discussed and illustrated below. Table 5-5 lists the pertinent points for each principle.

Table 5-4   Topics Involving Verbal Learning

Domains	Topics
Oral language: listening and speech	Compounds, contractions, and denotative meanings—specific labels, synonyms, and antonyms
Reading	Sight vocabulary, compounds, and contractions
Written language: spelling, handwriting, genre	Spelling specific words—frequently used words, spelling demons, and special words; and names—letters, punctuation marks, and Arabic numerals
Arithmetic	All topics in numeration except place value
Personal-social skills	Specific facts, e.g., names of particular people, places, or things; particular addresses and phone numbers; particular brands of food or clothing; particular insurance companies; particular governmental agencies; particular map routes; and so on

Source: Blake (1974, p. 230).

Table 5-5   Specific Principles Influencing Verbal Learning

Meaningfulness

When there is a choice, material should be high on one of the indices of meaningfulness: frequency, pronunciability, sequential dependencies, vividness, or concreteness. When there is no choice and low-meaningfulness materials must be used, procedures should allow more time for pupils to study and practice. When low-meaningfulness materials must be used and there is sufficient time, procedures should be used to familiarize pupils with the materials. In paired-associates learning, when one member of the pair is more meaningful than another, that member should be made the response member. (p. 231)

Intratask similarity

In tasks involving paired associates and serial learning, procedures should be used to reduce intratask similarity. If intratask similarity cannot be reduced, then more teaching and practice time should be allowed. In free-recall learning, formal similarity needs to be reduced, and meaningful, conceptual, and associative similarity increased. Here again, teaching and practice time need to be adjusted if intratask similarity cannot be manipulated. (pp. 233–234)

Serial position effect

Procedures should be used to take into account the serial position effect. In serial learning, attention should be focused on the last items in the list; in free learning, on the first items. Procedures should include such techniques as marking the items on which to focus attention, allowing more study and practice time for the critical items, and using verbal instructions about the critical items. (p. 234)

Organizational devices

The instructional procedures should capitalize on the intrinsic organization of the material. If the material has no intrinsic organization, it should be organized by extrinsic devices like coding, mediation, clustering, and stimulus selection. (p. 232)

Source: Blake (1974).

Meaningfulness

The meaningfulness of material is determined by its familiarity to the students. The material's concreteness or abstractness is also a measure of its meaningfulness. An item's familiarity is defined as the number of times the student has heard or seen the material. A concrete item is one that can be directly observed. An abstract item is one that must be inferred and is not as meaningful as a concrete item.

Meaningfulness greatly helps students' verbal learning (Blake, 1976a; Williams, 1975a, 1975b, 1975c). If possible, always start with concrete materials in paired-associates learning, since the pairs are learned faster when the more-meaningful item is made the response member of the pair. When teaching low-meaningful information, the teacher should use instructional strategies to familiarize students with the materials before they start working on them.

For example, consider the task of learning synonyms. The students' must learn a new word (e.g., *quick*) to go along with a word they already know (e.g., *fast*). The new words are lower in familiaity and therefore not as meaningful.

The teacher should increase the meaningfulness of the new words by exposing them to the students before they work on them in a learning task. This pretask familiarization should include pronouncing the new words and having the students read them. It also helps to post the new words on a wall chart or bulletin board. During the initial practice sessions the teacher should present the new words (*quick*, etc.) as the stimuli. This technique will allow the students to respond with words they already know (*fast*, etc.), i.e., the more meaningful words.

Intratask Similarity

Intratask similarity is the overlap among the elements of a task. Verbal learning materials can be similar in several ways: formal similarity, meaningful similarity, conceptual similarity, and associative similarity. Blake (1974) provided the following definitions of these types of intratask similarity:

> *Formal similarity*. Formal similarity refers to the overlap of letters and other physical factors.
> *Meaningful similarity*. Meaningful similarity refers to the overlap in definitions of items, such as synonyms.
> *Conceptual similarity*. Conceptual similarity is an overlap in the items' class membership.
> *Associative similarity*. Associative similarity is an overlap in the extent to which items within a list elicit a common response with respect to scaled association values. (p. 233)

The affect of intratask similarity on verbal learning is complex (Blake, 1975b). The influence depends on the type of similarity in combination with the type of verbal learning. Serial and paired-associates learning are made more difficult by all types of similarity. The overlap in the items causes confusion, and this confusion interferes with the learning. For example, consider the following two lists of phone numbers:

	List 1		List 2
355-3642	police emergency	355-5577	police emergency
764-4624	fire emergency	764-6689	fire emergency
542-6224	ambulance	542-4003	ambulance
387-6442	physician	387-2221	physician

List 1 has more within-task formal similarity than List 2. In other words, List 1 has more overlap of numbers within its list of phone numbers than List 2. This overlap makes List 1 harder to learn than List 2.

Free-recall learning is easier with high meaningful, conceptual, and associative similarity. In these types of similarity, associative connections exist among the items. Therefore, they tend to elicit one another easily. For example, consider learning to recall the following two lists:

List 1	List 2
house	automobile
table	boat
Charles	airplane
pickle	rickshaw

List 2 has more conceptual similarity than List 1. That is, everything in List 2 is a form of transportation. This overlap makes List 2 easier to recall than List 1.

Free-recall learning is harder with high formal similarity. Associative connections do not already exist among items. They must be learned. This makes the task a paired-associates task, and similarity causes confusion in associative learning. For example, consider learning to recall the following two lists:

List 1	List 2
golf	band
hamburger	banal
light	ball
floor	Baltic

List 2 has more formal similarity than List 1. The first two letters of all the words in List 2 are identical. This overlap makes List 2 harder to recall than List 1.

If possible, the intratask similarity should be manipulated to make the verbal learning task easier. If this is not possible, then teaching and practice time must be increased. The instructional strategies should also point out the helpful and harmful similarities.

Serial Position

Serial position is the position of an item within a series of items. The influence of serial position on learning depends on whether the task is free-recall- or serial learning. In free-recall learning, the last items in the list are learned best; the first items are learned next best; and the middle items are learned least (McManis, 1965). In serial learning, the order changes to become first items, last items, and middle items.

The application of this principle is straightforward. For example, consider the serial-learning task of spelling. Students will generally make more errors in the middle of the words. Teachers should direct students' attention to the critical letters in the middle and at the end of words. This can be done by color-coding, underlining, and using verbal instructions.

Organization

The principle of organization is used to impose structure on the verbal learning materials. Coding, mediation, clustering, and stimulus selection are frequently used as organizational devices. Organizing the material helps handicapped students' immediate recall and learning (Frye, 1973; Frost, 1976). These devices increase the meaningfulness of the material and reduces the number of separate items to be learned.

Blake (1974) defined the organizational devices as follows:

> *Coding.* Coding is changing the material to another form, usually a more meaningful one.
> *Mediation.* Mediation is the linking of items to be learned with additional items which are related to both and thus serve as connectors. Mediators may be pictures, words, sentences, and various formulae.
> *Clustering.* Clustering is recalling items in sets. Depending on the material, the total number of items may be grouped by concepts, synonym groups, or some other grouping dimensions.
> *Stimulus Selection.* Stimulus selection is choosing only a part of the total complex item for association, i.e., choosing the parts which have some prior relations; these may be letters or other distinctive features. Pupils deal with the selected part of the stimulus and thus gain a more precise unit to associate with the response. (p. 272)

She also presented the illustration of mediation shown in Figure 5-8.

Note that this specific learning principle of *organization* overlaps with the general acquisition learning principle of *structure* (presented in Chapter 4). All the organizational devices increase the material's meaningfulness, and this is critical in verbal learning situations. In short, structure helps in all learning situations but is especially important with verbal learning materials.

DISCRIMINATION LEARNING

Discrimination learning is learning to respond differently to distinctive features of stimuli. For example, consider the following objective. Given the sets of letters *b* and *d* and *a* and *o*, the student should mark each letter as it is named with 100-percent accuracy in 10 seconds. The student would base his or her differential response to the letters on the shape of the letters; i.e., on the presence of the vertical line and its size and position in relation to the circle.

Table 5-6 shows the domains and teaching topics Blake identified as involving discrimination learning. Below are some illustrative instructional objectives:

> Given the task of sorting 100 nuts and bolts, the student will sort them by size, with 90-percent accuracy in 15 minutes.

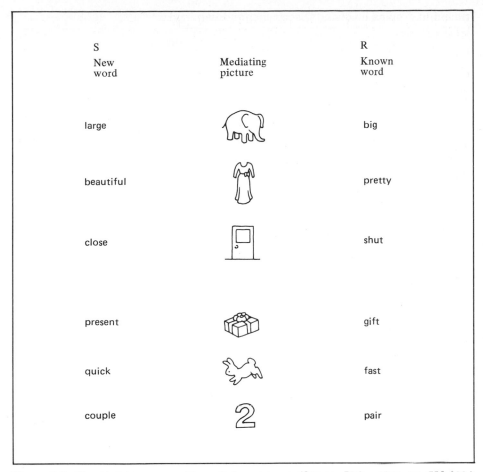

Figure 5-8 Teaching synonyms with mediating pictures. (Source: Blake, 1974, pp. 232-233.)

Given similar words like *cap/cat* and *sleep/deep*, the student can mark each word as it is named, with 100-percent accuracy at the rate of 20 per minute.

Four specific learning principles affect discrimination learning. Three of these relate to the nature of the materials: distinctive features, irrelevant features, and dimensionality. One principle, contiguity, pertains to the method of presentation. These four principles are described and illustrated below. Table 5-7 has the pertinent points for each principle.

Distinctive Features

Distinctive features are characteristics that identify a stimulus and make it different from other stimuli. For example, look at the shapes of the letters *b, d, a,* and *o*. The position of the vertical line in relation to the circle is the distinctive

Table 5-6   Topics Involving Discrimination Learning

Domains	Topics
Oral language: listening and speech	Differentiating sounds in words
Reading	Sight vocabulary, sound identification, sound discrimination, homonyms
Written language: spelling, handwriting, usage, and genre	Proofreading: letters, punctuation marks, Arabic numerals; arrangements and spacing—conventions; margins and headings—conventions
Arithmetic	None
Personal-social skills	All skills (e.g., discrimination among red, amber, and green traffic lights; busy signal, dial tone, and ring on the telephone); facial expressions indicating approval and disapproval; cleanliness in houses; freshness in food; quality in clothing; routes and areas on a map; and so on

Source: Blake (1974, p. 201).

feature. The instructional strategies should use techniques to emphasize the distinctive features of stimuli. In the above example, the vertical lines could be color-coded.

Overlap among distinctive features makes discrimination learning harder. The overlap makes it more difficult to find and respond to the unique features of the stimuli. Training strategies such as coding or stimulus pretraining have been effective with handicapped learners (Blake, 1975a; Tucker, 1973).

Blake (1974, p. 202) developed the following illustration of an instructional strategy applying the principle of distinctive features:

> The distinctive features for words are the letters/sounds which compose them. Consider the words *dog* and *pet* in relation to one another; each is characterized by a unique set of letters and sounds with no overlap. With our illustrative task, spelling homonyms, the difficulty comes precisely because of the overlap in distinctive features. They sound alike and have the same spelling with the exception, in most cases, of only one to three letters. As an example, consider the overlap among *too, two, to*; among *road, rode, rowed*; and among other homonym sets. With homonyms, we cannot reduce the overlap among distinctive features. However, we can focus attention on the overlap by various kinds of coding. For instance, suppose you are working on *stationary* and *stationery*. By color coding or simple underlining and pretraining with respective spellings, you could work out this arrangement.
>
> > stationary   *a* as in *stand*
> > stationery   *e* as in *letter*

Irrelevant Features

Irrelevant features are characteristics that do not define the positive stimulus. Discrimination learning is made harder by the presence of irrelevant features.

Table 5-7   Specific Principles Influencing Discrimination Learning

Distinctive features

The instructional procedures should include techniques to emphasize distinctive features of stimuli, e.g., stimulus pretraining techniques. Overlap among distinctive features of different stimuli should be reduced. When overlap cannot be prevented, instructional procedures should include techniques to focus attention on the overlap and nullify its confusing effects. (p. 202)

Irrelevant features

Instructional procedures should be used to control irrelevant features. They should be either reduced or marked and nullified. (p. 203)

Dimensionality of stumuli

In order to get more redundancy, three-dimensional stimuli should be used in preference to two-dimensional stimuli when possible. With three-dimensional materials, objects should be used in preference to pictures. With pictures, photographs should be used in preference to line drawings. (p. 204)

Contiguity

Instructional procedures should be used to increase contiguity. For example, the stimuli to be discriminated should be presented simultaneously rather than successively. Within simultaneous presentation, stimuli should be as close together as possible. (p. 205)

Source: Blake (1974).

They divert the student's attention from the distinctive features of the task (Klein, Lkein, Oscamp, & Patnode, 1972). Irrelevant features should be reduced as much as possible. If they cannot be eliminated from the materials, the teacher should identify them as irrelevant. It is important that the students know which features are relevant and which are irrelevant.

For example, consider the task of teaching a severely handicapped student the correct school bus to take home. In most cases the relevant feature will be the number printed on the side of the bus by the door. An irrelevant feature is the position of the bus in line outside the school. One day it might be first in line, the next day third, and so on. Identifying this as an irrelevant feature should be incorporated into the instructional strategies.

Dimensionality of Stimuli

Dimensionality of stimuli refers to the number of dimensions in the materials. The materials may either be two- or three-dimensional. Two-dimensional materials include line drawings and photographs. Three-dimensional materials include actual objects or cutouts. Three-dimensional stimuli provide more cues and thus make learning easier (Blake, 1974).

As an illustration, consider the materials used to teach a handicapped student the travel route from home to school. This task involves many discrimination learning situations, e.g., street intersections. The teacher could use many different types of materials to teach the student the correct discriminations. Photographs of the important intersections would be better than drawings, and a mock-up in the classroom would be even better. The teacher should include the actual street intersection in his training program.

Contiguity

Contiguity refers to how close together stimuli are presented in space or time. Stimuli can be presented all at one time and close together. This is called *simultaneous presentation*. Stimuli can also be presented separately at various time intervals. This is called *successive presentation*.

Increasing contiguity helps discrimination learning. Proximity enables the students to compare the stimuli and identify relevant and irrelevant features (Tucker, 1976). For example, review the following task on teaching homonyms (Blake, 1974, p. 205):

> High contiguity is an easy and important condition to arrange in teaching discriminations like those in our illustrative task homonyms. Look at these arrangements for simultaneous and successive presentation. The discriminations would be easier to learn with the simultaneous presentation.

Simultaneous Presentation

their	belonging to them
there	in that place
they're	they are
write	to make letters with a pencil
right	correct
some	a few
sum	the result of adding
too	also
two	one plus one

Successive Presentation

their	belonging to them
write	to make letters wih a pencil
some	a few
too	also
there	in that place
right	correct
sum	the result of adding
two	one plus one
they're	they are

LEARNING CONNECTED DISCOURSE

Connected discourse refers to oral and written material in sentences, paragraphs, and multiparagraphs. In learning connected discourse, students are required to grasp the meaning of the information, and to interpret and apply that information. Table 5-8 shows the domains and teaching topics Blake identified as

Table 5-8   Topics Involving Connected Discourse

Domains	Topics
Oral language: listening and speech	Context clues, genre, directly stated ideas, relations, descriptions, directions, inferences, analysis, processing, and critical listening
Reading	Context analysis, main ideas in paragraphs, supporting ideas in paragraphs, ideas in longer selections, and skimming and scanning
Written language: spelling, handwriting, usage, and genre.	None
Arithmetic	Connected discourse is used only indirectly in reading the problems
Personal-social skills	Connected discourse is used only indirectly here; this indirect use comes through the communication and arithmetic activities cited above

Source: Blake (1974, p. 236).

involving connected discourse. The following objectives are examples of those involving connected discourse:

> Given a description of the duties of a service station attendant, the student can recall the main ideas, with 90-percent accuracy.
> Given a set of directions for baking a cake, the student can follow them, with 100-percent accuracy.
> After listening to a lecture on fire hazards in the home, the student can recite nine out of the ten main points.

Three specific learning principles affect dealing with connected discourse. They are language maturity, sentence processing, and dimensions of material. These three principles are described and illustrated below. Table 5-9 presents the pertinent points for each principle.

Language Maturity

Language maturity is determined by the student's ability to deal with the four language components: phonological, morphological, syntactical, and semantic. These components are defined below:

> *Phonological Components.* The phonemes are the sounds which make up words, e.g., the *b* sound.
> *Morphological Components.* Morphemes are the irreducible units of meaning which make up words; e.g., *-s* and *-es* are morphemes which mean the plural noun and singular verb.
> *Syntactical Components.* Syntax refers to the structure of selections: the form classes (nouns, verbs, etc.) and the ways they are related.

Table 5-9   Specific Principles Influencing Learning Connected Discourse

Language maturity

The materials should be appropriate for the pupils language maturity. That is, the material should be adjusted to pupils' mental ages, sensory status, environmental background, dialect characteristics, and previous instruction. If the materials cannot be adjusted, the pupils should have more teaching and practice time. (p. 237)

Sentence processing

Materials should include more kernel sentences than double-base transformations. Right-branching structures should be used most often when double-base transformations are necessary. This is in contrast to left-branching structures and center-embedded structures. If the material does consist of the more difficult structures, the pupils should have more teaching and practice time. (p. 238) Materials also should include more kernel sentences than single-based transformations. (p. 238)

Dimensions of material

Materials should conform to dimensions which make processing easier. That is, main ideas should be directly stated, and redundancy, structure, and organization should be at a maximum. Complexity should be decreased as much as possible. More study and practice time should be allowed if these conditions cannot be obtained. (p. 240)

Source: Blake (1974).

Semantic Components. Semantics refers to the meaning of words, e.g., *happy* means *glad*. (Blake, 1974, pp. 236–237)

In general, students differ in language maturity. The differences correspond to mental age, sensory status, environmental background, dialect characteristics, and previous instruction. The teacher's instructions and materials should be appropriate to the students' language maturity. For example, look at the two reading selections below. Selection A is harder semantically; it has more unfamiliar words. Selection B is more appropriate for handicapped students.

Selection A. One of the greatest modern creations, the skyscraper, was initiated as a result of both necessity and capability. Exigencies related to space in already congested districts is the necessity while advances in modern engineering methods is the capability.

Selection B. The skycraper is one of the greatest new things we have today. Skyscrapers were started because we need them and because we are able to build them. We need them because we need more room in cities. We are able to build them because of new things in engineering. (Blake, 1974, p. 237)

Sentence Processing

Sentence processing is basically dependent on the complexity of the information. A simple declarative sentence in the active voice, known as a *kernel sentence*, is the easiest for students to process. When a kernel sentence is changed into another form such as a question or passive sentence, it is called a single-base transformation. Listed below is a kernel sentence and several transformations.

> *Kernel:* The teacher is helping the student.
> *Passive:* The student is being helped by the teacher.
> *Question:* Is the teacher helping the student?
> *Passive Negative:* The student is not being helped by the teacher.

Dealing with a transformed sentence involves recoding it, storing it in memory as a kernel, and tagging or footnoting what transformation took place. A student can more easily remember and recall kernel sentences than transformations; with transformations, he has more steps to go through and more to remember (Blake, 1975c; Semmel & Dolley, 1971).

Teachers should primarily give instructions and use materials with kernel sentences. If this is not possible, the students should have more teaching and practice time. To illustrate this principle look at the two sets of directions below. Set B is easier to understand than Set A.

> *Set A.* Late students are punished by the teacher. Students should not get out of their seats. When the teacher is talking, students should not talk.
> *Set B.* The teacher punishes late students. Students should stay in their seats. Students should be quiet when the teacher is talking.

Dimensions of the Material

Dimensions of the material refers to characteristics such as redundancy and explicitness of ideas. *Redundancy* is the amount of repetition in the material. *Explicitness* refers to whether the ideas are directly stated or implied.

Connected discourse is easier to learn when the main ideas are directly stated and when redundancy is increased (Ballagas, 1975; Osterhout, 1976). As an illustration, look at the story below. There is redundancy: the main idea is stated in the title, the opening paragraph, and the closing paragraph. The main ideas are directly stated and are in a consistent location— the first sentence of each paragraph. The sentences stating the main idea could be abstracted in an outline and they would convey the significant events in the story.

Pete Learns a Lesson

Pete learned a lesson in being polite. He learned it Saturday morning at the movies. Pete started out by making a mistake. He came running up to the movie house. There were many boys and girls waiting their turn in a long line. Pete took one look at the long line. He decided that he was not going to wait in that long line. No, Sir. He walked to the front of the line and pushed his way in there. Billy Wilson did something about Pete's mistake. Pete pushed in front of Billy. Billy did not say a word. But he pulled off Pete's hat and handed it to Joe, the boy behind him. Joe passed the hat to the girl behind him. And Pete's hat went down the line until it got to Betty at the very end.

Pete soon understood his mistake. He said to Bill, "Where's my hat?" Billy pointed down the line. There at the end was Betty holding up Pete's hat. Everyone smiled.

Pete made up his mistake. He did not smile when he saw where his hat was. He did not say a word. He walked back to the end of the line behind Betty.

Pete still remembers his lesson. He goes to the movies every Saturday morning. But he goes to the end of the line and waits his turn to buy his ticket. (Blake, 1974, p. 241)

SUMMARY

The general and specific principles of learning are the cornerstone of the basic teaching model. All instructional strategies should be based on these principles. The general principles influencing acquisition, retention, and transfer should be applied in teaching all skills. The instructional strategies should also be appropriate for the type of learning specified in the instructional objective. This chapter describes and illustrates learning principles specific to four types of learning: concept learning, verbal learning, discrimination learning, and learning connected discourse.

Concept Learning

Concept learning involves grouping or categorizing stimuli into sets. These sets may be either concrete or abstract. Concrete concepts can be observed. Defined concepts must be learned by definition. Students are required to use concept learning more than any other type of learning. The following principles should be used to develop instructional strategies for concept learning.

Nature of rules. Conceptual rules vary in difficulty. Teaching and practice time should vary according to the difficulty of the rule defining the concept.

Relevant and irrelevant dimensions. Relevant dimensions define the concept. Irrelevant dimensions are present but do not define the concept. The number of relevant and irrelevant dimensions should be reduced as much as possible. In addition, the relevant dimensions should be made more obvious than the irrelevant dimensions.

Taxonomic level. Teaching and practice time should be varied according to the hierarchical order of the concept. Higher-order concepts are harder to learn because they are further removed from concrete objects and events.

Contiguity of instances. Contiguity refers to how closely together instances of a given concept are presented when several concepts are being learned concurrently. Concepts are easier to learn in highly contiguous situations. In other words, concepts should be taught one at a time.

Positive and negative instances. Positive instances are examples of the concept. Negative instances are not. The instructional strategies should include more positive than negative instances.

Simultaneous and successive exposure. In successive exposure, the students see only one instance of the concept at a time. With simultaneous exposure, the student is allowed to look back to previous instances. Simultaneous exposure should be used to simplify concept learning.

Expository and discovery learning. With an expository method, the students are given information about the concept. With a discovery method, they are given a question and allowed to discover the information about the concept. Concept learning is faster with expository methods.

Verbal Learning

There are three types of verbal learning: paired-associates learning, free-recall learning, and serial learning. Paired-associates learning requires the student to pair, or learn the relations between, particular stimuli and responses. Free-recall learning requires the student to learn the items in a set or list and recall them in any order. Serial learning requires the student to learn the items in a set or list in a particular sequence. The following principles should be used to develop instructional strategies for verbal learning.

Meaningfulness. The meaningfulness of material is described by its familiarity to the students. Meaningfulness greatly helps verbal learning. If possible, always start with concrete materials. When teaching low-meaningful information, the teacher should use methods to familiarize students with the materials before they start working on them. In paired-associates learning, the pairs are learned faster when the more-meaningful item is made the response member of the pair.

Intratask similarity. Intratask similarity is the overlap among the elements of a verbal learning task. Serial- and paired-associates learning are made more difficult by all types of similarity. Free-recall learning is easier with high meaningful, conceptual, and associative similarity. It is harder with high formal similarity. Teaching and practice time should be adjusted to the type of similarity and type of verbal learning. The instructional strategies should point out helpful and harmful similarities.

Serial position. Serial position is the position of an item in a series. The instructional strategies should plan to counteract the serial position effect. In free-recall learning, the last items in a list are learned best; the first items are learned next best; and the middle items are learned least. In serial learning, the order changes to first items, last items, and middle items.

Organization. The material should be organized to help structure the situation for the students. Coding, mediation, clustering, and stimulus selection are methods which increase meaningfulness and make learning easier.

Discrimination Learning

Discrimination learning is learning to respond differently to distinctive features of stimuli. The following principles should be used to develop instructional strategies for discrimination learning.

Distinctive features. Distinctive features are characteristics that identify a stimulus and make it different from other stimuli. The instructional strategies should emphasize the distinctive features of the stimuli. Overlap among distinctive features should be reduced or pointed out to the students.

Irrelevant features. Irrelevant features are characteristics that do not define the positive stimulus. The instructional procedures should reduce the number of irrelevant features in the materials. If they cannot be eliminated, they should be identified as irrelevant to the students.

Dimensionality of stimuli. Dimensionality of stimuli is the number of dimensions in the materials. When possible, three-dimensional materials should be used to make learning easier.

Contiguity. Contiguity refers to how close together stimuli are presented in space or time. Increasing contiguity helps discrimination learning.

Learning Connected Discourse

In learning connected discourse, students are required to grasp the meaning, interpret, and apply oral and written information presented in sentences, paragraphs, and multiparagraphs. The following principles should be used to develop instructional strategies for learning connected discourse.

Language maturity. Language maturity is determined by the student's ability to deal with the four language components: phonological, morphological, syntactical, and semantic. The instructional strategies should be adjusted to the student's language maturity by increasing teaching and practice time.

Sentence processing. Sentence processing is dependent on the complexity of the information. Teachers should give instructions and use materials with kernel sentences. When transformations must be used, the students should have more teaching and practice time.

Dimensions of the material. Dimensions of the material refers to characteristics such as redundancy and explicitness of ideas. Connected discourse is easier to learn when the main ideas are directly stated and when redundancy is increased.

REFERENCES

Ballagas, L. D. Effects of attention-focusing techniques upon the learning of temporal relationships. *Journal of Research and Development in Education*, 1975, *8*, 110–111.

Blake, K. A. *Teaching the retarded.* Englewood Cliffs, N.J.: Prentice-Hall, 1974.

Blake, K. A. Coding relevant and irrelevant features and retarded and normal pupils' sight vocabulary learning. *Journal of Research and Development in Education*, 1975, *8*, 8–9. (a)

Blake, K. A. Intratask similarity and retarded and normal pupils' synonyms learning. *Journal of Research and Development in Education*, 1975, *8*, 29–31. (b)

Blake, K. A. Type of transformation and retarded and normal pupils' learning sentence material. *Journal of Research and Development in Education*, 1975, *8*, 89–94. (c)

Blake, K. A. Concreteness and abstractness and retarded and normal pupils' learning synonyms. *Journal of Research and Development in Education*, 1976, *9*, 59–60 (a)

Blake, K. A. *The mentally retarded: An education psychology.* Englewood Cliffs, N.J.: Prentice-Hall, 1976. (b)

Blake, K. A., & Williams, C. I. *Studies of the effects of systematic variations of certain conditions related to learning III, Task Conditions.* Washington, D.C.: U.S. Office of Education, Cooperative Research Program, 1963.

Blake, K. A., & Williams, C. I. Induction and deduction in retarded, normal, and superior subjects' concept attainment. *American Journal of Mental Deficiency*, 1968, *73*, 226–231. (a)

Blake, K. A., & Williams, C. I. Retarded, normal, and superior subjects' attainment of verbal concepts at two levels of inclusiveness. *Psychological Reports*, 1968, *23*, 535–540. (b)

Bourne, L. E., Jr. Knowing and using concepts. *Psychological Review*, 1970, *77*, 546–556.

Bourne, L. E., Jr., Goldstein, S., & Link, W. E. Concept learning as a function of availability of previously presented information. *Journal of Experimental Psychology*, 1964, *67*, 439–448.

Bourne, L. E., Jr., & Jennings, P. C. The relationship between contiguity and classification learning. *Journal of General Psychology*, 1963, *69*, 335–338.

Bugleski, B. *The psychology of learning applied to teaching* (2d ed.). New York: Bobbs-Merrill, 1971.

DeCecco, J. P., & Crawford, W. R. *The psychology of learning and instruction.* Englewood Cliffs, N.J.: Prentice-Hall, 1974.

Frost, D. Type of stimulus and retarded and normal pupils learning synonyms. *Journal of Research and Development in Education*, 1976, *9*, 53.

Frye, S. Verbal mediation in the learning of synonyms by retardates and normals. *Journal of Research and Development in Education*, 1973, 101–106. (Monograph Supplement)

Gagné, R. M. *The Conditions of Learning* (2d ed.). New York: Holt, 1970.

Hurley, O. Learning concepts: Positive to negative instances. *Journal of Research and Development in Education*, 1973, *6*, 131–137. (Monograph Supplement)

Hurley, O. Learning concepts: Mixed and unmixed contiguity. *Journal of Research and Development in Education*, 1975, *8*, 59–61. (a)

Hurley, O. Learning concepts: Ratio of positive to negative instances. *Journal of Research and Development in Education*, 1975, *8*, 62–63. (b)

Klein, H. A., Klein, G. A., Oskamp, L., & Patnode, C. Color distractors in discrimination with retarded and nonretarded children. *American Journal of Mental Deficiency*, 1972, *77*, 328–331.

McLaughlin, P. J. Retarded and normal pupils' learning attributes of conjunction, inclusive disjunction, and exclusion concepts. *Journal of Research and Development in Education*, 1976, *9*, 35. (a)

McLaughlin, P. J. Retarded and normal pupils' complete learning of conjunction, inclusive disjunction, and exclusion concepts. *Journal of Research and Development in Education*, 1976, *9*, 37. (b)

McLaughlin, P. J. Retarded and normal pupils' learning rules for conjunction, inclusive disjunction, and exclusion concepts. *Journal of Research and Development in Education*, 1976, *9*, 33. (c)

McLaughlin, P. J. Successive and simultaneous presentations and retarded and normal pupils' rule learning, attribute identification, and complete learning of an inclusive disjunction concept. *Journal of Research and Development in Education*, 1976, *9*, 44. (d)

McLaughlin, P. J., Eaves, R., & Fallen, N. Cognitive development. In N. Fallen (ed.), *Young children with special needs.* Columbus, Ohio: Merrill, 1978.

McManis, D. L. Position cues in serial learning by retardates. *American Journal of Mental Deficiency*, 1965, *70*, 471–473.

May, W. The role of relevant and irrelevant dimensions in concept attainment among retardates and normals. *Journal of Research and Development in Education*, 1973, *6*, 144–149. (Monograph Supplement)

Osterhout, J. Retarded and normal pupils' comprehension and recall of chunked and non-chunked connected discourse. *Journal of Research and Development in Education*, 1976, *9*, 104–105.

Semmel, M. I., & Dolley, D. G. Comprehension and imitation of sentences by Down's Syndrome children as a function of transformational complexity. *American Journal of Mental Deficiency*, 1971, *75*, 739–745.

Tucker, J. Amount of coding in learning of homonyms by retarded and normal children. *Journal of Research and Development in Education*. 1973, 113–118. (Monograph Supplement)

Tucker, J. Contiguity of transformation and retarded and normal pupils' learning sight vocabulary. *Journal of Research and Development in Education*, 1976, *9*, 10–11.

Williams, C. Association value and retarded and normal pupils' synonyms learning. *Journal of Research and Development in Education*, 1975, *8*, 34–35. (a)

Williams, C. Objective frequency and retarded and normal pupils' synonyms learning. *Journal of Research and Development in Education*, 1975, *8*, 36–38. (b)

Williams, C. Pronunciability and retarded and normal pupils' synonyms learning. *Journal of Research and Development in Education*, 1975, *8*, 39–40. (c)

Chapter 6

Instructional Strategies: Reinforcement Conditions

This chapter is concerned with ways to motivate handicapped students. In order to ensure that handicapped children perform at an optimum level, positive reinforcement is usually necessary.

Learning Goals

The questions below should key your reading of this chapter:

- What is positive reinforcement?
- What is the Premack principle?
- Describe three types of reinforcers.
- What is a token-reinforcement system? How do you reduce a child's dependency on token reinforcers?
- What are three means of reinforcer selection?
- How does immediacy of reinforcement relate to learning? What influence does a schedule of reinforcement have on the child's retaining a skill?
- How does pairing reinforcers help a child learn to respond more effectively to praise?

- What is contingency labeling? Why is it necessary for teachers to develop this skill?
- Why is it important for handicapped students to acquire self-management skills?

Motivating students is usually connected in some way to providing positive reinforcement. It is unrealistic to assume that an individual, handicapped or not, will perform a task for extended periods of time without some form of payoff. Even those who greatly enjoy their work would rarely stay on the job with no remuneration. This has been demonstrated by educators interested in eliciting optimum test scores from culturally disadvantaged children (Chadwick & Day, 1971). It has also been demonstrated in arranging conditions, which facilitates students' learning more quickly and staying "on-task" for longer periods of time (Axelrod, 1977; O'Leary & O'Leary, 1977). Positive reinforcement also facilitates transfer of training (Wehman, Abramson, & Norman, 1977).

What special educators must learn is how to use principles of reinforcement to their advantage in the classroom. There is little doubt that rewards have been used for years by teachers. Sometimes rewards have been used correctly and at other times in a less-than-optimum fashion. This chapter provides a description of guidelines which are relevant to using positive reinforcement. This involves how to select different types of reinforcers, specific ways in which reinforcers should be given to children, and how children can be taught to reinforce themselves.

POSITIVE REINFORCEMENT

Positive reinforcement refers to an increase in the frequency of behavior when followed by a pleasurable event or stimulus. Positive reinforcers may be money, food, attention, or any event which is instrumental in increasing the occurrence of behavior. While the terms *reward* and *positive reinforcer* are frequently used interchangeably, an important distinction between the two should be made. A reward is only a positive reinforcer if the behavior it follows increases in frequency.

For example, a child may consider candy or soda pop a reward for performing a certain behavior like cleaning his or her room. However, unless delivery of the candy following the room cleaning increases the regularity of this behavior, the candy would not be considered a positive reinforcer. A positive reinforcer has the functional effects of increasing and strengthening behavior.

Positive reinforcers fall into two basic, broad categories: primary and secondary. *Primary reinforcers* are those events which do not require special training to become reinforcing to the individual. The need for food, water, or sleep are basic needs of all individuals and are examples of primary reinforcers.

Secondary reinforcers correspond to the type of reinforcement found in everyday life. Secondary, or conditioned, reinforcers are events which gradually acquire reinforcing value through a pairing with other events which are already reinforcing. Through repeated presentation of a neutral event prior to or along with a reinforcing event, the neutral event eventually becomes a reinforcer. Examples of secondary reinforcers include money, tokens, praise, special privileges, or activity reinforcers (e.g., special playtime).

A good illustration of the development of a secondary reinforcer may be found in the work of Lovaas, Koegel, Simmons, and Long (1973). These researchers helped seriously emotionally disturbed children become more responsive to attention and praise through the systematic pairing of food reinforcers with attention and praise by the trainer. Previously, attention and praise were not reinforcing to these children. The pairing of consumable reinforcers with praise gradually increased the reinforcing value of social attention.

Premack Principle

The Premack principle (1959) is a further example of a secondary reinforcer. Based on experimental research, the Premack principle states that of any two activities in which an individual engages, the more-frequent one may serve as a reinforcer for the less-frequent one. For the child who has discovered the pleasurable aspects of play and engages in frequent use of leisure time (high-preference activity), play may be an effective reinforcer for increasing the amount of study time (low-preference activity) or the frequency of "good" behavior.

One of the obvious advantages of the Premack principle is that it is a natural type of reinforcer and does not require the use of food or liquid reinforcers. Furthermore, it is a relatively easy reinforcer to identify through extended observation and evaluation of the child's daily activities.

Role of Contingency Management

A contingency is the relationship between a behavior and the events following the behavior. This relationship is crucial in most behavior training programs. This has been readily demonstrated in a study conducted by Redd (1969). Children learned rapidly to discriminate between teachers who delivered reinforcement *contingently* for appropriate play and social behavior and teachers who gave reinforcement noncontingently. Other examples of the importance of contingent reinforcement are prevalent in the behavior modification literature (Hart, Reynolds, Baer, Brawley, & Harris, 1968; Redd & Birnbrauer, 1969).

TYPES OF REINFORCERS

Edible Reinforcers

A child who engages in appropriate behavior may receive consumable items. Frequently used types of edible reinforcers include candy, fruit, juice, milk, and snacks. Edibles have enjoyed widespread use with children who are severely handicapped and continually exhibit a lack of responsiveness to natural reinforcers such as attention, approval, free playtime, etc.

Edible reinforcers have been extremely effective in developing language, self-help, and social skills in autistic children (Lovaas et al., 1973) and in severely and profoundly mentally retarded individuals (e.g., Gibson & Brown, 1976). They are optimally used when:

1   The child is hungry or has not just finished eating
2   The child has demonstrated a definite preference for food and/or liquids.
3   They are administered in small amounts.
4   They are administered with social reinforcers at the same time.
5   They can be consumed rapidly by the child and do not take several minutes to eat.

It should be recognized that edibles represent a basic means of motivation, and, in fact, should be used only when no other consequences are successful. If edible reinforcers are used for too long, the child may become dependent on food for each task. Another limitation may involve preventing those children who are not receiving edibles from becoming upset and disruptive. When reinforcement systems are developed appropriately, however, this is usually not a major consideration (Christy, 1975).

Activity Reinforcers

There are a variety of activities which are frequently reinforcing to all ages and levels of handicapped students. These include such events as extra time at recess, helping the teacher, going home early, free playtime, use of the television, or use of phonograph headphones. In order to be effective, activities must be provided *contingent* on the performance of the target behavior(s).

Activity reinforcers may be used with students who appear nonresponsive to all types of events. For example, consider the following illustration. A mentally retarded adolescent, whom we will call Gary, had had his way at home and in school most of his life. He was now, however, being trained to learn vocational skills and become prepared for a work-study program. Unfortunately, Gary would become extremely stubborn when demands were placed upon him and refused to work for any substantial period of time. Many items were tried as reinforcers, and although Gary would accept them willingly, they had no significant effect on his behavior. Careful observation, however, did indicate that he would spend long periods of time sitting in the beanbag chair. It was hypothesized that this was a reinforcing event. Gary was allowed to sit in the chair for 5 minutes contingent initially on 15 minutes of on-task work. Although this time span was gradually expanded, the sitting "activity" in this case proved effective in strengthening work behavior. This is an illustration also of how the Premack Principle was applied in this classroom.

Social Reinforcement

Social reinforcement is praise or special attention given for desired behavior or performance. It is the type of reinforcement which tends to govern the interpersonal relationships between most people, and is no less effective with handicapped students. The advantages of social reinforcement have been summarized by Kazdin (1975):

1   Social reinforcement is easily administered by change agents.
2   Social reinforcement can be delivered without disrupting the behavior.
3   Attention and praise are more natural types of reinforcers.

Panda (1971) has suggested that social reinforcement provides two functions for the child: it gives informative feedback and also creates a positive feeling (affective feedback) in the child. Panda and Lynch (1972) have identified a major problem in the administering of social reinforcement which should be observed. This basically revolves around the lack of expression, or matter-of-fact manner, in giving praise or attention. Particularly with lower-functioning handicapped children, the need for affective praise and physical reinforcement is critical. The teacher must become visibly excited at the child's success. Without expressive reinforcement, the child will not become sensitive to the teacher's role in his or her success.

For social reinforcement to be effective, teachers must clearly identify which behavior(s) is to be reinforced. Reinforcement must be expressive and immediate, and inappropriate behaviors should be ignored. Frequently in large groups peers will reinforce a child's inappropriate behavior through attention. When this happens, the teacher should look to children who are behaving appropriately and reinforce them immediately. Withholding attention for "bad" behavior is a critical aspect of having the child discriminate between what type of behavior results in attention and what type results in being ignored.

Token Reinforcers

The implementation of a token-reinforcement program begins with the identification of behaviors to be altered. Tokens may be chips, happy faces, stars, money, checks on an index card, or any other tangible item which represents backup reinforcers, i.e., items or activities which the child may receive in exchange for token reinforcers. There are a number of advantages in implementing a token economy in a classroom with disruptive children who are off-task or highly distractible. For example, token reinforcers:

1   Bridge the delay between the target response and backup reinforcement
2   Permit the reinforcement of a response at any time
3   May be used to maintain performance over extended periods of time when the backup reinforcer cannot be given
4   Allow sequences of responses to be reinforced without interruption
5   Maintain their reinforcing properties because of their relative independence of deprivation states
6   Are less subject to satiation effects
7   Provide the same reinforcement for children who have different preferences in backup reinforcers
8   May take on greater incentive value than a single primary reinforcer

Although some teachers feel that token reinforcement in classrooms of handicapped and nonhandicapped children is unfair to those students not receiving tokens, and may subsequently lead to more behavior problems, a careful study performed by Christy (1975) did not support this notion. In fact, it was found that the behavior of peer observers remained the same or improved.

Token reinforcement has been an effective means of increasing on-task (Feindler, Taylor, & Wilhelm, 1975) and instruction-following behavior (Zimmerman, Zimmerman, & Russell, 1969) by retarded children, reducing thumb-sucking in preschoolers (Snell & Cole, 1976), and decreasing inappropriate social behavior of culturally disadvantaged children (O'Leary, Becker, Evans, & Savdargas, 1969) and predelinquent boys (Phillips, 1968). Studies of classroom behavior have shown that academic performance (Brigham, Groubard, & Stans, 1972) and standardized achievement test scores (Chadwick & Day, 1971) are accelerated with token reinforcement. The reader who is interested in excellent reviews and a more in-depth discussion of token-economy literature is referred to Kazdin (1977) and Kazdin and Bootzin (1972).

DESIGNING A TOKEN-REINFORCEMENT SYSTEM

The first step in devising a token economy for a group of children is to select the behaviors which will earn tokens. When the behaviors that earn tokens are specified, the teacher knows when to give tokens, and the children will know what to work for.

In identifying behaviors that earn tokens, it is necessary to specify quality of work as well as quantity of work. Initially, it will be best to provide token reinforcement frequently; however, as the child becomes more independent, the behavioral requirements for tokens may gradually be increased. For example, assume the children work successfuly for only 30 seconds at a time. When this criterion is met, the teacher can move on to 60 seconds of on-task work for one token. At a later point, the children might work 10 minutes for three tokens.

The second step involves developing a list of backup reinforcers. This is also called a *reinforcement menu*. Three classes of backup reinforcers may be considered:

Food	Activities	Play materials
Gum	Swinging outside	Makeup kits
Candied cereal	Having extra lunchtime	Boats
Peanuts	Helping teacher water plants	Cars
Raisins	Leading class	Dolls
Chocolate Kisses	Taking attendance slip to office	Balls
Lemon Drops		Yoyos
Raisins		Play-Doh
Apples		Coloring books
Lollipops		Painting sets
		Beanbags
		Puzzles

By involving the children in developing the reinforcement menu, there is a greater likelihood that the events will be more motivating. The menu should be changed weekly to avoid satiation of items, and there should be only ten to fifteen items at a time.

Once behaviors are identified and reinforcers are selected, prices and wages must be established to relate the two through tokens. In setting prices, the teacher should begin by selling store items at a reasonable price, which, hopefully, is in accord with retail store prices. Eventually, the reinforcement menu will have the number of tokens required next to the reinforcer so that students will have an expectation of how many tokens they need to earn. Adjustments in prices will have to be made as it becomes evident which items are more popular.

Once the teacher has established what type of token reinforcer (checks, plastic chips, etc.) will be used, then the system must be explained. With young children, start by handing out one token to each child and then requiring the children to use the tokens to get some treat. After several pairings like this, they should begin to get the idea. With older children, instructions alone may suffice.

When giving out the tokens, tell the children what they have done to earn them. It is important to focus on the behavior and not the tokens.

Initially, a token exchange can occur daily, but with older children a weekly exchange may be sufficient. The purpose of the exchange is to let the students know they are improving and doing a good job.

The structured contingencies which a token system provides is critical in the successful teaching of many handicapped children. In developing new skills in or managing inappropriate behavior of handicapped students, it is important that the teacher make the child aware of the expectations being placed on him or her. A token-economy system allows for careful specification of appropriate behaviors and positive consequences which should maintain those behaviors.

In getting the handicapped child off the token system, these guidelines should be followed:

1 Reduce the frequency with which tokens are given and increase behavioral requirements.
2 Reduce the number of tangible items available on the menu.
3 Increase the amount of social reinforcement and praise.
4 Increase the length of time between receipt of tokens and exchange time.

These methods, if done gradually, will move the child back to a more normal classroom arrangement. It is important that a planned follow-through and maintenance program be devised so that the child is not indefinitely working for tokens.

SELECTION OF REINFORCERS

Direct Observation

By careful observation and recording of the child's behavior in the natural environment, it may become apparent which types of items and activities are preferred. As noted in the case of the adolescent, not all handicapped students will respond to the same types of reinforcers. Candy, praise, and grades may not be effective in motivating the child. If the teacher records the types of foods and liquids which the child normally prefers at mealtimes or the toys which are played with most frequently, this can serve as an effective means of assessing items which may prove to be potential reinforcers.

Interviewing

Parents and other family members may also be interviewed in order to investigate which items and activities the child prefers. Since parents spend far more time with their child, frequently they have much more information about consequences which will motivate the child. A structured interview in the home can provide teachers with another source of locating effective reinforcers.

Testing for Reinforcers

If the previously discussed methods are not successful, it may be necessary to set up a more structured assessment. Systematic testing and recording will facilitate reinforcer selection.

Testing for Edible Reinforcers   There are several steps involved in testing for consumables. The first of these is to pick out a number of items, such as a peanut, cereal, marshmallow, M & M, and spice drop. You should have at least five. Allow the student to sample one of each of those items. After each of the items has been consumed, place the items on the table within easy reach in front of him or her so they are approximately 4 inches apart. Each item should then be pointed out one by one to make sure the child attends to the fact that there are five items there. The child can then choose one. This is done through a verbal cue (if the child's receptive language is good enough) such as, "Take one," or "Pick one." If receptive skills are limited, gently prompt the child's arm toward the table. After an item is selected, record on a data sheet which item was chosen. The order of the items should then be switched around, so that no item is in the same position it occupied during the previous trial or presentation. This is done because some children have a dominant-hand preference, or they have position habits, i.e., they consistently chose an item that is to the right or to the left of them depending on the hand preference. It is necessary that the items are placed randomly so that the position habit is controlled.

Assessing Activity-Reinforcer Preferences   This system for consumables can also be used to test for preferred toy items. Toys that are small enough can be placed on a table. Larger ones can be placed on the floor in front of the student. The same procedure is followed for testing toy preference, the only difference being that instead of allowing the child to consume the item, you simply let him or her play with each of the toys about 30 to 45 seconds. Take the first toy away and present the child with the next toy until all have been manipulated. As he or she selects each toy across the fifteen trials, randomize the presentation again, but make sure the child is allowed about a minute to play with each toy that is selected. This is done so the child doesn't feel punished for choosing a toy. It is important to allow enough time to play with it so that it serves as a reinforcer.

One possible problem with either of these procedures is that some children will see the whole array of edibles or toys on the table and grab frantically, scooping up three or four items at a time. To prevent this, obtain a piece of cardboard that is about 11 × 13 inches or bigger, and place it between the child and the items. In this way grabbing can be prevented, and it will not be necessary to physically restrain the child.

If liquids are being sampled as part of the edible reinforcers, give the child only a small amount in a glass. If a whole glassful is given, there may be a higher rate of toilet accidents.

A source of additional information regarding reinforcer testing can be gained from the following: Number the positions in which the items are placed. Number the edible furthest to the student's right number 1, and then number across 1 to 5. Record on the data sheet the number of the chosen item corresponding to its position in front of the student. What may occur is that the child will reach consistently to the midline or that the child may *not* ever cross the midline to choose an item. The child may always choose those items from the middle to the right, or to the left. This numbering system cues you to this behavior.

Typical Questions   One question which is frequently asked by teachers is: How long should a reinforcer be used in a program? This is answered in the following way: If two types of stimuli are about equally reinforcing (out of fifteen trials, one may be chosen seven times, another, eight), use both items randomly. If a child definitely has one preference (choosing it fourteen out of fifteen trials on consecutive days), use it until data from his or her programs starts to look bad, i.e., until the child's performance deteriorates. Another reinforcer test may be conducted at that point. When using edibles, however, it is wisest to combine them with verbal praise and affection, while trying to "wean" their use.

Reinforcer Sampling

Another means of identifying reinforcers for education programs is through providing children with *new* items or events. Many handicapped children, particularly those from low-income, inner-city areas, have not been exposed to activities, toys, and edibles which might prove to be highly motivating. It could be beneficial to expand the range of events which may be reinforcing to the child.

One illustration of how reinforcer sampling might be used during playtime is presenting the child with a variety of cause-effect toys. These play materials often require brief instruction before children understand their reinforcing qualities.

Reinforcer sampling has been used with chronic schizophrenic patients (Ayllon & Azrin, 1968). Meyerson and Bailey (1971) also found that a vibratory was an effective consequence in motivating profoundly mentally retarded invididuals. For students who are unresponsive to most items, it may be necessary to be creative and develop new sources of reinforcing events.

Reinforcement Menus and Schedules

A reinforcement-event menu may consist of a large board with a number of high-preference activities represented by stick figures or other symbolic figures to indicate the different reinforcing activities available (Addison & Homme, 1966). This is one method of presenting a variety of reinforcer options to the child. It also has value because it can be observed and is not totally abstract. Colored photographs or illustrations may be used to make the board more attractive and meaningful to younger children or the severely retarded child.

When working with mildly handicapped children, the Children's Reinforcement Survey Schedule (CRSS) may be employed (Phillips, Fischer, & Singh, 1977). Table 6-1 features the reinforcer categories included in the schedule, as well as sample reinforcers. The child is then asked to fill out a survey similar to the one illustrated in Table 6-2.

Table 6-1   Reinforcers

Food

1   Candy
        What kind?
2   Ice Cream
        Flavor you like best
3   Nuts
4   Potato chips
5   Cake
6   Cookies
7   Coke, other sodas

Toys

1   Racing cars
2   Electric trains
3   Matchbox cars
4   Bicycles
5   Dolls

Sports and Games

1   Football
        With other kids
        With your father
2   Swimming
3   Bike riding
4   Skating
5   Skiing
6   Basketball

Entertainment

1   TV
        Your favorite program
2   Movies
        Western
        Horror
        Comedy
3   Records
        A record you like
4   Play or puppet show

Music, Arts and Crafts

1   Playing a musical instrument
2   Singing
3   Dancing
4   Drawing
5   Building models
6   Working with tools
7   Working with clay

Excursions

1   Riding in the car
2   Going to work with your father
3   Visiting grandparents or other relatives
4   Visiting the seashore
5   Going on a family picnic
6   Vacationing with the whole family

Table 6-1 (Continued)

7	Horseback riding		7	Vacationing with your parents only
8	Tennis		8	Taking an airplane ride
9	Hiking		9	Going out to dinner with your parents
10	Chess		10	Visiting a friend
11	Checkers		11	Visiting a new city
12	Fishing		12	Visiting a museum
13	Baseball		13	Going to the store
14	Ping-Pong		14	Taking a walk in the woods
15	Pool		15	Hunting for frogs, snakes, etc.

Social

1 Playing with friends
2 Being praised
   By father
   By mother
   By teacher
   By friend
3 Being hugged or kissed
4 Participating in Girl Scouts,
   Boy Scouts or other clubs
5 Having a friend sleep over

School Work

1 Reading
2 Spelling
3 Science
4 Social studies
5 Gym
6 Maths

Personal Appearance

1 Getting new clothes
2 Putting on makeup
3 Dressing up in a costume
4 Dressing up in mother's clothes
5 Getting a haircut
6 Going to the beauty parlor

Learning

1 A new language
2 Piano playing

Helping around the House

1 Setting the table
2 Making the bed
3 Baking cookies
4 Repairing or building
5 Working in the garden
6 Going on errands
7 Picking flowers

Other

1 Reading books that are not for
   school
2 Staying up past bedtime
3 Earning money
4 Having free time
5 Having a pet
6 Giving a party
7 Going to a party
8 Getting an allowance

DELIVERY OF REINFORCEMENT

Once reinforcers have been selected and target skills chosen for instruction, the teacher must consider how reinforcers will be delivered. There are a number of factors which must be carefully adhered to if the reinforcement program is to be effective. These points are discussed below.

Immediacy of Reinforcement

Reinforcement must be immediate if it is to succeed. Many studies have confirmed that even a 10- or 15-second delay in reinforcement is too great for

Table 6-2   Children's Reinforcement Survey Schedule

Name _____

Age _____

Date _____

The items in this questionnaire refer to things and experiences that may give you joy or other pleasureable feelings. Check each item in the column that describes how much pleasure it gives you these days. In the blank spaces you may put in other things you particularly like that are not mentioned on this form.

	Not at all	A little	A fair amount	Much	Very much
1 Candy What kind?					
2 Ice cream Flavor you like best					

effective conditioning. Moreover, the reinforcing effect is associated with whatever behavior is ongoing during the moment immediately preceding the onset of the reinforcer. A delay of more than a few seconds often results in the diversion of a child's attention from work. If a child completes a task, sits half a minute and begins to daydream, then gets a reinforcer, it is daydreaming rather than on-task behaviors that will increase in subsequent frequency.

Immediate reinforcement is important in the early stages of an educational program when the target skill is developing. After a response is performed consistently, the amount of time between the response and reinforcement can be increased without a decrement in performance. For example, in classroom settings students sometimes receive points or candy daily while high rates of academic behavior develop. However, after behavior has stabilized, the reinforcers can be delivered every other day or at the end of several days without a negative effect on performances (Cotler, Applegate, King, & Kristal, 1972). If a program begins with delayed reinforcement, behavior might not change at all or as rapidly as when reinforcement is immediate.

Reinforcement Schedules

Reinforcement may be given on one of two types of schedules: continuous or intermittent. A *continuous schedule* of reinforcement requires that a reinforcer be delivered for each correct response made by the child. Continuous reinforcement schedules are the quickest way to develop behavior, but are frequently impractical in classroom settings in which there are many other children. Giving reinforcement for each correct response presents a number of logistical problems, and is not a very realistic analogy to normal reinforcement conditions in the natural environment. Furthermore, behavior which is continuously reinforced tends to decrease rapidly if reinforcement is immediately withdrawn.

On the other hand, *intermittent reinforcement* refers to reinforcers delivered only after a certain passage of time or certain number of correct responses are emitted. Intermittent reinforcement schedules correspond to the natural environmental conditions of reinforcement which we face daily. Examples of intermittent reinforcement include receiving a paycheck each Friday, gambling behavior (i.e., not knowing when to expect payoff), or an occasional compliment by a parent to child for good behavior. Behavior which is reinforced on an intermittent schedule is more durable, and is maintained longer than behavior which is reinforced continuously.

It should be noted at this point that there are more sophisticated types of intermittent reinforcement schedules. These include fixed interval, fixed ratio, variable interval, and variable ratio schedules, as well as chained, multiple, and concurrent schedules (Whaley & Malott, 1971). These schedules are beyond the scope of this text yet may be of interest to some teachers. The interested reader is also referred to Reynolds' *Primer of Operant Conditioning.*

Amount of Reinforcement

The amount of reinforcement delivered for a response also determines the extent to which a response will be performed. The greater the amount of a reinforcer delivered for a response, the more frequent the response. The amount can usually be specified in terms of quantity of food, number of points, or amount of money.

Although the magnitude of reinforcement is directly related to performance, there are limits to this relationship. A reinforcer loses its effect when given in excessive amounts. This is referred to as *satiation.* When teachers find effective reinforcers, they should not abuse them by overuse. Rather, new reinforcers should continually be sought out in order to expand the range of positive consequences for which the child may work.

The effect of the amount of the reinforcer on a child's behavior will depend upon: (1) the satiation state and (2) the deprivation state of the child with respect to that reinforcer. For example, individuals who are temporarily deprived of adult attention are more responsive to attention than are those who are not deprived of attention (Gewirtz & Baer, 1958). Similarly, children will be more responsive to food reinforcers before mealtime than after eating.

Pairing

Pairing reinforcers refers to giving two reinforcers at approximately the same time or in close temporal proximity. As noted earlier, this is an excellent means of strengthening reinforcers and expanding the range of events or stimuli which the child finds reinforcing.

Here are several examples of how reinforcer pairing should be performed by a teacher:

Skill	Paired reinforcing consequences
1 Child eliminates in toilet	a Fruitloop given b Praise and hug
2 Child completes 10 minutes of on-task work	a Token given b Praise given
3 Child self-initiates toy on Jack-in-the-Box	a Jack-in-the-Box pops up b Teacher and peers applaud

With the pairing of two consequences, each reinforcer strengthens the other. This is an excellent means of fading the use of artificial reinforcers, such as food and other consumables, and replacing them with "intrinsic" reinforcers, e.g., praise or toy play.

Labeling Reinforcement Contingencies

When a handicapped child acts in an appropriate manner or begins to acquire a desired skill, the teacher must reinforce this behavior. However, it is critical that the child be told *why* he or she is being reinforced. A common drawback of many education programs is the failure of teachers to label the reinforcement contingency placed on the target behaviors. For example, if a teacher is encouraging cooperative play between two children who frequently fight with each other, then any approximation of appropriate social interaction by either child should be reinforced with: "Good playing with Johnny!" and a pat on the back or a hug. Severely handicapped students may not connect the positive reinforcement consequence with the desired behavior unless the contingency is labeled.

It is important to be specific in selecting the skill which is being reinforced. The child will respond more consistently if the teacher is consistent in providing reinforcement for selected target skills.

In concluding this section on delivering reinforcement, a summary of the major points in providing reinforcement for handicapped students has been developed. In Table 6-3, there is a description of ten points with an illustration of how "good" versus "poor" teachers apply reinforcement principles. This table will provide a valuable checklist for the teacher in assessing individual reinforcement skills.

SELF-MANAGEMENT: IMPLICATIONS FOR DEVELOPING INDEPENDENT BEHAVIOR

Rationale for Developing Self-Management Skills

A major problem for special educators is that of developing self-directed behaviors in handicapped students. Many educators recognize this deficit as a primary obstacle in the community-integration process for handicapped individ-

Table 6-3   Instructional Guidelines for Providing Reinforcement

I Finds an effective reinforcer.

The importance of finding an effective reinforcer is obvious. The more effective a reinforcer is, the more a child will work for it; in fact, the measure of a reinforcer's effectiveness is the effort which a person puts out to get it.

Poor	Good
Poor teachers usually use the same reinforcers with all students and don't experiment to find the most effective one.	The good teacher usually has a number of different reinforcers and is prepared to find the most-effective one. This is usually determined before training starts.

II Give the reinforcer quickly.

Learning requires that the response and the reinforcement occur in close temporal proximity; that is, that they occur closely together. This means that the reinforcer should follow the desired response as quickly as possible—1 to 2 seconds is a good estimate.

Poor	Good
A poor teacher usually fumbles with the reinforcers, dropping them, forgetting to give them, and giving them slowly.	Good teachers usually have their reinforcers close at hand and give them quickly and smoothly.

III Give verbal reinforcement enthusiastically.

Handicapped children experience little success, so accentuating what success they do have is important. Verbal reinforcement (e.g., "Good boy") should be given in a dramatic fashion. It must also be given in conjunction with the primary reinforcement (food) and serves as a "bridging signal" between the response and the reinforcer. In other words, it is sometimes difficult to give the primary reinforcement immediately after the response; however, it is almost always possible to praise the child. This way, verbal praise becomes associated with the primary reinforcement and later can be used in its place.

Poor	Good
The poor teacher is apt to forget to give verbal reinforcement or gives it in a mechanical manner.	Good teachers have a flair for dramatics. Verbal praise is given with many changes in loudness and tone.

IV Give verbal reinforcement with primary reinforcement.

It is important that verbal praise be given immediately after the response, and thus serve as a bridging signal. Verbal praise can then be used instead of treats, since it has been associated with them in the past. This is an important step in the child's development because it represents the acquisition of a basic receptive vocabulary.

Poor	Good
Poor teachers often forget to give praise, or, if they do, the delay between praise and the treat is too long. Sometimes the praise follows the treat instead of coming before it.	Good teachers give praise immediately after the desired response and before the treat.

Table 6-3 (Continued)

V Give physical reinforcement enthusiastically.

Most handicapped children like physical contact (though there are exceptions). It is very effective to give most children physical reinforcement by patting them softly on the back, rubbing their backs, giving them a short swing, etc. Like verbal reinforcement, it should be given with the primary reinforcement. In short, try to reward the child in as many ways as possible at the same time, with a treat, by praise, and with physical contact. *Always,* individual differences between children must be taken into account.

Poor	*Good*
Poor teachers often forget to give physical reinforcement or give it mechanically.	A good teacher gives physical reinforcement initially following every desired response.

VI Give physical reinforcement with primary reinforcement.

As in the case of praise, it is important that physical reinforcement be associated with the primary reinforcement. In those cases where the physical contact is already reinforcing to the child, this presents no problem. In cases where the child is afraid of physical contact, association with primary reinforcements is essential. Without physical contact, training is very difficult, and adjustment to everyday life situations is impossible.

Poor	*Good*
Poor teachers often forget to give physical reinforcement, or the delay between the physical contact and the treat is too long.	Good teachers give physical contact immediately after the desired response and in conjunction with praise. Both are given before the treats.

VII Use the bridging signal in chaining.

Once a child is responding to verbal praise, it can be substituted for treats. In a simple task, like asking a child to sit down in a chiar on the other side of the room, one can first tell the child, "Come to me," then give him praise ("Good boy") followed by the next command, "Sit over there" (pointing to the chair), and then give the treat for the completed response. This chain looks like this:

"Come to me" —"Good Boy," "Sit over there" —"Good Boy" plus treat

Here the verbal praise has been used in a situation which before had required the treat. Of course, the time to begin using praise in establishing chains of responses will differ with each child.

Poor	*Good*
Poor teachers will begin using praise in chaining too early or too late. Sometimes they never even use it.	Good teachers use praise and substitute it once responses have been well established. Usually the child reacts normally to this change when it is introduced correctly.

VIII Change the reinforcer if necessary.

Sometimes in the middle of a training session the child becomes increasingly distractible and stops working. There may be a number of causes for this, one of which may be that the reward is no longer effective. Handicapped children, like the rest of us, become tired of the same thing —this is called *satiation.* If this is the case, a variety of rewards should be tried.

Table 6-3 (Continued)

Poor	Good
Poor teachers usually don't remember this important variable and end a session before considering it.	Good teachers take all the possible reasons for poor performance into consideration.

IX Withhold reinforcement correctly.

It is important to decide what the desired response will be before starting. This way it is clear what responses will be reinforced and which will not. For example, in taking off a pullover shirt, the first response may be holding the shirt. When the child does this, he or she is reinforced. The next response would be holding the shirt and pulling it off the end of the arm. Now the child is not rewarded for just holding the shirt. Reinforcement must be withheld until the desired response occurs. If it does not, it is usually appropriate to say "No" and then repeat the command. Removing the reinforcer with the word "No" is often effective. As always, you should be sure that the step which you are requiring is not too great for the child.

Poor	Good
Poor teachers are hesitant to withhold reinforcers. Often they forget to say "No" or to remove the reinforcer from sight when the child is not responding appropriately.	Good teachers correctly withhold the reinforcer when the child doesn't respond correctly. They always inform him by saying "No" and removing the reinforcer from sight momentarily.

X Give reinforcement correctly.

Of course, it is vital that reinforcement be given correctly. A child is reinforced when he or she emits a desired behavior. As has been said, there are individual differences between children and in the same child from time to time. This means that the teacher must adjust that response to the conditions of the training session. Nonetheless, the child must be reinforced for desired responses, and must not be reinforced for undesirable behaviors. A teacher should be able to justify each reinforcer given a child according to the goals of a particular training session.

Poor	Good
Poor teachers sometimes reinforce inappropriate behaviors, or they forget to reward the appropriate responses.	Good teachers know what responses to expect and reinforce them when they occur. They do not reinforce inappropriate or undesirable behaviors.

uals. Well-established self-control procedures could alleviate much of this difficulty.

There is a host of drawbacks associated with an external-control approach. Change agents like the workshop supervisor, counselor, or educator frequently miss many opportunities to reinforce the individual for appropriate behaviors. Also, change agents rather than natural conditions in the environment may become a cue for behavior to occur. This issue relates to the problem of transfer of training and generalization. It is much easier for generalization to occur if the individual is controlling his or her own behavior rather than having continually programmed sequences introduced with the onset of each new learning experience or situation. Furthermore, response maintenance, or the duration of behavior over time, is greatly enhanced through an individual's developing his or her own contingencies. Another advantage to a self-control approach is that the individual can have greater input into the behaviors being altered.

In short, the prospect of self-control skills with the handicapped person is most attractive because it allows for the normalization process to occur. Development of self-control behaviors is highly congruent with the developmental-growth model, which states that handicapped persons can and must continue to grow. By helping the individual develop self-management skills, the teacher is expanding the potential of the individual and removing the artificial "ceiling" which is frequently placed on the progress of many handicapped individuals.

Range of Settings Where Self-Control May Occur

It may be helpful to suggest some of the areas where self-control training is applicable. Often teachers become "trained" to the point where they see only external control, at least to some degree, as an essential to success for the individual. This is particularly true when dealing with a more severely involved population.

Workshop   There are two primary facets of workshop behavior: task performance and social skills. Self-control is required in both of these areas for optimum vocational adjustment. Many workshops operate on a token-economy system for which the supervisor gives workers tokens for criterion performance. It has been demonstrated that severely retarded workers can improve their work performance by determining their own work criterion and self-administering tokens, through use of a model initially (Wehman, Schutz, Bates, Renzaglia, & Karan, 1978). The modeling literature with the mentally retarded (Wehman, 1975), as well as the self-control observational-learning paradigm utilized by Bandura and his associates (Bandura & Perloff, 1967) suggests that modeling may facilitate self-reinforcement training in the workshop. Social behaviors, such as proper use of leisure time, giving social greetings, or being on time, can also be developed through self-management procedures.

Community   Without some development of self-control behaviors, handicapped individuals cannot succeed in the community independently. The whole process of independent living presents a number of potential decision-making situations. Self-control may be required in any of the following home-living settings:

1   Maintaining a balanced diet.
2   Staying on a regular work schedule.
3   Washing and caring for clothes.
4   Managing money.
5   Using discretion in choosing friends and deciding whom one trusts.

Self-control situations can arise in public places where tolerance to frustration may be low. Crowded buses, waiting in line, inability to follow directions, or hostile service clerks represent some of the everyday situations in which self-discipline is necessary. The mentally retarded adult in the community for the first time must be aware of the pitfalls in dealing with door to door salesmen, taxicab drivers, or store clerks.

Classroom   One of the major problems with the educational process is the reliance on an externally (teacher-) controlled system to teach different content areas. Educators have not allowed enough student participation or have defined the parameters of learning too narrowly. This is no less a problem in the special education classroom, and, indeed, may be a greater problem since it is probable that children with exceptional behavior and learning characteristics need individually prescribed areas of particular interest for optimum learning to occur. Different classroom instructional options should be open to the handi-capped student. This may be more appropriate in classrooms for the mildly handicapped, although the creative teacher may be able to devise innovative ways for trainable retarded students to develop greater self-direction. Self-determination and self-administered token economies could also be utilized to determine level of educational performance.

State Facilities   Perhaps in no other setting is there so little opportunity for handicapped persons to develop self-direction and choice behaviors than in a state institution for retarded persons. Traditionally, external control and uniformity represent the standard. Decision making and exercising self-control behaviors by residents is either frowned upon or completely inhibited. This is a primary reason for the tremendous difficulty many institutionalized adolescents and adults encounter in adjusting to the "outside world" when discharged. As it is highly unlikely that all state facilities will be phased out and closed in the near future, it is important for professionals working in institutions to create programs which are geared toward individuals' practicing self-control behaviors. To date, the orientation of many community preparation programs seems to be aimed at giving information or making students aware of community facilities. Participation tends to be directed toward the goal of having the patient perform simple survival skills, e.g., use of the telephone. These programs need to take the "ceiling" off the individual's potential, and be used to develop methods of training self-management which correspond to the real-life problem situations which arise daily.

Self-Control Strategies Available to the Mentally Retarded

There are a number of self-control techniques which have been advanced, and which rely on covert techniques or the use of imagery to change behavior (Thoresen & Mahoney, 1974). The present discussion, however, is limited to strategies which are directly applicable to the handicapped students and which do not require extensive cognitive sophistication or aversive procedures.

Self-Observation   One method which can facilitate self-control is self-observation. Self-observation has been used successfully with mentally retarded workers through use of behavioral graphs (Jens & Shores, 1969), and daily feedback from a videotape of work performance (DeRoo & Harrison, 1971). Observation of one's self appears to be a strategy which can enhance performance in a workshop or classroom. Also, it is a crucial prerequisite for more sophisticated types of self-control, such as self-determined reinforcement. Depending on the attending skills of the individual, the teacher may want to develop self-observation initially through giving immediate feedback of the task completed and displaying a visual mark or chip in a prominent place to be seen by the client. Gradually, self-observation can be faded to pictorial representations of progress, or film and videotapes.

Self-Reinforcement   Training the child to become aware of his behavior in certain situations is helpful in developing another self-control strategy, self-reinforcement. As noted by Skinner (1953), the major requirement for self-reinforcement is that the individual is free to reward himself at any time whether or not he performs a particular response. Self-reinforcement can be viewed as self-determined reinforcement and self-administered reinforcement. *Self-determined reinforcement* refers to the individual's setting his own work level or performance criterion (Glynn, 1970). A more limited concept of self-reinforcement is *self-administered reinforcement*. This refers only to the child's taking the reinforcer himself, but under a performance criterion determined by the teacher.

Recent research provides an indication that severely handicapped workers may be able to perform at equivalent production rates under supervisor-controlled or self-controlled reinforcement contingencies and with several different tasks (Wehman et al., 1978; Helland, Paluck, & Klein, 1976). The primary implication of these studies is that self-reinforcement training may become an integral part of incentive systems in vocational education as well as in other curriculum areas. The vast majority of positive reinforcement consequences which have been provided for mentally handicapped workers have been externally controlled (Bellamy, 1976). While results from these research studies must be regarded with caution because of the small number of subjects and lack of stringent experimental design, they do provide the basis for continued investigation. Figure 6-1 is an illustration of production rates of a moderately retarded worker under three different reinforcement conditions.

The first and most obvious advantage to providing training in self-management skills is the savings on staff time. In the Wehman et al. study, prior to the program implementation, at least two of the participating workers required one to one supervision. Acquisition of self-reinforcement skills by these trainees enabled the staff to devote more time to other more severely handicapped workers who required a greater amount of attention.

A second equally important facet of these programs was the development of self-control and independence in workers. Through self-reinforcement training,

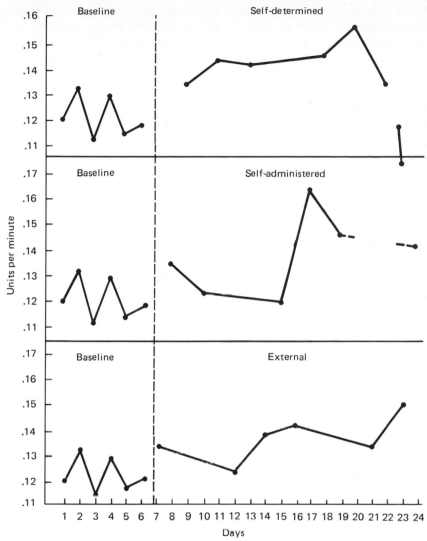

Figure 6–1 Production rates under three reinforcement conditions for moderately retarded worker. (Reprinted from Wehman et al., in press.)

workers were observed to be less dependent on the workshop staff and appeared to find their jobs more reinforcing.

The instructional methodology which was involved in developing self-reinforcement skills was the giving of verbal instructions initially by a teacher. This was followed by a demonstration or modeling if instructions were not successful. When neither of these methods was effective, physical guidance was provided. Each of the three workers who participated in the research required different levels of assistance. Not surprisingly, the amount of trainer intervention was related to the functional level of the worker. That is, the trainee in experiment 1 required physical guidance and modeling before learning to take the correct reinforcer for each unit completed. The worker in experiment 2 required limited amounts of demonstration and verbal cues. The moderately handicapped trainee in experiment 3 needed only instructions before being able to perform under the self-reinforcement contingencies.

Self-Instruction Kazdin (1975) suggested self-instruction as a self-control technique which can be effective in changing behavior. This involves the individual's directing language toward himself with the purpose of talking out a problem. Specifically, "The individual is trained to control his behavior in a fashion similar to being instructed by someone else" (Kazdin, 1975, p. 203). The applicability of this technique is limited to more behaviorally and intellectually developed clients. However, it would appear that this is a viable method for rehabilitation counselors to experiment with and perhaps develop in a more sophisticated manner. No research literature was found showing the retarded using a self-instruction-control technique, although Meichenbaum and Goodman (1971) have demonstrated the utility of this method with hyperactive and "impulsive" children. In this study, the experimenter modeled careful performance on the task, talking out loud to himself as he worked. The verbalizations modeled were: (1) questions about the nature of the task, (2) answers to these questions by mental rehearsal and planning, (3) self-instruction in the form of self-guidance, and (4) self-reinforcement. With mentally handicapped workers, social reinforcement by the counselor might be most helpful in encouraging this type of planning and problem solving.

Methods of Training in Self-Control Strategies

Special educators have at their disposal several methods of training in self-control. Unfortunately, little empirical research exists to substantiate self-control training with the handicapped, although most of the suggested methods have been successfully used before in other programming areas.

Modeling Extensive literature exists on the viability of modeling as a teaching approach with handicapped students (for a review see Wehman, 1976). Indeed, much of the self-control research has utilized the observer-model learning paradigm (Thoresen & Mahoney, 1974). Thus it would seem that physical and verbal modeling could be used to facilitate the acquisition of self-control behaviors. The counselor would have to vary the complexity of material presented according to the client's level of behavioral functioning. Ross and Ross (1973) have successfully used peer modeling and vicarious reinforcement to train educable mentally retarded (EMR) preschoolers in cognitive problem solving and planning skills.

Role Playing Similarly, role playing can be used to act out appropriate self-control strategies. Role playing can be carried out in group counseling sessions or in a one to one individual session between counselor and client.

There is some evidence to suggest the viability of a behavioral approach to counseling mentally retarded persons (Browning, Campbell, & Spence, 1974; Gardner & Stamm, 1971).

Social Reinforcement   Another suggested method for enhancing self-control behaviors is for the teacher to praise or compliment the individual for independent decision making and self-direction. This might be done quite often initially and gradually less as the individual becomes more confident in his development of self-control. It is recommended that an intermittent schedule of reinforcement be followed. In this way, self-control skills will become more durable over time.

To facilitate the initial development of self-control it may be necessary to physically guide or arrange certain environmental cues, such as using a bell to prompt self-directed behaviors. This would be done in conjunction with modeling. It is important to remember that in many cases no right or wrong decision may exist. Rather, of critical importance is that the individual makes the decision on his own. Prompting can be systematically eliminated as actions become more independent.

Although there is limited research, it is likely that the principles of reinforcement described above are applicable to self-management strategies also. Special educators attempting to develop self-management programs should utilize reinforcement principles in helping handicapped children develop independent behavior.

SUMMARY

The purpose of this chapter is to describe how positive reinforcement may be utilized in providing optimum special education programs. It is noted that selection and delivery of reinforcers are important skills which teachers must develop to motivate handicapped students. A substantial part of the chapter is devoted to discussing what self-management skills are, where they should occur, and how they can be developed in handicapped students. It is emphasized that for handicapped individuals to function independently in the least-restrictive environment they must be able to engage in self-directed behavior.

Positive reinforcement is defined as "an increase in the frequency of behavior when followed by a pleasurable event or stimulus." The distinction between a reward and reinforcer is made. A reward is a positive reinforcer only if the behavior it follows increases in frequency.

One example of positive reinforcement is the *Premack principle*, which states that in any two activities in which an individual engages, the more-frequent one may serve as a reinforcer for the less-frequent one. The Premack principle is relatively easy to identify through extended observation and evaluation of the child's activities.

Seveal *types* of reinforcers are described. Edible reinforcers include candy, fruit, and other consumables. It is emphasized that edibles should be used only when no other consequences have been successful. Activities are a second type of reinforcement. They include things such as extra free time, special privileges, or time listening with headphones. Social reinforcers, e.g., praise, attention, are also described as a very important type of activity reinforcer. For social reinforcement to be effective, praise must be expressive and immediate, and inappropriate behaviors should be ignored whenever possible.

Developing a token-reinforcement system is also described. The steps involved in this process include *identifying the behaviors which can earn tokens, developing a list of back-up reinforcers, and establishing prices for items and student requirements for earning items*. It is important in removing the child from the token system that social reinforcement be increased, the frequency with which tokens are given decreased, and the length of time between receipt of tokens and exchange time increased.

The selection of reinforcers must be a systematic and careful process. Direct observation of the child's behavior is one method. Interviewing parents and other family members is another technique. If these are not successful, it may be necessary to place different items in front of the child and have him or her identify preferences.

Immediacy of reinforcement is an important instructional variable which was discussed. In a new learning situation or when teaching a new skill, it is best to provide the reinforcer very quickly after the desired response occurs. If not done, the child may become confused about what behavior is being reinforced. The *schedule* of reinforcement is also critical. Reinforcers should be provided initially for every correct answer. Once the child has learned the skill, reinforcement can gradually be reduced. This will facilitate retention of the skill. A third instructional variable is *contingency labeling*. This involves telling the child *why* he or she was reinforced.

The final sections of the chapter discuss the importance of self-management and self-reinforcement in handicapped students. A variety of techniques, including role playing, counseling, and social reinforcement were described as ways of developing self-management skills. If handicapped children are to move to less-restrictive environments, it is crucial that they develop an ability to manage their own behavior and not require teacher-administered reinforcement constantly. This section outlines methods for developing self-control and those settings in which it is most applicable.

REFERENCES

Addison, R., & Homme, L. The reinforcing event (RE) menu. *National Society for Programmed Instruction Journal*, 1966, 5, 8–9.

Axelrod, S. *Behavior modification for the classroom teacher*. New York: McGraw-Hill, 1977.

Ayllon, T., & Azrin, N. Reinforcer sampling: A technique for increasing the behavior of mental patients. *Journal of Applied Behavior Analysis*, 1968, *1*, 13–20.

Bandura, A., & Perloff, B. Relative efficacy of self-monitored and externally imposed reinforcement systems. *Journal of Personality and Social Psychology*, 1967, 7, 111–116.

Bellamy, G. T. (ed.). *Habilitation of severely and profoundly retarded adults*. Eugene, Oreg.: University of Oregon, 1976.

Brigham, T., Groubard, P., & Stans, A. Analysis of the effects of sequential reinforcement contingencies on aspects of composition. *Journal of Applied Behavior Analysis*, 1972, 5, 421–427.

Browning, P., Campbell, D., & Spence, J. Counseling process with mentally retarded clients: A behavioral exploration. *American Journal of Mental Deficiency*, 1974, 79, 292–296.

Chadwick, B., & Day, R. Systematic reinforcement: Academic performance of underachieving students. *Journal of Applied Behavior Analysis*, 1971, 4, 311–319.

Christy, P. Does use of tangible rewards with individual children affect peer observers? *Journal of Applied Behavior Analysis*, 1975, 8(2), 187–196.

Cotler, S., Applegate, G., King, L., & Kristal, S. Establishing a token economy program in a state hospital program: A lesson in training student and teacher. *Behavior Therapy*, 1972, 3, 209–222.

DeRoo, P., & Harrison, L. Use of videotape feedback in maintenance of work performance. *Mental Retardation*, 1971, 9, 22-25.

Feindler, E., Taylor, C., & Wilhelm, P. Increasing on-task behavior of a retarded boy's contingent use of tokens and teacher attention. *School Applications of Learning Theory*, 1975, 8(1), 10–26.

Gardner, W. I., & Stamm, J. Counseling the mentally retarded: A behavorial approach. *Rehabilitation Counseling Bulletin*, 1971, 15, 46–57.

Gewirtz, J., & Baer, D. Deprivation and satiation of social reinforcers as drive conditions. *Journal of Abnormal and Social Psychology*, 1958, 57, 165–172.

Gibson, D., & Brown, R. (eds.). *Managing the severely retarded*. Springfield, Ill.: Charles C. Thomas, 1976.

Glynn, F. L. Classroom applications of self-determined reinforcement. *Journal of Applied Behavior Analysis*, 1970, 3, 123–132.

Hart, B., Reynolds, N., Baer, D., Brawley, E., & Harris, F. R. Effects of contingent and noncontingent social reinforcement on the cooperative play of a preschool child. *Journal of Applied Behavior Analysis*, 1968, 1, 73–86.

Helland, C., Paluck, R., & Klein, M. A comparison of self and external reinforcement with the trainable mentally retarded. *Mental Retardation*, 1976, 14(5), 22–24.

Jens, K., & Shores, R. Behavioral graphs as reinforcers for work behavior of mentally retarded adolescents. *Education and Training of the Mentally Retarded*, 1969, 4, 21–28.

Kazdin, A. E., & Bootzin, R. The token economy: An evaluative review. *Journal of Applied Behavior Analysis*, 1972, 5, 343–372.

Kazdin, A. E. *Behavior modification in applied settings*. Homewood, Ill.: Dorsey, 1975.

Kazdin, A. E. *The token economy*. New York: Plenum, 1977.

Lovaas, O. I., Koegel, R., Simmons, J., & Long, J. Some generalization and follow-up measures on autistic children in behavior therapy. *Journal of Applied Behavior Analysis*, 1973, 6, 131–166.

Meyerson, L., & Bailey, J. S. Vibration as a reinforcer with a profoundly retarded child. *Journal of Applied Behavior Analysis*, 1971, 2, 135-145.

Meichenbaum, D., & Goodman, J. Training impulsive children to talk to themselves: A means of developing self-control. *Journal of Abnormal Psychology*, 1971, *77*, 115–126.

O'Leary, K., Becker, W., Evans, M., & Savdargas, R. A. Token reinforcement in a public school: A replication and systematic analysis. *Journal of Applied Behavioral Analysis*, 1969, *2*(1), 3–13.

O'Leary, K., & O'Leary, S. Classroom management. (2d ed.). New York: Pergamon, 1977.

Panda, K. C. Social reinforcement: Theoretical issues and research implications. *Psychological Studies*, 1971, *26*, 319–339.

Panda, K., & Lynch, V., Social reinforcement: Theoretical issues and research implications. *Psychological Studies*, 1971, *26*, 319-339.

Premack, D. Toward empirical behavior laws, I. Positive reinforcement. *Psychological Review*, 1959, *66*, 219–233.

Phillips, F. Achievement place: Token reinforcement procedures in a home-style rehabilitation setting for "pre-delinquent" boys. *Journal of Applied Behavior Analysis*, 1968, *1*, 213–223.

Phillips, D., Fischer, S., & Singh, R. A children's reinforcement survey schedule. *Journal of Behavior Therapy and Experimental Psychiatry*, 1977, 8(2), 131—134.

Redd, W. H. Effects of mixed reinforcement contingencies on adults' control of children's behavior. *Journal of Applied Behavior Analysis*, 1969, *2*, 249–254.

Redd, W. H., & Birnbrauer, J. S. Adults as discriminative stimuli for different reinforcement contingencies with retarded children. *Journal of Experimental Child Psychology*, 1969, *7*, 440–447.

Reynolds, G. S. *A primer of operant conditioning*. Glenview, Ill.: Scott, Foresman, & Co., 1968.

Ross, D., & Ross, S. Cognitive training for the EMR child: Situational problem solving and planning. *American Journal of Mental Deficiency*, 1973, *78*, 20–25.

Skinner, B. F. *Science and human behavior*. New York: Macmillan, 1953.

Snell, R., & Cole, M. The use of a VI schedule of token reinforcement to effect all day control of thumbsucking in the classroom. *School Applications of Learning Theory*, 1976, *9*(2), 14–21.

Thoresen, C., & Mahoney, M. *Behavioral self-control*. New York: Holt, 1974.

Wehman, P. Behavioral self-control with the mentally retarded. *Journal of Applied Rehabilitation Counseling*, 1975, *0*, 27–34.

Wehman, P. Imitation as a facilitator of training for the mentally retarded. *Rehabilitation Literature*, 1976, *37*, 41–48.

Wehman, P., Schutz, R., Bates, P., Renzaglia, A., & Karan, O. Self-reinforcement programs for mentally retarded workers: Implications for developing independent vocational behavior. *British Journal of Social and Clinical Psychology*, 1978, *17*, 183-197.

Wehman, P., Abramson, J., & Norman, C. W. Transfer of training in behavior modification programs: An evaluative review. *Journal of Special Education*, 1977, *11*(2), 217–231.

Whaley, D., & Malott, R. *Elementary principles of behavior*. Englewood Cliffs, N.J.: Prentice-Hall, 1971.

Zimmerman, E., Zimmerman, J., & Russell, C. Differential effects of token reinforcement on instruction-following behavior in retarded students instructed as a group. *Journal of Applied Behavior Analysis*, 1969, *2*, 101–112.

Chapter 7

Program Evaluation

One of the more critical areas in special education is the issue of program evaluation and accountability. In recent years, there has been an increased emphasis on developing quantifiable performance objectives which can be objectively assessed and evaluated. Teachers of exceptional children are expected to meet program objectives and verify completion of objectives through systematic evaluation procedures.

Learning Goals

The following questions provide an overview of the information presented in this chapter:

- What is the relationship between the individualized education program (IEP) and program evaluation?
- How do reliability and validity of evaluation differ? Why is reliability of evaluation important?
- Which school personnel are involved in the evaluation process?

- What characteristics are critical in developing a report card for the handicapped student?
    - Describe the pretest-teach posttest design.
    - Describe the multiple-baseline design. Why is this design usually easier to utilize in a classroom than the reversal design?
    - Describe the changing-criterion program design.

As increased tax dollars are required for handicapped students, the potential for a legal backlash from parents of nonhandicapped children grows. There is little doubt that if special educators cannot justify the larger proportion of dollars allocated to exceptional children, then parents of nonhandicapped children will speak out. This is especially true because of two considerations:

1   Many nonhandicapped students, particularly in urban areas, are without up-to-date textbooks and equipment, and go to school in overcrowded classes. This can usually be attributed to lack of funds.
2   The gains which handicapped children make through special education have frequently not been documented regularly in an objective fashion. Objectives are not clearly specified and thus it is difficult to evaluate the impact of special education services. Many exceptional children are severely handicapped and tend to make gains very slowly.

Unless a system is devised that is sensitive enough to assess the advances made by severely handicapped children and evaluate the effectiveness of training programs, special educators will be unable to refute charges that public school services are not justified for these children.

Therefore, the focus of the chapter is to identify several important considerations in conducting evaluations. These include reliability and validity of evaluation, frequency of monitoring progress, and who should be involved in the evaluation process. A large part of this chapter is also devoted to describing individual-performance-evaluation designs.

RELATIONSHIP OF THE IEP TO EVALUATION FOR HANDICAPPED STUDENTS

Each child's individualized education program calls for an evaluation of short-term instructional objectives annually. The child's program also must be completely reevaluated once every 3 years. These are minimal standards for evaluation and, in effect, are far too limited.

In order that a child's IEP is properly evaluated, it is necessary for the teacher to make evaluation an ongoing process and not just follow arbitrarily set time periods. The teacher must be able to regularly communicate the child's current levels of performance. By using an assessment model similar to the one described in Chapter 2, evaluation of skill mastery will confirm the child's strengths and weaknesses in different domains at several junctures throughout the school year.

Ongoing evaluation is a critical aspect of the IEP for several reasons. After the initial assessment of the child's present performance levels, frequent follow-up assessments provide for tracking overall progress in each domain. Daily or weekly evaluation of specific skills indicates the effectiveness of instructional programs.

The dynamic process of regular evaluation of instructional procedures, as well as short-term objectives, will make the IEP a more viable blueprint of the child's educational progress and not simply a piece of paper to be shuffled onto one corner of the desk. The progress of each child should be systematically followed throughout the school year and reported periodically to parents.

CONSIDERATIONS IN EVALUATING A STUDENT'S PROGRESS

Frequency of Evaluation

A decision which must be made, usually by the teacher, is exactly how often short-term instructional objectives will be evaluated. Objectives may be evaluated at the end of each lesson, weekly, biweekly, or once a month. As a general rule, the child's progress on a specific skill should be monitored frequently enough so that the teacher:

1 Receives feedback as to the progress of the child. The more frequently the child's skill level is evaluated, the easier it is to assess problem areas.

2 Can make necessary modifications in methods or materials and ascertain whether the instructional sequence is effective or not.

3 Can verify that the child has attained the objective. Once the child has learned the skill, then the next skill in the instructional sequence can be taught with the newly acquired skill being reviewed periodically.

It is advisable, however, to implement continuous evaluation measures, i.e., evaluate progress each session, with children who do not display clear-cut gains in their programs. Marks on a chart or a graph will provide a gradual ascending trend of progress, if the program is working, thereby giving indications of the child's mastery of the skill as well as the rate of learning. For those who work with severely impaired children, this type of evaluative feedback is an important aspect of determining the child's progress (see Figure 3-2).

Reliability of Evaluation

The reliability with which data are collected will be indicative of how accurate the information is. Accuracy of monitoring the student's progress can be influenced by a number of factors. If the child or teacher are ill, if the same person always does the evaluating, or if there is confusion or inconsistency about the method of evaluation, the data collected will be suspect. Therefore, it will be erroneous to make any important decisions about the program effectiveness with the child.

One means of increasing the reliability of observations is to have a second person collect data independent of the teacher. For example, in order to achieve a reliability of agreement that the target behavior is actually occurring at a given rate, two or more independent observers must simultaneously view the response. In this way, an index of the consistency of agreement may be established. Reliable recording of behavior is the foundation of a good evaluation. Inconsistent agreement between observers casts serious doubt on the credibility of evaluation data.

Reliability may be determined two ways, depending on the assessment method employed. With a frequency measure of responding the smaller frequency is divided by the larger frequency and multiplied by 100. That is, if Observer A notes a child acting on 20 different toys, and Observer B counts only 18, then the reliability index would be 90 percent $\left[\frac{18}{20} \times 100 = 90\% \right]$.

The same procedure is used in duration recording with the smaller measure being divided by the larger measure, and then multiplied by 100. An illustration of this might be the length of a child's tantrums. The teacher may view the tantrum as lasting 10 minutes, but the teachers' aides would see it lasting 12 minutes. This would constitute 83 percent reliability $\left[\frac{10}{12} \times 100 = 83\% \right]$.

A slightly different formula is used in finding reliability of agreement with interval recording. Reliability is calculated in the following way:

$$\frac{\text{Total agreements}}{\text{Total agreements} + \text{total disagreements}} \times 100$$

Only intervals or cells in which behavior occurred are counted in the total agreements plus total disagreements. An examination of Figure 7-1 reveals how reliability of agreement for interval recording would be determined. During seven of ten intervals Observer A and Observer B agreed on the occurrence of the target behavior. In the other three intervals, numbers 4, 6, and 10, there was disagreement. Therefore a reliability index of 70 percent was established.

Validity of Evaluation

The validity of the evaluation technique addresses the question: Does the instrument which is used to assess the child's progress measure what it purports to? To a certain extent, this relates to Public Law 94-142 in terms of testing the child in the native language and using culture-fair tests. (See Table 2-2 for a review of these criteria.) However, it also reflects the importance of evaluating all children with instruments which will provide a true picture of the child's performance level on different specific skills.

One way to ensure validity of evaluation measures is to employ different types of techniques. For example, if a teacher of mildly retarded children is interested in improvement of the classes' reading comprehension skills, then an observational assessment of percentage of correct answers might be computed and recorded daily. This would be an example of *criterion-referenced* evaluation.

\+ = Behavior occurred

− = Behavior did not occur

Observer A	Cell number	1	2	3	4	5	6	7	8	9	10
		+	+	+	+	+	−	+	−	−	+

Observer B	Cell number	1	2	3	4	5	6	7	8	9	10
		+	+	+	−	+	+	+	−	−	−

$$\frac{\text{Total agreements} = 7}{\text{Total agreements} + \text{total disagreements} = 10} \times 100 = \frac{70\%}{\text{agreement}}$$

Figure 7–1 Reliability of agreement for interval recording.

As a second evaluation of reading comprehension, however, a standardized test such as the Durrell Analysis of Reading Difficulty could be employed. This test is *norm-referenced*, meaning that performance levels are computed on the basis of how a large number of other children have performed on the same test.

By utilizing two types of evaluations, classes' performance can be cross-checked. Although improvement on one measure (observational assessment), might not be mirrored by similar advances in the norm-referenced standardized tests, the use of two different measures allows for independent means of tracking a child's progress.

Who Should Conduct Evaluations?

Usually a school psychologist will be actively involved in collecting data on the child's behavior for the IEP committee to evaluate. This is done in conjunction with the teacher, who may have specific information about the child's level of functioning in relevant domains.

According to the public law, however, a variety of professionals representing disciplines such as occupational and physical therapy, social work, nursing, and nutrition should be involved in evaluations. Evaluations which meet the previously discussed standards of reliability and validity should be completed. They should be conducted in order to elicit an optimum appraisal of the child's strengths and weaknesses. Experts in each of the speciality areas are required because it is very difficult for a teacher or school psychologist alone to make useful recommendations about the amount and type of special services required to help the child.

Because handicapped children present such a diverse range of learning and behavior characteristics, special consultants may have to be called in to evaluate.

Consider the difficulty in evaluating the hearing capacity of a nonverbal blind child who is diagnosed as emotionally disturbed. If the child has a hearing impairment, clearly it will be difficult to develop effective instructional programs, assuming the teacher is unaware of this deficit. Through a special technique called operant audiometry (Sloane & MacAulay, 1968), however, audiologists can usually evaluate the hearing level of such children.

Parents must also be involved in evaluations. Since the public law mandates that parents have the right to participate in IEP committee meetings, their input should be actively solicited. Assuming that professionals know *how* and *what* to ask parents, the information gained through structured interviews can be extremely enlightening. The parents are the only individuals, other than the teacher, who see the child as a whole person and not only as someone with a hearing problem, a motor deficiency, or language limitations. They are able to observe the child for long periods of time in a natural context at home; furthermore, they will best understand family dynamics or a neighborhood situation which may be placing undue emotional stress on the child. The IEP committee must carefully interview parents in order to gather data which will either provide new information or cross-validate findings which have already been established.

A logical person to synthesize results of the evaluations and place them into a clear perspective is the teacher. Bricker (1976) has suggested that as special education increasingly utilizes more specialty areas to help handicapped children, the teacher must play a critical role in the synthesis and coordination of the program, in addition to being actively involved in classroom instruction. This will be especially true if a child remains in the same class for several years with one teacher, as so often happens. Only the teacher (and parents) will be aware of the progress or difficulties of the child and thus be able to integrate recommendations from all other evaluations.

PERIODIC EVALUATION: TOWARD AN OBJECTIVE "REPORT CARD" FOR HANDICAPPED STUDENTS

Although professionals within different disciplines have a way of communicating with each other about a child's skills through a mutual understanding of basic tests and the technical jargon associated with evaluation, this does not help the parent and frequently becomes a large source of frustration. Special educators must move toward giving parents regular evaluation reports which are objective, concise, and free of difficult-to-understand terminology. These reports may be distributed quarterly or every 9 weeks, or, in some cases, evaluations may be provided daily (Dougherty & Dougherty, 1977; Schumaker, Hovell, & Sherman, 1977).

We are familiar with few concentrated efforts at developing report cards which accurately reflect progress of handicapped children. There is a need to develop an evaluation report which parents can easily understand, even if the teacher must initially explain it during a conference. The majority of the report card evaluations which we have seen ask for the teacher's anecdotal records of the child's behavior. Since it is difficult for the teacher to reliably remember and record all students' behavior, this type of evaluation report alone would appear to be extremely limited in its value, particularly over a long-term period.

Doughtery and Dougherty (1977) have developed one type of report card which we feel is a good illustration of how handicapped children's progress can be evaluated and how parents can be involved as well. The section below outlines the instructions which were given to students, teachers, and parents.

THE DAILY REPORT CARD

The Daily Report Card is a tool designed to increase communication between teachers, students, and parents. By providing feedback regarding a student's behavior and performance, the card provides information about progress not usually available to parents. Moreover, students' successes as well as problem areas are pointed out for recognition or further remediation.

Instructions for Students

1   Put your name, date, and classes on the card before going to school.

2   Give the card to the teacher at the *end* of each class and request that the teacher rate your behavior and work by circling a number in each of the three columns titled, "Behavior," "Schoolwork," and "Homework." Make sure that the teacher crosses out the columns which might not apply for that class on that day. Also, the teacher *must* write his or her name in the last column.

3   If you have any questions about your rating, they should be discussed with the teacher. If you feel that you deserved a different rating, ask the teacher why you were given a particular number and what you could do differently next time.

4   Give the completed card to your parents each evening. Any missing ratings will be regarded as "Poor" (Number One) ratings. This means that a missing card will be regarded as a card with all "Poor" ratings.

Instructions for Teachers

1   You are to rate the child *only* when he or she remembers to give you the Daily Report Card at the end of your class.

2   Cross out all the numbers in a column which may not apply to your class on a particular day. For example, you may not have assigned any homework, or you may have a class with no schoolwork. Schoolwork and homework need not apply only to written assignments, but to class participation or other related performances.

3   Remember to sign your name in the last column.

4   Please discuss with the child why he or she received a particular rating, and what he or she could do to improve behavior or work.

5   Rating and discussion should take no longer than one minute on most days, and should not interfere with regular classroom functioning. Additional discussion should be scheduled at the teacher's convenience.

Instructions for Parents

   1   Please read your child's Daily Report Card every evening. Pay attention to and discuss the good ratings first, however small or few. The discussion should be positive and constructive, and aimed at helping your child find ways of doing better. This is not a system to emphasize faults or weak points.

   2   Save the cards to indicate progress. Use them to communicate more meaningfully with your child as well as teachers and other school personnel.

   A major advantage to this format is that the teacher can identify specific behaviors related to each column, "Behavior," "Schoolwork," and "Homework."

   A more general report card format outlined by Schumaker et al. is a simple yes-no choice which can be used either daily or weekly. It has particular application for the "socially maladjusted" child or culturally disadvantaged students who are inconsistent in their performance. Table 7-1 outlines the basic categories which were identified for teacher evaluation.

Table 7-1   Student Evaluation Form

Name _____

Date _____

Teacher _____

Did the student	Yes	No	
Come on time?			
Bring supplies?			
Stay in seat?			
Not talk inappropriately?			
Follow directions?			**Rules Section**
Raise his hand?			
Not physically disturb others?			
Clean up?			
Pay attention?			
Speak courteously?			
Were you pleased with his performance today?			**Teacher Satisfaction Section**
Points on today's classwork			**Classwork Section**
Grade on test assignment			**Grades Section**
Teacher's initials			

Source: Schumaker et al. (1977, p. 452)

Table 7-2   Teacher's Criteria for Classwork Points

When discussion is held:

4 pts	Student listens and contributes* 3 times to discussion.
3 pts	Student listens and contributes two times to discussion.
2 pts	Student listens and contributes one time to discussion.
1 pt	Student pays attention and listens to discussion.
0 pt	Student does not listen to discussion.

When in-class assignment is given:

4 pts	Student works all of class time on assignment.
3 pts	Student works three-fourths of class time on assignment.
2 pts	Student works one-half of class time on assignment.
1 pt	Student starts work on assignment.
0 pt	Student does no work on assignment.

In classes where there is no opportunity for participation (reading on own, movie, lecture, etc.):

4 pts	Student is extremely attentive to subject (movie, teacher, guest lecturer) throughout the class.
2 pts	Student is generally attentive to subject.
0 pt	Student does not attend to subject.

*Contributing to discussion was defined as raising one's hand, being called on by the teacher, and answering or asking an appropriate question.

It should be noted that measurements of these categories can be highly arbitrary and that a rating system would be fairer. This format would probably be most successfully employed when used in conjunction with anecdotal records. Assigning different amounts of points to more appropriate behavior is an even more effective means of evaluating the child's performance. One example of this is shown in Table 7-2.

Skill-Development Evaluation

Proficiency of skill development in students can be evaluated in a similar fashion. As noted in Chapter 3, task-analytic evaluation involves a simple process of recording the steps or phases in the skill sequence which have been acquired by the student. A more specific means of evaluation would be to indicate whether each step in a skill sequence was at one of the following three stages:

1   Was not reached yet, as the child had not come up to that skill level
2   Was in training and therefore in the acquisition phase
3   Had been learned and was now in the review (retention) phase

Although this would probably not be done daily or weekly, it could be completed quarterly with a minimal amount of difficulty, assuming the teacher teaches from a skill sequence format. It should be a fairly routine procedure to check off the level at which the child is functioning for certain skills within the different domains. As an illustration, consider the haircombing task analysis again; this sequence was earlier outlined in Chapter 3. Table 7-3 shows the task

Table 7-3   Evaluation Form for Task Analysis of Haircombing

Steps of task	Not yet in training	Training for acquisition	Review for retention
1 Child locates comb.			
2 Child picks up comb in one hand.			
3 Child raises comb to center of the head.			
4 Child combs hair in the center of the head forward by bringing teeth of comb one-fourth of the way through hair from center of head towards front of head.			
5 Child combs hair in the center of the head forward by bringing teeth of comb one-half of the way through hair from center of head towards front of head.			
6 Child combs hair in the center of the head forward by bringing teeth of comb three-fourths of the way through hair from center of head to-wards front of head.			
7 Child brings teeth of comb completely through hair in the center of the head using many strokes from center of head towards front of head.			
8 Child combs hair on one side of head by bringing teeth of comb one-fourth of the way through hair from top side to bottom of one side.			
9 Child combs hair on one side of head by bringing teeth of comb to one-half of the way through hair from top side to bottom of the side.			
10 Child combs hair on one side of head by bringing teeth of comb three-fourths of the way through hair from top side to bottom of side.			

analysis with a choice of three categories which the teacher can check for evaluation purposes:

This response format could also be modified to include the level of teacher assistance required under the training phase. For example, the following categories could be included:

1   Needs physical assistance
2   Needs gesture
3   Needs verbal cue only
4   Performs independently

Table 7-3 (Continued)

Steps of task	Not yet in training	Training for acquisition	Review for retention
11 Child brings teeth of comb completely through hair.			
12 Child combs hair on the opposite side of head by bringing teeth of comb one-fourth of the way through hair from top side to bottom of side.			
13 Child combs hair on opposite side of the head by bringing teeth of comb one-half of the way through hair from top side to bottom of side.			
14 Child combs hair on opposite side of the head by bringing teeth of comb three-fourths of the way through hair from top side to bottom of side.			
15 Child brings teeth of comb completely through hair.			
16 Child combs rear portion of hair by bringing teeth of comb one-fourth of the way through hair from top rear of head to bottom rear of head.			
17 Child combs rear portion of hair by bringing teeth of comb one-half of the way through hair from top rear to bottom rear of head.			
18 Child combs rear portion of hair by bringing teeth of comb three fourths of the way through hair from top rear to bottom rear of hair.			
19 Child brings teeth of comb completely through rear portion of hair.			
20 Child places comb back in its proper place.			

Although this would be more time-consuming, it would also be a more-precise means of evaluating a child's progress in a given skill sequence.

INDIVIDUAL PERFORMANCE EVALUATION

The balance of this chapter describes different program designs which may be employed by teachers to evaluate the child's progress. The designs outlined below range from simple to more-sophisticated, and several can be employed to specifically assess the effectiveness of instructional procedures. The program-evaluation designs discussed in this section are commonly used in behavioral programs. The interested reader can obtain a far more detailed explanation from Hersen and Barlow's text, *Single Case Experimental Designs*.

A number of instructional program designs are available for the evaluation of child progress (e.g., Kazdin, 1975). However, it is the purpose of this section to present a review of only the most basic and relevant program-evaluation formats which may be of value to special education teachers. It is emphasized that these evaluation designs can be employed with one, two, three, or as many children as the teacher wishes to evaluate.

Prerequisities to the Use of Individual Program Designs

For individual program designs to be valid, several prerequisites must be met. Performance objectives need to be stated in behavioral terms with a minimum of confusion as to the behavior being recorded. Ideally, two independent observers should be able to agree on the occurrence of a target behavior with a consistently high degree of accuracy.

Once a specific skill has been identified for instruction, data-collection procedures must be decided upon. Regardless of what type of data are collected (e.g., frequency, duration), a target behavior should be assessed regularly. In this way, close attention to and monitoring of program progress is enhanced, both through daily perusal of data as well as precision-teaching techniques. Often in the classroom, teachers find little time available for frequent data collection. When this is the case, a probe format is suggested where behavior(s) can be monitored periodically, such as once a week, and the teacher may still receive objective feedback as to the effectiveness of teaching procedures, results, etc.

Pretest-Teach-Posttest

The most common program design employed by teachers interested in quickly evaluating student performance is the pretest-teach-posttest design. In this design, the teacher identifies a skill for training and then assesses the preinstructional level of the skill. This is assuming the behavior is in the child's present repertory of skills. If it is not, then the teacher would indicate that it is occurring at a zero level, and begin teaching procedures. As the child acquires the skill, posttest measures of progress are taken to verify the meeting of performance objectives.

For example, assume that a young child placed in an EMR class cannot print or write. Assume further that the teacher wants the child to copy the entire alphabet as an initial first step in a writing program. Thus, data must be taken for a pretest measure of how many letters, if any, the student can copy legibly. Teaching procedures shall include a stimulus-fading technique, where initially there are very small spaces between broken lines or dots which, when connected, make the letter. Gradually the spaces may be lengthened to a point where the student is virtually copying the letter with no assistance. Evaluation consists of a periodic posttest check every 10 days or so to assess the number of letters which are being acquired with this teaching procedure and how many days are required for a letter to be learned. Figure 7-2 is an illustration of how the pretest-teach-posttest design might be employed.

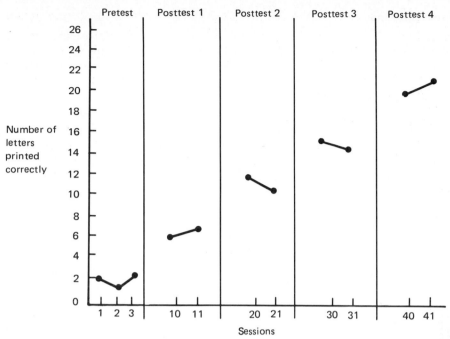

Figure 7–2 Pretest-teach-posttest program design.

The advantage of this design is that it is quick, economical, and easy to administer. However, this design can only be recommended when the teacher is absolutely certain of the validity of teaching procedures being employed, when evaluating the effectiveness of the teaching procedures is of little concern, or when there is little time available for data collection. The primary disadvantage of the pretest-teach-posttest is that without a control group (randomly selected or matched subjects who do not receive treatment), no definitive statements can be made about the experimental effectiveness of the teaching procedures being utilized. Change in behavior may occur as a result of outside-the-class room variables, such as alterations in student medication, greater attention at home, increased peer acceptance, etc. Therefore, the teacher may erroneously feel that certain instructional procedures may be used successfully with other students.

A goal which all classroom teachers of handicapped children should point to is the development of teaching practices and procedures which are replicable with other students, and which may be successfully implemented by inexperienced teachers. The value of teaching procedures which can only be performed by one teacher is limited.

This design should be used when a teacher has a large class of children and therefore has little time for continuous evaluation of lessons, yet desires an objective means of probing the child's acquisition of the skill. It is a good way for beginning teachers to get into a routine of systematic evaluation.

Multiple Baseline

Another design which may be considered for use is the multiple-baseline design. A multiple-baseline design is an excellent means of evaluating instructional methodology while also measuring the child's progress. With this instructional design, program variables may be evaluated across students, across settings or environments, or across behaviors. When using a multiple-baseline design across students, baseline (preteaching) data are taken on a target behavior for two or more students. For example, if baseline data for students in a class were consistent and stable with minimal fluctuation, a certain teaching procedure would be introduced with student Robert. Data would continue to be collected for all students in the multiple baseline, but instruction would be given only to Robert. When significant changes in Robert's behavior were noted, then the instructional procedures would next be introduced to Michael, with data still being collected on all other students in the design.

The same format can also be carried out across behaviors. For example, a teacher might wish to evaluate how effective a token-reinforcement procedure was in the acquisition of reading skills, writing ability, and computational behaviors with five students. Once specific skills were identified for each of the three domains, then data would be taken on the level of each student's pretoken-reinforcement performance. After a stable baseline was established, token reinforcement would then be delivered for the goal of 90 percent reading comprehension, while writing and arithmetic behavior would continue to be assessed but with no instruction. As reading comprehension increased with delivery of token reinforcement, then the same treatment could be used with writing, and eventually arithmetic skills.

As an illustration, consider evaluating the effectiveness of loud reprimands on inappropriate behaviors of autistic children. Figure 7-3 indicates how the reprimand was evaluated in a multiple-baseline design across three behaviors, taking shoes off, pulling hair, and flapping hands.

If noncompliant behavior or refusal to follow instructions seems to be a problem, and no one can influence the student, then a multiple-baseline design across time might be an appropriate format for evaluating management procedures. Once again an index of noncompliant behavior would be assessed during several times (e.g., percent of commands complied with) such as early morning, midmorning, and noon. The initial treatment procedure might be a 5-minute time-out from positive reinforcement contingent on each noncompliant episode. The treatment could be initiated during the first time period. If the plan is successful then, the time-out contingency could be extended into the second and finally third period. Figure 7-4 illustrates the logic of the design.

Reversal Design

An alternatve evaluation format available to the more experimentally oriented teacher is the reversal design. In this design, baseline data are gathered on a target behavior which the teacher may want to increase or decrease. A treatment procedure is then implemented and evaluated; if the procedure successfully

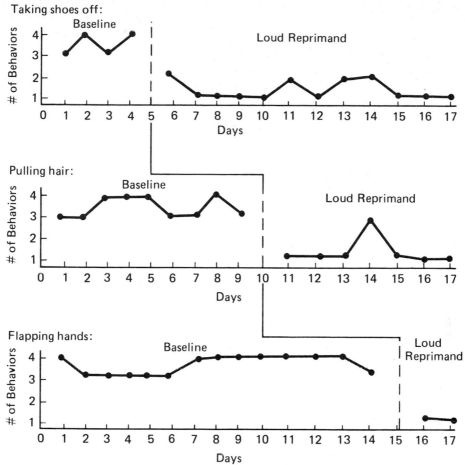

Figure 7–3 Multiple-baseline-across-behaviors program design.

alters the target behavior, the teacher removes the procedure briefly in a return-to-baseline phase. During this period the behavior should revert to the original baseline-response level, if the contingency was directly instrumental in effecting behavior change. Once the behavior returns to baseline level, the instructional intervention may be reinstituted and response-maintenance procedures developed. With subsequent reversals (e.g., replications), support is given to the efficacy of procedure or contingency being employed. Figure 7-5 provides an example of how token reinforcers were evaluated as being effective on talking out in EMR children.

The problems of reversal designs in applied settings, particularly in a classroom, should be readily apparent. Teachers laboring to develop academic skills in students are not enthralled with the possibility of losing the newly developed behaviors, regardless of replicability and efficacy issues. Further-

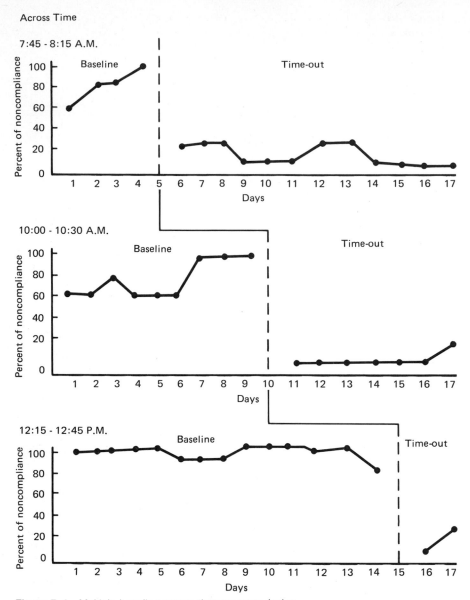

Figure 7–4 Multiple-baseline-across-time program design.

more, many academic skills do not lend themselves to reversal. Reading and speech skills, once acquired, come under control of naturalistic reinforcement contingencies such as the intrinsic joy of talking or reading certain types of materials. Finally, the ethical issue of reversing behavior is one which should be taken into consideration before employing the reversal design.

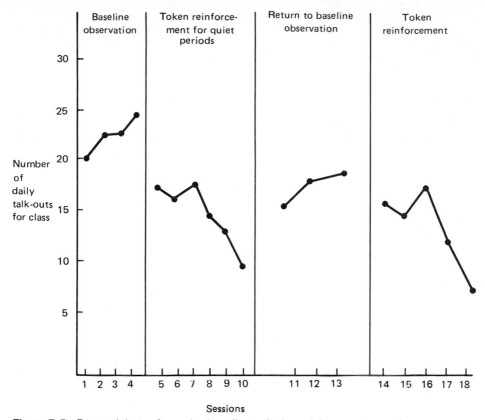

Figure 7–5 Reversal design for evaluating effects of token-reinforcement procedure.

Changing-Criterion Design

Perhaps the most viable alternative to the previously discussed evaluative methods is the changing-criterion design (Hartman & Hall, 1976). With a changing-criterion design, the teacher establishes an initial criterion to be obtained by the student, and then gradually through behavior-shaping procedures increases the criterion of trials-to-success to a higher level. Alternatively, if an error to criterion format is taking place, then the criterion level is steadily decreased. The changing-criterion design lends itself nicely to self-recording and self-evaluation by the student who may participate in the charting and graphing of his or her progress.

This is an especially effective design for evaluating programs which employ behavior-shaping techniques. Here are two examples of how it might be utilized with different problems exhibited by handicapped students. The first example involves a retarded girl who needs to lose weight:

Problem: Obesity

Student's Name: Rosie, a trainable mentally retarded adolescent
Goal: Decrease obesity and improve self-concept and general physical health
Specific Objective: Reduce weight from 220 to 106 pounds within 6 months
Method: Daily exercise and diet-control plus reinforcement for meeting criterion level
Evaluation: Changing-criterion design

Figure 7-6 is an illustration of the decrease in pounds. Rosie had to achieve 3 days in a row at the criterion level before the criterion was reduced. Each criterion change was 5 percent less until the final target weight was achieved.

Here is a second example for increasing behavior:

Student's Name: Dave, a physically and mentally handicapped adult
Goal: Increase work behavior and prepare for workshop placement
Specific Objective: Increase production rate on task by 100 percent
Method: Social and penny reinforcement for every other unit completed correctly and for meeting criterion work level
Evaluation: Changing-criterion design

Data from a similar program conducted by Bates, Wehman, and Karan (1976) are displayed in Figure 7-7. The manner in which this program was evaluated is also applicable to the case outlined above. It is evident that the gradual criterion change provides important short-term goals and structure for both student and teacher.

Hartmann and Hall (1976) have written an excellent paper reviewing the

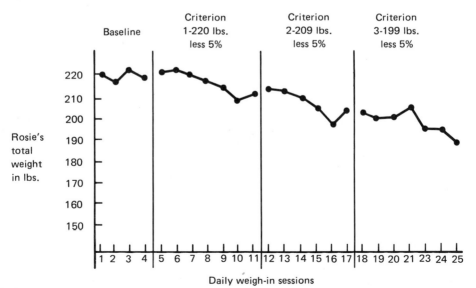

Figure 7–6   Use of changing criterion design to evaluate weight loss.

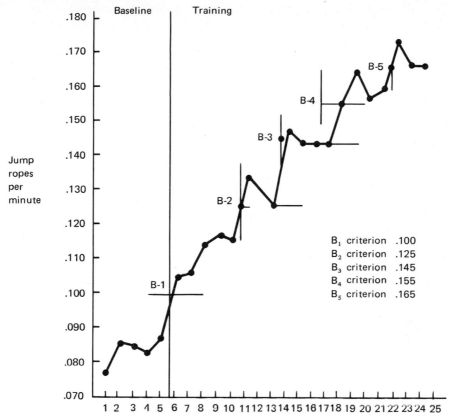

Figure 7–7 Program design for evaluating work productivity.

merits of the changing-criterion design and in doing so have outlined several points which must be considered in employing the design correctly. These include the following:

   1   All treatment (instructional) phases should be long enough to ensure that successive changes in a therapeutic direction are not naturally occurring due to either historical, maturational or measurement factors.
   2   Treatment (instructional) phases should differ in length, or if of a constant length should be preceded by a baseline phase longer than each of the separate treatment phases.
   3   Each treatment phase must be long enough to allow the rate of the target behavior to *restabilize* at a new and changed rate; it is stability after change that has been achieved, and before introduction of the next change in criterion, that is crucial to providing or convincing demonstration of control. (pp. 531–537)

The use of instructional design will come about only through the systematic education of teachers. In the past decade, many teachers have adopted such

instructional practices as instructional objectives, task analysis, operant conditioning technology, and data-based programming via tools such as precision
teaching. Utilization of these techniques has increased the sophistication of
educational services for children with learning and behavior problems. While
these strategies have influenced content and method of instruction, they have
not been effectively integrated into classroom program evaluation. In order to
maximize the quality of instruction, teachers need to adopt one more strategy—
program design. Program design enables the teacher to efficiently determine the
efficacy of an instructional technique and thus maximize the probability of
scholastic success for the learner. Through the application of criterion-
referenced measures and individual-performance evaluation the teacher may
match instructional needs with teaching techniques and achieve the best possible
instructional fit.

Integrating Individual-Performance Designs into the Classroom

The first step in the use of program design is having a working knowledge of the
advantages and disadvantages of each type of design that has been discussed.
The second step, given the selection of an appropriate design, is to develop skill
in coordinating instructional objectives; for example, those children who are in
the baseline data-collection phase awaiting instruction on one objective are
receiving instruction on another objective, thus making maximum use of
instructional time. For example, use of the multiple-baseline design, by its very
nature, requires the teacher to use data in making programming decisions. The
third step in applying design to program evaluation is using data once they are
collected. Since the teacher using multiple-baseline techniques is already
committed to determining the efficacy of a teaching technique, data will
necessarily be reviewed and program changes made on the basis of pupil
performance. The scheduling of data reviews will become an automatic part of
the classroom responsibilities of the teacher. In addition, the review of data may
become a reinforcer for the teacher, as it supports the competency of the teacher
in arranging special learning conditions. Table 7-4 depicts the logical sequence
involved in identifying appropriate teacher behaviors for effecting behavior
change in students as well as for providing evaluative feedback.

SUMMARY

This chapter is concerned with providing information about (1) basic issues
to consider in conducting evaluations, (2) report card formats which can be
employed to provide evaluation of the child's progress, and (3) program designs
which may be utilized by teachers to evaluate effectiveness of instructional
programs and training procedures.

Within the IEP, evaluation must be seen as a dynamic and constantly
evolving process which provides feedback to the child, teacher, and parent as to
the progress being made in the program. It is noted that federal guidelines are

Table 7-4 Planning an Instructional-Program Sequence

1 Task-analyze specific skill

2 Select assessment instrument(s)

3 Administer assessment instrument(s)

4 Select annual goals and identify instructional objectives

5 Establish data collection procedures
   a Frequency
   b Interval
   c Duration
   d Anecdotal

6 Select appropriate program design
   a Pretest-posttest
   b Multiple-baseline (across behaviors, students, or environments)
   c Changing-criterion (trials-to-error or -success)
   d Reversal

7 Select instructional technique
   a Write teaching routine and lesson plan
   b Determine schedule of reinforcement
   c Consider consequences of instruction

8 Collect baseline data

9 Employ treatment technique

10 Review data
   a Note changes in performance
   b Plan intervention for successive days/students

11 Establish accountability

---

neither stringent in evaluation requirements nor specific in the evaluation formats employed. However, it is strongly suggested that teachers and parents work as a team to continually track the child's gains in different skill domains.

Reliability of evaluations reflects the accuracy of the information collected. Reliable recording of behavior is the foundation of good evaluation. Inconsistent agreement between observers or faulty tests casts serious doubt on the credibility of evaluation data. Validity, on the other hand, refers to whether the instrument used to measure the child's progress does what it purports to. Validity of tests is especially important as it relates to testing children in their native language.

Usually a school psychologist will be actively involved in collecting evaluation data. The teacher often plays an important role in providing information about the child's classroom behavior. Because many handicapped children present such a diverse range of learning and behavior characteristics, special consultants may have to be called in for evaluation. This may include occupational and physical therapists, speech pathologists, and audiologists.

The development of objective, yet easy-to-understand report cards is also discussed. It is noted that special educators must move toward regular evaluation reports which are concise and free of technical jargon. It is important that report card formats be developed which are objective and which do not rely solely on teachers' anecdotal records.

The *pretest-teach-posttest design* assesses the child's behavior before instruction and then at different points during instruction. This design is quick, economical, and easy to administer. The primary disadvantage of the test-teach-test design is that without a control of the group, no definitive statements can be made about the experimental effectiveness of the teaching procedures.

In a *multiple-baseline design*, instructional variables may be evaluated across *students*, across *environments*, or across *skills*. An important consideration in using a multiple-baseline design is that the baselines not receiving intervention remain stable. Change should occur only as a result of the instructional contingency. A *reversal design*, on the other hand, leads to a temporary removal of the instructional contingency. Although this may be valuable to assess the effects of the contingency, it may not be advisable in a classroom learning situation.

The final program design discussed is the *changing-criterion design*. This design is similar to the test-teach-test design except that it requires the client to achieve a given criterion of performance. Once this level is attained, the criterion is gradually shifted toward the terminal criterion. This design is very helpful in shaping new behaviors.

REFERENCES

Bates, P., Wehman, P., & Karan, O. Evaluation of work performance of a developmentally disabled adolescent. In O. Karan (Ed.). *Habilitation Practices with the Severely Developmentally Disabled*, Vol. I. Madison, WI: University of Wisconsin Rehabilitation Research and Training Center, 1976.

Bricker, D. D. Educational synthesizer. In *Hey, don't forget about me, education's investment in the severely, profoundly, and multiply handicapped*. Reston, Va.: Council on Exceptional Children, 1976.

Dougherty, E., & Dougherty, A. The daily report card: A simplified and flexible package for classroom behavior management. *Psychology in the Schools*, 1977, *14*(2), 191–196.

Hartman, D., & Hall, R. V. The changing criterion design. *Journal of Applied Behavior Analysis*, 1977, *9*(4), 527–532.

Hersen, M. & Barlow, D. *Single case experimental designs*. New York: Pergamon, 1977.

Kazdin, A. E. *Behavior modification in applied settings*. Homewood, Ill.: Dorsey, 1975.

Schumaker, J., Hovell, M., & Sherman, J. An analysis of daily report cards and parent-managed privileges in the improvement of adolescents' classroom performance. *Journal of Applied Behavior Analysis*, 1977, *10*, 449–464.

Sloane, H., & MacAulay, B. (eds.). *Operant procedures in remedial speech and language training*. Boston: Houghton-Mifflin, 1968.

Part Two

Curriculum Development

Chapter 8

Self-Care Skills

The ability to attend to one's self-care needs is fundamental in achieving self-sufficiency and independence. The self-care domain involves eating, dressing, toileting, grooming, safety, and health skills. These skills should be considered a critical part of the educational curriculum for many handicapped children. With recent advances in behavior modification technology there is little doubt that most handicapped individuals can acquire many of these skills.

The development and maintenance of self-care behaviors contribute to efforts at deinstitutionalization by allowing many handicapped children to stay at home with their families. If a child is able to go to the toilet independently, can eat and dress with a reasonable degree of proficiency, and learns basic health and safety skills, then parents will be more comfortable with the child. Furthermore, with the current proliferation of home-based early intervention programs parents are increasingly becoming involved as partners in the self-help training process. Ultimately, the success of training efforts which emphasize skills such as eating and dressing depends on the effectiveness with which parents can follow through as well as implement self-help programs.

Learning Goals

You should be able to answer these questions when you have finished this chapter:

- What is an example of an instructional objective for toilet training?
- What is the Azrin-Foxx rapid-toilet training technique?

- Outline a normal developmental sequence for eating skills.
- Describe how the backward-chaining instructional technique can be employed to teach spoon feeding.
- What are three special devices which can be used to facilitate eating skills?
- What are two strategies for overcoming chronic regurgitation?
- Describe the optimum training techniques for teaching buttoning skills.
- What role do backward chaining and fading have in the sock-undressing program?
- Give an example of a safety-skill instructional objective.

This chapter is organized in the following way. First, a developmental sequence of skills within each self-care subdomain is provided. These sequences have been derived from examining developmental scales, behavioral checklists, and other rating scales. Second, from this array of skills, a number of short-term instructional objectives and task analyses are provided for each subdomain, i.e., eating, dressing, grooming. Within each subdomain is a description of how to employ learning conditions to teach self-care skills.

TOILETING SKILLS

Many toilet-training programs have been documented since early research by Ellis (1963) and Dayan (1964). Several reviews which discuss the merits and weaknesses of toilet-training studies conducted in the past decade have been written as well (Osarchuk, 1973; Rentfrow & Rentfrow, 1969). Table 8-1 provides the developmental sequence in which nonhandicapped children become toilet-trained.

Table 8-1   Toileting Skills Sequence

Age	Content
0–4 months	
4–8 months	
8–12 months	
12–18 months	Controls bowels on a shedule
18–22 months	Controls bladder on a schedule
22–24 months	
24–36 months	Verbalizes needs at toilet Self-initiates toileting
3–6 years	Cares for self at toilet unassisted
6–9 years	
9–12 years	
12–15 years	

Toileting Objectives

In developing an individualized education program (IEP) for a handicapped child, toileting objectives may have to be established. Below are objectives which may be relevant to students at different levels of functioning.

1 When taken to the toilet 3 times during the school day, the student will eliminate appropriately with less than 5 percent bowel accidents occurring over a 2-month period.

2 Given bladder and bowel pressure, the student will verbalize or use gestures to indicate to the teacher his need to go to the toilet with less than 5 percent accidents occurring over a 2-month period.

3 Having become toilet-trained, the student will care for himself independently at the toilet with 95 percent accuracy over a 2-month period.

Table 8-2 is a task analysis for toilet-training a handicapped child. Each component skill, when chained together into a logical sequence, will lead to independent toileting.

Table 8-2 Task Analysis of Toileting Independently

Behavioral Objective: Given bladder and bowel pressure, the student will go to the toilet independently and eliminate appropriately with less than 5% accidents occurring over a 2-month period.

Student follows these steps:

1 Approaches toilet
2 Puts toilet lid up
3 Puts seat down
4 Unfastens belt (Girl: pulls up dress)
5 Unfastens pants
6 Pulls pants down to hips
7 Pulls pants down to knees
8 Sits on front edge of toilet seat
9 Scoots back onto toilet seat
10 Eliminates appropriately
11 Reaches for toilet paper
12 Pulls toilet paper to proper length
13 Holds paper steady with 1 hand and tears off paper with other hand
14 Folds toilet paper
15 Wipes properly with toilet paper
16 Drops toilet paper into toilet
17 Gets off toilet
18 Pulls pants up to knees
19 Pulls pants up to hips
20 Pulls pants up to waist
21 Fastens pants (Girl: pulls dress down in front, back, and sides)
22 Fastens belt
23 Grasps flush valve
24 Pushes handle down to flush
25 Puts toilet lid down

Instructional Strategies

The basic instructional strategy employed in teaching toileting skills is behavior shaping, or the method of successive approximations. The efficiency of this method has been supported by numerous investigators (e.g., Mahoney, Van Wagenen & Meyerson, 1971).

Essentially what is involved is the sequencing of skills which are required for appropriate toileting. This includes finding the toilet, pulling down pants, sitting on the toilet, appropriately defecating or urinating, using tissue paper, pulling up pants, flushing the toilet, and washing and drying hands. Training usually takes place with the contingent reinforcement of each of these steps by a supervisor. Careful data and records are kept to indicate progress being made.

While applications of operant conditioning to toilet training have been successful, recent advances in behavior modification have led to even more dramatic improvements in the speed and effectiveness with which toileting skills can be acquired (Foxx & Azrin, 1973). As Azrin and Foxx (1971) note, many of the previous studies performed in the 1960s failed to provide conclusive follow-up data, leaving the maintenance of newly acquired toileting skills suspect.

The Azrin and Foxx rapid method of toilet training decreases training times to approximately 4 to 5 days. The several distinctive features of this approach include:

1   An artificial increase in the frequency of urination by providing more liquids.
2   Positive reinforcement given for appropriate toilet use; however, toileting accidents result in a brief time-out period.
3   Use of an automatic apparatus fastened to the pants and toilet which automatically signals moisture or appropriate elimination in the stool.
4   Full cleanliness training; that is, the child must clean up thoroughly following an accident.
5   Self-initiated toileting.
6   Positive reinforcement given for being "dry."

The emphasis on self-initiated or independent toileting is an important milestone in toilet-training research. This aspect of training eliminates the need for external prompts or control, and develops independent behavior in the individual. A fully described maintenance procedure is also available in the Azrin and Foxx (1971) report.

EATING SKILLS

The development of eating skills is an important aspect of self-help-skills training. For some children, such as those who are severely multiply handicapped, eating training may involve learning how to swallow and suck. Other children must learn how to eat neatly; and still other children may have to acquire family-style eating skills. Table 8-3 is the sequence of eating development through which normal children come.

Table 8-3 Eating Skills Sequence

Age	Content
0–4 months	Sucking-swallowing reflex (birth) Anticipates food on sight (16 weeks) Balances head (16 weeks) in midline
4–8 months	Takes solids well (20 weeks) Reaches for nearby objects Sits unsupported Begins to finger-feed Holds bottle with both hands
8–12 months	Drinks from cup assisted Demonstrates rotary chewing Grasps with thumb and finger
12–18 months	Gives up bottle Hands over empty dish
18–22 months	Unwraps candy Partially feeds self, much spilling Drinks from cup unassisted Uses spoon and does good scooping
22–24 months	Begins using a fork
24–36 months	Gets a drink unassisted, pours well Uses a straw
3–6 years	Uses a napkin Uses a drinking fountain
6–9 years	Uses a table knife for cutting Cares for self at table
9–12 years	
12–15 years	

Eating Objectives

As noted above, many handicapped children exhibit low entry-level eating skills. However, it is usually necessary for this sequence to be followed before progression to more advanced skills. The three objectives described below indicate varying levels of proficiency.

1 When presented a bottle containing formula, the student will demonstrate a sucking-swallowing reflex for 3 consecutive days.

2 When presented a piece of wrapped candy and given the verbal cue, "Unwrap the candy," the student will do so independently for 3 consecutive days.

3 When given the opportunity, the student will eat all foods independently at the lunch table without adult assistance for 3 consecutive weeks.

Tables 8-4 and 8-5 provide task analyses of eating with a spoon and using a napkin.

Table 8-4   Task Analysis of Spoon Feeding

Behavioral Objective: Given a spoon and plate of food and the verbal command, "Eat," the student will pick up the spoon and feed him/herself 3 out of 4 consecutive days.

Student follows these steps:

1   Reaches toward the spoon
2   Touches the spoon
3   Grasps the spoon
4   Picks up the spoon
5   Approaches the plate with the spoon
6   Touches the plate with the spoon
7   Scoops some food on the spoon
8   Lifts filled spoon away from plate
9   Lifts the spoon above the plate
10 Lifts the spoon halfway to mouth
11 Lifts the spoon 3 in. from mouth
12 Lifts the spoon 1 in. from mouth
13 Gets filled spoon to mouth without spilling
14 Puts filled spoon in mouth without spilling
15 Puts spoon back on plate
16 Will continue all steps until meal is eaten

Table 8-5   Task Analysis of Using Napkin

Behavioral Objective: Given a napkin, during mealtime the student will demonstrate appropriate use of the napkin 90% of the time.

Student follows these steps:

1   Seats himself at the table
2   Reaches dominant hand toward napkin
3   Graps corner of napkin with dominant hand
4   Lifts napkin off of table
5   Raises napkin to mouth with dominant hand
6   Wipes spillage from mouth
7   Returns napkin to table

Instructional Strategies

Teaching appropriate eating skills is a programming area which has received increased attention in recent years. For example, several reports describe the acquisition of independent spoon feeding achieved through dividing the behavior into smaller steps (Berkowitz, Sherry, & Davis, 1971; Christian, Holloman, & Lanier, 1973; Groves & Carroccio, 1971; Henrikson & Doughty, 1967; Zeiler & Jervey, 1968). With a backward chaining of responses, students are physically guided through most of the spoon-feeding behavior and are initially required only to empty the spoon into their mouths. As the children become more proficient, the trainer gradually fades hand support until total independence is achieved.

A critical component found in most of these programs is the use of a time-out procedure, or temporary removal of the food as punishment for inappropriate eating. The experimental efficacy of this procedure has been demonstrated with a series of socially unacceptable eating behaviors, such as "pigging" and food stealing (Barton, Guess, Garcia, & Baer, 1970).

Physical restraints have also been used temporarily in cases of children who constantly grab food with their free hand (Song & Gandhi, 1974). It has been suggested by these writers that the developmental level of arm and hand movement are important factors in selecting which children are good potential candidates for training.

The work of Azrin and his associates provides direction for the training and maintenance of eating skills in the profoundly retarded (O'Brien & Azrin, 1972; O'Brien, Bugle, & Azrin, 1972). In this research, the critical role of maintenance procedures is emphasized.

A major distinction between the research programs of Azrin's group and those of other workers is that Azrin's eating training includes a full chain of eating skills. Use of napkins, utensils, and other meal-time accessories is trained separately. One example of the success of this method is the "mini-meal" approach to rapid eating training of the profoundly retarded (Azrin & Armstrong, 1973). Characteristic of the "mini-meal" approach is a division of three daily meals into a number of shorter meals throughout the day. In this way the child receives numerous opportunities for training and practicing appropriate eating behavior. Furthermore, the problem of satiation encountered in using three large meals for training is minimized by using several smaller meals.

Specific Feeding Techniques

Because of the importance of eating skills and the complexity in teaching many handicapped children, specific techniques are provided below in areas such as positioning, swallowing, and using a straw and cup.

Positioning   Feeding in the correct position should start as soon as possible. When teaching parents to feed very young children, it is important to give clear and detailed instructions, preferably to both parents.

1   The child's head should be in a slightly downward position (the normal position during eating).

2   The spoon (with a small, shallow bowl in the beginning) should be placed into the mouth from either side rather than directly from the front, with a slight downward pressure to counteract the often-present tongue thrust.

3   Encourage the child to take off the food with his or her lips and not with the teeth.

4   To assist swallowing, stroke the child's throat slightly. If the child gags or chokes, put the head forward and down; the child will probably throw his or her head back and put a stretch on the esophagus, preventing the food from getting dislodged.

5   The child should sit in a correct position, with the feet supported and the

elbows resting on the table. It may be necessary to use special supports such as straps and sandbags to secure proper position. However, try to keep this to a minimum, because it may be hard to wean the child from these later.

Swallowing In order to teach voluntary swallowing the following points should be followed:

1 The head should be in a slightly downward position.
2 Use only a small amount of liquid in the cup; it is easier and keeps the child from being discouraged.
3 Stroke the throat to facilitate swallowing.
4 Discourage the child from biting the cup.
5 If there is no lip closure (due to overbite or involuntary motion), hold the upper and lower lips shut with a very slight pressure of your fingers.
6 Teach the child to take one sip and swallow.
7 If the child stiffens on approach of the cup, wait until he or she relaxes again. The child will soon learn that he or she will get food only when relaxed.

Strawdrinking This can be started if the hands are ready or not. Some of the important factors to remember are:

A It is a step towards independent feeding.
B It is a prespeech activity, i.e., it teaches breath control.
C It helps in controlling drooling.
D It is an excellent means of getting liquids into a severely involved child, when the following steps are used.
   1 Use a short plastic straw with a small circumference.
   2 Place only a small amount of liquid in the cup.
   3 Let the child take only one sip at the time, gradually increasing speed until it becomes a continuous procedure.
   4 Encourage the child to close only his or her lips and not the teeth. If lip closure is not present or insufficient, again apply slight pressure with your fingers to the lips around the straw.
   5 A good way to start is to use a small Tupperware cup, with a lid which has a straw running through it. It is possible to push milk into the child's mouth by pressing on the lid, after which the child will swallow and gradually get the idea of sucking up. Karo syrup applied to the tip of the straw also encourages sucking. Later several small holes may be punched into the lid to allow easier flow.
   6 Increase the length of the straw and change to liquid with a heavier flow (milkshakes) as the child progresses.
   7 Use a paper straw and see how many the child needs to empty a cup.

Chewing Start with semisolid foods (lima beans, carrots, etc.) which the child likes. Bread or vanilla crackers are soft and prevent choking. The child should be encouraged, with each bite, to chew before swallowing until it becomes a habit. By putting food between the teeth from alternate sides of the mouth you can set off a chewing reflex through stimulating the inside of the cheek; the same method seems to counteract the tongue thrust. Give more and more solid foods as chewing strength increases.

Self-Feeding The following assistive devices can be utilized to facilitate self-feeding:

    1 Use a built-up handle on the spoon, or a handcuff to hold the spoon. Use a fork as much as possible; it is easier to spear than to get food onto a spoon.
    2 Use a plate with sides, so food will fall back onto plate.
    3 Employ a cut-out board to hold the plate, if necessary.
    4 Give the child a cup which is not too large and which has a lip.
    5 Use a cup holder if the child cannot hold a cup.
    6 Try something sticky like mashed potatoes at first, or something that will not fall off the spoon so easily.

The following points are important to remember in feeding training:

    1 Be sure of a good body position.
    2 If indicated, stabilize the child's feet and other hand.
    3 Support the child's hands on the table.
    4 Let the child try out which hand he or she wants to use.
    5 Make a dry run until the child is familiar with the activity and understands exactly what he or she is supposed to do.
    6 Give the child some assistance at first, gradually reducing it.
    7 Let him or her try the task independently and see what the child does when he or she thinks there is no one observing; this might give you some helpful clues.

Eating-Proficiency Guidelines

Although the types of eating skills which have been discussed in the previous section are fairly comprehensive, separate behaviors, they are all alike in one way: the goal is to teach new skills or increase the frequency of selected eating behaviors. However, with some handicapped students, other types of eating difficulties may also involve:

    1 Refusal to eat
    2 Eating very sloppily or "pigging" food
    3 Throwing up food regularly

The guidelines provided here are attempts to present what researchers in this area have done. There are, unfortunately, only a limited number of published reports which deal with these frustrating eating problems.

Refusal to Eat Refusal to eat food occurs infrequently with severely handicapped students. However, one reason for its occurrence is the overprotective nature of many parents and families with handicapped children. Not placing normal behavioral requirements upon the child allows him to become dependent on the family. When others try to encourage independent eating responses, resistance by the child occurs, leading to an unpleasant eating period. There are at least three ways of attempting to cope with this difficulty:

    1 If parents are responsive and willing, begin to teach them how to develop self-feeding responses in their child.

    2 If the teacher must assume full responsibility, the selection of preferred foods and presentation of one preferred food at a time by a highly reinforcing person is desirable (Wehman & Marchant, 1978); when criterion is reached, i.e.,5 days in a row of accepting food, a second food can be used.

    3 Withhold food; this will lead to increased hunger and break down the student's resistance not to accept food. The obvious problem with this method is the ethical difficulty of depriving a child of food.

    Sloppy Eating Many young handicapped children play with food, spill it excessively, throw it, or show other similar behaviors. These inappropriate eating responses can be eliminated and good eating can be trained. Below are several suggestions:

1 The removal of the child's food immediately contingent on the sloppy eating behavior has worked repeatedly and is advised as one possibility. For this method the teacher should remove the food for only 10 to 30 seconds after the last bit of food has been swallowed and tell the child why the food was removed.

2 A second method is physical guidance of correct responses and then gradual removal of teacher assistance as the child becomes more proficient. Preferred foods may be used as reinforcers for "good" eating.

3 If the child persists in sloppy eating, a third strategy is the combined use of:
    a Preferred food as reinforcement for good eating.
    b Cleaning up the spilled food by rapidly guiding the entire clean-up process of washing the floor, wringing out the cloth, etc.

    Chronic Regurgitation Another inappropriate eating behavior which is exhibited by severely and profoundly handicapped students is throwing up after each meal. This is usually done for the attention which it inevitably brings. No teacher cares to let vomitus lay on the floor, and it is a typical reaction to believe the child is physically ill, "anxiety-ridden," or is suffering from some emotional distress. However, if the child vomits regularly, it may be that the teacher attention after each vomiting period is strengthening the vomiting behavior. Two possible methods of overcoming this problems includes:

1 Giving the child an extra portion of food at meals until he will take no more. The rationale behind this is that many of the children exhibiting this behavior bring up the food for the taste in their mouth, and complete food satiation at mealtime decreases this maladaptive response (Jackson, Johnson, Ackron, & Crowley, 1975).

2 If this strategy is not successful, then using a combination of two procedures:
    a Giving positive reinforcement and attention for *not* vomiting
    b Making the child complete the entire clean-up process of the vomitus very rapidly and with physical guidance (Azrin & Wesolowski, 1975).

    Certainly, these methods are not all-inclusive or detailed. However, they should provide some possible methods which can be implemented. If there are doubts about how to utilize these methods, a professional consultant trained in behavior modification should be brought in.

DRESSING SKILLS

There are a number of resources available which specify procedures necessary for the development of dressing and grooming behaviors in the severely and profoundly retarded (e.g., Anderson, Hodson, & Jones, 1975; Copeland, Ford, & Solon, 1976; Myers, Sinco, & Stalma, 1974). Each of these sources provides instructions or guidelines for implementing dressing programs. Table 8-6 shows a developmental sequence for dressing.

Dressing Objectives

When selecting dressing and undressing objectives it is important to pay careful attention to the child's fine motor skill level. Attempting to teach dressing skills such as zipping or lacing to a spastic child or a student with poorly developed eye-hand coordination will set up the child for failure. The following objectives are illustrations of an undressing skill, a dressing skill, and a higher-level dressing skill involving clothing selection.

   1   When given the verbal cue, "Pull off your socks," the student will do so independently for 3 consecutive days.

Table 8-6   Dressing Skills Sequence

Age	Content
0–4 months	Tugs at clothes
4–8 months	Cooperates in dressing
8–12 months	Pulls off shoes or socks Cooperates with dressing Enjoys removing hat
12–16 months	
18–22 months	Removes socks, mittens, shoes Unzips zipper
22–24 months	Removes coat or dress
24–36 months	Puts on coat or dress Puts on shoes Unbuttons accessories and buttons
3–6 years	Buttons coat or dress Dresses and undresses except for tying Laces shoes Distinguishes front and back of clothes
6–9 years	Ties shoe laces Personally decides on clothes needs
9–12 years	
12–15 years	Maintains complete care of dressing needs

2 When given the verbal cue, "Tie your shoes," the student will do so independently 5 days in 1 week.

3 When given the opportunity to select appropriate clothing to wear from his or her wardrobe, the student will choose appropriately with 95 percent accuracy.

A detailed task analysis for putting on a pair of long pants is provided in Table 8-7.

Table 8-7   Task Analysis of Putting on a Pair of Pants

Student follows these steps:

1 Grasps top of pants with both hands
2 Holds pants in front of stomach
3 Turns pants until zipper of pants is farthest (away from) from stomach
4 With left hand, holds on to pants at left side of snap
5 With right hand, holds on to pants at right side of snap
6 Sits down
7 Bends body over at waist
8 Holds pants in front of legs at calf level
9 Raises right foot
10 Moves foot over back of pants towards front
11 Points toes of right foot
12 Places right foot into inside of pants
13 With toes pointed, slides right foot into top of right leg hole
14 Extends right leg through right pants leg opening
15 Places right hand below knee on right pants leg
16 Pulls up right pants leg
17 Pulls up pants leg until bottom of right pants leg is at right ankle
18 Puts foot down
19 Lets go of pants leg
20 With right hand, holds on to front of pants at right side of snap
21 Raises up left foot
22 Raises left foot over back of pants
23 Points toes of left foot
24 Places left foot into inside of pants
25 With toes pointed, slides left foot into top of left leg opening
26 Extends left leg through left pants leg opening
27 Places left hand below knee on left pants leg
28 Pulls up left pants leg
29 Pulls up pants leg until bottom of left pants leg is at left ankle
30 Lets go of pants leg
31 Puts left foot down
32 Stands up
33 Places left hand on top of left side of pants
34 Places right hand on top of right side of pants
35 Grasps pants with both hands
36 Pulls up pants
37 Pulls up pants until over bottom
38 Lets go of pants
39 Places left hand at top of pants in on left side

Table 8-7 (Continued)

40	Holds top of pants
41	Places thumb and forefinger of right hand at bottom of zipper
42	Grasps zipper tab of zipper with fingers
43	Pulls up zipper tab of zipper
44	Pulls zipper tab of zipper until it reaches top of pants
45	Lets go of zipper tab
46	With right hand, touches snap on right side of pants
47	Places left hand on snap at left side of pants
48	With left hand, grasps pants at left side of snap
49	With right hand, places right snap on top of left snap
50	With right hand, places forefinger on top of snap
51	Places thumb underneath bottom of snap
52	Presses fingers together tightly until snaps fasten to each other
53	Lets go of pants

Instructional Strategies

Dressing skills are best taught in realistic situations such as toileting sessions, preparing to leave school, or removing garments in the morning. It is also necessary to schedule weekly sessions in the classroom to work on dressing behaviors needing special attention or on skills which do not lend themselves to daily classroom activities. The following dressing and undressing guidelines might be implemented during training sessions:

A   Each child should be assessed to determine which steps of a skill he or she is able to perform unassisted. A task analysis of each activity will help the teacher assess the child. Every person working in the classroom should be aware of what level of assistance each child needs so that no child is given more physical assistance than is required.

B   Undressing is usually easier for a child than dressing, so training should begin with this. Backward chaining is usually the best instructional technique for use in dressing since the child receives early satisfaction.

C   Several concrete suggestions for undressing-dressing instruction include:

   1   Use clothing about two sizes too big for the child so that he or she can remove it with ease.

   2   Use socks without heels (tube socks for children) for first sessions. Backward chaining helps the child learn to manipulate the heel area effectively. When the child can pull this type of sock on, introduce a stretchy-type cotton-blend sock with heel. Follow this with a regular nylon sock.

   3   For training in putting on or removing crew-neck shirts, first teach the child to raise and lower a hula hoop or similar aid over his or her head. When the child has learned these hand motions, introduce a dressing shirt which has only a hole for the head. Have the child learn to raise and lower this over his or her head using modeling and physical assistance. From this move on to an oversized T-shirt, followed by a regular shirt the child would wear. Some children take long periods of training to learn to

remove the shirt over their head and arms, so it is better to have them learn to pull their arms out before raising the shirt over their heads.

4   Putting on a coat is facilitated if the child is taught to lay the coat flat in front of him or her with the neck closest to the body. The child then places one arm in each sleeve, lifts both arms high to throw the coat over the head, and then pushes each arm through the sleeve.

5   For practical purposes, when teaching a child to remove a coat, carry the instruction further to include picking it up and hanging it in the proper place in the classroom.

6   Buttoning is facilitated if the following steps are used:
   a   Have the child learn to drop a wooden disc through a vertical and a horizontal opening in a box made of three pieces of wood.
   b   Have the child learn to pass the disc from one hand to another through the same slots.
   c   Repeat steps 1 and 2 using a large button and a piece of vinyl or leather.
   d   Use large buttons on regular material.
   e   Use smaller buttons and have them attached to the material.
   f   Use the child's regular clothing or dressing jackets with buttons large enough for the child to manipulate.

Individual Teaching Guidelines   The sequence presented below is directed to those teachers who must have a one-to-one training situation. This may occur because of additional staff or because of the extreme handicap of the child. The following points must be considered in preparing an instructional session in dressing:

1   *Room Selection*—select a room or area without distractions. Consider whether the curtains are pulled, the toys are removed, you and the child are together alone, and the room is quiet.
2   *Position*—the child and teacher should be facing each other. Sit on the chair the same level as the child so it is easy to reach him.
3   *Materials and Equipment*—have clothing laid out, and reinforcers and record-keeping materials ready before you begin the training session.
4   *Time of Day*—be as consistent as possible in teaching at the same time each day; perhaps morning, evening, or before and after naps.
5   *Length of Session*—this may vary, but an optimum time is about 15 to 20 minutes per session. It is better to teach for several short periods daily rather than for infrequent long sessions.

Group-Teaching Guidelines   A more realistic means of teaching is with two or more children. The points identified below indicate several considerations involved in training dressing skills to handicapped students in small groups.

When to use group teaching:

1   When there is insufficient staff or time for a detailed check of the child's progress.
2   At day care centers which do not see the child during the normal dressing and undressing times in the morning and evening.

3 When children can be grouped together for similar dressing skills, such as putting on coats, hats, mittens, etc.

Considerations when teaching handicapped children in a group:

1 Place children in a chair on their own level.
2 Be able to move freely from child to child, such as by the use of a chair on rollers.
3 If children cannot imitate each other or the teacher, work with each child individually and have the other children wait for their turns.
4 Work on only one dressing task at a time, such as putting on a T-shirt. You may need more than one item of clothing, depending on the size and the abilities of your group.
5 If the children do imitate, let the child who can do the most model for the other children.
6 If the children have accomplished many of the tasks but need practice in the dressing skills, play *dress-up games*. If dress-up clothing is used, check to make certain that the clothing:
   a Is not too big or too small.
   b Has fastenings which the children can reach.
   c Has fastenings that are large enough for the children to grasp and hold, such as on buttons and zippers.
7 Provide a mirror to help the child see his or her own accomplishments. Remember that the child does see himself in reverse, so a mirror is not appropriate for teaching—just as a reinforcer. Also, some children's behavior is affected by the use of shiny objects.

SAMPLE LESSON PLAN FOR UNDRESSING

An illustration of how the learning conditions described in Chapters 4, 5, and 6 can be employed to teach an undressing skill is provided below. The skill involves having the child learn to remove his or her socks independently. Close examination of this program indicates the role of the learning variables in different stages of instruction.

Scope: The following lesson plan will cover most instruction for the short-term objective listed below. The lesson encompasses four parts:
   A Initial presentation
   B Instruction and practice
   C Evaluation
   D Generalization

Intentional learning
Small amount of material
 in objective

Objective: Given the verbal cue, "Pull off your socks," Phil will do so correctly within 2 minutes on 3 consecutive days.

A *Initial presentation:*

Oral and visual presentation

"Phil, we are going to learn to pull off our socks this week! Do you know where your socks are? These are your socks and these are my socks. Say,

Modeling

'socks'.'' (Prompt Phil to touch his socks and say "socks.")

"To pull off our socks we put our thumb in the top of the sock and *pull* it off like this! Look, Phil, I'm going to *pull* off my other sock, too." (Pull off your socks enthusiastically!)

Orienting procedure

"There, I have pulled off my socks! Phil, pull off your socks."

Prompting

(If Phil does, reward him profusely with praise. If not, physically prompt him through the act of pulling off one sock.)

Positive reinforcement

"Good, you helped me pull off one sock! Now pull off the other sock!" (Repeat the procedure with the other sock.)

"That is good helping, Phil. If you learn to pull off your socks, you can help Mom undress you each night. When you learn more dressing skills, you can get dressed all by yourself! Won't that be fun!

Creation of a positive learning environment

(Give Phil a big hug!) "Let's get busy now and learn to pull off your socks!"

B *Instruction and practice:*

Training Program I

Instruction will involve carrying the child through the steps of the following task analysis using shaping, backward chaining, and fading procedures. The child will be required to complete each step independently on three trials prior to moving to the next step.

Instruction will be done for 20 minutes each day until the objective is mastered. Programming for overlearning will then begin.

Task analysis:

Progressive-parts presentation

1 Child pulls the socks off his toes when they are pulled down over the heel.
2 Child pulls the socks over the heels and off his feet.
3 Child grasps the tops of the socks, pulls them down over the heels, and off his feet.

Backward chaining

Procedures: Pull the child's socks down over his heels and say, "Phil, pull off your sock."

Shaping

If he moves his hand in the direction of the sock, say, "Yes, use your hand to *pull off your sock.*" If

Fading

he does not reach for the sock, physically prompt him to do so, but remove your physical prompt as you feel he is able to carry out the step. Repeat for the other sock. When he has pulled the socks off his toes three times correctly, move to Step 2 of the

Corrective feedback
Reaction time

task analysis and finally to Step 3, where he has to do the complete task. Use lots of praise to reward him.

Verbally tell him what mistakes he makes. Record the length of time it takes the child to carry out the task and, if necessary, remind him to work faster on the task. Physically guide him through it faster, if necessary, to give him the idea of working faster.

C *Evaluation:*

Overlearning for retention

When the child has demonstrated the ability to do each step of the task analysis as specified, the test on pulling off socks will be administered. This test involves verbally telling the child, "Pull off your socks," and recording the steps of the task which he does independently. When Phil has done the task independently for 3 consecutive days, practice on the whole task will continue half again as long as it took Phil to attain initial mastery. Then, evaluation will occur again.

Training Program II
Whole method of presentation
Massed practice

If Program I does not produce desired acquisition of the skill in a reasonable time period, Phil will be carried through a rapid training program of pulling off socks, in which he is physically guided through the complete task over and over again for 45-minute sessions each day. At the end of the 45-minute session, he will be requested to pull off his socks and required to do so independently. Evaluation and overlearning will then be carried out as for Training Program I. (See Azrin & Wesolowski, 1977.)

D *Generalization:*

Instructions and intent

Instructions throughout the strategy will emphasize the use of pulling off socks in other situations such as rest time, swim time, or other such occasions at school. The differences and similarities between pulling off socks and other dressing skills will be pointed out in regard to various transfer situations. For example:

Similarity situation

"Phil, remember how you pull your sock off when it's over the heel? Can you do that with your shoe, too? Show me!"

Across environments and trainers

In addition, the parents of Phil will be taught how Phil takes off socks at school so that he can be an active participant in the transfer situation of undressing at home.

GROOMING AND HEALTH SKILLS

Personal hygiene and grooming include skills such as haircombing, toothbrushing and bathing. Health skills involve knowledge of balanced meals and principles of weight control. In Tables 8-8 and 8-9 are representative skills

Table 8-8   Grooming Skills Sequence

Age	Content
0–4 months	
4–8 months	
8–12 months	
12–18 months	
18–22 months	
22–24 months	
24–36 months	Washes and dries hands
3–6 years	Washes face Brushes teeth Bathes self when assisted Blows nose Coughs politely
6–9 years	Bathes self unassisted Shampoos hair Combs or brushes hair
9–12 years	Uses deodorant Uses mouthwash
12–15 years	Uses cosmetics Uses sanitary pads
15–20 years	Shaves

which make up grooming and health subdomains. Although there are obviously many more skills, the important aspect of the tables is the logic of the sequence.

Grooming- and Health-Skills Objectives

The objectives listed below are skills which may be relevant for most handicapped students.

    1 When given the verbal cue, "Wash your hands," the student will do so independently for 3 consecutive weeks.

    2 When given the verbal cue, "Shampoo your hair," the student will do so for three consecutive training sessions.

    3 When given the verbal cue, "Shave your face," the student will do so for three consecutive training sessions.

    4 When coughing, the student will cover his or her nose and mouth correctly three out of four coughs when observed during a 30-minute period.

    5 When presented with twenty-five foods to choose from, the student will plan three balanced meals with 95 percent accuracy.

    6 When presented with ten illness situations, the students will identify which ones need immediate medical attention with 95 percent accuracy.

A task analysis for brushing teeth is presented in Table 8-10. The detail

Table 8-9 Health Skills Sequence

Age	Content
0–4 months	
4–8 months	
8–12 months	
12–18 months	
18–22 months	
22–24 months	
24–36 months	
3–6 years	Blows nose correctly Covers nose and mouth when coughing
6–9 years	Maintains proper posture
9–12 years	Understands principles of weight control Has knowledge of balanced meals Has knowledge of appropriate clothes for weather conditions
12–15 years	Gets proper sleep Has knowledge of reproduction processes
15–20 years	Has knowledge of birth control methods Has knowledge of first aid Seeks medical attention when needed

provided in this sequence will be helpful in working with more severely involved students.

Instructional Strategies

Grooming A variety of instructional techniques have been used to train grooming skills. Chaining and task-analytic approaches have proven successful in training toothbrushing (Horner & Kelitz, 1975) and handwashing and facewashing (Treffry, Martin, Samuels, & Watson, 1970). Both of these studies also involved the use of positive-reinforcement procedures.

Verbal cues, modeling, and physical prompting are techniques which have been employed to teach grooming skills (Wehman, 1974). Treffry, Martin, Samuels, and Watson used these strategies in combination with a 15-second time out for wrong responses in their study to teach hand- and facewashing skills to thirty severely retarded girls.

With moderately and mildly handicapped individuals, activities utilizing a multimedia approach have proven helpful in teaching grooming skills. Numerous films, filmstrips, and packets of illustrative pictures are available for use in such activities, as well as free supplies from companies which sell grooming aids such as toothbrushes (Hamre-Nietupski & Williams, 1976).

Counseling or discussion sessions are helpful in teaching the value of good grooming habits in work and social situations. It is also important for teachers

Table 8-10   Task Analysis of Brushing Teeth

Student follows these steps:

1   Removes toothbrush and toothpaste from cup
2   Unscrews toothpaste cap
3   Squeezes appropriate amount of toothpaste onto brush
4   Lays toothbrush down
5   Screws cap back on tube
6   Picks up brush in preferred hand
7   Leans over sink
8   Brushes in down motion over top teeth from one side of mouth to the other
9   Spits out excess at least once
10 Brushes in up motion over bottom teeth from one side of mouth to the other
11 Spits out excess at least once
12 Brushes in down motion over back of top teeth from one side of mouth to the other
13 Spits out excess at least once
14 Brushes in down motion over back of bottom teeth from one side of mouth to the other
15 Spits out excess at least once
16 Brushes back and forth over crowns of top teeth from one side of mouth to the other
17 Spits out excess at least once
18 Brushes back and forth over crowns of bottom teeth from one side of mouth to the other
19 Spits out excess at least once
20 Picks up cup
21 Turns on cold water faucet
22 Fills cup with water
23 Rinses mouth with water
24 Spits out excess at least once
25 Pours excess water out of cup into sink
26 Replaces cup next to sink
27 Rinses toothbrush in water
28 Turns off cold water faucet
29 Replaces brush and paste in cup

and other adults working with handicapped individuals to serve as appropriate models for the students by practicing good grooming themselves.

Health   The development of good health skills is essential in the education of mentally handicapped students if they are to function independently. Exceptional individuals go through the same biological and emotional stages as other individuals, and need instruction to help them understand how to deal with varying health situations ranging from planning a balanced diet to handling an emergency first aid situation.

There are a number of ways in which the teacher might plan lessons across all areas of the curriculum in order to develop needed health skills. For example, mathematics could be incorporated into meal planning and weight loss, and language arts into reporting first aid procedures. A multimedia approach should also be utilized with films, posters, and available kits incorporated into the instructional procedures. In addition, the procedures should provide for transfer of training by affording the student the opportunity to apply health skills in other situations outside the classroom. Social clubs, such as the Girl Scouts, can afford opportunities for students to participate in health activities at nursing homes or hospitals.

Knowledge of bodily functions should include information regarding adolescent bodily changes as well as family-planning information. (See Hamre-Nietupski, 1976 for a well-developed curriculum on teaching body parts to trainable retarded students.) Bass (1972) discusses the importance of sex education for mentally retarded individuals, and points out that mildly and moderately handicapped students need information as much or more than other young people for reasons which include confusion about their identities and a need for help in understanding acceptable and expected forms of social behavior.

Several authors suggest having students visit ministers or pastors for information on sex (Lawson, 1965), but in view of the fact that many families are not affiliated with churches, the school staff must assume some responsibility for sex education. Bass (1972) suggests that the school administration should inform parents of the need for sex education for the handicapped. She gives outlines for three planning sessions with parents in which the need for and methods of instruction for family-living units would be presented. Each school district would have to adhere to local and state guidelines in these instructional procedures, and in some locales parents would have the right to refuse to allow their child to participate.

After these planning sessions, family-living training would be incorporated into the curriculum. Bass (1972) suggests that family life should be integrated into other courses, and as much use as possible should be made of the "teachable moment." Multimedia approaches are once again suggested, and many good audiovisual materials are available and listed by the Sex Education and Information Council of the United States and the American Association for Health, Physical Education and Recreation.

Since retarded girls may become pregnant, it is suggested that some emphasis be placed on prenatal medical care and on care of a young child (Lawson, 1965). Field trips to nursery schools where the students serve as helpers provide concrete experiences in child care for these adolescents.

Discussion groups, dialogue, and role playing for which the students are encouraged to express their feelings are often more successful than lectures (Bass, 1972). Concrete experiences such as a field trip to a child-placement home where a child is waiting for adoption might have a greater impact than any classroom experiences.

Contraception is viewed as a very controversial area, and Bass suggests that parents be involved or give approval before any teacher advises a student to use contraceptives. Teachers are reminded (Bass, 1972) that parents have emotions regarding their handicapped children which are often deep or unconscious. Many parents have been encouraged to deal with their adult retarded offspring as children and are not prepared to deal their sexuality. However, the rights of the unborn child and of the retarded individual in understanding his or her feelings are also involved, and outside counselors or medical personnel may be of use to the parents and teachers.

In the area of health skills, a well-rounded community program of supervision and care would be helpful. Such a program could assist adults and adolescents by offering counseling in sexual behavior, marriage, and health care. School personnel could carefully coordinate programs with local community agencies, and both could help inform the community of the needs of exceptional individuals in the health care area.

SAMPLE LESSON PLAN FOR HEALTH

One area of health and safety which has not been discussed is teaching handicapped children not to drink poisonous substances. This is an important health skill which many parents constantly worry about. The lesson plan designed for instruction in this skill is characterized by application of specific learning conditions. Careful attention to the instructional sequence of this program will help teachers prepare an effective lesson.

Scope: The following lesson plan will cover most instruction for the short-term objective listed below. The lesson plan encompasses four parts:
   A Initial presentation
   B Instruction and practice
   C Evaluation
   D Generalization

Objective: When presented with twenty items, Bill will identify the poisonous ones with 100 percent accuracy (concept learning).

A *Initial presentation:*
   "Bill, today we are going to begin to learn about things which are poisonous. Do you know what poisonous means?" (Wait for reply)
   "Right, Bill. Poison is something which will make you very sick or maybe kill you if you eat it of drink it when you are not supposed to. Look at the picture I have. This little boy is eating pills which the doctor gave his mother. This other picture shows the doctors at the hospital pumping his stomach to get the poisonous pills out of him. Do you know of any poisonous things in your house or in the school room here?" (Give corrective feedback)
   "That's right. Drano is poisonous. It is very important that you learn about other things which are poisonous. Can you tell me why?" (Wait)
   "Right. You do not want to poison yourself. Another reason is that you may need to warn your little brother about things he should not eat or drink." I have brought several poisonous things with me today. I have bleach, ammonia, and lighter fluid. How can these poison you?

Overlap—liquid
Redundant—smell
Few items

"Right, if you drink them, they may poison you. Look at these other items."

Expository presentation

(Show a plant leaf, D-Con rat tablets, and lye.) "How can these poison you?"

Oral and visual stimuli

"Right. They are poisonous if you eat them. You have a good idea about how poisonous items do damage to our bodies. Do you have any questions?" "Well, you may have some later as we learn about many household items which are poisonous. I will give you practice activities to help you learn the poisonous things, and later I will give you a test to be sure that you know what things you must not eat or drink."

B *Instruction and practice:*

Low contiguity
Three-dimensional items
3:1 positive to negative instances

Bill will be presented three poisonous items at a time. Each of these will be discussed with the child, who will then explain to the teacher how poisoning might occur. A nonpoisonous item will be presented also, and the student will identify the poisonous ones. The poisonous items will be grouped so that relevant dimensions facilitate learning. The relevant dimensions are the uses of the items.

Group I: bleach, ammonia, furniture polish, Coke.
Group II: Campho-phenique, prescription pills, aspirin, tomato.
Group III: lye, Drano, lighter fluid, lettuce.
Group IV: poisonous berries, poisonous plant leaf, poisonous flower, candy bar.
Group V: gasoline, motor oil, antifreeze, milk.

Stimulus fading

Procedures: Bill will be told, "Poisonous items may or may not be identified with this sign for poison (skull and bones). To help you learn the poisonous items I have put the poison sign on all the poisonous items. As you learn the items, you will not need the sign.

Progressive parts

Groups I through V will be presented in week 1; each previously learned group will be reviewed daily. When each group is introduced, the three poisonous items will be presented successively. The class will be defined as being poisonous with the relevant dimension being what the items are used for.

Example: "Bill, we are going to learn about three new poisonous items today. The first one is bleach.

Successive exposure

Pick it up and smell it."

"The next item is ammonia. Pick this one up and smell it."

"The third poisonous item is furniture polish. Smell it."

"Good work! All three of these are household

cleaning agents which are poisonous if taken into the body. Now that you have identified them, I want you to practice choosing these items from others. I'm going to give you four things and ask you to choose the poisonous ones. Are there any questions before we begin?"

3:1 positive to negative instances
4:1 practice to initial instruction
Corrective feedback

(Present randomly at least four times the three items with a fourth nonpoisonous item, such as Coke. Provide corrective feedback and continue practice until Bill identifies the poisonous ones with 100 percent accuracy. Then move on to Group II and go through the same procedures.)

C *Evaluation:*

Overlearning to facilitate transfer and retention

When Bill has demonstrated the ability to identify all five groups of poisons, give a test by presenting twenty items out of which Bill must identify the poisonous ones with 100 percent accuracy. When he does so, provide one-half again as much practice to achieve overlearning of 150 percent.

D *Generalization:*

Intent and instructions

Throughout instruction and practice, Bill will be reminded where the poisonous items might be found outside the classroom, and similarities between these items and other poisonous ones will be pointed out.

Similarity relationships

If possible, accompany Bill to other environments, such as the janitorial storage room or his kitchen at home, to point out how knowledge concerning poisons can be transferred to other situations.

SAFETY SKILLS

If handicapped children are to approach normalization in society, they must acquire certain independent safety skills. Basic skills include correct usage of sharp objects, safe bicycle riding, and moving safely about the comunity. Teachers can assist in this normalization process by helping students acquire the necessary skills. Table 8-11 is a developmental sequence of safety skills.

Safety-Skills Objectives

The objectives below are illustrations of the types of safety skills which might be identified for instruction on the IEP. They may be appropriate and relevant for most handicapped students.

1   When entering the school building, the student will demonstrate using the steps and corridors with no running or pushing behaviors for five mornings.
2   When presented with twenty items, the student will identify the ones which are poisonous with 100 percent accuracy.
3   When given three examples of emergency situations, the student will

Table 8-11   Safety Skills Sequence

Age	Content
0–4 months	
4–8 months	
8–12 months	
12–18 months	
18–22 months	
22–24 months	
24–36 months	Avoids simple hazards
3–6 years	Uses steps and corridors safely
	Knows dangers of matches, stove, and careless fires
	Travels in a car or bus safely
	Crosses streets correctly
	Goes to nearby neighborhood places alone
6–9 years	Uses sharp objects safely
	Uses electrical items safely
	Identifies poisonous items
	Adheres to bicycle safety rules
	Knows how to report emergencies
9–12 years	Can extinguish a small fire
12–15 years	Goes about hometown freely
15–20 years	Knows how to report infractions of safety rules
	Goes to distant places alone

demonstrate techniques for reporting them to the proper authorities with 100 percent accuracy.

Instructional Strategies

Teacher-developed activities are one method used to foster acquisition of the needed safety skills. In planning such activities, student input should be sought as well as parent involvement to determine what skills they feel their children need. These activities should be multisensory and should actively involve the students. With younger handicapped students this might mean actually experiencing the feeling of "hot" during a discussion of safety with matches. Students should also be given the opportunity to actually use sharp objects under adult objections after participating in discussions concerning the dangers of their use. Direct instruction is suggested as being the most sensible method to teach safety to exceptional individuals.

Many illustrative pictures and simple written pamphlets are available from the National Safety Council (5 Pennsylvania Ave., Washington, D.C.). Many of these materials suggest projects for students to carry out and report back to the class about. Role playing or play action can be incorporated into learning activities in this area, as students' acting out whom they should contact in an emergency. Learning centers can be developed where students practice dialing emergency numbers and recording the situation. Also, language activities from the *Peabody Language Development Kits* can be used as the basis for discussions about how students should respond in certain situations such as house fires. Community helpers such as firemen can help teach children safety habits, and field trips to community facilities also assist in making safety concepts concrete enough for children to acquire and retain (Virginia State Department of Education, 1973). Pre- and posttests in all activities, however, should be used to measure the learning of individual students. These tests will allow the teacher to modify specific activities where individual students still need practice.

With moderately and severely handicapped students, Certo and his associates (1976) found that using coding cues and highly structured learning activities can help students acquire skills such as riding the public bus. The bus would be coded for the student so he would know which one to catch, and he would initially be physically guided through all the steps of using public transportation. Such structured lessons could help other populations acquire community-living skills. In such activities, it is essential that the teacher has laid groundwork in the community so that the citizens understand what the school personnel are attempting to teach the students.

SAMPLE LESSON PLAN FOR SAFETY

Many children run in school halls and may push or shove needlessly. This is an inappropriate social skill. However, more importantly, it can be hazardous to the child as well as to others. The lesson plan below represents one effort at overcoming this problem.

The following lesson plan will cover most of the instructional programming for the short-term objective written below. The lesson encompasses four parts (concept learning).

    A Initial presentation
    B Instruction and practice
    C Evaluation
    D Generalization

Objective: Charles will demonstrate correct use of the school corridors and steps (i.e., no running, loud talking, or shoving) for five consecutive mornings when entering the school building.

A *Initial presentation*

Student involvement

"Charles, we want to learn how to use the school hallways and steps correctly. Can you help me determine how students should act in the school halls? Let's figure out several rules which might guide us in behaving well in the halls and on the steps."

"O.K., Good. Rule 1 is *'No loud talking in the hall'*. Any other ideas?" (Write the rule on the board.)

Simple definitional rules

Expository method

High contiguity—few concepts the student has to grasp

"How about running? Rule 2 can be *'No running in the halls'.*"

"Could rule 3 be *'No pushing or shoving others?'* How about going up the left steps and coming down the right steps? Would that help avoid crowding on the steps?"

"Charles, now that we have made up the rules and have written them on the board, we want you to practice using them. When you have a good idea of how to use the hallway correctly, I'm going to observe or watch you each morning to test how well you are using the rules. Do you think you will have any problems following these rules?

B *Instructions and practice:*

Oral practice

4:1 practice to original input

Written practice

"Charles, do you remember the rules about using the hallway, which we made up and I put up here on the board? I have a notebook for you. Would you please take time now to read the rules to me again? (Provide an opportunity for him to read the rules three other times during the day—before lunch, play, and dismissal.)

"Good. Now I want you to write each of them and draw a picture to show someone using the rule correctly. Where would you like to put the rules in this notebook?"

Active student involvement

"Charles, I have the camera here today. Do Do you remember how to use it? Good! Could you take pictures of your friends using the halls and steps correctly as our rules suggest? We will use the pictures on our bulletin board showing what rules we have made up."

Positive reinforcement

"Good work, Charles! You seem to understand how to use the hallway and steps correctly. When you use these rules all the time, you will be able to go from place to place in the school without any watching by teachers."

"Today I have lots of photographs of students in the hallways here. Can you select the ones who are following our rules?"

3:1 positive to negative instances
Corrective feedback

Simultaneous exposure

Procedure: Present in random sequences: (1) three photos of students walking, one running; (2) three other photos of good behavior, one student shoving; (3) three other photos of good behavior, one student sliding on the bannister; (4) three other photos of good behavior, one student hollering with hands at the mouth to amplify his or her voice. Give immediate feedback after each set. Leave preceding sets of photos out so Charles can review them if he wishes to.

Fading teacher prompts
Backward chaining

"I think we are ready to use the rules in our everyday schedule. We have been sending Mildred (the aide) with you in the hallway. Today she will go only to the end of the hall with you. Can you go on to the cafeteria using the good rules for the hall?" (Provide feedback as needed on his way to the cafeteria.)

"Great! You did well in the hallway on the way to lunch. Can you go the the bus from the library? Remember to keep the rules in mind."

When Charles has demonstrated the ability to use the hallways correctly for several days, administer the evaluative posttest.

C *Evaluation:*

Overlearning for facilitating retention and transfer

Charles will be observed for five consecutive mornings to determine if he uses the hallways with no running, shoving, or loud talking, and to see if he uses the steps correctly. When he does so for five consecutive mornings, practice will continue for one-half as long again to accomplish 150 percent mastery level.

D *Generalization:*

Instructions and intent

Throughout instruction, it will be pointed out to Charles how the rules can be applied in everyday school and home situations. Similarities between home and school situations will be mentioned and instructions will be given to Charles as to how to act in transfer situations.

Field trips will afford opportunities for the rules to be generalized across environments and parent contacts will be made to facilitate generalization of the rules to home situations and across people.

The lessons for caring for oneself at the lunch table will follow exactly the same procedures as these, i.e., establishing the rules, providing practice situations with pictures, fading adult intervention, and evaluation for 1 week.

SUMMARY

The purpose of the present chapter is to describe self-care skills program development. This chapter addresses toileting, eating, dressing, grooming, health, and safety skills. Developmental sequences are provided for each content area. These sequences facilitate program planning for teachers as they conduct initial assessments.

Toilet training is discussed in traditional terms of habit or clock-regulated training, and rapid toilet training is described as well. A number of relevant toileting studies are reviewed. The major features of rapid toilet training include: providing more fluids, reinforcing the child for being dry, giving frequent opportunities to go to the bathroom, and cleaning up accidents by the child.

Eating is also discussed. Program guidelines for spoon feeding, chewing, swallowing, and using a straw are detailed. Special prosthetic devices and techniques of helping the physically handicapped individual acquire eating skills are suggested. These include devices such as built-up handles on spoons, plates with sides, and special cup holders with lips.

In a similar fashion, dressing and undressing skills are presented. Step by step guidelines are provided. Within these guidelines are also special techniques for working with physically involved persons. An explanation is given of how a backward-chaining technique can be used to teach taking off socks. This helps the child through all of the steps except the last one. At the last step the child practices with reinforcement the correct step in the taking-off-the-sock chain.

The importance of teaching safety and health skills is also discussed. A sample program for good health and safety skills, i.e., understanding the concept of poison, is presented.

This chapter, similar to those that follow, is concerned with demonstrating how principles of learning can be applied to self-care skills. Many of the major principles such as instructions, modeling, chaining, reinforcements, corrective feedback, etc. are presented in the sample programs. It is necessary for teachers to be capable of identifying which types of learning should be employed to develop specific self-care skills.

REFERENCES

Anderson, D., Hodson, G., & Jones, W. *Instructional programs for handicapped students.* Springfield, Ill.: Charles C. Thomas, 1975.

Azrin, N. H., & Armstrong, P. The "mini-meal"—A method for teaching eating skills to the profoundly retarded. *Mental Retardation,* 1973, *11*, 9–13.

Azrin, N. H., & Foxx, R. A rapid method of toilet training the institutionalized retarded. *Journal of Applied Behavior Analysis,* 1971, *4*, 89 99.

Azrin, N. H., & Wesolowski, M. Eliminating habitual vomiting in a retarded adult by poitive practice and self-correction. *Journal of Behavior Therapy and Experimental Psychiatry,* 1975, *6*(2), 145–148.

Barton, F. S., Guess, D., Garcia, E., & Baer, D. Improvement of retardates' mealtime behaviors by time-out procedures using multiple baseline techniques. *Journal of Applied Behavior Analysis,* 1970, *3*, 77–84.

Bass, G. *Sex Educational Informational Council of the United States.* Washington, D.C.: Department of Health, Education, & Welfare, 1972.

Berkowitz, S., Sherry, P., & Davis, B. Teaching self-feeding skills to profound retardates using reinforcement and fading procedures. *Behavior Therapy,* 1971, *2*, 62–67.

Certo, N., Schwartz, R., & Brown, L. Teaching severely handicapped students to ride a public bus. In H. Haring & L. Brown (eds.), *Teaching the severely handicapped* (Vol. II). New York: Grune & Stratton, 1976.

Christian, W., Holloman, S., & Lanier, C. L. An attendant operated feeding program for severely and profoundly retarded females. *Mental Retardation,* 1973, *11*, 35–37.

Copeland, M., Ford, L., & Solon, N. *Occupational therapy for mentally retarded children*. Baltimore, Md.: University Park Press, 1976.

Dayan, M. Toilet training retarded children in a state residential institution. *Mental Retardation*, 1964, *2*, 116–117.

Ellis, N. R. Toilet training the severely defective patient: A stimulus response reinforcement. *American Journal of Mental Deficiency*, 1963, *68*, 98–103.

Foxx, R., & Azrin, N. H. *Toilet training the retarded*. Champaign, Ill.: Research Press, 1973.

Groves, I., & Carroccio, D. A self-feeding program for the severely and profoundly retarded. *Mental Retardation*, 1971, *9*, 10–11.

Hamre-Nietupski, S., & Williams, W. Teaching selected sex education and social skills to severely handicapped students. In L. Brown, N. Certo & T. Crowner (eds.), *Papers and programs related to public school services for severely handicapped students* (Vol. VI). Madison, Wis., 1967.

Hamre-Nietupski, S., Williams, W. Family-life curriculum. In L. Brown, W. Williams, & T. Crowner (eds.), *A collection of papers and programs related to public school services for severely handicapped students* (vol. IV). Madison, Wis., 1977.

Henrikson, K., & Doughty, R. Decelerating undesirable mealtime behavior in a group of profoundly retarded boys. *American Journal of Mental Deficiency*, 1967, *72*, 42–44.

Horner, R. D., & Keilitz, I. Training mentally retarded adolescents to brush their teeth. *Journal of Applied Behavior Analysis*, 1975, *8*, 301–310.

Jackson, G., Johnson, C., Ackron, G., & Crowley, R. Food satiation as a procedure to decelerate vomiting. *American Journal of Mental Deficiency*, 1975, *80*, 223–227.

Lawson, P. *Special education curriculum for self-care*. Richmond, Va.: Virginia State Department of Education, 1965.

Mahoney, K., Van Wagenen, R., & Meyerson, L. Toilet training of normal and retarded children. *Journal of Applied Behavior Analysis*, 1971, *4*, 173–182.

Myers, D., Sinco, R., & Stalma, M. *The right-to-education child*. Springfield, Ill.: Charles C. Thomas, 1974.

O'Brien, F., & Azrin, N. J. Developing proper mealtime behaviors of the institutionalized retarded. *Journal of Applied Behavior Analysis*, 1972, *5*, 389–399.

O'Brien, F., Bugle, C., & Azrin, N. H. Training and maintaining a retarded child's proper eating. *Journal of Applied Behavior Analysis*, 1972, *5*, 67–72.

Osarchuk, M. Operant methods of toilet training of the severely and profoundly retarded: A review. *Journal of Special Education*, 1973, *7*, 423–437.

Rentfrow, R., & Rentfrow, D. Studies related to toilet training of the mentally retarded. *American Journal of Occupational Therapy*, 1969, *23*, 425–430.

Song, A., & Gandhi, R. An analysis of behavior during the acquisition and maintenance phase of self-spoon feeding skills of profound retardates. *Mental Retardation*, 1974, *12*(1), 25–28.

Treffry, D., Martin, G., Samuels, J., & Watson, O. Operant conditioning grooming behavior of severely retarded girls. *Mental Retardation*, 1970, *8*, 29–33.

Virginia State Department of Education. *Curriculum guide for training mentally retarded*. Richmond, Va., 1973.

Wehman, P. Maintaining oral hygiene skills in geriatric retarded women. *Mental Retardation*, 1974, *12*, 20.

Wehman, P., & Marchant, J. Reducing multiple problem behaviors of a profoundly handicapped child. *British Journal of Social and Clinical Psychology*, 1978, *17*, 149–152.

Zeiler, M., & Jervey, S. S. Development of behavior: Self-feeding. *Journal of Consulting and Clinical Psychology*, 1968, *32*, 164–168.

Chapter 9

Motor Development and Programming

Ferol Menzel, Ph.D.

Registered Occupational Therapist

The development of motor skills has been and continues to be an integral part of instructional programming for handicapped students. Indeed, basic motor skills are necessary prerequisites and/or components of self-care activities, play, and cognitive and academic tasks. The handicapped student who does not grasp will not gain independent dressing. The child who is immobilized by physical handicaps will be unable to engage in group play activities. The handicapped child whose physical disability restricts movement will have difficulty attaining the cognitive and social skills necessary for maximum independence.

Learning Goals

Upon completion of this chapter you should be able to answer these questions:

- How is motor skill defined?
- What is the difference between a discrete and a continuous motor task?
- What are the very early stages of gross motor task development?
- How do they relate to working with the young handicapped child?
- Write sample objectives for three gross motor skills.

- Why is it important for a physical or occupational therapist to be involved in motor skill programming?
- Why is the pregrasp sequence an important fine motor skill?
- Give a curriculum example of the pincer grasp and explain why this is a critical fine motor skill.
- Identify several functional fine motor skills which special education teachers should emphasize.
- What are three techniques which can inhibit or reduce spasticity?
- What role does positioning the physically handicapped child have in motor skill programming?

Planning the motor-development component of a curriculum requires knowledge of the child's current level of functioning in gross and fine motor skills. In addition, assessment of muscle tone and the child's patterns of movement are necessary. Third, some understanding of the relationship between motor skills as a means to the development of social, cognitive, and self-care skills is needed. Finally, when planning for the physically handicapped student, consultation with a physical and/or occupational therapist is necessary. Physical and occupational therapists are knowledgeable in motor development, appropriate assessment tools, medical precautions, adaptive equipment, and therapeutic techniques to facilitate motor training.

The purpose of this chapter is to provide general information on both gross and fine motor development. Included in this information are skill sequences, sample instructional objectives, and instructional strategies to assist in program development. At the end of the chapter is a glossary containing terms used by physicians, physical therapists, and occupational therapists when reporting on physically handicapped students. This information should prove useful for those required to read medical-educational reports of children with cerebral palsy or other physical disabilities.

The chapter begins with an overview of motor skills and an introduction to some of the terminology used by educators as well as therapists.

WHAT IS A MOTOR SKILL?

Motor tasks range from simple tasks such as standing up or sitting down to complex tasks such as playing the piano or playing tennis. To understand the motor domain some definitions are necessary.

First, motor implies movement. *Fine motor* refers to delicate, sensitive, accurate responses often involving eye-hand coordination (Singer, 1975). *Gross motor* refers to movement of the whole body in activities such as the broad jump, riding a tricycle, or playing football. This does not imply that accuracy or precision is not required in gross motor tasks. Riding a bicycle does require precision, balance, and coordination. But gross motor movement requires the large muscles or muscle groups of the legs, trunk, or shoulder as opposed to the small muscles of the hand.

In addition to being categorized as gross or fine, motor tasks may be discrete or continuous. *Discrete motor tasks* have an obvious beginning and an end, although they may contain a series of sequential movements which must be carefully coordinated.

Continuous motor tasks involve a series of movements, constantly flowing and adjusting. Cursive writing, walking a balance beam, or running the hurdles are examples of continuous activities. The distinction between discrete and continuous tasks is useful when considering an approach to task analysis. Continuous tasks require a certain amount of judgment, adjustment, and coordination on the part of the individual which may be difficult to capture in a task analysis. It may be advisable to first train on discrete tasks or a series of component tasks before combining them into a continuous task. For example, when training an infant to crawl, it may be advisable to train in pushing up onto all fours, maintaining all fours (hands and knees position), and weight shift on all fours before training in the actual reciprocal crawl sequence.

To this point, the term *task* has been used to refer to discrete and continuous movements. To apply the word *skill* to a motor task requires some additional conditions. Singer (1975) believes that for a motor skill to be present the individual must have acquired the motor task plus perform with speed, accuracy, form, and adaptability. Speed refers to the time in which a task is completed; accuracy is the precision with which the task is completed; form refers to the economy of effort; and adaptability refers to how the individual performs under varying conditions.

Motor training therefore should include both the acquisition of the motor task and the development of skill (speed, accuracy, form, adaptability) in that task. In Chapter 14, on vocational training, these two phases are referred to as acquisition and production, but the concept of task and skill development applies to self-care and recreational tasks as well as to vocational and motor tasks.

Finally, as will be seen in the section on gross motor development, balance, postural control, and proprioception are basic to the development of motor tasks and skills. The automatic responses of postural control provided through the nervous system by proprioceptors facilitate the development of balance and motor skills. These automatic responses are often lacking or diminished in the individual with cerebral palsy. The presence or absence of automatic postural control will determine the nature of the motor training.

GROSS MOTOR DEVELOPMENT

Gross Motor Skills

The end product of gross motor development for the handicapped infant during the first year of life is the attainment of the upright position. Once children have overcome the effects of gravity and developed balance, they are free to pursue the climbing, running, and jumping skills of the toddler and preschooler. Some handicapped infants spend many years struggling with the effects of gravity, and some seem never to adequately develop the balance basic to preschool skills. The developmental tasks discussed in this chapter and outlined in Table 9-1 will aid the teacher in planning a developmentally appropriate gross motor program.

Table 9-1   Gross Motor Development

Age range	Skill	Postural mechanism	Reference
0–4 months		Asymmetrical tonic neck reflex (ATNR) Foot grasp Moro response	Bobath
	Rolling	Nonsegmental rolling from back to side, often associated with the moro response	McGraw
		Turning face and extending neck so that shoulder lifts; head flexes to complete the roll	McGraw
	Crawling	Newborn remains in total flexion Spinal extension—head lifts up Spinal extension—back extends Attempted movement leads to pivot	McGraw
	Sitting	Head lags when child pulled to sitting position Head maintains alignment with body; legs remain inactive when child pulled to sitting position	
	Standing	Flexed position—child does not aid	McGraw; Peiper
	Locomotion	Automatic (reflex) stepping When child held under arms, stepping is inhibited; head erect	McGraw

4–8 months		Disappearance of:
		  ATNR
		  Foot grasp
		  Moro response
		Development of:
		  Labyrinthine righting
		  Optical righting
		  Landau response
		  Propping
		  Equilibrium reactions in prone and supine
			Bobath

	Rolling	Segmental rolling with no trunk extension until child is in prone; leg pulls over first, followed by shoulder Segmental rolling followed by legs flexing to assume either crawling or sitting position	McGraw
	Crawling	Assuming position with abdomen off the floor; rocking back and forth	McGraw
		Progression: right arm and left leg move together, followed by left arm and right leg	McGraw

	Sitting	Ventral push
		  Prone
		  All Fours	

Table 9–1 (Continued)

Age range	Skill	Postural mechanism	Reference
		Raising trunk and abducting one leg	
		Sitting	
		Dorsal push	
		Lateral position	
		Pushing against floor with one arm	
		Raising legs off floor slightly	
		Pushing to sitting position	McGraw
	Standing	When held under arms, child places feet on surface and pushes into extension; aligns pelvis and shoulders	
	Locomotion	When held under arms, child flexes knees but keeps feet on ground	
		When held by hand, child steps, flexing knees and lifting feet off the floor	McGraw
8–12 months		Primitive reflexes absent	
		Development of:	
		Propping	
		Body righting	
		Equilibrium reactions in prone, supine, sitting	Bobath
	Rolling	Sequence complete	McGraw
	Crawling	Most efficient means of mobility	White
	Sitting	Dorsal push to sitting most frequent	McGraw
		Protective responses now apparent to the front, side, and back	Milani-Comparetti & Godoni
		Falling to sitting from standing	Gesell
	Standing	Pulling to standing on furniture	
		Standing alone momentarily	Bayley
	Locomotion	Taking steps with both hands held	Bayley; McGraw
		Beginning to climb on furniture	
12–18 months		Increased equilibrium in prone, supine, sitting, kneeling, and standing	Bobath
	Rolling	Sequence complete	
	Crawling	Sequence complete	
	Sitting	Protective and equilibrium responses well established	Bobath
	Standing	Assuming standing independently from a quadraped position	McGraw
	Locomotion	Independent steps: high guard, high steps, toe grip, plantigrade	
		Heel-toe progression: normal base heel of forward foot touches when toe of back foot touches	McGraw

Table 9–1 (Continued)

Age range	Skill	Postural mechanism	Reference
		Lowering to sitting position	
		Vestibular stimulation	White
18–24 months		Equilibrium and protective reactions established	Bobath
	Rolling		
	Crawling	Sequence complete; used in play	McGraw
	Standing	Standing from sitting position to squat to upright	McGraw
	Locomotion	Variations on walking/running	
		Walking sideways, backwards	
		Walking stairs unaided, 2 ft per tread	
		Standing on one foot	
		Jumping from step	
		Walking on tiptoes	Bayley
24–36 months		Alternating feet on stairs	Gesell
		Jumping rope 3 in off the ground	R.I.S.E
		Throwing ball with stiff arm	Cratty
		Stopping rolling ball; catching large ball with extended arms	Cratty
36–48 months		Balancing on a walking board	Gesell
		Running, changing direction	Rural Infant Stimulation Environment (R.I.S.E.)
		Skipping 5 ft	R.I.S.E
		Dribbling a ball with direction	R.I.S.E.
		Riding a trike with skill	R.I.S.E.
		Kicking a ball	R.I.S.E.
		Climbing a ladder	R.I.S.E.
		Jumping rope	R.I.S.E.
		Throwing a ball, shifting body weight toward the throw	Cratty
		Catching ball, arms in front in vice like position	Cratty
48–60 months		Stepping forward with foot on opposite side of throwing arm when throwing a ball	Cratty
		Mature catching with arms at side	Cratty

A physical or occupational therapist should be involved in curriculum planning, especially when programming for a cerebral palsied child.

Newborn The newborn infant arrives with a set of primitive reflexes which will eventually disappear as the child's central nervous system develops. The newborn spends much of this time in a flexed posture (Figure 9-1a)—much as he

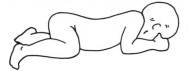

Figure 9-1a Totally flexed posture of the newborn (McGraw, 1945).

Figure 9-1b Moro response. Stimulus: Head movement or loud noise. Response: Extension of neck back, arms, and legs, followed by flexion.

Figure 9-1c Asymmetrical tonic neck reflex. Stimulus: Head turned to the side. Response: Arm and leg on the side the child is facing, extend. Arm and leg on the opposite side, flex.

Figure 9-1d Grasp Reflex. Stimulus: Object is placed on palm of hand firmly or under toes. Response: Fingers or toes grasp the object and do not release.

was in the womb. Activity at this age is general and random. The infant does, however, display reflex activity. Monnier (1970) defines a *reflex* as an automatic, purposeful, orderly response to a sensory stimulus. The reflexes in the newborn may be simple like the knee jerk, involving only one part of the body, or they may be complex, involving the entire body as in the moro response (Figure 9-1b). Table 9-2 outlines some of the reflexes present in the newborn. The Moro reflex, asymmetrical tonic neck reflex (Figure 9-1c), and hand and foot grasp (Figure 9-1d) are seen at birth and are a part of the flexed and asymmetrical pattern seen in the newborn (Fiorentino, 1963). These reflexes will disappear over the course of the first 4 months as the child matures and practices new patterns of movement. The occurrence of cerebral palsy may limit the child's ability to overcome these reflexes. The presence of abnormal muscle tone such

Table 9-2   Natural Course of Developmental Reactions

Type of reaction	1–4 weeks	2 months	4–6 months	7–12 months	12–14 months	2–3 years	3–5 years	After 5 years
Primitive								
Moro (startle)	+	+	=	+				—
Asymmetrical TNR	+	+	=	+			+	
Grasp reflex	+	+	=	+				
Sucking reflex	+	=	=	+				
Neck righting	+	+	=	=	+			
Mature								
Labyrinthine righting of the head		+	+	Partly and increasingly inhibited by optional righting reactions				=
Landau reaction			+	+	+			
Propping (parachute) reaction			+	+	+	+	+	+
Body righting on body				+	=	=	=	
Equilibrium reactions								
Prone			+	+	+	+	+	+
Supine				=	+	+	+	+
Sitting				=	+	+	+	+
Kneeling					+	+	+	+
Seesaw reaction					+	+	+	+
Standing					=	+	+	+

Key: + = Present
     = = Inconsistent or weak
    — = Not present

Source: Bobath and Bobath (1972, p. 52).

as spasticity or athetosis will alter the child's ability to use his or her body in a coordinated fashion. Thus the teacher and therapist must consider the following factors when programming for the physically handicapped child:

1 Functional gross motor skills (head control, sitting, etc.)
2 Present abnormal reflexes
3 Muscle tone (spastic, athetoid, hypotonic)

Table 9-1 outlines normal development by age and should be helpful in understanding how the various gross motor skills interact. However, for the purpose of developing skill sequences each skill will be discussed separately.

Rolling   The first rolling to occur may be part of the reflex activity discussed above. The child's body will simply flop over in a "nonsegmental roll" (Figure 9-2a). Slightly later he or she may extend the neck and back to start rolling, flexing the legs to complete the turn (Figure 9-2b). This type of rolling is often seen in the child with cerebral palsy and should not be encouraged. By the time normal children approach 6 months of age they begin a segmental rolling (Figure 9-2c). It is not always obvious how this is initiated (McGraw, 1945), but

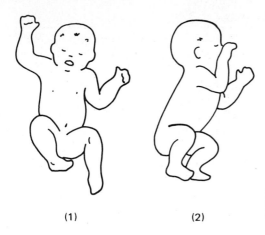

(1)   (2)

Figure 9-2a Nonsegmental roll. Head, body and legs all move together. (McGraw, 1945).

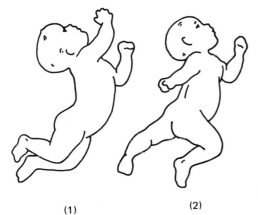

(1)   (2)

Figure 9-2b Roll with neck and trunk extension. To be discouraged in the Cerebral Palsy child. (McGraw, 1945).

(1)   (2)

Figure 9-2c Segmental roll with leg moving over the body first, followed by pelvis, trunk, shoulder, and head.

usually children pull one leg over their bodies, followed by the trunk, shoulders, and head. Once children are over on their stomachs (prone position), their heads lift up (extend) and they rest on their elbows or forearms (Figure 9-3). The ability to hold the head up and look around is one of the first victories against gravity. This position may also serve as a starting point for crawling.

Initial attempts at rolling in the normal child may seem automatic and without a goal, but as the child progresses, rolling becomes the first means of moving about the environment at ages 4 to 6 months.

Rolling is important because it (1) is a starting point for crawling, (2) is the child's initial attempt at rotation or segmented movements, and (3) can provide the child's first means of movement in the environment. The therapist should encourage segmental rolling. An objective for rolling might be as follows:

> When placed on his or her back and given the command, "Roll over" (or a toy to go after), the student will roll segmentally, starting with legs and hips, to the stomach and maintain the prone-on-elbows position for 10 seconds 85 percent of the time on 4 consecutive days.

Crawling Progress toward crawling requires more time than rolling and involves sequential components. As was pointed out previously, infants begin in a flexed position when placed on their stomachs (see Figure 9-1a). By the age of 4 months, they can lift their heads, extend their backs and legs (see Figure 9-3). At this point they may move their arms and legs in some rhythmic movements which result in a pivot turn on the stomach. The pivot is not, however, well-coordinated or purposeful. As indicated previously, the child's assuming the prone-on-elbows position and then prone-on-straight-arms (see Figure 9-3c) may be the first step in a sequence toward crawling.

Normal infants then spend a great deal of time learning to assume the all-fours or crawl position. In order to do this they must overcome the influence

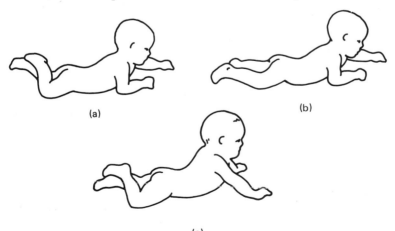

(a)

(b)

(c)

Figure 9-3 (a) and (b) Infant in extended prone-on-elbows position. (McGraw); (c) infant in extended prone-on-straightarms.

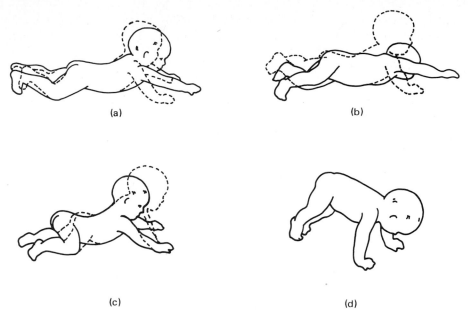

(a)   (b)

(c)   (d)

Figure 9-4   Influence of symmetrical tonic neck reflex. (McGraw)

of the symmetrical tonic neck reflex (Figure 9-4). They begin by pulling their legs up under them as if to crawl (Johnston, 1976), but if their legs push up into the crawl position, their arms collapse. Likewise, if their arms push up, their legs collapse. Normal children will spend 1 to 2 months rocking back and forth like this until they can coordinate their efforts and maintain the crawl position. The rocking behavior is often seen in the cerebral palsied child, who, rather than working through it to develop a reciprocal crawl, may bunny hop as a means of mobility (Finnie, 1975). The bunny hop (Figure 9-5a) and "W" sitting (Figure 9-5b) should be discouraged if possible while attempting to train in the reciprocal pattern. Assuming the crawl position is an example of a discrete skill composed of many subcomponents which must work together. Head, arms, trunk, hips, and legs must coordinate to accomplish this skill.

Normal children can also assume the crawl position from sitting (Figure 9-6). They simply place their hands down on the floor to one side, rotating the trunk, and lift their hips, placing knees on the floor. Either approach to the crawl position is acceptable. The second approach has the advantage of encouraging trunk rotation in the process and may help to avoid the "W" sitting.

Once the normal child assumes the all-fours position the reciprocal crawl begins: right hand and left foot forward followed by left hand and right foot forward. One or two steps may be taken initially before the child collapses. The reciprocal crawl quickly becomes the child's most efficient means of mobility, replacing rolling. By 8 to 10 months (McGraw, 1945) the child can move fluidly from floor to sitting to crawling.

Crawling is important therefore as (1) a means of mobility, (2) an

(1)   (2)

Figure 9-5*a*   Position for bunny hop.

Figure 9-5*b*   W sitting (Finnie).

opportunity to develop trunk rotation, (3) an opportunity for further development of righting reactions (antigravity responses), (4) a first attempt at
reciprocal movement necessary for walking.

An objective for crawling might be as follows:

The student will assume the all-fours position from sitting and crawl
reciprocally to a toy placed on the floor 3 feet away 90 percent of the time
on 3 consecutive days.

This objective could also be broken down into two parts, the first requiring
the child to assume the position, and the second requiring the reciprocal crawl.
Training the child to crawl has become a focal point of controversy

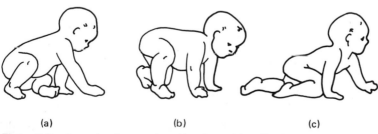

(a)   (b)   (c)

Figure 9-6   Assuming the crawl position from sitting. (McGraw)

(Neman, Roos, McCanns, Menolascino, & Heal, 1975). A teacher and/or therapist must use judgment when choosing motor objectives. If a child has progressed to the walking stage or has developed a functional means of mobility, it may not be necessary to train for crawling. Functional skills as well as developmental progression must be considered in planning a program for a handicapped child. There is no clear-cut evidence that training or retraining in crawling is beneficial to a child who has progressed beyond this stage (Cratty, 1969).

Sitting The development of sitting closely parallels the development of crawling. Mastery of independent sitting may preceed crawling by 1 or 2 months in the normal child.

Infants have no sitting ability. When placed in a sitting position, they sit with rounded back, bent at the waist, and head down (Figure 9-7a, 2). When pulled to sitting, their heads fall back (lag) (Figure 9-7a, 1) and they do not assist in pulling up. By the end of 4 months infants will sit with rounded backs, but their heads will stay in line with their bodies (Figure 9-7b). This may well be an initial objective for training a severely handicapped child in sitting.

By 6 to 8 months (Touwen, 1976) the child can sit alone for 3 minutes. The

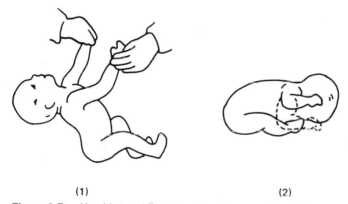

(1)   (2)

Figure 9-7a   Head lag and flexed position of the newborn infant.

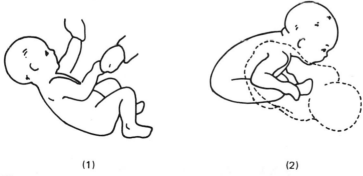

(1)   (2)

Figure 9-7b   Four-month-old with head and body in alignment.

child does this by first propping him- or herself up with the hands (Figure 9-8a, 1) and eventually freeing the hands to hold objects and play (Figure 9-8a, 2). The final objective of a sitting program is this independent "hands-free" level.

By 6 months the infant will have also adopted one of two ways to get to the sitting position. McGraw (1945) refers to these as the ventral push and the dorsal push.

The ventral push is illustrated in Figure 9-8b. Children start on their tummies (prone position), raise up to the all-fours position, rotate their trunks, and sit down, pushing themselves into position with their arms.

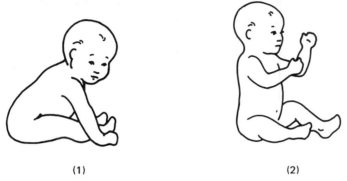

(1)   (2)

Figure 9-8a   Early sitting with propping and hands-free position.

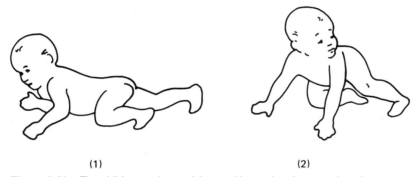

(1)   (2)

Figure 9-8b   The child assuming a sitting position, using the ventral push.

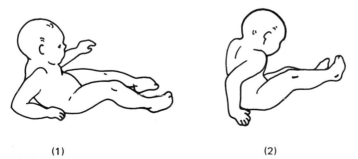

(1)   (2)

Figure 9-8c   The child assuming a sitting position, using the dorsal push.

The dorsal push is illustrated in Figure 9-8c. The child starts on the back (supine), rolls to the side (lateral position), pushes against the floor with one arm, raising one leg (opposite of the pushing arm) off the floor. The child pushes up to the sitting position using arm and trunk control. Children over 2 years are able to get up to sitting using a modified dorsal push requiring less of a lateral movement and more of a "sit-up" movement.

In the normal developmental progression children will be able to sit with arms propped before assuming the sitting position as previously described. The hands free sitting and pushing up to sitting come at about the same time. Sitting independently and assuming the sitting position require a similar degree of balance and trunk stability resulting in their parallel development.

The hands-free sitting is an important milestone in the child's development. Not only is he or she free to play, but finger feeding rapidly develops as the child becomes comfortable in sitting. The beginning of effective hand use therefore corresponds to the development of sitting.

The development of sitting is important for (1) continued development toward the upright position, (2) further development of balance and equilibrium to free the hands for play and functional activities.

A sample objective for sitting is as follows:

When placed in sitting on a mat, the student will maintain sitting (hands propping) for 3 minutes, keeping his or her back at least at a 45° angle to the floor for 3 consecutive days.

Standing   Newborns can "walk" across an examining table minutes after birth using a reflex known as the *stepping reflex*. This reflex disappears quickly (Figure 9-9a), and not until children are 6 to 8 months (McGraw, 1945) can they stand supported (Figure 9-9b). Between 9 and 12 months (Touwen, 1976) children can pull themselves up to their knees at a chair or couch (Figure 9-10a). By 12 months they can pull to standing by going from kneeling to half-kneeling to standing (Figure 9-10b). At this point, children can crawl or climb up on the furniture, greatly enhancing their mobility. In terms of preparation for standing, this sequence is often used by therapists:

1   Kneeling at a chair
   a   Independent kneeling
   b   Stepping-in kneeling
2   Half-kneeling at a chair
   a   Independent half-kneeling
3   Pulling to a stand from half-kneeling
4   Standing at chair
   a   Movement in standing with assistance, particularly weight shifting
5   Assuming standing independently

These skills could be incorporated into a training skill sequence, developed with the assistance of a therapist. A sample objective for Skill 1 is as follows:

(1)   (2)

Figure 9-9a   Newborn standing; no weight bearing.

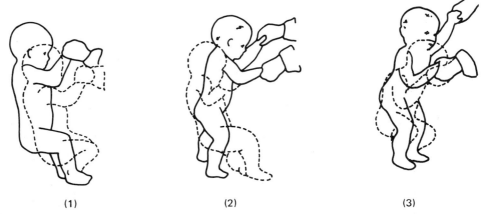

(1)   (2)   (3)

Figure 9-9b   Supported standing between 8 and 12 months.

The student will pull up on his or her knees at a 12-inch chair and maintain the kneeling position independently for 2 minutes for 3 consecutive days.

The fifth skill in the above sequence, assuming standing independently, is approached by the nonhandicapped child in two ways. First, the child just walking will assume standing by bending at the waist (legs straight) and pushing up from the floor (Figure 9-10c). By 3 years the toddler can go from sitting to standing as shown in Figure 9-10d. The child who continues to require furniture or pushes to standing from the floor may be experiencing balance problems and may require special training.

Locomotion   Once the child begins to pull to standing, walking is not far away. The cruising (sideway walking) around furniture usually precedes independent walking. It provides the child with an opportunity to practice the balance and weight shift (from foot to foot) required to walk. At the same time,

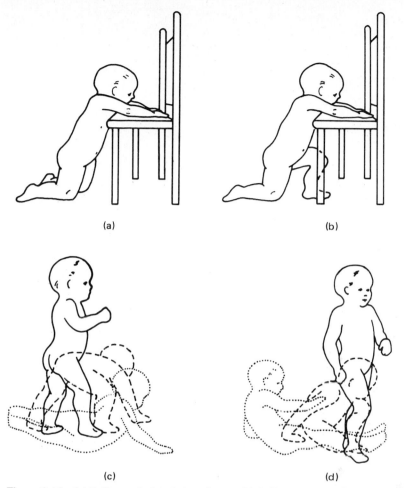

Figure 9-10 (a) Pulling up to the chair on knees. (b) Pulling up to chair in half-kneeling position. (c) Pushing up to standing, 12 to 15 months. (d) Assuming standing independently.

parents can usually encourage walking by holding the child's hands and slowly fading their assistance. As the child develops balance, and trunk, hips, and legs coordinate, he or she will begin the first independent steps. The nonhandicapped child often takes one or two steps, falls, gets up, and repeats the process.

Posture during the first steps includes hands up in front or "high guard" and a wide-base (legs-apart) gait (Figure 9-11). As balance develops through practice, the arms begin to lower and the legs move together. Just as the infants use arms for balance during early attempts at sitting, they use arms for balance during early attempts at walking. Parents should not interfere with this posture until balance is established.

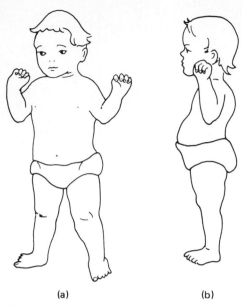

(a)   (b)

Figure 9-11   Child in high guard and wide base gait.

As coordination improves, the child adopts the mature heel-toe walk around 15 to 20 months. McGraw (1945) describes this as follows: "The heel of the forward foot strikes the surface as the back foot is raised on the toes" (p. 82). The final stage of walking involves the synchronous swinging of each arm in movements with the opposite leg. This occurs at about 2 years (McGraw, 1945).

It is especially important to include a physical therapist in programming when training for walking. The child with cerebral palsy may have congenital hip, knee, or foot deformities which will interfere with walking. Adaptive equipment such as walkers may be helpful but should be used only under the guidance of a therapist. Training a child to walk with abnormal patterns may result in problems which will prohibit walking at a later date.

A sample skill sequence for walking may include the following:

1   Maintaining standing
2   Walking with two hands held
3   Walking with one hand held
4   Independent steps
　　a   Hands in high guard; wide-base gait
　　b   Hands in medium guard
　　c   Hands in low guard; narrow-base gait
5   Heel-toe gait
6   Heel-toe gait with reciprocal arm swing

A sample instructional objective for Step 4 in the above sequence may be as follows:

The student will take three independent steps from chair to teacher, without falling (hands may be in high guard) 90 percent of the time on 3 consecutive days.

Equilibrium Throughout the first year of life, the normal child is developing equilibrium, or balancing responses. These responses, along with the righting reactions, assure that the child will be able to maintain and/or regain the upright position. The Bobaths (1972) suggest the following sequence for equilibrium development:

1 Equilibrium in prone and supine (develops as the child learns to sit)
2 Equilibrium in sitting (develops as the child learns to pull to standing
3 Equilibrium in standing (develops as the child learns to walk)
4 Equilibrium in walking
5 Equilibrium in running

Figure 9-12 illustrates the equilibrium reactions in sitting and standing. These responses are complex, allowing the body automatically to adjust to changes in position. The child under 2 years of age will struggle to maintain the upright position even when turned upside-down in play. Once equilibrium and righting reactions are established around the age of 2 years, vestibular stimulation becomes fun and the upside-down position becomes a common occurrence in the life of a toddler.

Equilibrium responses are subtle responses to changes in position. When there is a sudden, unexpected change, the adult relies on protective extension (Figure 9-13) of the arms to save him from injury. The protective responses begin to develop between 4 and 6 months (Peiper, 1963). The propping seen in sitting is a forerunner of this response. Initially children thrust their arms out forward, then learn to protect laterally (to the side), and then back.

Variations on Walking Espenchade and Eckert (1967) outline several gross motor activities which develop from walking as children grow in strength, coordination, and control. Walking sideways and backward, for example, occurs at about 16 months. *Running* begins at 18 months but becomes more refined as heel-toe walking develops. Running in a straight line is possible between 2 and 3 years of age, but running with abrupt starts, stops, and turns comes after 3 years of age. The ability to run faster and for longer distances depends on the child's increased strength and body size. As legs grow and leverage improves, running speed will increase (Espenchade & Eckert, 1967).

Climbing Stairs Stair climbing starts when the child can crawl. Ascending stairs in the upright position begins between 12 and 23 months in the normal child (Bayley, 1969). Initially the child requires two feet per step rather than the alternating stair climbing typical of an adult. As the child develops balance, particularly one-foot balance, the alternating step will occur. In the normal child

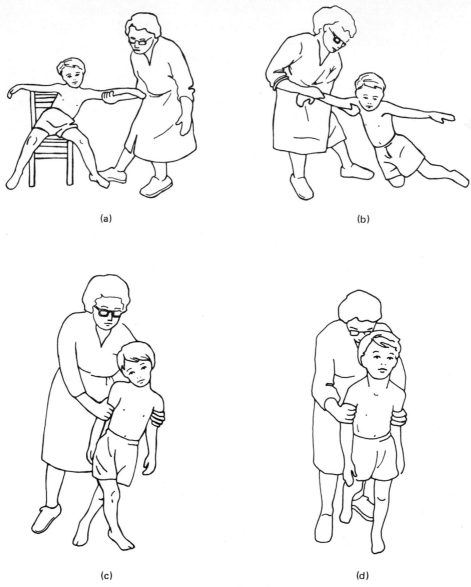

(a)   (b)

(c)   (d)

Figure 9-12 Equilibrium reactions in sitting and standing.

alternating stair climbing begins at about 30 months (Bayley, 1969). Espenchade and Eckert (1967) suggest the following sequence of stair-climbing skills:

  1 Ascend stairs in upright position, two feet per step, holding on to rail. Descend stairs crawling.

Figure 9-13 Protective extension.

2 Ascend stairs, alternate feet with support. Descend stairs in upright position holding on to support, two feet per step.

3 Ascend stairs, alternate feet, no support. Descend stairs, alternate feet with support.

4 Descend stairs, alternate feet without support.

Skipping This is a skill acquired rather late in a child's development. By 36 months a child begins to gallop (Espenchade & Eckert, 1967), combining a hop with the same foot always leading. Reciprocal skipping follows at about 4 to 5 years (Guttridge, 1939). Skipping involves the reciprocal pattern of the walk plus elevation of the hop. The component skills require a degree of coordination and balance before skipping can occur.

Jumping Figures 9-14 and 9-15 illustrate two types of jumping seen in the young child. The jumping in Figure 9-14 is a logical extension of stair descent. It starts with a one-foot takeoff and eventually goes to a two-feet-together takeoff. Hillebrandt, Rarick, Glassow, and Carns (1961) emphasize the importance of head position and the righting reflexes in jumping. In addition the cooperation of arms as "stabilizers" and "brakes" is important. The child who has difficulty with balance in the static upright position or whose righting reactions are not functional will not accomplish jumping skills.

The development of the broad jump follows the stair jump. Bayley (1969) suggests the following sequence for jumping and hopping on one foot:

Figure 9-14 Illustrations of the inability of the very young child (Willie) to jump from two feet simultaneously. Rows 1 and 2, stepping off an elevation at 17 months of age. Row 3, momentary suspension during a jump made at 18 months. Row 4, signs of incipient two-footed jumping at 21 months. Observe beginning shoulder girdle and arm retraction. (From F. A. Hellebrandt, G. L. Rarick, R. Glassow, and M. L. Carns, "Physiological Analysis of Basic Motor Skills. I. Growth and Development of Jumping." American Journal of Physical Medicine, 40:14–25, 1961. By permission of the publisher, Williams and Wilkins.)

Figure 9-15 Row 1, the earliest jump from a two-footed take-off observed in David at 32 months of age. Row 2, standing broad jump at the age of 3 years. Note the same shoulder girdle and arm retraction seen in Figure 16. (From F. A. Hellebrandt, G. L. Rarick, R. Glassow, and M. L. Carns, "Physiological Analysis of Basic Motor Skills. I. Growth and Development of Jumping." American Journal of Physical Medicine, 40:14–25, 1961. By permission of the publisher, Williams and Wilkins.)

1   Broad jump, 14 to 24 inches—25 to 30 months
2   Jump over a string 2 inches high—24 to 30 months
3   Broad jump, 24 to 24 inches—28 to 30 months
4   Hop on one foot two or more hops—30+ months
5   Jump over string 8 inches high—28 to 30 months

It is important to understand that training in jumping and hopping will provide the teacher with an opportunity to improve the child's balance and coordination as well as provide the student with age-appropriate play skills for activities such as jump rope, hop scotch, or games adapted for recreational purposes.

Kicking   The ability to kick a ball develops as one-foot balance develops. Initially a child may "kick" by simply walking into a ball, as Gesell described (Gesell, 1940). However, by 2 years the child can lift his or her foot off the ground. Eventually the kick involves a back swing and follow-through with the body leaning forward (Deach, 1951).

The development of jumping, hopping, stair climbing, kicking, and skipping reflect the child's continued development of balance in the upright posture, coordination of body parts, and the development of skill components (speed, accuracy, form, and adaptability). Stair climbing has a clear, functional value for the handicapped child. Is there any value associated with training for jumping, hopping, etc.? As stated above, many of these skills are important for the further development of balance, coordination, and recreational skills. However, the teacher in conjunction with the adaptive physical education instructor and therapist must sometimes make judgments regarding priorities. For the profoundly retarded child who does not learn to walk until he or she is 5 or 6 years old, working toward skipping may not be practical. Choosing a lower-level skill as part of a play program, however, may be appropriate. Once again motor skills must be chosen carefully to be functionally as well as developmentally appropriate.

Gross motor development presents some interesting dilemmas for educators and therapists. So much of the early development leading up to walking and the upright position is dependent on a combination of central nervous system maturation and practice. Much of the early literature on motor development refers to the "unfolding," or maturation basic to motor development. Once motor development progresses past the preschool stage where balance in the upright position is established, skill development becomes very task-specific. Sage (1977) suggests that past a certain stage there is no general motor ability. Research has shown that a motor activity requires balance, coordination, and response time specific to that task (Fleishman, 1972). Thus, training for specific skills related to performance of an activity should be more beneficial than a generalized motor program designed to "enhance" motor development. Research has shown that when it comes to learning higher-level motor skills, "individual differences in initial proficiency have relatively little relation to ultimate proficiency" (Sage, 1977, p. 386). The reader is cautioned to remember that this statement refers to nonhandicapped individuals who have developed some basic abilities in balance and equilibrium. It should serve as a reminder, however, that programming without specific functional objectives may not be productive.

Sample Instructional Objectives

The preceding section of this chapter outlines normal gross motor development and lists selected skill sequences and objectives. There are several manuals which outline objectives that may be useful to teachers and therapists. These include *Infant Stimulation Curriculum, Developmental Programming for Infants and Young Children, The Behavioral Characteristics Progression (BCP) Observation Booklet*, and *Rural Infant Stimulation Environment* (R.I.S.E.). There are not, however, many tasks analyses of motor skills available. At this time the *Teaching Research Curriculum for Moderately and Severely Handicapped* is the only published attempt at task-analyzing motor skills. The task analyses included in this section have not been field-tested and are therefore subject to modification. Chapter 3 presents guidelines for the development of task analysis (TA) when new TAs are necessary.

As was previously indicated, pulling to standing is an important milestone in the development of the upright position. The sequence suggested in normal development includes:

1 Pulls to kneeling at furniture
2 Pulls to half-kneeling at furniture
3 Pulls to standing at furniture
4 Pushes up from floor to standing without assistance

An objective for Item 3 would be as follows:

When placed in a kneeling position, facing a chair, the student will, on command, stand up and maintain standing for 2 minutes.

Prerequisites for this skill include maintenance of kneeling at a chair for 30 seconds.

The task analysis follows. The student

1 Maintains kneeling for 5 seconds with hands on the chair
2 Flexes right hip to 90°
3 Places right foot flat on the floor (one-half-kneel position)
4 Shifts weight to right side (teacher should be able to put one finger under the left knee)
5 Extends right leg, pushing the child into the upright position
6 Shifts weight to extended arms, leaning body forward slightly
7 Extends left leg

   8   Places left foot flat on the floor
   9   Distributes weight from arms to legs
10   Maintains standing   5 seconds
                              10 seconds
                              20 seconds
                              30 seconds
                              60 seconds
                             120 seconds

Independent sitting is an important goal if hands are to be used functionally. Children who must support themselves with their hands will not have them free to play, eat, or dress. A sequence for establishing independent floor sitting would be as follows. The student

1   Maintains supported sitting, both hands on the floor
2   Maintains supported sitting, one hand on the floor
3   Maintains supported sitting, both hands on the knees
4   Maintains supported sitting, one hand on knees
5   Maintains independent sitting, balance undisturbed
6   Maintains independent sitting, balance disturbed forward
7   Maintains independent sitting, balance disturbed to the side
8   Maintains independent sitting, balance disturbed backward
9   Maintains independent sitting during play

A task analysis for a skill involving durations will look slightly different from a sequential skill. The following is an example of a task analysis for independent sitting. The objective is:

The student will maintain an unsupported sitting position (hands off the floor), head in line with the body, and hips at a 70 to 90° angle, for 60 seconds, 90 percent of the time for 3 consecutive days.

Task Analysis: The student

1   Maintains ring-sitting (or long-sitting), hands on knees for 10 seconds
2   Lifts right hand off right knee for 5 seconds, maintaining balance
3   Lifts left hand off left knee for 5 seconds, maintaining balance
4   Maintains both hands off knees, touching the floor only to stop a fall
        5 seconds
        10 seconds
        15 seconds
        30 seconds
        60 seconds

Rolling from back to tummy (supine to prone) is an important milestone in development and one which many children with cerebral palsy never accomplish. Some children with cerebral palsy learn to roll but in an abnormal pattern which limits higher-level skills. The following task analysis incorporates the normal sequence of rolling and may require a great many therapeutic techniques to accomplish it. In the next section on instructional strategies, an explanation of how to couple the task analysis with therapy procedures will be given. For the moment only the normal sequence is presented. This may not be the only sequence for rolling. The movement may initiate at the head with remaining body segments following. The rolling sequence is an acceptable, normal pattern, adopted from McGraw (1945).

1   Left leg flexes at the hip and knee
2   Left leg moves over the body to the right
3   Head turns to the right
4   Right arm reaches above the head (optional)
5   Right leg maintains extension
6   Left arm reaches across the body to the right; wrist remains in neutral position
7   Head flexes off the mat
8   Body rolls to the right
9   Head extends after sidelying
10   Left arm contacts the floor
11   Right arm contacts the floor
12   Student assumes prone on elbow (fisted hands are ok)
13   Left leg extends
14   Student maintains prone-on-elbows position at a 45° angle, 10 seconds (15 seconds, etc)

FINE MOTOR DEVELOPMENT

Fine Motor Skills

Studies of normal development provide special education teachers with skill sequences appropriate for training the handicapped. Table 9-3 outlines the normal development of fine motor skills, the age range, and the reference from which the item was taken. This checklist or commercially available assessment tools, such as the Bayley infant scales, Developmental Programming for Infants and Young Children, or the R.I.S.E., may be used to pinpoint the students current fine motor skills.

It is important during assessment and training to be aware of the interaction between fine and gross motor skills. For example, Touwen (1976) points out that the development of walking and fine pincer grasp are highly correlated. They are likely to occur at about the same time. Therefore, attempting to train a child who is just beginning to sit to pick up a raisin using pincer grasp would be inappropriate and inefficient use of training time. Likewise, one should attempt to train following the normal developmental sequence before moving out of sequence.

Table 9-3 Fine Motor Development

Age range	Skill	Reference
0–4 months: pregrasp period	Eyes converge on hand and fixate 5–10 seconds	White, Castle, & Held
	Regard for objects 6 in away Frequent regard for hands Hands fisted Immediate interest in objects Accurate swipe with one hand (forward and downward movement); no grasp	White, Castle, & Held Bruner
	Raising hand to object and shifting visual regard back and forth to object Hands predominantly open	White, Castle, & Held Bayley Towuen
	Bilateral hand activity Hands clasped at midline (arms extended) Immediate visual regard of object	White, Castle, & Held
	Hands raised in midline Midline activity—fingering clothes, playing with fingers	White, Castle, & Held
	First crude grasp—fumbling at object Possibly opening hand in anticipation of contact	White, Castle, & Held
	Accurate reach; successful palmer grasp in supported sitting, supine Bringing object to mouth	Bayley White, Castle, & Held Touwen
4–8 months: discovery of the effects of child's own action (Flavell)	Palmar grasp Radial grasp Scissors grasp Picking up one toy at a time; repeating motor activities such as banging, mouthing, fingering, shaking Unilateral reach Pronation-supination of forearm Dropping object rather than placing it down Transferring objects from hand to hand Using hands in cooperation, i.e., retaining two cubes No more overreaching	Gesell Bayley Touwen Fenson Connolly Bayley
8–12 months: motor skills used in purposeful goal-directed play (Flavell)	Inferior pincer grasp Pointing Pincer grasp Simple relational play: beginning to combine two objects such as spoon and cup, blocks and cup; attempting to stack blocks, scoop, place, and replace Releasing toys on purpose	 Fenson

Table 9-3 (Continued)

Age range	Skill	Reference
	Beginning means-end play, i.e., pulling string to obtain toy	Bayley
12–18 months: motor skills used in trial and error exploration	Accomodative reactional acts: combining objects appropriately based on physical or functional similarities	Fenson
	Smooth and accurate pincer grasp and release which enables exploration of small objects	White
	Motor skills used as a means to play and functional skills, as reflected in typical assessment items:	
	Placing 1 in peg in hole	
	Turning page of book	
	Removing lid of a box	
	Building block tower	
	Placing forms in form board	Bayley
	Holding crayon; scribbling	Bayley
	Finger feeding	Rural Infant Stimulation Environment (R.I.S.E.)
	Drinking from a cup	R.I.S.E.
	Attempting use of spoon	R.I.S.E.
18–24 months: symbolic play (Flavell)	Refinement of basic fine motor skills of grasp and release to develop the use of tools; dexterity, control and precision	
	Typical functional or play skills, as found on assessments:	
	Holding crayons, scribbling, imitating horizontal line	
	Attaining toy with stick	Bayley
	Replacing body parts on doll	
	Placing pegs in hole	
	Lining up blocks for train or tower	R.I.S.E.
	Beginning to develop hand preference	
24–36 months	Pouring from a container	
	Copying + and *H*	
	Placing forms on formboard	Bayley
36–48 months	Cutting with scissors	
	Copying circle	
	Stringing beads	
	Copying *T*	
	Isolated finger movements	Bayley Gesell

Pregrasp Sequence   Profoundly retarded individuals with cerebral palsy may well be at the pregrasp level of development. Programming for them would require training toward the target behavior of a crude palmar grasp. White, Castle, and Held (1967) have described the normal child's progression toward grasp during the first 4 months of life.

The pregrasp sequence begins with infants looking at (regarding) the objects around them as well as their hands. Newborns, when lying on their backs, tend to keep their arms bent (flexed), and hands fisted, eliminating the possibility of extending their arms and hands into the line of vision. As infants' general activity moves toward extension, arms will begin to reach and will come into the line of vision.

Once both object and hands are visible to children, they will begin to reach for or swipe at an object suspended over their heads. Their hands will remain fisted but there will be an accurate approach to the object. During this process children attempt to coordinate their visual and motor efforts by constantly looking back and forth from object to hand.

An objective at this point might be:

When lying on his or her back, the student will regard and make contact with an object suspended 12 inches above the nose 90 percent of the time on 4 consecutive days (Figure 9-16).

If the child is blind the objective might be:

When lying on his or her back, the student will make contact (hands fisted) with a music box (or rattle) suspended 12 inches above the head 90 percent of the time on 4 consecutive days.

Although the above objectives involve rudimentary skills, they may be too difficult for a severely handicapped child. Short-term goals involving tracking, scanning, and auditory localization may be more appropriate. The following three objectives were developed for a profoundly retarded student with cerebral palsy:

Figure 9-16 Pregrasp reach

Given an object placed before student and moved horizontally to the left or right, the student will track the object 80 percent of the time for 3 consecutive days.

Given a visual stimulus of two objects placed 16 inches apart at midline on a lap tray, the student will alternately look at the objects two times within 5 seconds when given the verbal cue "Look," 80 percent of the time for 3 consecutive days.

Given an auditory stimulus for 3 seconds, the student will look in the direction of the sound within 5 seconds 80 percent of the time for 3 consecutive days (head must turn at least 45°).

Once children have accomplished reach with a fisted hand, their hands remain open and the flexed posture is less restricting to movement. They will then begin to engage in bilateral activity with the hands coming together at the center (midline) of the body. When an object is placed in children's hands, the grasp reflex may still assist them in holding onto the object, but they will now move their arms to the midline in a clapping motion. In addition, midline activity will involve playing with fingers or fingering clothing or objects (White, Castle, & Held, 1967). A sample objective at this stage might be:

The student, when lying on his back, will contact an object suspended 6 to 12 inches over his chest, with both hands (hands open), 90 percent of the time on 4 consecutive days.

As children approach 4 months, muscle tone and movement patterns will have shifted from the flexed posture of the newborn (see Figure 9-1a) to the extended posture (see Figure 9-3) as seen in prone-on-elbows. This shift corresponds with increased control of extension needed to open the hand and grasp. At 4 months infants can extend their arms to reach, open their hands, and grasp an object using palmar grasp (see Figure 9-16). An objective for the terminal behavior in this sequence would be:

When lying on her back, the student will reach for, grasp (palmar grasp), and retain for 3 seconds, an object suspended over her chest, 90 percent of the time on 4 consecutive days.

Four to Eight Months   The child's ability to use his hands improves rapidly during the 4- to 8-month period. Palmar grasp develops into radial grasp where thumb, index, and middle fingers rather than the child's entire hand are involved in grasping. Finally scissors grasp develops (Figure 9-17). The hand is almost flat on the table, the thumb pushing the object toward the index finger. The scissors grasp allows children to pick up small objects such as Cheerios, raisins, and crackers.

	Sequential Development of Prehension	
	Age (weeks)	Description
	12	Reflective, ulnar side strongest; no reaching before eye contact.
	16	Mouthing of fingers and mutual fingering; retains object placed in hand; no visually directed grasp until both hand and object in field of vision.
	20	Primitive squeeze, raking; fingers only, no thumb nor palm involved; immediate approach and grasp on sight.
	24	Palmar or squeeze grasp; still no thumb participation; eyes and hands combine in joint action.
	28	Radial-palmar or whole-hand grasp; radial side stronger; thumb begins to adduct; unilateral approach; transfer from one hand to the other.
	32	Inferior scissors or superior-palm grasp; known as monkey grasp because thumb is adducted, not opposed.
	36	Radial-digital or inferior forefinger grasp; fingers on radial side provide pressure on object; thumb begins to move toward opposition by pressing toward PIP joint of forefinger; finer adjustment of digits.
	40	Inferior-pincer grasp; thumb moves toward DIP joint of forefinger; poking finger, inhibition of other four digits; beginning of voluntary release.
	44	Neat pincer or forefinger grasp with slight extension of wrist.
	52	Opposition or superior-forefinger grasp; wrist extended and deviated to ulnar side for efficient prehension; release smooth for large objects, clumsy for small objects.

Figure 9-17 Reprinted from Erhardt, R. P., Sequential levels in development of prehension. *American Journal of Occupational Therapy* 28 (10), 1974.

The child's reach and grasp has become accurate by this age, but release continues to need refinement. At 4 to 8 months the child has the ability to voluntarily release, but objects tend to be dropped rather than placed on the table.

The child develops an additional important skill at this time. During play the child begins to pronate (turn palm down) and supinate (turn palm up) the forearm (Figure 9-18a). The ability to pronate and supinate is required in activities as diverse as shaking a rattle and turning a door knob. Children with cerebral palsy are very often restricted in this movement thus restricting functional hand use.

During this time period, infants are exploring the effects of their own activities (Flavell, 1977). They repeat their few motor skills over and over, enjoying activity for its own sake. Babies are in the process of learning about objects and their properties. Fine motor control is an integral part of this cognitive development. Shaking, banging, fingering, exchanging objects from hand to hand are typical "exploring" activities at this age. Children can also imitate behaviors of a model that they themselves have produced (Flavel, 1977). Thus objectives for development of fine motor skills may need to be paired with cognitive objectives. Two objectives will make this point.

> When placed in a supported sitting position and given a block, the student will reach for and grasp (palmar grasp) for 10 seconds, a 1-inch cube placed 6 inches from the edge of the table, 90 percent of the time on 3 consecutive days.

> When placed in a supported sitting position and given a rattle, the student will reach for, grasp, and shake the rattle for 10 seconds 90 percent of the time on 3 consecutive days.

Eight to Twelve Months The period of 8 to 12 months involves the continued refinement of the scissors grasp to an inferior princer grasp (see Figure 9-17). In addition, a pointing response with index finger is refined so that the index finger and thumb begin to approximate.

Cognitive development leads the child at this age into purposeful goal-directed play (Flavell, 1977). Assessment items such as "pulls the string to obtain toy" (Bayley, 1969), requires both fine motor ability and the knowledge

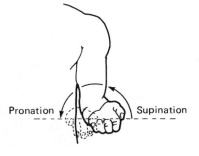

Pronation   Supination

Figure 9-18a Forearm pronation and supination (Lippincott).

that the string can be used as a tool to obtain the toy. Two levels of training may occur during this period. First, training to establish the inferior pincer grasp must occur:

> When placed in a sitting position and presented with a finger food placed 6 inches from the table edge, the student will pick it up (inferior pincer grasp) and lift it to his mouth 90 percent of the time on 4 consecutive days.

Then comes training in using pincer grasp in a cognitive or means-ends activity:

> When placed in a sitting position and presented with a string attached to a toy train, the student will grasp the string, using inferior pincer grasp, pull the string toward him or her, and retain the toy train, or

> When placed in a sitting position at a table and presented with a bowl and a spoon, the student will pick up the spoon and place it in the bowl within 5 seconds, releasing his or her grasp of the spoon, 90 percent of the time on 3 consecutive days.

Twelve to Eighteen Months   The child between 12 and 18 months develops smooth and accurate pincer grasp. Continued exploration of objects to enhance cognitive development is made possible by the improved motor skills. The child can now turn pages in a book, remove the lid of a box, build a tower of blocks, and place pegs in a hole (Bayley, 1969).

Again, cognitive development and the development of play skills interact with fine motor development. Objectives should continue to include a sequence of fine motor and cognitive skills. It should be noted that the acquisition of the motor skill itself is no longer the goal of the child. Rather, once a motor skill such as fine pinch is accomplished, it is employed in the play routine. Just as walking initially required the child's total attention, once established, it becomes a means to other goals.

Another development is the beginning of tool use. Being able to use a spoon, drink from a cup, and scribble with a crayon are some examples of the child's increased ability to use objects as tools. Tool use will continue to improve as the child's skills in drawing, hammering, and eating improve throughout the preschool years. A cluster of skills during this age period designed to improve accuracy of grasp and release and/or improve tool use include:

1   Unwrapping a cube (covered in paper)
2   Turning pages in a book
3   Using a spoon
4   Obtaining a toy with a stick

Eighteen to Twenty-Four Months   At this stage, the fine motor skills of grasp and release have been achieved. Refinement of these skills and development of tool use begin to occur in the process of symbolic and imitative play.

Thus pretending to open doors with toy keys, helping to stir pancake batter, and helping to dust afford the normal child an opportunity to try out newly acquired skills in the course of a day. Play programs should be designed to allow for this type of learning.

Prewriting activities begin during this period also. Random scribbles begin this sequence. By the end of the second year the child can scribble a circular mark and draw a horizontal and verticle line when given a model (Cratty, 1969). Scribbling may remain in the page or within a 6×6 inch area. Development of drawing skills from 24 months on includes:

24 to 36 months: Copies a +, first –I–, then a +
                   Copies an *H*

36 to 48 months: Copies an *O*
                   Copies a *T*

48 months: Copies a square
                   Copies a triangle

Evaluation of drawing skills can be done with the Developmental Test of Visual Motor Integration (VMI) (Beery & Butinica, 1967). The manual of the VMI is especially useful in identifying the development of drawing geometric forms.

Children's grasp of a pencil or a crayon changes from their initial attempts at 15 months to the achievement of an adult grasp. The grasp of a crayon starts with a palmar grasp, the forearm either in the neutral position or in a pronated position. Gesell (1940) describes the pencil grasp of the 3-year-old as being the thumb and the index finger in opposition while the tip of the middle finger rests near the point of the pencil. By 4 years of age the child holds a pencil like an adult; the thumb and the index finger are in opposition and the middle finger rests laterally on the pencil.

Drawing and Writing   Drawing skills consisting of geometric figures, and drawing a man and simple pictures are predominant during the preschool years. During late kindergarten and first grade the child makes the transition from drawing geometric forms to writing. Several factors appear to be involved in this transition. These include the ability to match like letters, to hold pencil and maintain posture, and finally to reproduce the letter.

Motorically the child must be able to adequately hold a pencil, assume the correct sitting position, and initiate a motor response. One method of training which incorporates these factors is the Palmar Method (1973), currently used in kindergarten and first-grade classrooms. Palmar starts with geometric forms already familiar to the child, such as circle, verticle line, and horizontal lines, and puts these together to make letters; for example, *1 o = p*. Johnson and Myklebust (1967) suggest that letters be made on a large scale initially and made smaller as the child's coordination improves.

The sequence for training handicapped students to write seems to begin with tracing, then copying, and finally reproducing from memory (Hallahan & Kaufmann, 1976). Two programs based upon behavioral training include one by Staats, Brewer, and Gross (1970) and Rajek and Nesselroad (1970). In the latter program, writing was taught using shaping procedures, working through the sequence of shaping, copying, writing from dictation, and finally functional writing.

Merkley (1972) recommends training in forming letters in the following order:

A   Uppercase letters:
   1   O C G Q—counterclockwise
   2   D B P R—clockwise
   3   L T H I F E Z—straight lines
   4   U Y J—combined letters
B   Lowercase letters:
   1   o d q e g
   2   b p
   3   l i t k v x w z
   4   h f m n r u y j

Prior to being trained in letter formation the child must be able to grasp the pencil correctly and maintain a correct sitting position. Pencil grasp starts around 2 years of age with a palmar grasp, the forearm in the neutral or pronated position (see Figure 9-18a). Gesell describes the pencil grasp of the 3-year-old as being the thumb and the index finger in opposition, with the tip of the middle finger resting near the point of the pencil. By 4 years the child holds a pencil like an adult with the thumb and the index finger in opposition and the middle finger resting beside the pencil.

Forty-Eight months   At this stage, fine motor skills continue to interact with intellectual and perceptual tasks. For example, preschool intelligence tests include items such as drawing a man, stringing beads, unraveling mazes, folding paper, cutting with scissors, and doing block designs. The Osterestky Tests of Motor Proficiency (Doll, 1946) purports to measure motor proficiency rather than intellectual ability. Introductory material for the Osterestky suggests it measures static coordination, dynamic coordination, and motor speed to name a few. The items on the test are in some cases similar to neurological tests done by physicians including one-foot balance, finger to nose test, walking on tiptoes, placing match sticks in a box, and others.

The Ayres Southern California Sensory Integration Tests (1972) present yet a third approach to assessing perceptual-motor skills in the preschool, school-age child. All or some combination of these assessments are appropriate when planning programs and provide a broad view of motor abilities. In fact, Singer (1975) suggests the literature is "replete with tests of motor ability" (p. 342). It is important, however, to read carefully the rationale behind these tests and understand their theoretical implications, as well as their implications for training.

In terms of training for functional fine motor skills during the preschool, early-childhood periods, the following lists from Bleck (1975) should be considered:

Functional fine motor skill	Age
Stirs ingredients in a bowl	3 years
Cuts with scissors	3–4 years
Unscrews lid from a jar	3–4 years
Turns handle of egg beater	3 years
Squeezes tube	3 years
Opens and closes safety pin	6 years
Dials phone	7 years
Draws line with a ruler	7 years
Unlocks door with key	7–8 years

Sample Instructional Objectives

Several objectives are suggested in the preceding section on fine motor development. Additional objectives and task analyses are presented below. These task analyses will be developed further as therapeutic techniques are added. They have not been field-tested and may need modification. The objective is:

> When placed in a supported sitting position, the student will reach for a 1-inch block placed 12 inches from the body, grasp it, and retain it with a palmar grasp for 10 seconds 90 percent of the time.

> Task Analysis: The student

> 1 Extends arms toward object (Figure 9-18b)
> 2 Keeps wrist in neutral, not flexed (optional), position
> 3 Touches object
> 4 Opens hand
> 5 Closes hand around the object
> 6 Maintains grasp for 2, 4, 6, 8, 10 seconds

Turning pages of a book consists of the motor task (turning the page) as well as the opportunity to learn once access to a book is possible. The analysis and sequence below is adapted from the Infant Stimulation Curriculum (Nisonger Center). The objective is:

> The student, when seated at a table and presented with a book, will turn four pages individually within 30 seconds 85 percent of the time on 3 consecutive days.

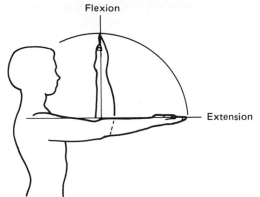

Figure 9-18*b* Flexion and extension of forearm.

Task Analysis: The student

 1 Reaches with the dominant hand for the book
 2 Touches the book with the dominant hand
 3 Places the thumb on top of the page at the upper right-hand corner
 4 Places the index finger on the right-hand edge of the page
 5 Lifts the page 1 inch, using the middle finger if necessary
 6 Moves the dominant hand under the page, pushing it to the left-hand side of the book
 7 Grasps the page with the left hand
 8 Releases the right hand
 9 Places the page flat on left side of the book
10 Repeats

These training materials can be adapted for completing the task analysis above:

 1 Book made of file folders with tabs still attached
 2 Same book with one-half of the tab cut off
 3 Same book with the remaining tab cut off
 4 Construction paper book
 5 Regular paper book

Additional fine motor objectives include:

The student will copy the letters *O* and *T* using an upright posture and adult pencil grasp 90 percent of the time on 3 consecutive days.

When standing (or sitting in a wheelchair) facing a door, the student will reach for the door knob and turn it until the door opens 5 inches, 90 percent of the time on 3 consecutive days.

When seated at a table, the student will pick up a pencil in her dominant hand and draw a closed circle (copying from a model) 90 percent of the time on 4 consecutive days.

When presented with a milk carton, the student will open it (using a one- or two-handed method) to produce a spout which will allow milk to pour, 95 percent of the time on 3 consecutive days.

INSTRUCTIONAL STRATEGIES

To this point, discussion has centered around motor development and establishing skill sequences and objectives. The final section of this chapter will discuss instructional strategies emphasizing the incorporation of therapeutic techniques appropriate for physically handicapped students. A program format in Table 9-4 will be developed as a model for teachers working with the physically handicapped.

It bears repeating that an occupational and/or physical therapist should be involved in evaluation and program development. Although the techniques presented here are relatively simple, they should not be attempted without some demonstration or assistance from a therapist. Therapists do not all agree on one approach to training in motor skills in the cerebral palsied child, just as educators do not all agree on one approach to training in reading. It is important

Table 9-4   Program Format

Student's Name: _____ Date Initiated _____
Objective:

Preparation:

Position:

Instructional Strategy:

Task Analysis:

Student behavior	Teacher behavior	Therapeutic techniques
1		
2		
3		
4		
5		
6		
7		
8		

for educators and parents to work closely with the therapist and attempt to understand the rationale behind the therapeutic techniques. Finally, the approach taken in this chapter concerning therapeutic techniques and intervention is a conservative one. It is necessary for the teacher to be aware of his or her liability when working with the physically handicapped and of the laws which govern the practice of occupational and physical therapy in the state. One needs to understand precautions, both medical and physical, and act accordingly. Those people who are uncertain or unclear about an intervention technique should not proceed. This caution should not serve to decrease enthusiasm and creativity but should encourage a proper mix of action and judgment.

Cerebral Palsy

At the beginning of the chapter, it is suggested that three factors be evaluated before developing motor instructional programs. The first item has already been described: motor skills and sequences. The second factor is primitive reflexes (see Table 9-2) which we want to inhibit during the course of training. The third factor is muscle tone. We want to evaluate these factors because the child with cerebral palsy has (1) motor development delay; (2) abnormal or primitive reflexes; and (3) altered or abnormal muscle tone.

Treatment or training programs for cerebral palsy must attempt to develop motor skills, decrease the presence of primitive reflexes, and decrease the influence of the abnormal muscle tone.

Briefly, *muscle tone* refers to the degree of tension or contraction of the muscle (Johnston, 1976). Muscle tone in the normal individual provides us with the ability to maintain posture, as well as move in a coordinated fashion. The child with cerebral palsy experiences abnormal muscle tone. The spastic child has too much tension or contraction, thus limiting movement. The athetoid has constantly fluctuating muscle tone so that movement is often unpredictable or uncontrolled. The hypotonic child has too little muscle tone and will have difficulty maintaining posture.

Muscle tone in the normal child allows antagonistic muscles to maintain a balance. For example, the biceps flex the arm at the elbow and the triceps extend the arm (see Figure 9-18b). In the normal individual these two muscles are in balance. When the triceps are causing extension of the arm, the biceps are relaxed. When carrying a book, the biceps contract and the triceps relax to allow that movement. The cerebral palsied child does not have this balance. The muscles which flex tend to be in a constant state of contraction. Even when the child attempts to reach or extend it is difficult.

The combination of abnormal muscle tone, muscle imbalance, and primitive reflexes results in some predictable postural and movement patterns. Figure 9-19, for example, illustrates a child under the influence of the asymmetrical tonic neck reflex. When the child's head is turned or he turns it voluntarily, the remainder of his body is pulled into a pattern of flexion on one side and extension on the other. If the child is a severe spastic, he may not be able to

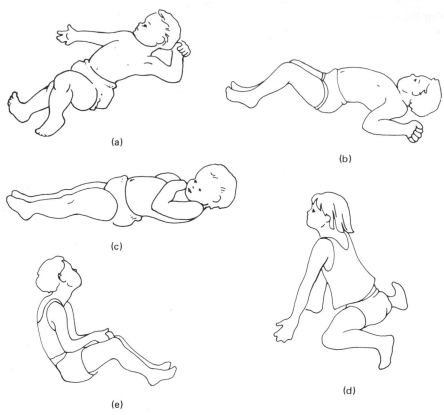

(a)

(b)

(c)

(d)

(e)

Figure 9-19 Examples of abnormal postures, due to the position of the head, which affect the whole body. These postures will result in abnormal patterns of movement, preventing the normal development of righting and balance reactions. *Note*: These postures will be more permanent in the spastic child, intermittent in the athetoid child, and seen on the affected side only in the hemiplegic child. (*a*) The child turns his or her head, which may also be bent to the side, and in the very severe child pulled back. The arm and leg toward which the face is turned are straight, the hand open, the arm and leg away from which the head is turned are bent and the hand is fisted. This pattern is seen most clearly when the child lies on his or her back or stands and is often present, but modified, when lying on his or her tummy or in sitting. (*b*) The head and shoulders are pulled back and the back arches. The athetoid child's legs may remain bent–the spastic child's legs will be straight and stiff. If the child is as severely affected as shown in our sketch, he or she may even show the same pattern when lying on the tummy. (*c*) The head is pulled forward, the arms are bent and are pulled over the chest, the hips and legs stiffen. If the child shows this pattern while lying on the back, it will be even more accentuated when lying on the tummy. (*d*) Lifting the head up and back, as illustrated, results in the arms stiffly extending and the hips, legs, and ankles bending. Sometimes, as shown in the sketch, the child will sit between his or her legs. (*e*) Bending of the head has the opposite effect, i.e. the arms bend and the hips and knees extend. This pattern can also be seen when the child sits. (Adapted from Finnie, N., *Handling the Young Cerebral Palsied Child at Home*.)

move out of this position. If an athetoid or mixed type, the child may use this position in activities. For example, a child or parent may learn that the child's left arm extends when he or she faces left. Therefore to put the left arm through a sleeve the child turns the head to the left. This clearly is an inappropriate use of muscle tone and patterns, but it exemplifies how influential patterns can be.

Training Techniques

There are several approaches to the treatment of cerebral palsy. Although these approaches are not mutually exclusive, one will find centers treating children with cerebral palsy which are influenced to a great extent by one or the other.

The first approach is the orthopedic approach. This approach usually includes surgery, bracing, and/or exercise. This was one of the earliest approaches to cerebral palsy and is still valuable. Children who are severe spastics can become so bound up in their spasticity that tendon-release surgery or bracing may be the only alternative.

There have been, however, several new approaches developed over the last 20 years which do not include or limit the use of surgery. Pearson and Williams (1972) list the following as the most promising contemporary approaches: Bobath's Neurodevelopmental Treatment (NDT), Kabat proprioceptive neuromuscular facilitation, and Rood's sensory motor approach. The suggestions included in this chapter are based on the latter approaches. The treatment techniques included here may not be appropriate or realistic for children in braces. Again, it is advised that the teacher work closely with a therapist when planning a program using therapeutic techniques.

Preparation

Once objectives have been established as indicated in Table 9-5, information concerning preparation should be included. In this program format, preparation refers to techniques which are designed to either inhibit or facilitate muscle tone. In the case of the spastic or hypertonic child one would work to decrease overall muscle tone. More specifically, if the child is dominated by spastic flexor tone, the therapist or teacher would want to decrease or inhibit the flexor tone. If extensor tone predominates, then extensor tone needs to be decreased.

In the case of a child who is hypotonic or floppy, an attempt should be made to increase overall tone. A word of caution is appropriate here. Children who are hypotonic are difficult to train. Hypotonicity requires powerful intervention techniques such as vibration and vestibular stimulation. It is recommended that the teacher does not try to use these methods since they also have a powerful effect on the central nervous system. It is the opinion of this author that spinning and vibration should be used by therapists only.

Preparation to Inhibit Hypertonicity   In general, the environment should be as quiet and comfortable with as few distractions as possible when working with hypertonic children. Loud noises, sudden movements, or visual stimulation may cause a startle or withdrawal response and accompanying spasticity. The following suggestions are designed to inhibit spasticity.

Inversion. Farber and Huss (1974) suggest that the inverted position (Figure 9-20) facilitates or stimulates extension of the neck, trunk, and extremities. This position plus the influence of the optical righting reaction should inhibit or decrease flexor spasticity and increase extension.

The most common means of using the inverted position is to place the child

Table 9-5   Program Format with Sample Objectives

Fine motor

Student's Name _____ Date Initiated _____

Objective: Using his right hand, John will reach for, grasp, and retain for 5 seconds a 1-in cube.

Gross motor

Student's Name _____ Date Initiated _____

Objective: When placed in kneeling, facing a chair, Mary will on command stand up and maintain standing for 2 minutes.

prone (on tummy) over a beach ball holding onto the pelvis. After the child is positioned, slowly rock him or her back and forth. An inviting toy or toys in front of the child will encourage him or her to look and reach using the extension pattern being facilitated.

Buttram and Brown suggest that children can also be inverted over the teacher's lap where their heads are lower than their feet. They warn that straight alignment of the back should be maintained. This exercise should be discontinued for children pulled into a S curve or with scoliosis.

This position should be used with caution. The trainer needs to watch for signs of distress, such as red face or sweating. Students with shunts or hearing conditions should not be put in this position.

Figure 9-20 Inverted position on beach ball.

Rotation. Buttram and Brown also recommend rotation as a means of "breaking up" patterns of spasticity. Trunk rotation involves the movement associated with the twist: shoulders and upper trunk rotate to the right while hips rotate to the left. This movement can be encouraged with the child in a sitting (Figure 9-21a) or a sidelying (Figure 9-21b) position. Rotation should be done to both sides to maintain symmetry.

Neutral warmth. Neutral warmth must be used cautiously. Individuals with severe spasticity or rigidity can be wrapped for short periods in a cotton blanket. The individuals should not get hot but should remain warm until they start to relax (Farber & Huss, 1974). The environment is again important. Bright lights, loud noises, and lots of activity will encourage hypertonicity.

Slow rolling. Farber and Huss (1974) describe slow rolling as follows: "The therapist places one hand on the patient's pelvis and one hand on his rib cage. The patient is then rolled from supine to side and return. The patient is always rolled away from the therapist so that his extremities will not come into contact with the therapist's. Slow rolling should be repeated for several mniutes until the patient shows signs of relaxing" (p. 41).

Slow rocking in developmental patterns. Slow rhythmic rocking will result in inhibition according to Farber and Huss (1974). Slow rocking may be done in the

(1)   (2)

Figure 9-21a Rotation in sitting.

(1)   (2)

Figure 9-21b Rotation in sidelying.

prone or inverted position, as well as in the sitting-, the all-fours-, or the standing position. The amount of time spent rocking depends on the individual, but it should not exceed 5 to 10 minutes.

Preparation to Facilitate Muscle Tone in Hypotonic Children   Only a few techniques are listed here, and these should be used with care. It is possible to facilitate muscle tone within abnormal patterns. If you feel a child pulling into an asymmetrical or abnormal pattern, then you should stop immediately and seek the advice of a therapist.

Pressure. Applying pressure to a muscle belly should stimulate or facilitate that muscle (Farber & Huss, 1974). Pressure should be applied firmly with the pads of the fingers or heel of the hand so that bruising does not occur. Pressure to the tendon will inhibit the muscle, so you must know exactly where to apply pressure.

Fast rocking in developmental patterns. Instead of slow rocking, a fast irregular rocking is used in the positions of prone, sitting, all-four, and standing. Again one needs to be sure abnormal patterns are not facilitated.

Inverted position. The inverted position is again used to facilitate extension of the head, trunk, and extremities.

Response to these techniques will vary with the individual child. If slow rocking results in more muscle tone rather than less, then discard the method for that child.

Once teacher and therapist have determined the most effective preparation techniques, they should be entered on the program format as in Table 9-6.

Positioning

One of the most important factors influencing the success of training for the cerebral palsied child is position. For example, if we took normal 1-month-old babies, put them in a sitting position, and tried to get them to swipe at an object, they couldn't do it. But if we put the babies in their cribs or infant seats where the head and back are supported, they would succeed with the pregrasp sequence.

Although it is important to offer support, it is imperative that the support be appropriate. The child in Figure 9-19 is supported, but he is in the asymmetrical tonic neck reflex and cannot swipe at an object or roll over when caught in that position. If, however, the child's head were turned to the midline and his shoulders and arms pulled forward, he too might succeed in swiping at an object.

Finally, the child must have the opportunity for movement as well as proper static positioning. The child must learn to move in the appropriate way and should not be so positioned that he never has the opportunity to move.

Before any training begins, it is necessary to ask the following questions in regard to positioning.

Table 9-6   Program Format with Sample Objectives and Preparation

Fine motor

Student's Name: John   Date Initiated: 9-16-78

Objective: Using his right hand, John will reach for, grasp, and retain for 5 seconds a 1-in cube.

Preparation: Slow rocking over a beach ball to facilitate head, neck, back, and arm extension and decrease flexor spasticity.

Gross motor

Student's Name: Mary   Date Initiated: 9-16-78

Objective: When placed in kneeling, facing a chair, Mary will on command stand up and maintain standing for 2 minutes.

Preparation: Slow rocking in a sitting position, feet on the floor, to decrease general muscle tone and give her the feeling of weight bearing on her feet.

   1   Is the position appropriate to the task? If self-feeding is being taught, the child must be in an upright position, not lying down or semireclined.
   2   Does the position encourage normal posture and movement?
   3   Is movement allowed and if so is it normal movement?

As seen in Figure 9-19, children with cerebral palsy have typical patterns which they assume. Some of the movements they exhibit include:

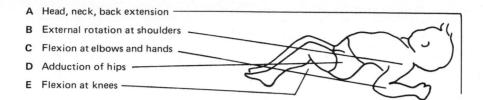

A Head, neck, back extension
B External rotation at shoulders
C Flexion at elbows and hands
D Adduction of hips
E Flexion at knees

Other movements are:

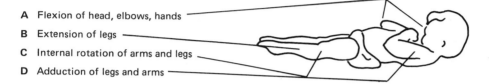

A Flexion of head, elbows, hands
B Extension of legs
C Internal rotation of arms and legs
D Adduction of legs and arms

Take a few minutes to try these positions yourself. Imagine how uncomfortable and nonfunctional these positions are. The child in the top figure will have difficulty turning over in this position. He or she will be unable to rotate shoulders and hips segmentally to initiate the rolling response described for the normal child.

Finnie's book *Handling the Young Cerebral Palsy Child at Home* is an excellent resource for positioning techniques. It is well-illustrated and should be a part of your library. No attempt will be made to duplicate her work; however, some examples of *static* positioning useful for program development will be presented.

Prone over a bolster   This position (Figure 9-22a, 1) can be used for several purposes. First, it can be used to facilitate head control as well as neck and trunk extension. Secondly, it can be used as a play position, freeing the child's hands to play on the floor in front of the child. Sitting over a *bolster* (Figure 9-22a, 2) may be used for the more-advanced child.

Sidelying   Sidelying is an alternative to supine (on back). If the child has a great deal of extension as seen in Figure 9-22b. The sidelying position allows children to pull their shoulders and arms forward to play with toys. If children cannot maintain sidelying independently, they may need to be propped into position (Finnie, 1975).

Sitting   Two props for training in sitting are:

1 Beanbag chair: An ordinary beanbag chair may be used for a child with no sitting balance (Figure 9-23a). The chair can be molded to the child to place him or her in an upright or semireclining position. This positioning may be

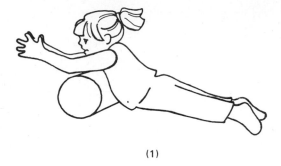

(1)

(2)

Figure 9-22a (1) Prone over the bolster.
(2) Sitting over a bolster.

Figure 9-22b Sidelying.

appropriate for reaching and grasping activities or to inhibit extension during feeding activities.

2 Chair: There are limitless variations on the common chair (Figure 9-23b). In some centers a full-time carpenter is employed to adapt straight chairs and wheel chairs to fit the needs of children with cerebral palsy. Several basic principles underlie the use of a chair:

   a Feet should always be supported, never dangling because the chair is too high.

Figure 9-23a Bean bag sitting.

Figure 9-23b Sitting in a chair.

Figure 9-23c Tailor sitting.

Figure 9-23d Side sitting.

Figure 9-23e Ring sitting.

  b Hips and knees should be flexed at a 90° angle. The child with extensor tone can push himself out of a chair unless this rule is followed.

  c Trunk and head should be upright and in alignment, and hips should touch the back of the chair.

  d The lap tray on the table should be at or slightly below the elbows so the child can support himself if necessary.

3 Floor sitting: Sitting on the floor has developmental and physical advantages. Several types of sitting are recommended and these include tailor sitting (Figure 9-23c), (a good alternative to W sitting), side sitting (Figure 9-23d), and ring sitting (Figure 9-23e). These positions will encourage sitting balance and protective extension.

    Prone board The prone board (Figure 9-24) is designed for children who do not stand independently. Buttram and Brown (N.D.) suggest that it provides weight-bearing stimulation as well as leaving the hands free for other activities.

    Once a child is positioned one cannot assume he will stay in that position. Normal individuals get tired of sitting and automatically change throughout the day. The same holds true for the child with cerebral palsy. If you position a child at the beginning of a project, you may well have to reposition several times during the project. One must continually check for the presence of abnormal postures.

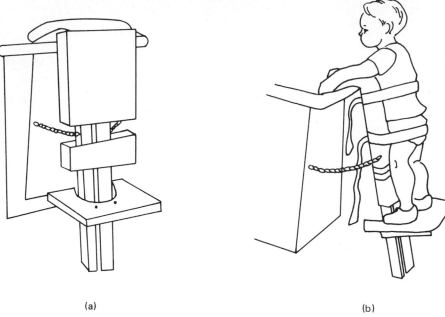

(a)   (b)

Figure 9-24   Prone board.

When the position for the project has been determined, it should be entered on the program format (see Table 9-7).

Facilitating Movement Responses

Once the child has been prepared and positioned, the final step involves facilitating normal movement patterns during training. It is possible, as illustrated in the example of dressing, to teach the child to use abnormal patterns of movement. Many cerebral palsied children, for example, grasp objects with wrist flexed and deviated and elbow flexed. This is not only abnormal but it eliminates the development of higher-level hand skills. There may be a time when abnormal patterns have to be accepted, but initially training should encourage normal patterns.

The following are some suggestions on how to incorporate therapeutic techniques into a training sequence.

Backward chaining   When possible, backward chaining should be used to provide tactile-kinesthetic feedback concerning the normal response. The fine motor task in Table 9-8 is an example. If the trainer moves the child through the normal reaching pattern (arm extended, forearm in neutral, wrist in neutral), the child will benefit from this repetitive feedback. The trainer can then release physical assistance to allow the child to complete the last step in the chain (hold for 2 seconds). As the child moves through the training procedure, physical

Table 9-7 Program Format with Objectives, Preparation, Position

---

Fine motor

Student's Name _____ Date Initiated _____

Objective: Using his right hand, John will reach for, grasp, and retain for 5 seconds a 1-in cube.

Reinforcement: "Good Boy"

Preparation: Slow rocking over a beach ball to facilitate head, neck, back, and arm extension and decrease flexor spasticity.

Position: Placed in Bobby-Mac chair, legs in tailor sitting, 3-in square pads on either side of his head to hold head in midline.

Gross motor

Student's Name _____ Date Initiated _____

Objective: When placed in kneeling, facing a chair, Mary will on command stand up and maintain standing for 2 minutes.

Preparation: Slow rocking in a sitting position, feet on the floor, to decrease general muscle tone and give her the feeling of weight bearing on her feet.

Position: Placed on her knees, facing the chair, hands on the seat of the chair. Trainer holds her hips.

---

assistance will be eliminated. This is not the traditional approach to backward chaining, but it has merit for the cerebral palsied child.

There may be instances where backward chaining in the above manner is

Table 9-8   Program Format

Fine motor

Student's Name _____ Date Initiated _____

Objective:	Using his right hand, John will reach for, grasp, and retain for 5 seconds a 1-in cube.
Reinforcement:	"Good Boy" plus gold star on performance chart
Preparation:	Slow rocking over a beach ball to facilitate head, neck, back, and arm extension and decrease flexor spasticity.
Position:	Placed in Bobby-Mac chair, legs in tailor sitting, 3-in square pads on either side of his head to hold head in midline.

Student's actions	Teacher's command
1 *S* extends arm toward object	(*T* holds shoulders forward to prevent extensor thrust) **a** John, hold the block. **b** John, reach. **c** John, reach. (Facilitate by tapping triceps; model.) **d** John, reach. (Physically prompt; hold John at elbow, moving his arm into extension.)
2 *S* touches object	**a** John, hold the block. **b** John, touch the block. **c** John, touch the block. (Model; tap wrist extensors.) **d** John, touch the block. (Physically prompt, holding John at the elbow as you prompt.)
3 *S* opens hand	**a** John, hold the block. **b** John, open your hand. **c** John, open your hand. (Model; tap wrist extensors.) **d** John, open your hand. (Prompt, holding John at elbow and wrist as you prompt.
4 *S* closes hand around object	**a** John, hold the block. **b** John, hold the block. (Model.) **c** John, hold the block. (Physically prompt. You will probably not need to facilitate finger closure, but will want to maintain wrist in neutral.)
5 Maintains grasp for 5 (3, 1) seconds	**a** John, hold the block. **b** John, hold the block. (Model.) **c** John, hold the block. (Physically prompt —see Step 4.)

unrealistic, such as in walking the length of a parallel bar. Therapist and trainer will need to consider what is appropriate.

Stability of positioning of proximal joints   The Bobaths (1972) and Finnie (1975) refer to "key points" of the body which may affect what the rest of the body does. These key points include the head, shoulders, and hips. The suggestions on static positioning have already illustrated the importance of these key points which need to be controlled during a program. If John exhibits extensor tone in his back, pulling his shoulders and arms back, it may be necessary to hold his shoulders forward as as he proceeds through training. A gradual release of this assistance as he gains independence during training will occur.

Controlling the head may be important also. If, for example, Mary tends to throw her head as she stands, the teacher may want to hold her head forward as she stands and fade that assistance throughout training. Likewise she may need some stability at her hips. The teacher may wish to hold her hips, applying some downward pressure to provide stability for standing.

Tapping   Tapping is described under the preparation techniques, but it can also be used during the training. The Bobaths (1972) suggest that tapping can be used to:

1   Increase postural tone for maintenance of posture
2   Activate weak muscle groups
3   Obtain proper grading of reciprocal innervation (p. 172)

In the example of John's program, tapping the triceps and wrist extensors should facilitate arm extension and wrist extension. This in combination with positioning and preparation should increase the likelihood of John's performing in a normal pattern.

Tables 9-8 and 9-9 illustrate how the program format would look after the trainer and therapist worked out all the teacher behaviors and therapeutic techniques.

Table 9-9   Program Format

	Gross motor

Student's Name _____ Date Initialed _____	
Objective:	When placed in kneeling, facing a chair, Mary will on command stand up and maintain standing for 2 minutes.
Reinforcement:	Raisins and "Good Girl, you stood up."
Preparation:	Slow rocking in a sitting position, feet on the floor, to decrease general muscle tone and give her the feeling of weight bearing on her feet.
Position:	Placed on her knees, facing the chair, hands on the seat of the chair. Trainer holds her hips.

Student's action	Teacher's command
1 S flexes right hip to 90°	1 Mary, stand up.
	2 Mary, bend your knee.
	3 Mary, bend your knee. (Model.)
	4 Mary, bend your knee. (Physically prompt. (Facilitation will probably not be necessary here.)

Table 9–9 (Continued)

Student's action	Teacher's command
2 *S* places right foot flat on floor	**a** Mary, stand up. **b** Mary, foot on floor. **c** Mary, foot on floor. (Model.) **d** Mary, foot on floor. (Prompt; place hand on Mary's knee and give downward pressure until foot is flat. Foot should not curl in or out. If it does, stop.)
3 *S* shifts weight to right side	**a** Mary, stand up. **b** Mary, shift. **c** Mary, shift. (Model; raise left leg.) **d** Mary, shift. (Prompt; lift Mary's left leg to shift the weight.)
4 *S* extends right leg, pushing into upright position	**a** Mary, stand up. **b** Mary, stand up. (Model; tap firmly on quadriceps.) **c** Mary, stand,up. (Physically prompt; stand behind Mary, place your arms under hers, your right hand on her knee, and with a forward motion, stand up.)
5 *S* shifts weight to extended arms, leaning body forward slightly	**a** Mary, stand up. **b** Mary, stand up. (Model.) **c** Mary, stand up. (Prompt—see step 4.)
6 *S* extends left leg to follow	
7 *S* places left foot flat on floor	**a** Mary, stand up. **b** Mary, foot on floor. **c** Mary, foot on floor. (Model; gesture by tapping quadriceps.)
8 *S* distributes weight from arms to legs	**a** Mary, stand up. **b** Mary, stand up. (Model.) **c** Mary, stand up. (Physically prompt; tap at front of shoulders with both hands until weight is shifted.)
9 *S* maintains standing 120 (60, 30, 20, 10, 5) seconds	**a** Mary, stand up. **b** Mary, stand up. (Model; gesture by tapping front of shoulders.) **c** Mary, stand up. (Physically prompt; hold at hips to maintain standing.)

Note: This is an example and has not been field-tested. Teacher behaviors will differ depending on the child.

SUMMARY

In this chapter, normal gross and fine motor development are discussed. Also discussed is the influence of cerebral palsy on that development and how teachers and therapists must adapt training procedures to fit the needs of cerebral palsied children.

This is not "everything you ever wanted to know about motor development and training." Teachers are encouraged first to continue to develop their skills by observing normal children. Normal infants are in constant motion, always challenging their balance and coordination. We should not lose sight of that fact. Training should be geared not just to the acquisition of a motor task but to the developing of that task as a skill. It is not enough to meet a goal such as "takes four independent steps," but is necessary to expand that goal until the student has a functional skill: "walks 50 yards on three kinds of surfaces."

Secondly, it is important to work closely with an occupational and/or physical therapist. No two cerebral palsied children are alike, and program planning, especially preparation and positioning, should be the product of problem-solving sessions between therapist and teacher. There is not, unfortunately, a cookbook for training the child with cerebral palsy.

Finally, continued study of the literature describing normal development and suggestions for handling cerebral palsied children will aid the teacher in providing the best services possible to handicapped students.

REFERENCES

Ayres, A. G. Southern California Sensory Integration Tests. Los Angeles: Western Psychological Services, 1972.

Bayley, N. *Bayley scales of infant development*. New York: The Psychological Corporation, 1969.

Beery, K. E., & Buktenica, N. A. *Developmental test of visual motor integration*. Chicago: Follett Educational Corporation, 1967.

Bleck, F. E., & Nagel, D. A. *Physically handicapped children: A medical atlas for teachers*. New York: Grune & Stratton, 1975.

Bobath, K., & Bobath, B. Cerebral palsy. In P. H. Pearson & C. E. Williams (eds.), *Physical therapy services in the developmental disabilities*. Springfield, Ill.: Charles C. Thomas, 1972.

Brosius, K. Instructional program for teaching tracking, scanning and auditory localization. Unpublished manuscript, 1978.

Buttram, B., & Brown, G. *Developmental physical management for the multi-disabled child*. University, Ala.: University of Alabama, N.D.

Connolly, K. *Mechanisms of motor skill*. New York: Academic, 1970.

Cratty, B. J. *Motor activity and the education of retardates*. Philadelphia: Lea & Feberger, 1969.

Deach, D. F. Genetic development of motor skills in children two through six years of age. *Microfilm Abstracts*, 1951, *11*, 287.

Doll, E. A. The Oseretsky tests of motor proficiency. Circle Pines, Minn.: American Guidance Service, 1946.

Espenchade, A. S., & Eckert, H. M. *Motor development*. Columbus, Ohio: Merrill, 1967.

Farber, S. D., & Huss, A. J. *Sensorimotor evaluation and treatment procedures for allied health personnel*. The Indiana University Foundation, 1974.

Fenson, L., Kagan, J., Kearsley, R. B., & Zelazo, P. R. The developmental progression of manipulative play in the first two years of life. *Child Development*, 1976, *47*, 232–236.

Finnie, M. *Handling the young cerebral palsy child at home*. New York: Dutton, 1975.

Flavel, G. H. *Cognitive development*. Englewood Cliffs, N.J.: Prentice-Hall, 1977.

Fleishman, E. A. Structure and measurement of psychomotor abilities. In R. N. Singer (ed.), *The psychomotor domain*: *Movement behavior*. Philadelphia: Lea & Febiger, 1972.

Florentino, M. R. *Reflex testing methods for evaluating central nervous system development*. Springfield, Ill.: Charles C. Thomas, 1963.

Gesell, A. *The first five years of life*. New York: Harper, 1940.

Guttridge, M. V. A study of motor achievements of young children. *Archives of Psychology*, 1939, *244*, 1–178.

Hallahan, D. P., & Kauffman, G. M. *Introduction to learning disabilities*: *A psychobehavioral approach*. Englewood Cliffs, N.J.: Prentice-Hall, 1976.

Meyer Children's Handicapped children in head start centers. Rehabilitation Institute Teaching Program for Young Children. Reston, Va., The Council for Exceptional Children, 1974.

Hillebrandt, F. A., Rarick, G. L., Glassow, R., & Carns, M. L. Physiological analysis of basic motor skills I, Growth and development of jumping. *American Journal of Physical Medicine*, 1961, *40*, 14–25.

Infant Stimulation Curriculum (2d ed.) Ohio State University: The Nisonger Center for Mental Retardation and Developmental Disabilities, 1976.

Johnson, D. G., & Myklebust, H. R. *Learning disabilities educational principles and practices*. New York: Greene & Stratton, 1967.

Johnston, R. B. Motor function: Normal development and cerebral palsy. In R. B. Johnston & P. R. Magrab (eds.), *Developmental disorders, assessment, treatment, education*, Baltimore: University Park Press, 1976.

Levy, J. *The baby exercise book*. New York: Pantheon, 1973.

McGraw, M. B. *The neuromuscular maturation of the human infant*. New York: Hafner, 1945.

Merkley, E. *Becoming a learner in early childhood curriculum*. Columbus, Ohio: Merrill, 1972.

Milani-Comparetti, A., & Godoni, E. Routine developmental examination in normal and retarded children. *Developmental Medicine and Child Neurology*, 1965, *90*, 631–638.

Monnier, M. *Functions of the nervous system. Motor and psychomotor functions* (vol. 2). New York: Elsevier, 1970.

Newman, R., Ross, P., McCann, B., Menolascino, F. G., & Heal, L. W. Experimental evaluation of sensorimotor patterning used with mentally retarded children. *American Journal of Mental Deficiency*, 1974, *79*(4), 372–384.

Palmer Method Manuscript. Schaumberg, Ill.: A. N. Plamer Co., 1973.

Pearson, P. H., & Williams, C. E. *Physical therapy services in developmental disabilities*. Springfield, Ill.: Charles C. Thomas, 1972.

Peiper, A. *Cerebral function in infancy and childhood*. New York: Consultants Bureau, 1963.

Piaget, G. *The origins of intelligence in children*. New York: W. W. Norton, 1952.

Rayek, E., & Messelroad, E. Applications of behavior principles to teaching of writing, spelling, and composition. In G. Semb (ed.), *Behavior analysis and education*. Lawrence, Kan.: Kansas University, Department of Human Development, 1972.

Rural Infant Stimulation Environment (R.I.S.E.). University, Ala.: University of Alabama, 1979.

Sage, G. H. *Introduction to motor behavior: A neurological approach*. Reading, Mass.: Addison-Wesley, 1977.

Schafer, D. S., & Moersch, M. S. (eds.), *Developmental programming for infants and young children*. Ann Arbor, Mich: University of Michigan Press, 1977.

Singer, R. N. *Motor learning and human performance*. New York: Macmillan, 1975.

Staats, A. W., Brewer, B. A., & Gross, M. C. Learning and cognitive development: Representative samples, cumulative-heirarchical learning and experimental-longitudinal methods. *Monographs of the Society for Research in Child Development*, 1970, *35* (8, Serial No. 141).

Teaching Research Infant and Child Center. *Teaching research curriculum for moderately and severely handicapped*. Springfield, Ill.: Charles C. Thomas, 1976.

Santa Cruiz Education Management System. The behavioral characteristics progression (BCP) observation booklet. Palo Alto, Calif.: VORT Corporation, 0000.

Touwen, B. *Neurological development in infancy*. Spastics International Medical Publication, Lavenham, Suffolk England: Lavenham Press, 1976.

White, B. L., Held, R., & Castle, P. Observations on the development of visually-directed reaching. In J. Hellmuth (ed.), *Exceptional infant* (vol. 1), *The normal infant*. New York: Brunner/Mazel, 1967.

White, B. W. *First three years of life*. Englewood Cliffs, N.J.: Prentice-Hall, 1975.

Appendix for Chapter 9: Glossary

Anatomical Terms

Axilla   Area under the arm.

Distal   Parts of the body away from the midline.

Dorsal   Refers to the back.

Kyphosis   Increased convexity of upper back.

Lordosis   Increased concavity in the lower spine.

Midline   Center of the body from head to toe.

Pelvic girdle   Area of the lip including the hip joint.

Prone   Lying down on stomach.

Proximal   Parts of the body close to the midline.

Scoliosis   Lateral deviation of the spine into a S curve.

Shoulder girdle   Area of the scapula; joint where shoulder and arm meet.

Supine   Lying down on the back.

Range of Motion

Abduction   Moving body part away from the midline (see Figure 9-25).

Adduction   Moving body part toward the midline (see Figure 9-25).

Dorsiflexion   Lifting foot up (see Figure 9-26).

Eversion   Moving or turning foot outward (see Figure 9-27).

Extension   The act of straightening (see Figure 9-18b).

Flexion   The act of bending (see Figure 9-18b).

Inversion   Moving or turning foot inward (see Figure 9-28).

Plantar flexion   Pushing foot down toward the floor (see Figure 9-29).

Pronation   Hand palm-down (see Figure 9-18a).

Rotation   Internal—turning inward; external—turning out (see Figure 9-30).

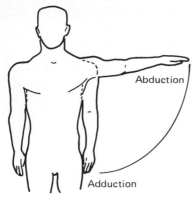

Figure 9-25   Abduction, adduction.

Dorsiflexion
Figure 9-26   Dorsiflexion.

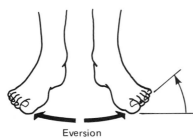

Eversion
Figure 9-27   Eversion.

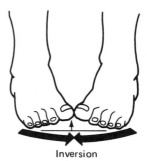

Inversion
Figure 9-28   Inversion.

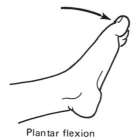

Plantar flexion
Figure 9-29   Plantar flexion.

Supination   Hand palm-up (see Figure 9-18a).
  Reflexes
Asymmetrical Tonic Neck Reflex   Stimulus: head turning. Response: fencing position (see
  Figure 9-1c).
Equilibrium Reactions   Stimulus: Body disturbed off balance. Response: righting
  response of head and trunk on one side and protective response on the other (see
  Figure 9-12a).
Grasp Reflex   Stimulus: object placed in palm of hand. Response: palmar grasp (see
  Figure 9-17).

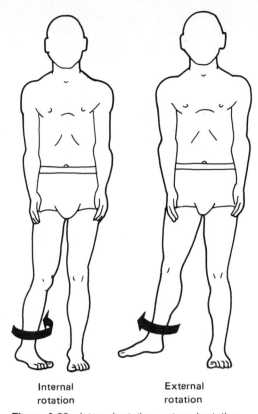

Internal
rotation

External
rotation

Figure 9-30 Internal rotation, external rotation.

Moro Response Stimulus: loud noise or quick change in head position. Response: extension of extremities and head (see Figure 9-1b).

Protective extension Stimulus: sudden movement of body off balance. Response: arms extend in direction of fall (see Figure 9-13).

Righting Reactions Stimulus: body moved out of alighnment. Response: head pulled into the upright position.

Stepping Reaction Stimulus: body moved off balance in standing. Response: several quick steps to regain balance (see Figure 9-12b).

Miscellaneous

Athetoid Involuntary writhing movements.

Ambulation Means of mobility, usually referring to walking.

Diplegic Distribution of abnormal tone throughout the body but more on one side than the other.

Hemiplegic Distribution of abnormal tone on one side of the body.

Long sitting Sitting on the floor with legs out in front.

Muscle tone Automatic tension on a muscle; tone is basic to movement and posture.

Paraplegic Refers to distribution of abnormal muscle tone limited to lower limbs and trunk.

Palmar grasp Grasp involving the entire hand.

Pincer grasp   Grasp involving the thumb and index finger in opposition.
Quadriplegic   Refers to the distribution of abnormal muscle tone to entire body.
Sidelying   Lying on the floor on the side rather than on the back or tummy (Figure 9-22b).
Side sitting   Sitting on the floor with legs flexed at knees and rotated to one side (Figure 9-22b).
Tailor sitting   Indian-style sitting (Figure 9-23c).
W sitting   Sitting on the floor with legs flexed at knees, feet behind the body making a W (see Figure 9-5b).

Chapter 10

Language and Speech: Developmental Programming

C. Milton Blue, Ph.D.

Professor of Speech
Pathology and Audiology
University of Georgia

All persons who work professionally with developmentally disabled children and youths encounter individual problems in the area of communication. Problems, from one subject to the next, are seldom similar for communicative behaviors are exceedingly complex, are developmentally acquired over an extensive period of time, and vary in numerous ways from the behaviors demonstrated by an average communicator. This chapter was prepared (1) to increase the reader's understanding of the developmental nature of the various dimensions of communication; (2) to assist the reader in differentiating between language problems and speech problems; and (3) to provide a basis for direct classroom assistance for the language-delayed child.

Learning Goals

This chapter should help you to answer the following questions:

- What is communication? What are the two basic components of the communicative act?

- What is language? What are its critical dimensions?
- What is speech? What are the critical dimensions of this behavior?
- What are the personal and environmental factors that influence language and speech acquisition?
- What behavioral differences lead to the designations language-delayed versus speech-defective?
- What information is available that can assist in evaluating the language-delayed child, with consequent program planning?
- What principles should the parent, teacher, and therapist apply in their dealings with the language-delayed child?
- What are some instructional objectives that can be pursued for children at varying levels of language functioning?

BASICS OF COMMUNICATION

Bill B. was an 8-year-old cerebral palsied child with virtually no ability to willfully move the muscles of his body. Upon hearing an acquaintance state, "The Yankees are a lousy baseball team," the muscles of Bill's chair-bound body became rigid, a contorted scowl appeared on his face, and a soft, spasmodic, guttural sound could be heard. Even an observing stranger would have judged that Bill had interpreted that message and desired to respond with an intellectually planned retort. Unfortunately the production of any appropriate spoken utterance was beyond his capabilities.

Mary, a 10-year-old educable mentally retarded child, when asked her name and age, correctly interpreted the question and was successful in producing the response, "My na id Mawy an I a teuh."

Mark, a 14-year-old trainable mentally retarded adolescent, was asked, "What is your name and how old are you?" His beautifully articulated response was an almost perfect fractional echo, "old are you."

Bonnie, a 6-year-old Down's Syndrome child, responded to the teacher's question, "What happened?" by holding the baby doll toward the teacher and stating, "Baby fall. Fik it."

Each of the foregoing exceptional children can be described as having a communication problem, but the specifics of those problems are grossly different: the first two children exhibited problems in the act of speaking; the latter two produced acceptable speech but with notable differences in language content and/or form from expectations based on chronological age. A differentiation between the language of human beings, the methods used for the transmission of language, and the problems that may be encountered in each sphere is critical to the understanding of communication differences in children and adults.

Language Defined

In its broadest sense, language is any human-devised symbol system that is representative of, i.e., substitutes for, the objects and events of reality, and the feelings and ideas that result from real experiences. The effect of such symbol systems is (1) to serve as an internalized shortcut for the storage and recall of experiences and the subsequent planning of action, i.e., the tool of thought, and (2) to allow for the sharing of those experiences with others through some form of overt expression, i.e., the tool of intrapersonal correspondence (Carroll, 1964).

Pictures, whether machine-produced as photographs or human-produced as drawings, are symbolic in nature inasmuch as they are representations of reality or the artist's perception of reality. Similarly, the movements of the face, hands, and other portions of the body in gestural production are also representations of an internal or external state of affairs.

In a narrower sense, language is defined as a spoken symbolic code. The building blocks of this code are individual speech sounds (phonemes) which are organized in isolation or in groups (words) to designate a referent as agreed upon by members of the speaking community. These meaning units are then strung together to form phrases or sentences in accordance with formative rules (rules of syntax), which have likewise been agreed upon by that community. Such a singular system is referred to as a spoken mother tongue, e.g., Spanish, English, Russian. Variations in words, and rules for word ordering, are encountered within subgroups of a generic community. This subgroup variation is referred to as a *mother tongue dialect*, e.g., the Southern, Mountain, and black dialects of the English language.

Two other systems of symbols, written numbers and alphabetical letters, are in daily use by the reader. These systems can be thought of as secondary systems for the average person inasmuch as they are a direct outgrowth of the spoken system. That is, the written word *cup* is representative of the spoken word "cup" which is representative of the object; the written symbol *4* is representative of the spoken word "four" which is representative of a quantity in reality. Other less commonly used secondary symbol systems are Morse Code, semaphore, and the printed system recently developed for use with nonspeaking persons, Blissymbolics.

Speech Defined

Speech is the neuromuscular vehicle for the transmission of language across distance. It is a learned motor activity which is initiated as neural energy within the central nervous system and terminates with the coordinated muscle action of three systems:

1   The respiratory system, where controlled exhalation serves as the energizer for speech.

2   The vocal system, where muscle movement of the vocal folds, in coordination with the movement of the air stream, results in the production of voice.

3   The articulatory system, where muscle movement of the lips, tongue, and palate results in the modification of that voice into distinct speech sounds

(phonemes). The sounds flow together as a result of rapid sequential articulatory movements to form the carriers of meaning, words.

The act of speaking is an extremely complex neuromsucular act—far more complex than learning to strike a golf or tennis ball or manipulate the fingers across the keys of a piano or typewriter. Amazingly, estimates indicate that 95 percent (Eisenson & Ogilvie, 1977) of the children in the United States acquire that skill simply as a result of being in contact with it from birth. That is, the act of speaking is not taught in the traditional sense.

Two other commonly used neuromuscular systems for the transmission of language must be identified because of their importance in a human being's daily functioning, gesturing, and writing. The latter serves not only for transmission but also as a sytem for storage.

Communication Defined

Communication is the summative effect of (1) language, plus (2) motor expression of that language, with the added requisite of (3) a receiver who has had comparative experiences and knowledge of the motor form of language expression. A simplified schema of the communicative act is as follows:

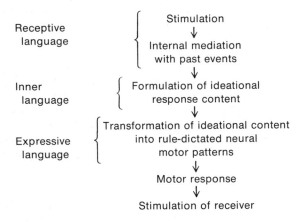

Jenny, a 24-month-old child, picked up a jagged leaf, examined it closely, and stated, "Weaf bwoke. Fik it." Within the communicative sequence, outlined above, the listener can identify only the stimulus and the verbal motor response. Essential to an understanding of the nature of that response are the inferred mediating steps. To *mediate* is to act as a go-between or to tie together. Language is the mediator of humankind, the internal bridge that ties together the past with the present and forms the substance for the transmitted response. In Jenny's case, the mediation is instantaneous as the healthy brain compares the present stimulus (the jagged leaf) with other events held in memory, selects the few appropriate symbols that are available at her level of development as being representational of those events, and then translates those symbols into neural energy to the muscles of expression. The resultant utterance is not adultlike in content, length, form, or sound (articulated phonemes), for these characteristics of language and speech are developmentally acquired over many years. Her statement, and the speech that carries it, is entirely "normal" for her chronological age.

In the opening paragraph, Bill B. received symbolic stimuli through the ear (rather than reality stimuli through the eye, as in Jenny's case). Judgment indicated that his brain also instantaneously derived meaning from the statement, à la comparisons with symbols acquired in the past, and the ideational content of a verbal retort was formulated. However, because of brain damage prior to birth Bill could not trigger the appropriate neural pattern for the muscle act of a spoken response. The conclusion of professional evaluators was that the breakdown was in the motor formulation for speech, not in the language formulation of a desired response.

Bonnie, the fourth of the children initially presented, also received auditory stimuli, and correctly interpreted the intent (question) and the content. Considering only chronological age (6 years), a listener would anticipate a verbal response such as, "My doll fell off of the table and broke. Please fix it." The actual statement, "Doll broke. Fik it", was essentially complete in meaning and was spoken understandably. However, it lacked certain semantic elements, arranged according to standard linguistic rules; the statement was telegraphic in construction and comparable to that expected of an average 2-year-old child, leading to the professional conclusion that the child was language-delayed.

The message to be derived from this discussion can be summarized: Anyone dealing with children should not make judgments about a child's knowledge of language on the basis of *how* he or she speaks. Speech is simply the observable symptom of language which can lead to erroneous conclusions.

> The little girl, newly assigned to the first-grade classroom, entered, looked at the teacher, and said, "Hewo Mith Thmith. I'm gwad to be in our woom."

In this example, the words expressed by the child were correct, as was the order in which the words were placed. The meaningful content of the message was clear and obviously appropriate. The only notable difference was in one dimension of speech, i.e., the articulated phonemic makeup of the utterance. That child's teacher must guard against the instant evaluation, "What a sweet, little, immature child. I doubt if she has the language to succeed in the academics of my classroom." Such a judgment can become a self-fulfilling prophecy.

It is important at this point to briefly consider the dimensions of language and those of speech which are gradually acquired during childhood and ultimately contribute to acceptable communicative skill. The dimensions noted are those most commonly investigated in the evaluation of the language and speech functioning of individual children.

THE CRITICAL DIMENSIONS OF LANGUAGE AND SPEECH

Children are born devoid of formal language and neurally incapable of dealing with the millions of stimuli which impinge upon them from the new, alien world. Thus, the newborn engages in protective sleep except for brief moments when biological need must be fulfilled. However, children are predestined, biologically and psychologically, to gradually attend to, manage, and organize the incoming reality stimuli, to learn to deal with them meaningfully, and to discover the existence of, and learn, a systematic symbolic code that is representative of that reality. The changes occur gradually as the sensory and motor systems reach maturational readiness and the experiences, plus language models, are provided within the environment. Communicative competence is gradually developed over a number of years. Cazden (1972) has noted that such competence

> has two aspects. It includes both knowledge of language (in the more usual and narrow sense of syntax, phonology, and semantics) and knowledge of the social world and of rules for using language in that world so that speech is appropriate as well as grammatical and creative within both linguistic and sociolinguistic rules. Together, these aspects of communicative competence are realized in the child's actual speech behavior, or performance. This performance includes both speaking and comprehending. (p. 3)

Language Behavior

Observable language performance is divisible into two interactive segments, receptive and expressive. In general, the ability to deal meaningfully at the receptive level with any of the dimensions of language precedes expressive use. For example, the average child will respond appropriately to the word "No," the vocal characteristics which are an integral part of the mother's use of the word, her head shake, and even her facial expression several months before he produces any one or combination of these interrelated expressive behaviors. The reader has within his or her receptive vocabulary many words which bring instant meaning when heard or read but which are seldom (and perhaps never) revealed when speaking. In the evaluation of exceptional children it is not uncommon to find a receptive level of functioning that is significantly higher than the expressive. Each of the following are components of both receptive and expressive language.

Communicative Interaction, Appropriateness, and Continuity At 10 months of age a child extends his or her hand, clenching and unclenching the fist in a "gimme" gesture. The child notes the mother's reactive frown and vigorous head shake, and he or she, in turn, reacts—rudimentary communicative interaction has occurred although a word has not been spoken. That is, there is evidence that the child perceives the act of communication as reciprocal in nature; an act where one continuously shifts from the role of initiator to that of respondent and vice versa. Although the average child is using and being influenced by some words during the period of 10 to 24 months, communicative interaction is largely physical, with the child's producing and responding to gestures, pulling, pointing, and even experimenting with temper tantrums to manipulate those around him. As the child increases in age, the expectations of him or her by others also increases, and he or she rapidly learns that there are differing limits of acceptability as one grows older. Therefore, as formal language is developmentally acquired, interaction becomes more and more sophisticated. This is evidenced in the child's gradual development of strategies (Wood, 1976) that are appropriately varied in differing social circumstances. For example, there is a time to speak and a time to be silent; daddy is very accepting of verbal forthrightness at one time but polite acquiescence is more politic at another.

Increasing content appropriateness accompanies social appropriateness as vocabulary and linguistic skills grow. By school age the average child is quite adroit in the use of language in varying situations which involve his or her family and, to some extent, peers. In familiar settings, the child is truly a conversationalist who enjoys the recripocal nature of communicative interaction and whose utterances have topical continuity until his or her knowledge and feelings are exhausted.

At ages 5 to 6 the child enters a new setting, the school, where other limits are imposed and new sociolinguistic strategies must be developed. Blue (1975) has cautioned that in making judgments about the language and speech functioning of the school-age exceptional child, observations must be made in at least three interactive settings in order to estimate the child's true level of functioning: (1) response to adult-initiated communication, (2) self-initiated communication with adults, and (3) self-initiated communication with peers. In some instances, children who are considered to be virtually nonverbal in the classroom are found to be highly sophisticated language users on the playground

Vocabulary   The first intellectually meaningful word is discovered receptively by the average child at approximately the tenth month and is used expressively at 12 to 14 months. Word learning does not immediately leap forward as a result of the discovery, for the child is acquiring new skills in many developmental areas during the next 12 to 14 months. The word-learning explosion occurs from 24 to 36 months, and new words will be continuously added to the individual's lexicon throughout life. It has been estimated that children have an expressive vocabulary of 1540 words at 4 years and 2072 at 5 (Berry, 1969). Receptive vocabulary is, of course, indeterminably greater. Apparently the type of word acquired is of greater significance than the number of words to the expressive interaction of preschool-age children. Newman and Bailey (1973), in an extensive review of studies of word usage in preschool-age children, found that 66 words accounted for 52 percent of all words spoken. The additional rank-ordered list of 934 words contributed 34 percent. Predictably, the most frequent word was *I*.

Morphologic Variations of Vocabulary   Within the second and third years of the average child's life the discovery is made that there are rules for the modification of some words which effect their meanings. The types of words that can be manipulated and the basic rules for their modification are acquired by the sixth birthday. For example, plurality can be indicated by the spoken addition of the sounds of *s*, *z*, or *ez*, depending on the final sound of the singular form; one element of time can be indicated by the addition of the sounds of *t*, *d*, or *ed*, again depending on the phonemic makeup of the verb. Some exceptions to the rules are learned during these early years, but their acquisition will continue well past school entrance as will more subtle rule variations.

Ordering of Vocabulary into Constructions   The 20-month-old child astounds mother one day by suddenly stating, "Daddy go," his first two-word utterance and evidence that the child is aware that rules exist for the orderly arrangement of words into more meaningful constructions. (It is significant that that first statement was not "Go Daddy.") These rules of syntax begin to be acquired at approximately 18 months of age and extend through the elementary school years (Wood, 1976). Rules of morphology and syntax, plus vocabulary, allow for the receptive understanding and the expressive production of infinite constructions, since "Few sentences are spoken or heard more than once. Each spoken sentence must be constructed anew to express and communicate particular meanings to particular individuals—oneself or others" (Cazden, 1972, p. 6).

Length of Utterance   From the modest beginning of two-word telegraphic utterances the child gradually expands his or her productions until at school age they are of indefinite length. Brown (1973) dealt with morphemes in the determination of mean length of utterance (MLU) in children at varying levels of language development and considered it to be an "excellent index of grammatical development because almost every new kind of knowledge increases length . . ." (p. 53). Lee (1974) employed a similar scoring approach which supported the clinical judgment that increasing age in childhood brings a corresponding lengthening of responses. Earlier studies, as summarized by Johnson, Darley, and Spriestersbach (1963), focused on word counts in individual sentences, rather than on morphemes. There is, of course, great variability in the length of utterances in young children, but the following averages are generally accepted:

Age, years	Average sentence length (words)
2	2
2½	3
3	3–4
4	4–5

Muma (1978) cautions against the use of such information for children older than 4 years: "above the age of four, MLU reflects situational and status variables more than developmental variables . . ." (p. 22).

Prosodic Variation of Meaning   By 16 months the average child is already aware that a softly produced tentative "no" spoken by mother carries a different meaning than a sharp, emphatic "*No!*". The first is interpreted as "maybe"; the latter as "she means it." Similarly, the meaning of the spoken phrase "I love you" can be altered by tone of voice, inflectional variation, and the intensity or stress that is placed on individual words. These variations in pitch, rate, intensity, and juncture (pauses) are referred to as the *prosodic features* of a spoken language. These nuances of spoken language defy precise demonstration in written form. Little is known about children's acquisition of prosody, but such variations are clearly in evidence in the expressive experimentation of the average child as early as 15 to 18 months of age, when a jargon is practiced which sounds almost adultlike although no words may be detected. From 18 to 20 months a child varies the meaning of a single word by changing prosody. For example, the way in which the child says "more" clearly indicates whether it is a question, a description, or a demand. Wood (1976) concludes that such features are well established in the average child by kindergarten age, although refinement undoubtedly continues well past that point.

Speech Behavior

Speech does not result from some magical gift. Rather, it, like the language that speech will transmit, results from maturational learning with gradual changes appearing over an extended period of time. The infant enters the world as a sound producer whose utterances, from the beginning, have an effect on those around him or her. These early cries are reflexive in nature with the instant, unlearned coordination of exhalation with closure of the vocal folds to signal distress. At that point the child has no speech organs; he or she does have biological systems whose primary functions are the maintenance of life, and the infant will learn to superimpose his or her will on these operations for the performance of a secondary function—speech. The basic mechanisms and their primary (vegatative) and secondary (speech) functions are:

1 Lungs and associated muscles
   a Primary: intake of oxygen and elimination of waste
   b Secondary: energizing source for the production of voice
2 Vocal folds and associated muscles
   a Primary: protection of the lungs
   b Secondary: vibratory body for the production of voice
3 Open passages (throat, nose, and mouth)
   a Primary: movement of the air stream, intake of food, and drainage
   b Secondary: modification of voice, through resonation, into a sound quality that is characteristic of that one individual

4 Facial structures (lips, tongue, teeth, jaw, and palate)
  a Primary: preparation of food
  b Secondary: articulated modification of voice into identifiable sound units

The ultimate function of the foregoing organs for the act of speech is dependent on the early strengthening and development of manipulative skill of those organs in vegetative functioning. For example, gradual movement to an erect position, followed by walking, is intrinsically related to the strengthening of the upper torso, which, in turn, is related to respiratory control for speech; vegetative movement from liquids to semiliquids (baby foods) and finally to table foods strengthens and develops manipulative skill in those muscles ultimately responsible for the articulation of speech sounds. Therefore, the first months of a child's life are a time of preparation for the act of speech. From that point through puberty children listen to the speaking models around them, experiment with their own vocal productions, monitor and compare those productions with the models, and gradually modify their speech into acceptable adult forms. The critical dimensions of speech which undergo modification are voice, articulation, and fluency.

Voice   Simply stated, voice refers to the way a person sounds to others. It, like all dimensions of language and speech, changes with physical and psychological maturation. Voice is similar to fingerprints in that it is distinctive of each individual. Wilson (1972) has succinctly described the characteristics of a normal voice as:

> (1) pleasing voice quality, (2) proper balance of oral and nasal resonance, (3) appropriate loudness, (4) an habitual pitch level suitable for age, size, and sex, and (5) appropriate voice inflections involving pitch and loudness. The rate of speaking should be such that it does not interfere with the five essential characteristics . . . (p. 1)

There are no precise normal limits that can be delineated for any of the foregoing characteristics, for there is wide acceptable variance from person to person. There is also variance in the characteristics within an individual as physical growth and learning occur.

Articulation   The act refers to the modification of voice into two classes of distinctive sound units, vowels (e.g., *a* as in c*a*t, *e* as in s*ee*) and consonants (e.g., *b* as in be, *g* as in go, *ch* as in ou*ch*). These sound units, or phonemes, are combined to form the carriers of meaning, words. The act of articulation results from precise, intricate movements of the movable structures of the oral cavity (primarily the lips and tongue) in conjunction with the fixed surfaces (primarily the teeth and roof of the mouth).

Phonemes differ greatly in their complexity. This difference pertains to the ease with which they are heard and discriminated, as well as to the number of muscles involved, and the speed and precision with which muscle movements must be carried out during production. Comparatively speaking, vowels are easier to hear and produce than consonants; therefore, they appear earlier in a child's speaking life. When there is difficulty in phoneme acquisition (resulting in the child's being said to have an articulatory problem), consonants are generally the sounds involved.

Articulatory complexity is further increased in the combining of phonemes into words, for there must be rapid movement from one sound position to another. Individual phonemes appear in varying positions in words. For example, the sound of *p* occurs in four positions: (1) initial, as in pie; (2) medial, as in happy; (3) final, as in up; and, (4) blends (where two or more consonant sounds are "blended" together) as in plate or help. Production of a sound in the initial position of words is usually acquired by the average child before production in other positions. Blend production is particularly difficult, with many blends not expected to be produced accurately until the early school years.

There is a gradual refinement in the articulatory abilities of average children over an extended period of time. Most children are quite intelligible by 3 years of age, although there are phoneme differences that will take an additional 3 to 5 years to reach adult form. Figure 10-1 shows that no precise age level can be specified for the use of each speech sound. Rather, consideration of an age range for each sound is more appropriate, with the outermost limit for articulatory competence for all sounds being 8 years of age.

Articulatory norms, such as in Figure 10-1, are useful in determining when a child's phoneme difference is developmentally acceptable or defective. For example, a child's production of "*pun*" for "*fun*" (or comparable *f* change) would be acceptable at 3½ years but significantly different at 4½; "*wook*" for "*look*" is of no concern at 5 years, but at 6½ the *l* sound would be considered defective.

Fluency Nicolosi, Harryman, and Kresheck (1978) define speech fluency as the "Smoothness with which sounds, syllables, words, and phrases are joined together during oral language," or conversely as the "lack of hesitations or repetitions in speaking" (p. 85). In truth, no human being, child or adult, opens his or her mouth and produces strings of utterances with unerring accuracy and fluidity. If careful note is taken, even the most sophisticated adult speaker will be found to pause in an interruptive manner, interject "uh—ah—well," prolong an occasional phoneme or word, and in other ways disturb the flow of what is being said.

Fluency is greatly influenced at all ages by both physical and psychological factors. A speaker who is in poor general health, or one with lowered food intake and perhaps lack of rest, will tend to increase interruptions in the flow of speech. Perhaps of even greater importance to the fluency of young children is the attitude of those around the child toward him or her as a speaker. The greater the degree of stress placed on the child by the listener, the greater the probability that speech nonfluencies will appear.

One thing is certain, nonfluencies do appear in the speech of all children, to varying degrees, during those years that are critical in the development of

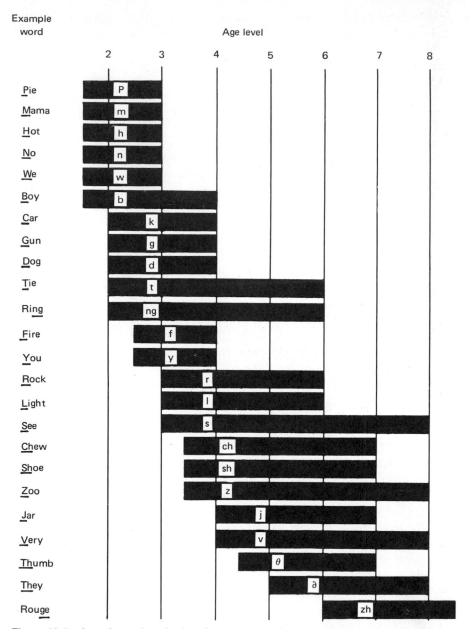

Figure 10-1   Age of sound production. Average age estimates and upper age limits of customary consonant production. The solid bar corresponding to each sound starts at the median age of customary articulation; it stops at an age level at which 90 percent of all children are customarily producing the sound. (After Sander, 1972)

connected, interactive speech—2 to 8 years. There are two points within this time span when nonfluencies have the greatest probability of occurrence, between the third and fourth birthdays, and again between the fifth and sixth. The interruptions of speech flow take the form of hesitations, sound and word repetitions, and sound prolongations. Such interruptions may also be observed in the delayed child who is functioning at the level of the aforementioned periods even though the chronological age is much higher. These breaks in fluency should be viewed as a natural stage of expressive development and should never be labeled "stuttering," for if the child

> can be kept from developing situation and word fears, if he can be helped to withstand the communicative frustration, if he does not become ashamed or troubled by his simple repetitions and prolongations, then he has an excellent chance of becoming as fluent as any other child. (Van Riper, 1978, p. 316)

The listening adult must avoid any negative response to the interruptions of speech flow demonstrated by such a child. Do not attempt to help him or her with verbal directions such as "Slow down and think about what you are saying" or "Relax, take a deep breath, and start over." *The best positive advice to any listening adult is to devote the same respectful attention to the nonfluent speaking child as the listener would expect when speaking to another adult.*

FOUNDATIONS OF LANGUAGE AND SPEECH ACQUISITION

At this point, the reader has been introduced to communication development as being two-dimensional: (1) the substance and form that is received, interpreted, and transmitted—language symbols—and (2) the vehicle that transmits—speech. In addition, attention has been devoted to the major parameters of language and speech. To further aid in the understanding of communication development in children, attention must now be directed to personal and environmental factors that influence language and speech acquisition. An understanding of these factors greatly aids the evaluation of, and programming for, children who exhibit delayed language and speech development, or defective speech.

Factors Influencing Language and Speech Acquisition

Biological Prerequisites   The fundamental basis of language is experience. Experience refers to those environmental events, objects, and behaviors of others that impinge upon the sensory receptors of the young language-acquiring child. Therefore, a prerequisite for normal language acquisition is adequate acuity of all sensory mechanisms to receive and transmit sensory stimuli to the central nervous system. If there is an alteration in one or more of the sensory mechanisms, a child's internalized experiences will differ to some degree from those of the "normal" child and the language base will be altered. For example, the normal child, who enjoys good muscle movement and muscle kinesthesia, acquires the vocabulary terms *walk* and *run* quite early in life. Sonny, a nonambulatory child, with restricted kinesthesia, did not acquire those words early, although *brace* and *pinch* were learned at a comparable time. Interestingly, the same word problems were apparent when he began a reading program at age 6. All senses are important, but that sense which is most critical to the discovery and learning of speech is hearing. Even a mild loss during the early years will have an adverse effect.

A second biological prerequisite is sufficient integrity of the central nervous system to attend to, perceive, evaluate, interpret, and store for recall those experiences that are received by the receptors. Central nervous system disfunction which negatively influences the development of these skills will, to varying degrees, alter language learning. The term *central nervous system disfunction* generally denotes specific damage to the brain, but it is important to note that many exceptional children have such disfunction superimposed upon them during the early language learning years. The drug, phenobarbitol, is a prime example. Dietary and other general health factors also have a role in normal brain functioning.

Psychological Prerequisites   A child may be born with complete biological integrity, but if locked in a closet, will not acquire language; if cloistered by overprotective parents, the child will have diminished language learning. There are psychological as well as biological prerequisites. Fortunately, the average infant gradually reveals two innate drives which, if allowed freedom of expression, move him continuously toward new experiences: (1) the drive toward independence and (2) the drive to become a social creature. At first glance these two drives appear to be operating at cross purposes but they are not; they operate in an equalizing manner. The locomotive 6-month-old infant, for example, spies the electrical outlet in the wall and independently moves toward it to investigate. The mother, to whom the child now responds socially, instantly interrupts the movement physically with accompanying words of warning, "Stop, hurt Billy." At this point, the words carry no intellectual meaningfulness, but the vocal behavior, along with the physical act, demonstrates to the child that there are limitations to the emergence of independent behaviors. There are comparable events that reward independence; e.g., the earliest effort of the young child in the high chair to lift and manipulate a cup are met with positive physical and verbal responses from those around him.

Positive Modeling and Reinforcement   Implied in the foregoing examples is the third prerequisite, a positive modeling and reinforcing environment that is conducive to language and speech learning. In such an environment the people around the child:

1   Take pride in, and socially reward, the developmental changes that the young infant demonstrates.
2   Provide opportunities for new experiences and do not unduly interfere with the child's independent searching and investigative behaviors.
3   Present good language and speech models.
4   Exude an aura of expectancy that the child will speak.
5   Change their behavior as a result of the emerging vocal and gestural utterances with continuing expectancy that further developmental changes will occur.

Point 5 of the above is paramount to the child's discovery of the existence and usefulness of spoken language. The motivational birthplace of the speech act is an extension of the previously discussed drives toward independence and socialization which interact to produce the egocentric urge to reach out and manipulate others. The discovery that hands reach out, obtain, and manipulate is made during the first 10 months; these tools have very limited range. The discovery is then made that vocal utterances act as a third hand with far greater range. It is certainly no accident that the first spoken words of the young child are not labels of things but rather are demands for action as in the following:

Child's word	Meaning
Mama (or Daddy)	Get over here, I'm in need.
Bottle	Feed me.
Up	Hold me in your arms.
Pottie	Get me there or you will be sorry.
More	Do it again.

The use of even approximations of such words brings instant success in manipulating the behavior of others. Success serves as the reinforcer that leads the child to the discovery of other effective words.

Other Prerequisites   The development of normal speech carries additional prerequisites. First, the brain must have sufficient integrity to formulate ideational content and to translate that content into the firing of motor neurons to the speech structures. Second, those structures, discussed earlier, must be adequate in form and function for the highly sophisticated, coordinated movements that are required. Third, the kinesthetic and tactile feedback senses from the muscles of speech must be functional, for these mechanisms, operating in conjunction with hearing, allow for self-monitoring with resultant developmental change over time.

Any biological, psychological, or environmental interference to one or more of the foregoing prerequisites will result in some discrepancy in language and speech acquisition and that child's being designated as having (1) delayed language and speech and/or (2) defective speech.

DELAYED LANGUAGE AND SPEECH AND DEFECTIVE SPEECH

This designation is descriptive and not etiological inasmuch as it is applied relative to a child's performance rather than to cause. The critical referent is time, and the use of the descriptive term means that the child's performance in language and speech reception and/or expression is at a level lower than that expected on the basis of chronological age. Generally speaking there is no implication of "defective" responding or producing, for such a child's performance is quite acceptable when contrasted with that of normal children of an earlier age. Thus, statements such as the following are found in the evaluative summaries of delayed children:

> Billy (chronological age) (CA) = 5) is functioning receptively and expressively at the 3-year level.
>
> Mary (CA = 4-4) is functioning receptively at the 3-year level with a more significant discrepancy in expressive language. Her restricted use of a few isolated words, plus jargon, indicates expressive functioning at the 18-month level.

Comparison of performance with chronological-age norms for language and speech functioning is not all that is required in the designation of delay. Observation of performance in other areas of learning is required. If there is an equivalence of functioning across all areas (as there often is in mental retardation), that child should not be considered to have a specific problem of language and speech delay. The following is such an example.

> Jerry (CA = 3-6) was a Down's Syndrome child. He was determined to be at the level of the average 18-month-old child in motor-, self-help, and social skill development. He responded accurately to many spoken words, used isolated words (at least fifteen) in directing those around him, and had been heard to produce an infrequent two-word phrase such as "un wa" (want water). This child's language functioning was only slightly above other areas of learning.

Jerry should not be considered to have the specific problem of language delay, although elevated language functioning must be a classroom and home objective.

The speech-defective child has kept pace with the norms for receptive and expressive language. The discrepancy in function lies in one or more of the three dimensions of speech: (1) voice, (2) articulation, and (3) fluency. A definition of speech defectiveness that is highly useful because of it's criterial nature is that of Van Riper (1978):

> Speech is abnormal when it deviates so far from the speech of other people that it calls attention to itself, interferes with communication, or causes the speaker or his listeners to be distressed. (p. 43)

A child may exhibit both delayed language and speech defectiveness. Tony, for example, responded to and expressed language at the 5-year level although he was 8 years of age. Virtually every utterance that he produced was marked by the extreme hesitations, repetitions, and struggle behaviors that characterize stuttering.

Causes

Volumes have been written about the known and suspected biological, psychological, and environmental factors that are associated with delayed language and defective speech. It is beyond the scope of this chapter to attempt to summarize such information. However, there are three somewhat subtle factors that are often overlooked in working with the language- and speech-delayed child that demand attention.

Hearing Loss Even a mild hearing loss that is permanent or recurrent during the first 5 years of life has an adverse effect on language and speech development. Mild to moderate losses are seldom obvious, for the children show evidence of hearing by responding to their names, environmental sounds, and situational commands such as "Time to eat" and "Take a nap." Normal hearing is not required for such responses. The hearing acuity of any child suspected of delay should be investigated immediately and periodically thereafter. An evaluation requires the services of a specialist in the measurement of hearing acuity, an audiologist.

Parent's Expectations A second factor that is frequently overlooked is the true expectancy demonstrated by the child's family that their child will acquire spoken language and employ it projectively to make things happen. Parents of a delayed child who are interviewed by a teacher or other authority figure can be expected to verbalize the desire for their child to speak, but the true picture of environmental expectancy may differ significantly. This factor comes into play most frequently in those children in which a congenital deviation, such as cerebral palsy or Down's Syndrome, is detected soon after birth. Such diagnoses often result in the lowering of expectations for development in all areas. Families of these children, like all others, look forward to the developmental evidences of emerging speech. When they do not appear on schedule, the parents gradually become overly accepting of the child's limitations, anticipate his needs, protect him from the eyes of the public, and make few demands for communication development. The true attitudes of those in the child's environment must be carefully observed and evaluated as an integral part of the efforts to plan an educational program for the language-delayed child. The parents must be helped to understand that spoken language will not appear if there is no expectancy and need.

Problems in Vegetative Functioning Earlier this chapter notes the importance of the progressive development of vegetative functioning to the acquisition of the neuromuscular act of speaking. Problems in this area are not encountered as frequently as problems in hearing and parental attitudes, but, on occasion, gross as well as subtle deviations go undetected. Problems often begin in early infancy when, for important medical reasons, a child is kept on a bottled formula or puréed foods when children would normally be advancing to a more mature feeding pattern. Too frequently this infantile vegetative routine is continued long after the medical need has passed, for it does satisfy the child's biological needs and it becomes an accepted part of the family routine. This, in turn, further influences negatively the expectancy of the family for developmental changes in function. Carefully evaluate the vegetative habits of the language-delayed child. Clues that there may be difficulty resulting from either biological or environmental causation include:

1 Use of the bottle before and after school although the teacher never sees it.
2 Consistent rejection of hard foods (apples, carrots, etc.)
3 Failure to suck through a straw
4 Difficulty with swallowing, revealed by the child's tilting the head backwards so that gravity aids the movement of liquids and solids into the stomach
5 Chewing by pressing food upward with the tongue rather than grinding with the teeth
6 Drooling

Suspected problems in vegetative functioning should be called to the attention of a speech therapist for assistance in planning a program for change. An occupational therapist, when available, can also be of great assistance. Parental cooperation and active participation is mandatory.

The remainder of this chapter is devoted to instructional concerns for the language-delayed child. The following texts are suggested for the reader who is interested in greater depth of study of the nature and etiology of delayed language and/or speech problems.

Introductory information regarding delayed language and all types of speech problems is given by Van Riper (1978) and Eisenson and Ogilvie (1977). Berry (1969), Lahey (1978), and Wood (1964) supply information specific to language differences. For information about speech differences see Wilson (1972) on voice, Van Riper (1973) on fluency, and Winitz (1969) on articulation.

BASIS FOR LANGUAGE INTERVENTION

The preparation of this chapter has relied heavily on published information concerning landmark behaviors in the receptive and expressive language development of normal children. It is this information that forms the basis for the total programming for any language- and speech-delayed child. Normative sequential schedules are valuable for (1) evaluating the language functioning of a given child, (2) specifying what the child does do and what the next objective should be, i.e., program planning, and (3) understanding the conditions which will influence the child's language learning, i.e., methods for obtaining the specified objective.

Three extensive evaluative instruments, based on knowledge of normal development, have recently appeared on the commercial market: (1) *Portage*

Guide to Early Education (Bluma, Shearer, Frohma, & Hilliard); (2) *Learning Accomplishment Profile* (Griffin, Sanford, & Wilson); and (3) *Brigance Diagnostic Inventory of Early Development* (Brigance). These instruments are comparable in that they provide developmental information, in sequence, concerning language and speech along with other areas of learning. Comparisons can be made across a number of developmental areas for the detection of specific delay. For example, the Brigance investigates the following areas:

Preambulatory motor skills and behaviors
Gross motor skills and behavior
Fine motor skills and behaviors
Self-help skills
Prespeech
Speech and language skills
General knowledge and comprehension
Manuscript writing
Math
Reading skills

Note that the Brigance taps symbol-manipulation skills in sections other than the two specifically designated: the General Knowledge category focuses extensively on word knowledge and the last three categories also involve the management of symbols. This instrument further assists the evaluator by providing example statements of objectives for the individual educational program (IEP) for each child.

Language-development norms provide the basis for the last section of this chapter, which contains suggested objectives for children at varying levels of language and speech behavior. Norms have also led to the recent publication of a number of language-intervention programs. Among them are: (1) *Language Acquisition Program for the Retarded or Multiply Impaired* (Kent); (2) *Emerging Language 2* (Hutten, Goman, & Lent); (3) *Functional Speech and Language Training for the Severely Handicapped* (Guess, Sailor, & Baer); (4) *A Language Intervention Program for Developmentally Young Children* (Bricker, Dennison, & Bricker); and (5) *Distar, Language I* (Engelmann & Osborn).

The user of developmental information must be cautious, for norms always denote averages rather than absolute points for the emergence of a specified language behavior. For example, first meaningful word production occurs for the great majority of children between the tenth and fourteen months with the twelfth month being the average. The application of such a range also calls for caution, for some normal children delay production of their first word to as late as 16 or even 18 months; if later, there is certainly cause for concern.

Jennifer produced her first meaningful word at 18 months, a 50 percent delay relative to the 12-month average. At 24 months the child was producing a limited number of two-word utterances, and by 30 months she was in step with the average-age expectancies.

In general, the age range for the appearance of the early behaviors will be less than that for the later acquired behaviors.

PRINCIPLES OF LANGUAGE INTERVENTION

Success in the elevation of language and speech functioning of the delayed child is largely dependent on the interactive cooperation of the parents, classroom teacher, and, where available, the speech therapist. Too often, the latter is viewed as a specialist who sees a child from two to five times a week in a highly structured setting for brief sessions called language therapy. *In truth, language instruction must encompass the entire day if language is to become the child's interactive tool in all environmental settings; the classroom teacher should be considered the primary language instructor.* The speech therapist is a valuable aide in the evaluation of a child, the determination of goals, and the delineation of methods to pursue those goals. The therapist also contributes by directly guiding the parents (Falck, 1978). However, it is the teacher who can best coordinate the efforts of all to see that pursuit of day to day objectives is a cooperative effort. Lack of cooperation leads to confusion and frustration for the child and failure to obtain carryover of specific objectives into daily usage. A language/speech behavior that occurs only in a highly structured language-therapy setting is useless.

Common Major Objectives

An aura of expectancy that a child will increase his language performance must be exuded by everyone. Agreement on common goals for a child should be reached through collaborative effort with expectancy reflected in carefully considered realistic demands that language be used. The major objectives to be pursued by all are:

1 Increased understanding and responsiveness to the spoken language symbols that are received
2 Quantitative and qualitative increase in the child's expression of spoken language symbols in communicative interaction with others

On rare occasion these objectives must be modified to involve receptive and/or expressive use of nonspeaking symbol systems such as signing, typing, and Bliss symbols (Bigge, 1976). These communication aids have extremely limited environmental usefulness inasmuch as few people have knowledge of the systems. Therefore, aids should be employed only when (1) early efforts directed toward spoken language have failed, (2) the child shows frustration resulting from ineffective communicative efforts, and (3) there is evidence of organic involvement that negates the probability that spoken language will be acquired.

Chart Progress The achievement of the broad objectives will, in general, be achieved slowly and laboriously. The successful language team includes at least one professional person, teacher or therapist, who is able to identify and break up major objectives into small day to day or week to week targets. Everyone then concentrates on the specified target. Each team member should chart any progress in a manner that is recognizable to the child and others involved; charting is often more important to the morale of the parents and teacher than it is to the motivation of the child. Focusing on small successes avoids the undue frustration that results from the failure to move rapidly.

Day to Day Goals

In the determination, and pursuit, of day to day goals there are several principles for the language team to consider.

Reception Precedes Expression Follow the general rule: Receptive language precedes expressive language. That is, in the pursuit of any specific language element the initial goal is the establishment of receptive understanding followed by efforts to obtain expressive use. Two occasional exceptions to this rule are (1) when there is a need to work for the improvement of a child's imitative skills independent of his intellectual knowledge and (2) when a child's receptive functioning is significantly higher than the expressive.

Language Level A language objective, at any given moment, should be slightly above the language level daily employed by the child even though the objective itself does not meet adult standards. For example, in working for phrase production by a child who consistently produces one-word utterances, the goal may be production of "Gimme _____." It would be unrealistic at that point to work for "Gimme a _____"; article usage can be pursued later. Similarly, movement from one objective to the next must be minimal with no large steps in the sequence.

Functional and Immediate Effect Selected short-term goals should be highly functional and have the probability of having an immediate effect in the child's daily living. Words and/or phrases and/or complete sentences that are naturally present day after day and which have the potential effect of bringing an immediate reward to the child will be acquired more rapidly than objectives which are artifically contrived. In the selection of early target words Bowerman (1978) has noted that

> Entities that move or upon which the child himself can act are more likely to be conceptualized and labeled earlier than static objects such as rooms, furniture, and trees. . . . Attributes and activities involving change and motion are also highly salient for young children. Thus, words to do with disappearance (all gone, away, no more), recurrence (more) falls and bumps (fall, uh-oh), . . . are among the earliest learned. (p. 170)

Observe each child and work to relate targeted objectives to those experiences toward which the child moves independently. Consider the following two examples:

> Billy stepped on a sharp stone on the playground. Whimpering, he sat down, picked it up, and began to investigate it. Immediately the teacher sat down, picked up another stone, and repeated "rock." She then pressed the stone into her hand and his hand while repeating, "Hurt—rock hurt." Over the next several days the teacher was certain to repeat the experience with the same words spoken each time.

> The teacher has selected pictures of a number of animals in their natural habitats. As she presents each picture she verbally describes it with telegraphic statements such as "Monkey—monkey swings," "Rabbit—rabbit eats."

In the first example, the teacher has spontaneously made use of a language learning experience that is concretely related to the child and one that has a probability of reoccurrence every time the child is barefooted in the yard. In the second, animals bear little relationship to the child's daily life. Furthermore, the labels are being attached to pictured representations (symbols) of reality rather than to the reality that is directly experienced and acted upon.

The foregoing examples involving the teacher's use of two-word telegraphic statements relates to another concern of all who implement the objectives for the language-delayed child. Teachers should consistently use words, utterance length, and constructions that are judged to be within the capability of the child. They should say those words and/or phrases in the manner that they are commonly heard by the child in his daily living. For example, "Gimme _____" is far more realistic than "Give me _____"; "ă (thĕ) car" is encountered constantly whereas "ā (thē) car" is heard only in structured drill. Other aspects of a child's verbal models are considered in the following section.

Stress Effectiveness   Pursuit of expressive language goals stresses effectiveness rather than beauty or perfection. Of course, increasing intelligibility is desired as the language goals are elevated, but the focus should be on the language intent, content, and form rather than on precision of speech production. As a general rule, intelligibility improves as language facility increases. Beware of random correction that is intended to increase understandability.

> Billy, a 6-year-old educable child, judged to be at the 3-year level of language development, struck his thumb, and the following conversation ensued: *Child*: "I hurt my fum." *Teacher*: "My goodness. Billy say *th*. Say *Th*umb."

Reward was called for rather than correction inasmuch as Billy's statement (1) was a complete sentence, (2) was quite intelligible, (3) employed correct pronoun usage, (4) contained the correct label for the act and the injured digit, and (5) was an act of communicative interaction. Spontaneous correction has its place in language instruction but only when it pertains to a designated objective and occurs at an appropriate time.

Random correction has little positive lasting effect. In fact, it is a clear indicator to the child that his communicative effort was unsuccessful. Language progress results from success, not failure. All listeners must strive to make any utterance produced by the language-delayed child a successful experience. As an extreme example, the teacher of a child who is just beginning to verbalize may not understand an apparently directive utterance or even be certain if it has interactive content. However, by observing the child's eyes, facial expression, gestures, and the context within which the utterance occurred she or he can force it to have meaningful results; i.e., the act of speaking becomes rewarding.

Plan for Generalization   Initial efforts to obtain a targeted receptive or expressive language response usually requires individual attention in a pre-planned, structured setting with instant reinforcement following any success. Worthley (1978, p. 1) has outlined the progression of steps as follows:

    I. Clinician models
        Student is physically assisted
    II. Clinician produces
        Student produces simultaneously
    III. Clinician models
        Student imitates
    IV. Clinician cues
        Student produces
    V. Student produces spontaneously

The foregoing progression will be diligently pursued over many days with some children, particularly the severely involved. However, attention at one level may be momentary or eliminated completely for other children who spontaneously demonstrate more rapid movement. These steps seek only to obtain a previously absent response and do not ensure that the child will generalize that response. Once a response is obtained, specific efforts to force generalization are mandatory, for "studies indicate clearly that we should not expect generalization to occur automatically" (Snyder, Lovitt, & Smith, 1975, p. 13). Generalization is pursued in two ways: (1) movement of the specific response from structure to semistructure to environmental usage and (2) extension of the response to comparable stimulus conditions that have not received direct attention. For example, adherence to the outlined steps has resulted in a child's accurate responding to "open door" during structured work. Efforts are now directed to obtain that response in the midst of other school day activities and to extend it to other articles such as "open box (sack, mouth)."

METHODS OF LANGUAGE INTERVENTION

There are three methods which are available to the language instructor in working to obtain a receptive or expressive response from a child: (1) visual cuing, (2) physical assistance and cuing, and (3) expressive modeling. A combination of two or all of these techniques is often necessary. They are important, not only in structured pursuit of a specific goal, but also during spontaneous communicative interaction throughout the child's waking hours. The teacher, therapist, and parents must be consistent in using them.

Visual Cuing

The gestures, facial expressions, and other visual information provided by those around the normal child in the first 3 years of life are important aids to that child's learning the usefulness and meaningfulness of spoken words, the sentence constructions in which they appear, and the subtleties of the language. Visual information is of no less importance to the learning of the language-handicapped child, and the need for such cues extends well beyond the 3-year level of language functioning. A teacher talks to the language-delayed child throughout the class day as they engage in physical activities, self-help training, etc. When a word of a phrase is given, and the child's understanding is questionable, the utterance should be accompanied by hand, facial, and other bodily cues. An appropriate tone of voice also assists understanding. At the simplest level, this means that the statement "No, no" would be accompanied by a frowning face, an emphatic voice, and a shaking finger and head. Other examples, at succeeding higher levels are:

"Billy, come here.": Hand extended outward, palm up, and then moved toward the body.
"Billy, jump.": Both hands extended, palm up, moved vigorously in an upward direction.
"Where is the dog?": A searching motion of the head and eyes.
"Draw a circle.": Extended finger tracing a circle in the air.

Visual cues in the form of printed symbols can be used when working with a child at a higher level. For example, the objective of compound-sentence production for the child who consistently produces complete simple sentences can be introduced in an "I see" game.

1 Select pictures of objects for which the child knows the labels.
2 Present pairs of pictures separated by any simple geometric symbol such as ◇. This symbol is designated "and."
3 Present the complete model "I see a _____ and a _____," pointing to the object, symbol, and object as named.
4 Use sentence completion, with the child producing "and a _____" as the pointing cue is given.
5 Require the complete utterance from the child, first with the printed cue, then without.

Any visual cue that accompanies a spoken expression should be consistent and gradually withdrawn. The goal is to obtain a response to, or use of, spoken words without a cue. This means that the successful instructor must maintain an internal catalog of gestural and other cues that have been used successfully with each child so that they will be consistent and gradually reduced until eliminated.

Physical Assistance and Cuing

In the infinite universe of acts that comprise receptive language, expressive language, and the act of speech, very few lend themselves to direct manipulation by the language instructor. This technique is most useful in obtaining receptive language responses and only rarely works for expression. In building a receptive vocabulary, a child's finger can be guided in an appropriate response to "Point to _____" as common objects are presented. Response direction in this instance relates to the verb as well as to the names of various objects. Similarly, one can physically assist a child in correctly responding to some simplified commands such as "Sit," "Stand," "Kick," and "Throw." Consider the following sequence of steps to obtain a response from a child to the command "Close door." Contrast the sequence with the earlier presented progression outline by Worthley (1978) and note that visual cues accompany direct assistance. Reinforcement must be given at each step.

    1 Standing with the child beside an open door, give the command with two gestures: "Close (pushing motion with the hand) door (pointing to the door)." Instantly take his or her hand and push the door closed.
    2 Give the command with gestures; lift the child's hand and hesitate expectantly.
    3 Give the command with gestures, with face and eyes moving from the child to the door. Wait for a response. If not forthcoming, provide the physical cue.
    4 Give the command without gesturing, except for the movement of the head and eyes from the child to the door.
    5 Give the command with no visual or physical cue.

The lifting of the child's hand in this example is considered a physical cue (or prompt) rather than direct assistance inasmuch as the child must complete the act. Physical cuing is an important intervening step for many children in the pursuit of responses to the spoken word.

The obtaining of imitative verbalization can be assisted by the physical cue of placing the forefinger on one's chin with the tip lightly tapping the lip as the model is presented: "Ball—say it—ball." The forefinger is immediately placed similarly on the child's chin. A comparable procedure can be used to obtain imitative vocalization. Place the child's finger tips lightly against the larynx (voice box) as sound is produced. The finger tips are immediately transferred to the child's larynx with the command "Say it."

Direct physical assistance should become physical cues as rapidly as possible. In turn, physical cues must be reduced gradually until they are eliminated and the child is responding consistently to the spoken word.

Expressive Modeling

The technique that is most frequently used by any instructor, regardless of the level of the language objective, is that of carefully producing a desired utterance or physical behavior with the command "Say it" or "Do it." The effectiveness of the procedure is dependent on the care with which the instructor has established (1) antecedent behaviors, (2) a reason for the child's attending to the behavior and attempting to produce it, (3) an ability on the part of the child to differentiate between the usually produced behavior and the model, and (4) a situation with no interferences (physical, sensory, or affective) to the child's replication.

Vicarious modeling is an excellent technique for use in a classroom. It involves one or more persons in addition to the instructor and the child, i.e., an aide, parent, and/or another child who has the targeted language skill. This person plays the role of a subject, attending carefully to the model and giving the required response. That person then monitors the response given by the subject. When progress is observed the roles are reversed so that the child who is the primary target not only gives the response but also monitors the acceptability of the response of others. Monitoring aids response habituation. The involvement of parents in such an activity has additional value inasmuch as it provides instruction for carryover into the home.

Modeling is not only important during structured goal pursuit, it is also useful during communicative action throughout the day. Two modeling techniques, expansion and extension, have been identified in the response of parents of young, normally developing children (Wood, 1976). These techniques have application in the instruction of language-delayed children.

Expansion occurs when the parent or instructor repeats the utterance of the child but in a more complete and accurate form:

Child: Daddy work.
Adult: Yes, daddy is going to work.

In this instance, verification is given while the utterance is modeled in a more complex form. The use of expansion with a language-delayed child calls for careful planning as to the extent of the expansion that can be handled by the student. Note that in the following examples the effort is not to correct the child but to provide approval of the content of the statement with an example of a higher-level construction.

Child: Ball fall.
Adult: Yes, the ball is falling.
Child: Want water.
Adult: Oh, you want some water.

The second type of modeling, extension, focuses on meaningful content of a child's production rather than on the structural form (Cazden, 1972). This is a useful tool for work for both receptive and expressive language as long as care is taken to keep the extended utterance brief.

Child: Betty fall.
Adult: Yes, Betty hurt her knee.

Child: Want water.
Adult: Oh, Billy is thirsty.

As earlier noted, modeling for the specific purpose of correction is a tenuous technique. Muma (1971) has stated that there is "general agreement that this is a destructive model from the standpoint of language usage, particularly when it is used too frequently" (p. 7). Negative feedback does tend to squelch a child's use of expressive language. However, it can be an important technique when used in the correct way at an appropriate moment; i.e., the instructor accepts the child's effort and intent and corrects only that element or elements that he or she has attended to successfully in a previous teaching situation. Haphazard correction must never be employed; all correction should be preplanned and clearly specified to the child. In the following, success in the use of "is (verb)ing" has been achieved in a structured setting, and the child's statement is spontaneous.

Child: Cat run.
Adult: Yes, cat *is* running. Say it, Cat *is* runn*ing*.

It takes planning and practice to use spoken language in both structured and nonstructured settings, in a manner that will aid the individual child's learning. Do not use words in the same manner as with the grocer, spouse, or school principal for such language contains elements that confuse the child. Carefully consider vocabulary, sentence construction, and length in giving instructions or statements.

LANGUAGE TO AVOID

There are five types of language expressions used every day by sophisticated speakers of the English language which may be detrimental to the language-learning child. These expressions are so much a part of the adults' verbal repertoire that the user tends to be unaware of the confusion that results for the unsophisticated.

Scarcasm

Scarcasm has been described by Wood (1976) as conflict messages resulting when the information transmitted through the vocal, verbal, and visual channels is incongruent.

> "You are such a hard worker"   (Verbal)
> Frowning face   (Visual)
> Sarcastic voice   (Vocal)

Wood's conclusion, concerning average children, is that they "do not learn to interpret conflict messages correctly until they are well into their teens" (p. 228). Scarcasm should never be used with the language-delayed child. The interpretation of such messages requires the intellectual skills of dealing with subtle cues which have not been acquired. If the skills were present the child would not be language-delayed.

Idiomatic Expressions

Idiomatic expressions are individual words or groups of words whose meaning, in the context used, differs from the usual or dictionary meaning. In the preparation of *A Dictionary of Idioms* (Boatner and Gates), 10,000 possible entries were gathered from the English language; obviously, the mother tongue is replete with such problematical statements. When one considers that the language-delayed child has difficulty acquiring the standard meaning of individual words he encounters in daily functions, it is easy to understand the confusion that can result when he is faced with statements such as:

> "Bear down and get it."
> "Doggone it."
> "For heaven's sake."
> "That's neat."
> "You're a ham."

Ambiguous Statements

Ambiguous statements require interpretation inasmuch as the precise intent is obscured. Statements such as "Billy, we don't put things in our mouths" result from the adult's desire to be directive in a kind, nondirective manner; an ambiguous impulse. Similarly, the statement, "That's pretty good, but . . ." would be interpreted by an adult as an indication that effort was good but performance was not. The language-delayed child cannot be relied upon to make such an interpretation and will frequently repeat the response in an effort to do "pretty good" again. Directive statements can be clear, precise, and concise, and still be kind.

Alternative Statements

Alternative statements (or indirect requests) also contain ambiguity for they involve the rephrasing of direct statements into question forms when questioning is not intended. Examples of such statements are:

Statement	Alternative statement
Say Billy	Can you say Billy?
	Will you say Billy?
Shut the door.	Can't you shut the door?
	Won't you shut the door?
Do not tap the pencil.	Must you tap the pencil?
Get the box.	Why don't you get the box?
Put that away.	When are you going to put that away?

Leonard, Wilcox, Fulmer, and Davis (1978) investigated the responses of normal children to the first three types of statements indicated above. Correct interpretation of all three was not present until 6 years of age, a time when normal children are relatively sophisticated language users. Straightforward requests eliminate the need for interpretation by the language-delayed child and result in more rapid acquisition of responses.

Words with Multiple Meanings

Words with multiple meanings cause confusion for any young language-acquiring child until he achieves the skill of detecting literal meaning from the context in which a word occurs. For example, *hand* has more than a dozen definitions in the *Webster's Seventh New Collegiate Dictionary*. It is no wonder that confusion ensues when a teacher, who has worked diligently on the labeling of body parts, looks at the child and says, "Hand me the _____."

> Mary had made good progress in the understanding of the word *up* as an indicator of direction. The teacher had wisely helped the child into a standing position, ascend stairs, and place articles on a shelf in response to the word. The session was concluded by the statement "Mary, put the toys up." Search as she might, the child could not find an elevated position for the toys.

No instructor can be totally successful in the use of words precisely as they relate to individual objectives. However, one must be aware of potential problems and work to be as consistent as possible. Observe each child for indications of confusion resulting from statements such as the following, and reword the phrase to clarify the intent:

> "Take your seat."
> "Line up."
> "You don't feel good."
> "Don't show off."

An effort has been made in the foregoing to clearly differentiate five types of common language utterances that often produce confusion in the instruction of the language-delayed child. There is much obvious overlap. For example, the alternative statement, "Can't you close the door?" is ambiguous, and, depending on other cues, may also be scarcastic. No instructor can stay constantly on guard and totally eliminate these utterances during daily interaction with children (although scarcasm should never be present). Total restraint would greatly reduce the spontaneity of communication and lead to other problems. However, all persons involved should be aware of the importance of being verbally direct and precise in communication with the child.

ESTABLISHMENT AND PURSUIT OF LANGUAGE OBJECTIVES

The knowledge of man concerning the orderly acquisition of language in children and the influencing factors is still quite limited. However, much progress has been made since the publication of Chomsky's 1957 landmark work, *Syntactic Structures*, which, in association with other political and professional concerns, established the drive for the recent study of child language. Significant sequential language behaviors of normal children have now been described and, as noted earlier, form the basis for the determination of the functioning of a child and the specification of objectives to be pursued. The remainder of this chapter is devoted to a discussion of some recorded landmark language behaviors that normally occur during the chronological age periods of (1) birth to 10 months, (2) 10 to 18 months, (3) 18 to 24 months, (4) 24 to 36 months, (5) 36 to 48 months, and (6) 48 to 72 months. The discussion is far from exhaustive, for the intent is to give examples of behaviors with comments related to instructional concerns. Many intervening behaviors are omitted. Therefore, the reader must consider any noted behavior as a point within a continuum of incremental steps which require careful consideration.

Birth to Ten Months

The first 10 months of life, commonly designated the *prelinguistic stage*, culminate with a child's intellectual discovery that spoken language exists. Before that discovery is possible, maturational changes occur within the central nervous system that result in a child's turning toward a sensory event and maintaining attention for at least a brief period of time. Length of attention increases during the period, as do efforts to move toward and manipulate stimulus objects. Some nonverbal children do not acquire the skill of attending selectively to environmental objects and events. The development of selective attention becomes an important objective in such cases. There are other developments that are important forerunners to the discovery of spoken language and require consideration in programming for the nonverbal child.

Selective Attention   Selective attention merges into the first behavioral evidence that there is internal retention and recognition of some objects and events that are present daily. The assumption is that the retention of functional associations occurs through the internal process of imagery, an important prerequisite to spoken language. Some early behaviors that are indicative of the retention of functional associations are:

Day after day the child strikes at the butterfly mobile that hangs over the crib.

When mobility is acquired, the child consistently scoots to the corner where the dog normally sleeps.

When a cup is placed in his or her hand, the child consistently moves it toward the mouth.

When mama enters his or her line of vision, the child's arms instantly stretch outward.

The objects and events that the child first deals with in a consistently meaningful physical manner form the basis for the first words that are acquired.

Instructional implication. Work to establish consistent physical responding by the child to a few common environmental objects. Select objects that move when acted upon and which allow for the instructor to produce the child's action, e.g., a ball, a toy that rotates when struck, a car that rolls easily, blocks that fall when struck. The behavior is first demonstrated by the instructor with the command "Look" and an appropriate gesture. Immediately lead the child through the action. Repeat the actions in a play setting many times each day always using precisely the same objects. Go from direct physical assistance to physical cuing as quickly as possible. When consistent responses are obtained add more objects that move and others that have an auditory result, e.g., a bell, a toy piano, a cow that moos when squeezed.

Receptive and Expressive Behaviors   Prior to the tenth month the average child has become conditioned, both receptively and expressively, to a number of spoken words. These are not intellectually recognized labels (true words) but rather are sound events which have been paired with positive or negative reinforcement to the extent that the child's responses have become consistent. Examples of such behavior are:

A   Receptive behaviors:
   1   The spoken command "No, no" (or, "Don't," "Stop it") has been paired with physical intervention to the extent that the spoken command alone will interrupt the child's activity.
   2   The child's name, as spoken by others, has been paired with positive reinforcement to the extent that the saying of the name produces instant attention.
B   Expressive behaviors:
   1   The child's self-motivated production of "ma-ma" during the stage of lallation has brought instant reinforcement by the parents who interpreted the utterance as a word. The sight of mother, or a need state such as hunger, then triggers the production of these syllables.

2   The child's lalling production of the syllables "ba-ba" has brought reinforcement from those around him as it is interpreted as a statement for bottle. "Ba-ba" then becomes a conditioned production when the child is hungry.

Instructional implication. When working with a nonverbal child, carefully select a few isolated words that will be consistently used in equivalent situations throughout every class day. Produce those words in exactly the same way followed instantly by consistent reinforcement. For example, if "No-no" is used as a command, stick with it. Do not say "Stop that" one time, followed by "Quit that," and then "Don't." This consistent command should be instantly reinforced negatively if the behavior is not interrupted. Expressively, carefully observe the child for any spontaneous utterance that can be interpreted as an approximation of a word in a specific setting. When it occurs, instantly repeat it and give it meaning, positively reinforcing the child for the utterance. During snack time, for example, the child's vocalization of the vowel *oo* should be instantly repeated by the teacher, followed by her or his statement of the word *juice* and the provision of the juice to the child.

Imitation   The young child discovers and begins to practice the skill of imitation prior to the tenth month. The discovery is generally assisted by the parent who, for example, models a clapping motion, followed by moving the baby's hands in a similar motion. First imitated behaviors are physical, and practice at this level is an important forerunner to the vocal imitation which the average child begins to demonstrate at 9 to 10 months. First efforts at either physical or vocal imitation are inaccurate approximations, but the intent is obvious. With increased physical maturation and practice, accuracy increases. Children's efforts at imitation are truly complimentary of the one being imitated and invariably lead to positive reinforcement that results in greater effort and success. An accompanying accomplishment is children's increasing skill in attending to the behaviors of others who are their learning models.

Instructional implication. The nonverbal child will require direct attention to the establishment of imitative behaviors, physical first and then vocal (Kent, 1974). Any efforts on the part of the child to imitate, physically or vocally, should receive instant reinforcement and pursuit, at that moment, of further imitation. The first directed efforts, i.e., the lowest level, should involve gross motor imitation rather than fine, e.g., clapping and standing, rather than touching the nose or blinking an eye. The progression should involve:

1   Gross motor
2   Fine motor
3   Vowels
4   Nonsense syllables, e.g., bah, mah
5   One-syllable words

Spoken Words   It is at approximately the tenth month that the average child discovers that there is such a thing as a spoken word. That is, he makes the magnificent intellectual discovery that by moving one's mouth the behavior of others is influenced. The effective range of the child's arms in reaching for his mother is no greater than 14 to 16 inches, but the effective range of what might be called a third arm, the spoken word, extends from the bedroom to kitchen. It is impossible to specify how this discovery can be "taught," for it is the result of maturation plus those behaviors and experiences that have occurred in the first 10 months.

Instructional implication. This is the first major objective in carrying any child forward in the acquisition of the formal mother tongue. Previously noted behaviors, imitation, conditioning, etc., are subobjectives leading up to this major event. Attention should be constantly directed to any evidence of a child's receptive awareness of the meaningfulness of a word. Since receptive awareness precedes the expressive use of language, the instructional emphasis should be reception, not expression. Although attention to the development of imitative skills is important, a focus upon imitative drilling may result in simple parroting.

Ten to Eighteen Months

The fourteen-month period from the intellectual discovery that spoken words exist until approximately 24 months can best be described as a period of "learning how to learn" language rather than a period of learning language per se. Certainly the average child acquires words, receptively and expressively, and by 24 months is even producing rudimentary phrases. Probably of greater importance is the fact that during this stage the child attends closely to the language utterances of others, the social context in which they occur, the interactive effect they have upon others, and the physical and vocal characteristics people demonstrate during the act of communication. Through observation the child determines elementary strategies for acquiring interactive language.

The tenth through the eighteenth month is an extremely busy time. Not only does the child discover and investigate the use of language, but learning demands are being made upon him in the areas of ambulation, feeding, bathing, socialization, etc. Observable growth in formal language learning is minimal and focuses primarily on isolated word learning. However, the changes that do occur, receptively and expressively, are of great fundamental importance.

Functional Associations   The number of functional associations, which are first observed in the latter half of the first 10-month period, increases dramatically. The child has become quite mobile and moves throughout his environment investigating those objects which attract his attention. Many behaviors are in evidence that indicate he is dealing with environmental objects through memory. There are appropriate motor responses to objects such as door knobs, light switches, shoes, hats, pets in the home, and familiar toys.

Instructional implication. The teacher should carefully observe the delayed-language child and record those objects which the child deals with meaningfully. The parents make similar observations and recordings in the home. The receptive and expressive vocabulary that is to be taught to the child will be derived from these recordings. Efforts should be made to increase the number of functional associations retained by the child, including object-sound associations. For example, select a few toy models of objects that the child comes in contact with daily. When playing with the child with each of the models, produce one sound consistently. The objective is the child's association of a unique sound with a specific object. For example,

a   Toy car (um . . . um)
b   Toy plane (er . . . er)
c   Toy telephone (ring . . . ring)
d   Toy dog (woof . . . woof)

Demanding Behavior   Very early in this 6-month period the average child shows evidence of an intellectual desire to obtain from and otherwise manipulate others. That is, vocal utterances, and facial and bodily movements, are varied in a directive manner; the child communicates, rudimentarily, without words.

Instructional implication. Leonard (1978) has noted that "Training for a non-verbal child should commence at the single-word utterance level only if he shows evidence . . . of gaining adults' attention by showing and pointing to objects and gaining access to objects by enlisting adults as vehicles to such access" (p. 85). Establishing the need to produce communicative behavior can best be attacked by varying times in the school day and in the home, rather than through a preplanned instructional period. Make note of a few environmental objects that are highly desirable for the child. Place them where they are easily seen within the room but unobtainable to the child. When the child moves toward one of the objects immediately take it and hold it enticingly out of reach. Any vocalization or gestural movement that can be interpreted as demanding is immediately rewarded by the child's obtaining the object. *The adult must not give the object to the child unless there is some change in behavior that can be interpreted as demanding*. With the most resistant cases, the temporary withholding of water during and after eating has been found to be quite effective.

Isolated Words   At some point within this period the average child begins using isolated words to act upon those in his environment. That is, the words are produced with intellectual intent rather than being simple conditioned utterances. The first word or two is expected of the average child by the fourteenth month, but some normal children do not use their first meaningful word until shortly thereafter. A speaking vocabulary of ten words is expected of average children by the end of the eighteenth month. Commonly, these are words designating specific individuals and objects in the home environment. However, there are usually one or more words which specify action, such as "more" (to demand repetition) and "up" (to demand someone to hold her or him). At this point the child's receptive vocabulary will certainly exceed ten words.

Instructional implication. Although the major focus of instruction during this period should be upon receptive understanding of labels, the child is encouraged to imitate the speaker as receptive understanding is being sought. The sequence, relative to a particular object over a number of days, would be as follows:

1 Repeatedly say "ball" as it is placed in the child's hand. Rub his or her hands over it, and assist the child in throwing or rolling it.

2 Place the object in front of the child with another object (and then with two other objects) with the command "Ball—point to (hesitation) ball." If needed, take the child's hand and place it on the object.

3 Once the child is giving an appropriate identification response, engage in the same activity, adding, "Yes, ball . . . say it, ball" (while directing the child's attention to the speaker's mouth). Immediately reinforce any approximation.

4 When there is vocal imitation, present the object and demand that the child generate the response on his or her own. "Ball, say it, ball"—(response)—"Good . . . what is this?" If the response is not forthcoming, the model should be presented again with the command "Say it."

A similar sequence will be used for other objects. It is important that the first few words include the labels mama and daddy; large, colored photographs of the two people are required.

Jargon Jargon is an important behavior acquired by the average child between the fifteenth and eighteenth month. Jargon is composed of connected sound utterances containing variations in pitch, loudness, and stress patterns. It is an experimental phase during which the child sounds as if he is carrying on a conversation except for the fact that there are no (or very few) understandable words; the rhythmical characteristics of spoken language are being practiced.

Instructional implication. Two techniques have been found to be useful in encouraging connected sound production, music and the use of a Voice-Lite. The latter is an instrument containing a microphone which, when stimulated by vocalization, results in the flashing of a light. That is, it gives instant visual feedback as a result of vocalization. The teacher, with a child or a group, can vocalize vowels or nonsense syllables (e.g., lah-lah-lah) in a musical manner varying loudness, pitch, and the rate of production. It may be necessary to assist the child in attending to the flashing light by engaging in the activity in a darkened room. A tape recorder is also a valuable tool. With or without such devices, music is important at this level of functioning. It matters not whether the child attempts imitation of the words to a song, but it is important that he vocalize in a continuous manner. Success in the variation of vocalization will occur over an extended period of time.

Eighteen to Twenty-Four Months

The child continues "learning how to learn" during this period, and at 24 months an astonishing change in formal language knowledge is demonstrated. The expressive vocabulary of approximately ten words at 18 months is suddenly discovered to approximate 300 words, and they no longer appear just as single-word utterances; there are frequent two-word combinations and, on occasion, utterances of greater length. At 24 months the child appears to understand statements that are of great length. The following comment by a father brings about instant, appropriate action on the part of the child: "Mary, go get your coat and I will take you outside." The child is thought to be responding to one or two key words, coat and outside in this instance, rather than to the total, complex message. The child is demonstrating a rule that has been discovered: The meaning of a total sentence can be determined by being alert for known, key elements. This rule aids the child in detecting unknown words within a message with subsequent determination of their meaning. There are a number of significant language changes that occur within this period which lend themselves to instruction with the language-delayed child.

Picture Interpretation   As previously indicated in this chapter, pictures are symbols. Although the average child attends to pictures and greatly enjoys being read to prior to 18 months, it is at about this point that the child will demonstrate meaningful interpretation of realistic colored pictures that are related to personal experiences. For example, when looking at a Christmas catalog a child may suddenly run to the bedroom and return with a tricycle as a result of having seen such a pictured object. He is demonstrating matching ability of a pictured representation to an object in the real world. At this point he may not express nor even respond to the spoken word "tricycle," but such response will undoubtedly occur shortly.

Instructional implication. The first objective related to picture use with the language-delayed child should be that of the matching of a picture with its counterpart in reality. An instant camera that returns a colored photograph of each of the objects for which a child has learned functional associations is useful in the classroom. As the teacher works with the child for matching, the spoken label should be produced in conjunction with each object/picture pair.

Gestures   Prior to 18 months the child has discovered that gestural information is an important communication aid in understanding spoken utterances. There is an obvious visual attentiveness in each communication setting. Learning the meaningfulness of gestures aids the child in learning the accompanying words. Whereas pointing, pulling, and reaching were predominant directive behaviors up to 18 months, the following 6-month interval results in increasing sophistication of gestural production, used extensively when the child cannot immediately find a word to express his thoughts.

Instructional implication. Caution must be exercised in deliberately programming for increased responding to, and use of, gestures because language-delayed children often demonstrate a relatively high level of dependence on visual communication, to the exclusion of the spoken word. Specific attention to the understanding of gestures, and subsequent use, is called for when spoken and gestural communication are equally depressed. Select a limited number of environmental commands that occur every day. Carefully preplan the gestures that will accompany the spoken command so that they will be consistent during both structured and unstructured work and used by everyone who communicates with the child. Examples of commands are:

"Close the door." (Head and eye movement in the direction of the door, hand describing a pushing motion.)

"Turn on the water." (Appropriate head and eye movement, hand describing a turning motion.)

"Turn on the light." (Appropriate head and eye movement, a flipping movement of the extended hand.)

Physical Action Words A few words that specify physical action are added to the child's receptive and expressive vocabulary between 18 and 24 months. The sequence of acquisition is (1) labels for what happens to oneself, e.g., fall, sit, (2) labels for what one does to things, e.g., play, throw, and (3) labels for the actions of things, e.g., bark, break. The learning of action labels is an important step toward two-word phrase production in the form of subject-verb constructions such as "Billy hurt," "Stick broke," "Cup broke," etc.

Instructional implication. Two specific instructional goals are the appropriate responding of the child to commands that specify (1) what he is to do in positioning his body and (2) what action he is to take on environmental objects. Initially, a gesture should accompany the spoken command and, if necessary, physical assistance in responding should be given. That is, when the command "Stand" is given, the instructor instantly places her hands under the child's arms and raises him or her to an upright position, followed by reinforcement. Reduce assistance and then physical cues as quickly as possible. A suggested sequence follows:

1 Work for the child's accurate responding to words related to his or her own body movements: stand, lay, sit, run, jump. Work on one word at a time.

2 Work for responding to action words related to the child's use of a ball, e.g., throw, kick, roll.

3 When consistent responses are obtained at Level 2, work to assist the child in generalizing the verbs to other objects. For example: roll ball, roll car, roll wagon. Be certain that the object label is well established before working at this level.

When appropriate responding has been established for a few commands, reverse roles, waiting expectantly for the child's command followed, if necessary, by verbal modeling ("Say it") for the child to imitate.

Prepositions   Toward the end of the second year of life the average child discovers that there are words that designate position, words that adults call prepositions. The first words that are learned specify static position, e.g., under, between. Directional terms such as to, with, and toward are acquired later.

Instructional implication. The prepositions *in* and *on* are taught first. It is much easier to introduce the concept of locative labels in association with the child's body position than it is to introduce them relative to the position of environmental objects. Place the child on the chair (table, box, step, tricycle) with the statement "On—on chair." Repeat the sequence many times over several days and then add "in" which requires an enclosure large enough for the child, "In—in box," "In—in bag."

After the terms have been used descriptively during several sessions introduce the command form "Get on chair," "Get on table," "Get in box." Vocal emphasis and gesture should be on the preposition and it may be necessary to physically assist the child into the correct position. Immediate positive reinforcement always follows.

When the child is responding appropriately to the commands relative to body position, work for responding relative to the position of environmental objects when the subject is indicated. For example, handing the child a block, the teacher states, "Put in box." The word "in" is emphasized and the response is assisted if necessary.

After establishing correct responding to the terms "in," "on," and the phrases "*put in (on)*" and "*get in (on)*," the instructor should reverse roles, in your-turn—my-turn format, to work for the child's expressive use. Modeling will be required.

Twenty-Four to Thirty-Six Months

At 24 months the average child responds with understanding to a large number of situational commands and statements (for examples see words below). In addition, there are responses to many novel utterances that are brief in length and contain a known word accompanied by prosodic and physical cues. By careful observation of novel utterances the child adds extensively to his receptive vocabulary during this 12-month period. Phrase production, at the beginning of this period, is telegraphic in nature, most frequently composed of two words in the forms of (1) subject-verb, e.g., "car broke" (2) verb-object, e.g., "push car," or (3) subject-object, e.g., "daddy car." By the end of the 12-month period the child's statements have become complete simple sentences averaging three to four words in length.

Words that are gradually revealed in the child's expressive repetoire reflect increasing knowledge of the rules of his mother tongue. It is quite probable, for example, that at 24 months Billy will state, as he clutches his car, "Billy car." Very quickly this utterance will be modified to "mine car" and by 36 months the adult form "my car" will be heard.

It is significant that parents often think of this period in their child's life as the "bossy" stage, for he has discovered the usefulness of spoken words and practices the act extensively to make things happen.

There are, indeed, extensive changes in the child's receptive and expressive use of language during this period. A few of the changes that lend themselves to direct attack in the classroom and in the home of the language-delayed child follow.

Situational Words and Phrases   There are large numbers of situational words and phrases that the child has learned by approximately 24 months and the number increases greatly by 36 months. Interestingly, one can often note the appearance of these productions in the child's speech as he plays with a doll, pet dog, cat, etc. Bangs (1968) has produced an extensive list of such statements as related to children under 3 years of age. The following is a modification of that list:

No	Come here	Point to
Stay here	Get it	Hold my hand
Stop it	Get _____	Ah oh!
It's hot	Family name (mama, daddy)	Gimmie a hug
Don't touch it	Up, down	Gimmie a kiss
Put it down	Good	Go to bed (nite-nite)
All-gone	Let's go	Let's eat
Hi	I see you	More
Bye-bye	Yes	Water
Child's name	Find _____	

Instructional implication. The words and phrases listed above do not lend themselves to structured, one to one instruction. Rather, they are statements that require consistent use in the class and in the home under specific, consistent conditions. There should be a deliberate effort on the parts of the teacher and the parent to employ these statements in a comparable manner daily. Note that the first seven in the list are terminal statements to be given with an appropriate tone of voice and gesture. The term *good* consistently follows any appropriate response given by the child during the day.

Picture Stories   The average child becomes increasingly alert to pictures of individual objects and also to "story" pictures that contain a limited number of objects with a central action theme. He responds appropriately by pointing when a consistent directive is given such as "Show me" or "Point to." Many pictured objects are labeled spontaneously or as a result of the request "What is that?"

Instructional implication. First, begin a picture workbook for each language-delayed child. The first pictures should be photographs of objects for which the child has learned the label. Gradually add other pictures of objects which are important in the child's world. Be concerned first that the child responds receptively to the label of each picture when the command "Point to _____" is given, then work for expressive labeling in response to the command "What is that?" Allow the child to take the notebook home each day with follow-up work for the parents.

Second, daily reading of a story from a child's book is an excellent language-development activity. Such books commonly contain sequentially pictured material. Select two or three books that contain activity pictures that are closely related to the language-handicapped child's own world. Do not select books containing caricatures, e.g., dogs talking, monkeys rowing boats. Tell the story in very simplified language repeatedly over many days. After repeated contact the child may spontaneously interject portions of the story and this should be reinforced. The same activity, again using only two or three books, should be carried out daily in the home.

Telegraphic Sentences As previously noted, the child of 24 months combines two words in the production of telegraphic sentences. The concept of open versus pivot words (Braine, 1963) is quite useful in working with the language-delayed child. Open words are labels of things or actions, i.e., concrete identifiers such as shoe, car, doggie, run. Pivot words are those that act upon open class words, e.g., see, all-gone, more.

Instructional implication. Two pivot words that lend themselves to structured activity are gimme and where. Using articles for which the child has acquired labels, receptively and expressively, the teacher can structure an activity in which the child is to respond to the command "Gimme _____." Establish a your-turn–my-turn mode of functioning and require the child to produce the utterance with appropriate labels; the articles are immediately given to the child.

In a similar your-turn–my-turn setting, locate the objects around the room. With searching physical action and questioning inflection ask, "Where _____?" Assist the response if necessary. The child is then stimulated to question the teacher.

Body Part Labels Many body part labels are acquired by a child prior to 36 months of age. For the average child the first labels are related to the head, e.g., eye, ear, nose, for they are the body parts named repeatedly by parents.

Instructional implication. In working with language-handicapped children the author has found certain cautions to be aware of in teaching labels for body parts:

1 Begin by working for the understanding of names for those body parts which the child can view directly upon himself: hand, foot, leg, tummy; parts of the head do not allow direct observation.
2 Work first for the identification of the child's body parts: "Where is Billy's hand?"
3 When five labels have been established relative to the child's own body,

broaden the identification task by including self (teacher) and a baby doll with the following questions:

a "Where is Billy's (pointing) hand?"
b "Where is my (pointing) hand?"
c "Where is baby's hand?"

4 Do *not* deal with toy animals or the child's image in a mirror.

When the child has acquired these labels receptively, the question "What is this (pointing)?" should be used, indicating the child, then the self, then the baby doll. Move forward by gradually adding a new word after each success.

Thirty-Six to Forty-Eight Months

The spoken language produced by the average child changes significantly from that produced in the previous 12-month period in two major ways. First, it no longer serves the simple purposes of directing the actions of others or responding concretely to their verbalizations. Its use broadens to the description of personal experiences and the expression of feelings and desires. Receptively, language can be used to reason with the child, who, in short, becomes a communicatively interactive person, a conversationalist.

Second, the grammatical nature of the child's language production undergoes significant change as the appearance of whole words and variations in word endings indicate awareness that there are grammatical rules which signify (1) time, (2) plurality, (3) gender, and (4) possession. Descriptive words also begin to appear.

Nominative Pronouns Children at the age of 35 months are using nominative pronouns including *I* to designate the subject of a statement. As a prerequisite to this acquisition the child must recognize that people are divisible into two classes with appropriate labels, boy-girl (later, male-female). This knowledge is then extended to the labels he-she and, in the possessive case, his-hers.

Instructional implication. Children in a classroom can be separated into two groups using the appropriate statement "a boy" or "a girl" with each child. In a one to one instructional setting the teacher can use pictures of the children in the class. Caution: Be certain that the characteristics of each pictured child clearly depict the sex, e.g., skirt versus long pants, short hair versus long hair. Work with the child to separate the pictures into two labeled groups as they are randomly presented. Once the child is successful in silent differentiation, present the pictures randomly, encouraging the child to verbally label them with a model and to imitate them when needed.

The next step involves the same pictures, plus others of both adults and children, with the expressive goal of "*He* is a boy," "*She* is a girl."

Present Participle Children in this age bracket are responding to and producing the present participle, *is +-ing*, of those verbs that have been previously acquired. In fact, during this period many more verbs are added to the child's vocabulary and the past tense begins to appear.

Instructional implication. Using action pictures of verbs that have been previously established, say the questioning phrase "What is the boy (the girl) doing?" Verbally emphasize the "doing" for it serves as a clue to the form of the expected response. Model the appropriate response with emphasis on the *ing* ending, e.g., jump*ing*, sleep*ing*. Rhythmical clapping should be used by the teacher to emphasize the two syllables.

When the child is responding spontaneously, rather than imitatively, the next objective can be introduced, *is +-ing*. This is presented in a sentence-completion format with the teacher stating the subject, "the boy," and the child producing the verb phrase, "is jumping." Subsequent objectives should be (1) the child's production of the complete sentence "The boy (The girl) is _____-ing," followed by (2) the use of the pronoun in the sentence construction "He (She) is _____-ing."

Descriptive Attributes Words which are descriptive of the attributes of objects in the child's world are important acquisitions during this age period. These words are dealt with as comparatives in adult language with a label for the polar opposites, e.g., tall-short, big-little. In the first learning of such words a child acquires one as an absolute. For example, Jenny used the label "big" as a designator for every object, no matter how small, for a lengthy period before the label "little" began to appear to specify difference in size between two objects.

Instructional implication. Attributes which have the greatest sensory impact should be the first to be named with the language-delayed child. Size has great impact for it has permanency and provides visual, tactile, and gravitational (weight) information. The first label to introduce is "big," and success is mandatory before adding others for this descriptor sets the stage for those that follow.

Pairs of objects are selected that are as identical as possible except for size, the attribute that must be grossly different. With both objects visible to the child, the teacher should name the one that has the positive characteristic, e.g., big ball, big spoon, big car. Move to the command "Point to the big _____." When consistent responding has been established, introduce the phrase "not big" relative to the second of each pair. The term "little" should be inserted later as a synonym for "not big."

In the introduction of subsequent pairs of comparative terms the positive of each pair (that which has greatest sensory impact) should be introduced first.

Plural Endings The discovery that the addition of *s*, *z*, and *ez* designates a group is an important linguistic step. This learning is aided by the additional clue that frequently accompanys such modified words, i.e., the preceding terms *a*, *the*, and *some*.

Instructional implication. In the pursuit of the objective of the recognition and use of plural endings the first target objects (or pictures of objects) should be those that employ the sound of *z* as the plural marker, e.g., guns, boys, girls, apples. Work first to ensure that the child differentiates receptively the singular and the plural. This can be accomplished by using groups of two pictures for which one is an isolated article and its counterpart contains two or more similar articles. The task is to separate each of the pair into an appropriate pile, those that are singular and those that are plural. The stated phrase should vocally emphasize the critical elements, e.g., "*a* car," "*some* cars." Although there is no intent at this point to teach counting, it will be helpful on each plural picture for the teacher to count the items then follow with the summary statement. For example, "one, two, three (as she points), *some* cars." The child should then be encouraged to separate each pair into its appropriate stack with physical assistance from the teacher.

A modified game of "go fishing" can be used to work for the child's expression of singular and plural forms. Initially, the reduced form "a _____" and "some _____s" should be all that is necessary to request of the other player the desired picture. When success is achieved, the required utterance is expanded to a complete sentence, "I want a _____" or "I want some _____s."

Forty-Eight to Seventy-Two Months

At the age of 48 months average children are quite loquacious, engaging in relatively elaborate interactive conversation with both adults and other children. However, their expressed language will contain noticeable errors of grammar and occasional misuse of words (by adult definitions). Language structure has remained simple up to 48 months, with sentences relatively brief in length. The words the child has acquired have, for the most part, been concrete labels for objects, actions, positions, etc. Between the fourth birthday and the sixth birthday great changes occur in language functioning as it rapidly approaches adult standards. This is a period of concept learning with major growth in the cognitive areas of abstraction and generalization. By the end of this 2-year period the average child's knowledge of the rules of syntax and grammar of his or her mother tongue is essentially complete except for language irregularities.

Abstract Labels Children acquire many abstract labels that describe sensory experiences during this period. Of course, some labels were acquired prior to the fourth birthday, but there is now a veritable explosion of word learning relative to hearing, vision, taction, smell, taste, etc.

Instructional implication. Teachers should take every opportunity to use abstract, descriptive words to describe a single experience that the children have had. They should work specifically for an increase in vocabulary related to each sense. For example, each day for a week during a specific time, the focus should be on tactile experiences with activities such as:

a The blindfolded teacher takes the classroom object that was placed in her hands by the child, uses words to describe its shape, texture, weight, etc., and finally identifies it by name. Each child then has a turn.

b A walk is taken around the school yard with even the most obvious objects (a rock, a fence post, a concrete block) being discussed in terms of tactile sensations.

In subsequent weeks similiar activities are conducted relative to one sensory input channel at a time.

Comparing and Grouping Children not only add greatly to their vocabulary of descriptive words, they also make use of those words for purposes of comparing and grouping experiences, that is, for making associations. "Soft" is discovered to be an attribute of cotton, pillows, and one's own cheek, and the label aptly describes all three.

Having acquired a degree of skill in judging and labeling likenesses, children begin to evidence attention to characteristics that are "not alike," i.e., different.

Instructional implication. Engage in specific activities for which the children look for articles in the classroom that are similar on one labeled sensory dimension, e.g., relative to vision: all things that are round, are red, are worn on the body (function). The emphasis is on likeness.

The foregoing type of activity, once successful, should then be extended to "not alike," or "not the same." The word "different" should be inserted as a synonym by the teacher when the child is responding appropriately and making use of the descriptive phrase "not alike," or "not the same."

Compound Sentences The average child is producing compound sentences at approximately the fourth birthday. For the most part, such statements will be simple sentences joined by the conjunction "and"; "The ball is red and the ball is round"; "The ball is red and the car is red." Shortly thereafter the child collapses such structures into the adult form, "The ball is red and round"; "The ball and the car are red."

Instructional implication. Employing the sensory experiences previously established, set the specific objective of each child's verbal description of the events with a multiple subject or object. A sentence-completion activity may be used to establish the expected structure. The teacher provides the subject and the child adds the descriptive words, as in the following example:

Teacher: "The ball is . . ." *Child*: ". . . red and round."

Complex Sentences Toward the end of this 2-year period complex sentence construction will be employed. The average child can be observed using words to hypothesize outcomes and evaluating possible alternatives in a situational problem. Phrases such as "I hope . . .," "What if . . .?" and "I wonder . . ." are observed.

Instructional implication. A sentence-completion activity using situational pictures can be used for verbal hypothesizing:

(Picture of a child on a wall)
Teacher: "If the boy falls . . ."
Child: "then he will hurt himself."

(Picture of a child reaching for a cookie jar)
Teacher: "If he hits the jar . . ."
Child: "he will break it."

A similar sentence-completion approach can be used to establish why-because statements relative to something that has already occurred.

Refined Articulation   Refinement in the articulation of speech sounds within words occurs during this period. At the fourth birthday the average child is expected to be producing pronunciations such as "wabbit" for rabbit, "hewo" for hello, and "bwue" for blue. However, within the sixth year speech is produced that approaches adult standards except for difficult combinations of sounds such as *str*ing, ba*thr*oom, and bir*thd*ay.

Instructional implication. Engage in activities that are designed to assist the children to become aware of the individual speech sounds that go together to make up words.

The major objective should be the listening for, and identification of, individual speech sounds, rather than the corrected production of those sounds. A sound a week can be selected by the teacher for attention during language time. In week 1, for example, the teacher may select the sound sh for concentration. Give the sound a name—the be-quiet sound in this case—rather than an alphabetical designation. Stories and rhymes involving the particular sound are then read to the class on succeeding days. Such materials are available in *The Big Book of Sounds* (Flowers), and *Speech Correction Through Story Telling Units* (Nemoy). In addition, the teacher and the children should search during the class day for words that contain the target sound. A different consonant sound should be selected each week with immediate reinforcement being provided to the child who spontaneously produces the sound correctly.

SUMMARY

An adult communicator usually detects intuitively the presence of a difference in the communicative skills of a child. The precise delineation of that difference poses a problem greater than simple detection and begins with the question: Is the difference related to language functioning, speech functioning, or both?

Language is herein defined as the substance of communication, i.e., the symbolic content and form. Speech is defined as the vehicle that transports one's language across distance, culminating in the individual's interacting with others as both an initiator and respondent. Intervention programming can begin only after careful evaluation of (1) a number of dimensions that comprise a child's receptive and expressive language functioning and (2) the coordinated neuro-muscular skills of vocalization, articulation, and fluency during the act of spontaneous speech. Complete evaluation also requires careful consideration of the many prerequisities for language and speech acquisition, and when problems are detected steps must be taken for their alleviation.

The child that is determined to be delayed in language and speech acquisition can be assisted to further development if there is a coordinated, cooperative effort by the parents, teachers, therapist, and others who are with that child daily. Fragmented, sporadic efforts lead only to confusion and failure to obtain carryover of goals into daily functioning. Everyone should adhere to the following principles:

1 Goals must be cooperatively determined and pursued.
2 An aura of expectancy of success must be exuded by each person.
3 Any success, no matter how small, must receive instant positive reinforcement.
4 The focus should be on receptive understanding first, followed by emphasis on expression.
5 The selected goals must be both realistic and functional.
6 Focus should be placed on short-term goals.
7 The incremental steps from subgoal to subgoal must be small.
8 The method for obtaining a behavior (visual, physical and/or verbal cuing) employed by one person should be used by all.
9 The verbal models presented to the individual child must be consistent and not include confusing language.
10 There must be a specific effort to obtain generalization of newly acquired behaviors into other situations.

Information regarding language and speech development in average children forms the basis for language programming for the delayed child. Such information is drawn upon for the many examples of targeted behaviors that are discussed in the latter half of this chapter. The examples range from objectives for the child who does not respond meaningfully to a spoken word to objectives for the verbally interactive child whose utterances are complete and meaningful although simple in construction and concrete in content. The behavioral sequence, as presented, cannot be used with an individual child for many intervening behaviors are omitted. However, any one of the behaviors cited may serve as a satisfactory starting point for language intervention for some children.

REFERENCES . . .

Bangs, T. E. *Language and learning disorders of the pre-academic child.* Englewood Cliffs, N.J.: Prentice-Hall, 1968.

Berry, M. F. *Language disorders of children.* New York: Appleton-Century-Crofts, 1969.

Bigge, J. L. Severe communication problems. In J. L. Bigge, *Teaching individuals with physical and multiple disabilities.* Columbus, Ohio: Merrill, 1976.

Blue, C. M. The marginal communicator. *Language, speech and hearing services in the schools*, 1975, *6*(1), 32–38.

Bluma, S., Shearer, M., Frohman, A., & Hilliard, J. *Portage guide to early education* (revised edition). Portage, Wis.: Cooperative Educational Service, 1976.

Boatner, M. T., & Gates, J. E. *A dictionary of idioms*. West Hartford, Conn.: American School for the Deaf, 1966.

Bowerman, M. Semantic and syntactic development. In R. L. Schiefelbusch, *Bases of language intervention*. Boston: Little, Brown, 1978.

Braine, M. D. S. The ontogeny of English phrase structure: The first phase. *Language*, 1963, *39*, 1–13.

Bricker, D., Dennison, L., & Bricker, W. *A language intervention program for developmentally young children*. Miami: Mailman Center for Child Development, 1976.

Brigance, A. H. *Brigance diagnostic inventory of early development*. Woburn, Mass.: Curriculum Association, Inc., 1978.

Brown, R. *A first language: The early states*. Cambridge: Harvard University Press, 1973.

Carroll, J. B. *Language and thought*. Englewood Cliffs, N.J.: Prentice-Hall, 1964.

Cazden, C. B. *Child language and education*. New York: Holt, 1972.

Chomsky, N. *Syntactic structures*. The Hague: Mouton, 1957.

Eisenson, J., & Ogilvie, M. *Speech correction in the schools* (4th ed.). New York: Prentice-Hall, 1977.

Engelmann, S., & Osborn, J. *Distar, language I*. Chicago: Science Research Associates, Inc., 1976.

Falck, V. T. Communication skills—Translating theory into practice. *Teaching Exceptional Children*, 1978, *10*(3), 74–77.

Flowers, A. M. *The big book of sounds*. Danville, Ill.: Interstate, 1963.

Griffin, P. M., Sanford, A. R., & Wilson, D. C. *Learning accomplishment profile*. Winston-Salem, N. C.: Kaplan School Supply Corporation, 1975.

Guess, D., Sailor, W., & Baer, D. *Functional speech and language training for the severely handicapped*. Lawrence, Kan.: H & H Enterprises, Inc., 1976.

Hatten, J., Goman, T., & Lent, C. *Emerging language 2*. Tucson: Communication Skill Builders, Inc., 1976.

Kent, L. R. *Language acquisition program for the retarded or multiply impaired*. Champaign, Ill.: Research Press, 1974.

Lahey, M. *Readings in childhood language disorders*. New York: Wiley, 1978.

Leonard, L. B. Cognitive factors in early linguistic development. In R. L. Schiefelbusch, *Bases of language intervention*. Baltimore: University Park Press, 1978.

Leonard, L. B., Wilcox, M. J., Fulmer, K. C., & Davis, G. A. Understanding indirect requests: An investigation of children's comprehension of pragmatic meanings. *Journal of Speech and Hearing Research*, 1978, *21*(3), 528–537.

Muma, J. R. Language intervention: Ten techniques. *Language, Speech and Hearing Services in Schools*, 1971, *1*(5), 7–17.

Muma, J. R. *Language handbook*. Englewood Cliffs, N.J.: Prentice-Hall, 1978.

Nemoy, E. M. *Speech correction through story-telling units*. Magnolia, Mass.: Expression Company, 1954.

Newman, M. A., & Bailey, B. E. *A compilation of preschool children's word frequency counts*. Unpublished manuscript, Austin, Tex.: Texas Department of Human Resources, 1973.

Nicolosi, L., Harryman, E., & Kresheck, J. *Terminology of communication disorders*. Baltimore: Williams & Wilkins, 1978.

Sander, E. K. When are speech sounds learned? *Journal of Speech and Hearing Disorders*, 1972, *37*, 55–63.

Snyder, L. K., Lovitt, T. C., & Smith, J. O. Language training for the severely retarded: Five years of behavior analysis. *Exceptional Children*, 1975, *42*(1), 7–15.

Van Riper, C. *The treatment of stuttering*. Englewood Cliffs, N.J.: Prentice-Hall, 1973.

Van Riper, C. *Speech correction—principles and methods* (6th ed.). Englewood Cliffs, N.J.: Prentice-Hall, 1978.

Wilson, K. S. *Voice problems of children*. Baltimore: Williams & Wilkins, 1972.

Winitz, H. *Articulatory acquisition and behavior*. New York: Appleton-Century-Crofts, 1969.

Wood, B. S. *Children and communication: Verbal and nonverbal language development*. Englewood Cliffs, N.J.: Prentice-Hall, 1976.

Wood, N. E. *Delayed speech and language development*. Englewood Cliffs, N.J.: Prentice-Hall, 1964.

Worthley, W. J. *Sourcebook of language learning activities*. Boston: Little, Brown, 1978.

Chapter 11

Functional Academics

Functional academics refers to the basic cognitive skills of reading and arithmetic. Teaching functional reading and arithmetic skills to handicapped students is crucial. The long-term goal of personal and vocational independence depends on some understanding of reading and arithmetic. This chapter presents reading and arithmetic skills ranging in difficulty from simple to complex. The purpose is to give you a range of options as you develop programs for handicapped students.

Learning Goals

You should be able to answer the following questions when you finish this chapter:

- What is the goal of a functional academic program? Specify the decisions that must be made to structure and manage a program.
- What notions should guide the characteristics of a functional academic program? Describe the implications of these notions.

- Define reading. What are the student's reading tasks?
- List the three categories of reading skills. Briefly describe the major broad and specific reading skills. Identify the type(s) of learning required for each specific skill.
- Using the general and specific learning principles, construct lesson plans for three specific reading skills.
- Define arithmetic. What is the key question to ask about arithmetic skills?
- Briefly describe the major broad and specific arithmetic skills. Identify the type(s) of learning required for each specific skill.
- Using the general and specific learning principles, construct lesson plans for three specific arithmetic skills.

This chapter is organized in the following way. First, some basic information on structuring and managing a functioning academic program is presented. This information focuses the program-development process on the decisions required to produce a viable program. Second, the functional academic subdomain of reading is presented. This section includes the set of reading skills appropriate to teach handicapped students and a sample lesson plan. The sample lesson plan is based on the principles of learning presented in Part One. The final section of the chapter presents the subdomain of arithmetic. As usual, skills within the subdomain and an illustrative lesson plan are presented.

STRUCTURING AND MANAGING A FUNCTIONAL ACADEMIC PROGRAM

Structuring a program requires decisions about scope, instructional objectives, sequences, placement level, and entering behavior (Blake, 1976b). Managing a program includes decisions on scheduling and allocating personnel and resources (Blake, 1976b). Most of these topics are covered in depth in Part One. The purpose here is to briefly review these topics in relation to a functional academic program.

Scope/Instructional Objectives

Many handicapped students can attain most of the same reading and arithmetic instructional objectives ordinarily proposed for normal students at the elementary school level. *However, they should have objectives pertaining to reading and arithmetic skills they will need in their adult personal and vocational tasks.* They should also have objectives pertaining to their deficits in prerequisite reading and arithmetic skills.

Sequences

Handicapped students should have the same sequence of instructional objectives as normal students. Within a category, e.g., numeration in arithmetic, skills should be ordered on the basis of complexity; less-complex skills should be learned before more-complex skills. Among categories, e.g., numeration and operations with whole numbers in arithmetic, skills should be ordered on the basis of similarity. The most similar skills should be presented closest together.

Placement Level

Placement level is the level at which reading and arithmetic skills are located for instruction. That is, placement of a skill indicates a point in the student's development at which we expect him to be able to learn that skill.

Reading and arithmetic instructional objectives should be based on handicapped students' mental ages (MA), not their chronological ages (CA). That is, we should expect handicapped students to master instructional objectives at the mental ages where they are achieved by intellectually normal students who have corresponding chronological ages.

Note that we are referring here to expectations about what students should be able to do, other conditions being favorable. We need these expectations to make judgments about goals, underachievement, and so on. In addition, though, as we describe below, at any given time, we should expose the student only to the skills he has the prerequisites for.

For example, consider a retarded student who has a chronological age of 12 years and a mental age of 9 years. We should expect him to achieve about at the level of a normal child in the third grade who has a chronological age and mental age of 9 years. We should not expect him to achieve like a normal child in the seventh grade who has a chronological age and mental age of 12 years. However, when we meet this student who has a MA of 9, he may be achieving at the level of a student with a mental age of 7. That is, he may be underachieving. We should base our general goals of helping him achieve up to his mental age expectancy. As we begin to teach him, though, we should begin at a level appropriate for those prerequisites he has attained.

Entering Behavior

Entering behavior is the student's status on an instructional objective at the outset of instruction, that is, his status on prerequisite skills. Handicapped students should have entering behavior about like a normal student who has the same mental age. However, we can expect that handicapped students will have attained the entering behavior required for an instructional objective less often than normal students.

Handicapped students often underachieve; i.e., they often do not attain prerequisite skills appropriate for students at their mental age levels. When this underachievement occurs, there are two choices:

Procedures should be used to give the student the prerequisites he or she needs.

Instructional objectives lower in the hierarchy of instructional objectives should be chosen.

Stated another way: our expectations are about what a student should be ready to do. Given those expectations, we still should base instructional level on what the student actually is ready to do.

Scheduling

Scheduling refers to the time allocated for pupils to learn the reading skills. Over a short period of instruction, mildly handicapped students should have the same time allocations as normal students *who have similar mental ages* for most skills. For a few skills, handicapped students should have more time. That is, within a limited time, most handicapped students learn at about the same rate as normal students and no adjustment is needed. Over a more-extended period of time, handicapped students should have more time allocated for learning particular skills. That is, we need to adjust for their slower rate of mental growth. The more severe the handicap, the more adjustment that needs to be made.

Allocating Personnel and Resources

Allocating personnel and resources includes the organization of people for teaching and the obtaining of media. Since placement levels of reading and arithmetic skills for handicapped students should be based on their mental age levels rather than on their chronological age levels, special attention should be devoted to administrative organizations. Commonly used patterns are the following:

Handicapped students may be placed in regular classes with other pupils who have the same chronological ages. This placement should be accompanied by tutoring by a resource teacher, intraclass grouping, and individual tutoring with systems like individually prescribed instruction.

Handicapped students may be placed in self-contained classes with other pupils who have similar CAs, IQs, and MAs.

Since handicapped students show a slower rate of mental growth, they will need instruction in reading and arithmetic beyond the elementary school years; therefore, provision for reading and arithmetic instruction at the secondary school level should be made.

Since handicapped students may have interest levels similar to those of their CA peers while they have achievement potentials like those of their MA peers, they should have special materials with interest levels appropriate for their CAs and difficulty levels appropriate for their MAs.These materials are called high-interest-level/low-difficulty-level materials.

GUIDING NOTIONS ON A FUNCTIONAL ACADEMIC PROGRAM

Several notions should guide the characteristics of a functional academic program (Blake, 1976a). These notions and their implications are presented below.

Intraindividual and Interindividual Variations

Students show intraindividual and interindividual variations in progress. Across skills, any one student will progress at different rates in the several skills. That is, he may make faster progress in sight vocabulary than in phonics or vice versa. Similarly, among students, each will progress at different rates through any one and all skills. Therefore, the teaching system should be organized so that each student's progress through each skill can be monitored for him as an individual and his instruction placed accordingly. That is, provisions need to be made for assessing each student's status and progress, gearing his instruction to that assessment, and recording both the results of the assessments and the nature of the instruction.

Need for Multiple Presentations

Students seldom show one-trial learning. In order to attain an objective, students may need a number of presentations of information. *These presentations cannot be merely repetitions.* Instead, they need to be multiple presentations in a variety of settings. Therefore, there should be a wide range of instructional procedures for each objective.

Variety of Procedures

Students and teachers need a variety of instructional procedures. Interests and preferences vary. An activity, story, etc. that one may prefer another may dislike. Therefore, again, there should be a variety of instructional procedures for each instructional objective.

READING

Reading is a complex act and can be defined in many ways. We have adopted the following definition from a reading research program (Blake, Williams, Aaron, & Allen, 1971–1976).

> Reading is the process of grasping the message conveyed in written symbols (comprehension following decoding), determining what the message means (interpretation following literal comprehension), and determining what the message means for a particular situation (application following interpretation).

This definition specifies the students' reading tasks as grasping information presented visually and interpreting and applying that information. These tasks parallel the student's tasks in listening within oral language. In listening, the student deals with oral material; in reading, with written material.

The student uses a variety of skills to accomplish the reading tasks of grasping, interpreting, and applying information. These skills can be classified as word recognition, word analysis, literal comprehension, interpretation, and application. Table 11-1 shows the broad and specific reading skills.

Table 11-1   Reading Skills

Broad skill	Specific skills
Prereading	
Language behavior	Understanding and using vocabulary (labels, concepts, etc.)
	Understanding and using connected discourse (conversations, stories, etc.)
	Interpreting pictures
	Hearing rhymes
Perceptual behavior	Using left-to-right progression
	Differentiating between figure and background
	Discriminating among sounds
	Discriminating among visual stimuli
	Maintaining sustained attention
Cognitive and social behavior	Showing awareness of common cultural experiences
	Making inferences beyond present stimuli
	Following simple directions
	Showing elementary work habits (independence, responsibility, etc.)
	Relating pictures and written material to own experiences
Word recognition	
Sight vocabulary	Learning a basic sight vocabulary
	Learning words which deviate from pronunciation principles
	Learning words for special purposes
Phonetic analysis	Hearing sounds in words
	Discriminating among sounds
	Blending sounds
	Identifying consonant letter-sound correspondences
	Using consonant-pronunciation principles
	Identifying vowel letter-sound correspondences
	Using vowel-pronunciation principles
	Using syllabication principles
	Using principles for accent
Analysis	
Structural analysis	Identifying root words
	Identifying meanings of compound words
	Identifying meanings of contractions
	Identifying inflectional suffixes (endings)
	Identifying derivational suffixes

Table 11-1   Reading Skills (Continued)

Broad skill	Specific skills
	Identifying prefixes Interpreting irregular forms Identifying roots of words which had spelling changes when suffixes were added
Context analysis	Determining word functions (nouns, verbs, modifiers, connectives) Using context clues (comparison, contrast, examples, elaboration, experience, definition) Using picture clues Differentiating homographs Differentiating homonyms
Denotative meanings	Learning specific labels Learning synonyms and antonyms Learning concepts
Figurative language	Interpreting idioms, similies, etc.
Dictionary use	Using types of dictionaries: regular dictionaries, picture dictionaries, thesauruses, lists of synonyms and antonyms Learning principles of alphabetic organization Using guide words Finding definitions Selecting definitions Using diacritical marking (pronunciation symbols) Noting information about words (pronunciation, syllabication, form class, inflected and derived forms, history, multiple definitions, examples, synonyms and antonyms, etc.) Using other information in a dictionary (rules for punctuation and capitalization, lists of geographic names, etc.)

Literal comprehension

Using previewing, detailed reading
Skimming and scanning; using punctuation and guides to coherence
Finding ideas in phrases and sentences
Finding main ideas in paragraphs
Finding supporting ideas and details in paragraphs
Finding main ideas in longer selections
Finding supporting ideas and details in longer selections

Table 11-1   Reading Skills (Continued)

Broad skill	Specific skills
Interpretation	
Identifying relations	Cause-effect Time Space Comparison and contrast Size Part-whole General-specific, Specific-general Sequence
Dealing with description	Objects Events Ideas Emotional states Motivations Sensory images Directions for performing in action
Drawing inferences/ conclusions	Content portrayed in pictures Implied ideas and feelings Events around described events (between, before, after) Character Plot and levels of meaning
Evaluating material	True and false information Pertinent and nonpertinent information Fact and opinion Faculty reasoning Rhetorical tricks (slanting, stereotypes, etc.)
Application	
Processing	Pinning down purposes Checking relevance Analyzing and outlining selections Summarizing and note taking Synthesizing information from several sources
Location	Using a book's structure (contents, index, etc.) Using reference materials (maps, charts, directories, encyclopedia, indexes, etc.) Finding materials in the library

Source: Adapted from Blake (1976).

The major broad skills are briefly described below. A sample lesson plan illustrates how to apply the principles of learning to reading instruction. You will need to use other resources, e.g., Alexander (1979), Bond and Wasson (1979),

Heilman (1976), Otto and Chester (1976), for detailed information on the broad and specific skills of reading.

Word-Recognition Skills

The student uses word-recognition skills to identify a word's pronunciation. Once he can pronounce the word, the student can attach it to a meaning in his oral vocabulary. Or, if the word is not in his oral vocabulary, he can learn a meaning (Blake, 1974). There are two broad word-recognition skills: learning sight vocabulary and phonetic analysis.

Learning Sight Vocabulary   Identifying sight words is recognizing the word instantly. The student does not analyze the word in any way. There are three categories of words where learning to identify words at sight is needed: words students need special help on, maverick words which do not conform to familiar pronunciation principles, and advanced words students need in current activities (Blake, 1976d). The following objectives illustrate the three categories of sight words.

> Given her problem words *this*, *their*, *above*, *have*, and *here*, Patty can identify them at sight with 100 percent accuracy in 10 seconds.

> Given the maverick words *your*, *very*, *often*, and *near*, Jean can identify them at sight with 100 percent accuracy in 10 seconds.

> Given the words *hospital*, *drugstore*, *medicine*, and *emergency* from the health unit, Susan can identify them at sight with 100 percent accuracy in 8 seconds.

The student uses discrimination learning and verbal learning when he or she learns to identify words by sight. He or she looks at the word, noting the general configuration and distinguishing features (Blake, 1976d).

Learning Phonics Rules   Phonics involves figuring out how to pronounce a word on the basis of letter-sound relationships, i.e., phoneme-grapheme correspondences. All vowels and many consonants stand for more than one sound. Particular pronunciations depend on the sounds' phonetic environments. These phonetic environments are described by spelling patterns called pronunciation principles (McLaughlin, 1975).

Table 11-1 lists all the types of principles within the broad skill of phonetic analysis. Table 11-2 shows some of the specific vowel pronunciation principles. These principles apply to one-syllable words or to a given syllable in a multiple-syllable word. The following instructional objective is an example of a short-term objective for a specific vowel pronunciation principle.

> Given the mixed group of words below, the student can identify those conforming to the final *e* principle and pronounce the vowel before the *e* long and keep the *e* silent with 100 percent accuracy in 2 minutes.

> safe   bed   hope   pot   line   complete

Table 11-2   Vowel Pronunciation Principles

1   Open Syllable principle: A vowel in an open syllable is usually long.

  hi   go   me   say   pupil

(Note: An open syllable is one where the vowel is the last letter pronounced; it is not followed by a consonant sound even though it may be followed by consonant letters.)

2   Final *e* principle: When a word ends in *e,* the *e* is usually silent and the vowel before it is usually long.

  safe   complete   hope   line   cute

3   Closed syllable principle: A vowel followed by one or more consonants usually has the short sound.

  at   bed   lip   pot   rut   hymn

4   The vowel *i* is usually long when it is followed by the consonant combination -*ld*, -*gh*, or -*nd*.

  mild   sigh   kind

5   The *o* is usually long when it is followed by the consonant combination -*ld* or -*st*.

  fold   post

6   When *y* is the last vowel pronounced in a one-syllable word, it is sounded as long *i*.

  try   fly   by

7   When *y* is the last letter in a word of two or more syllables, it usually is pronounced short *i*.

  happy   pretty

Source: Blake (1974, p. 66).

When students use the letter-sound relationships to recognize a word, they figure out the sounds of the letters in the word. For letters where there is more than one pronunciation, they use the consonant-pronunciation principles or the vowel-pronunciation principles. They synthesize the sounds into a word. They check the word with their memories or within the sentence context. If it makes sense, they know that they have figured out the unknown word. If it doesn't make sense, they use another word-recognition method (McLaughlin, 1975).

Students need to learn two things to use letter-sound relationships: phoneme-grapheme correspondences and vowel- and consonant-pronunciation principles. They use concept learning and discrimination learning to grasp these phoneme-grapheme correspondences and pronunciation principles. They also use concept learning and discrimination learning to become familiar with the other phonetic principles, e.g., syllabication and accent (Blake, 1976d).

Word-Analysis Skills

Students use word-analysis skills to figure out the meaning of words not in their oral language vocabulary. There are five broad word-analysis skills: structural analysis, context analysis, denotative meanings, figurative language, and dictionary use. Table 11-1 presents the specific skills with these four broad skills. Structural analysis and context analysis are considered below as illustrative word-analysis skills.

Structual Analysis   Structural analysis is figuring out a word's meaning by breaking it down into morphemes, i.e., roots, prefixes, suffixes, etc., and looking at the morphemes' meanings by themselves and in relation to one another. For example, suffixes are bound morphemes placed after a root. Inflectional suffixes come at the end of a word and change its number, tense, or degree. Derivational suffixes change a word's form class (part of speech) and meaning. Derivational suffixes may end a word or be followed by inflectional suffixes. Table 11-3 shows some common inflectional suffixes. Table 11-4 has some frequently used derivational suffixes. The following is an illustrative instructional objective on suffixes and roots.

> Given the complex words below, John can identify the roots and suffixes and tell the meaning of each with 100 percent accuracy in 2 minutes.
>
> boys   fixed   greener   player   hopeful   tallness

There are four steps in using structural analysis (Blake, 1976c). When the student meets a new word, he finds the root and then the affixes which are used, if any. He figures out the meanings of the root and affixes. He puts together the meanings of the root and affixes to get an idea about what the word probably means. He tries the probable meaning of the word in the sentence to see if it makes sense. If not, he analyzes the morphemes further or looks the word up in a dictionary.

To perform structural analysis, the student needs to learn two things: the meaning of some morphemes and the principles covering the way the spelling of roots changes when affixes are added. The pupil uses concept learning and verbal learning to learn these two things.

Table 11-3   Common Inflectional Suffixes

Suffix	Meaning	Example
s	Plural—noun	boys
es	Third person singular—verb	boxes she plays he reaches
ed	Past tense—verb	she worked
ing	Progressive tense—verb	walking
en	Past perfect tense—verb	have given
er	Comparative adjective	greener
est	Superlative adjective	greenest

Source: Blake (1974, p. 37).

Table 11-4   Common Derivational Suffixes

Suffix	Meaning	Example
er (or, ar)	one who acts	player: one who plays
ness	state/quality	shortness: state of being short
ship	state/quality	friendship: state of being friends
th	state/quality	warmth: state of being warm
able (ible)	can be, fit to	washable: can be washed
ish	like	boyish: like a boy
like	like	childlike: like a child
less	without	blameless: without blame
ful	full of	graceful: full of grace
ous	full of	courageous: full of courage
y	having, like, quality of	hilly: having hills
ize	make, turn into	legalize: make legal
ly	manner, being	sadly: sad manner

Source: Blake (1974, p. 38).

Context Analysis   A word's context is its setting, the way it fits in with the other words and phrases around it. For example, read Blake's (1976c) illustration presented below.

> The power saw was a *lethal* tool. It ripped through the board in a few seconds. It knocked a hidden nail across the room. It nearly cut off Jim's finger. (p. 37)

The definition of lethal as meaning dangerous is shown by the elaboration that follows its use as an adjective in the first sentence. Table 11-5 has definitions and illustrations of six common types of context clues.

The student does these things as he uses context analysis (Blake, 1976c). He gets an idea of the function an unknown word has in a sentence, whether it acts as a noun, verb, adjective, adverb, or connective. When he knows the word's function, he reduces the number of possible words and meanings he has to choose from. He decides what the word probably means by using the context clues, i.e., comparisons, contrasts, examples, elaborations, experiences, or definitions. He looks at the other words and sentences surrounding the word. He sees if one of the types of context clues is present. He figures out the relation of the unknown word to the known words. He checks the meaning he decides on by putting it in the sentence to see if it makes sense. The student uses discrimination learning and learning-connected discourse when he uses context analysis.

Literal Comprehension and Interpretation Skills

The student uses literal comprehension and interpretation skills to identify and respond to ideas presented in connected discourse. The main task is to figure out

Table 11-5   Common Types of Context Clues

Comparisons

In comparisons, word meanings are shown by direct comparisons, similes, or metaphors.
   She jumped around *friskily,* just like a playful kitten.

Contrast

In contrasts, word meanings are shown by telling what something is not like. Words like *not, instead of, rather than,* and *nevertheless* are used.
   He was *cantankerous,* not very nice and pleasant at all.

Examples

Examples show the meaning of a word by giving instances of it.
   All of the boys are well *occupied.* Charles is washing the windows. Mike is cutting the grass. George is painting the porch.

Elaboration

Elaboration consists of details or explanations which show what the word means.
   The good worker is *punctual.* He gets to work on time. He takes the right amount of time on breaks. He is never late getting back from lunch.

Experience

Experience means connecting a word with an event which is familiar to the listener.
   Mary was *extremely* pleased. She wanted a new car very much and she was glad when she got one.

Definitions

With definitions, the word's meaning is given right in the sentence with a synonym or a longer definition.
   She was very *fatigued,* very tired.

Source: Blake (1974, p. 46).

what the writer intends to tell the reader. Table 11-1 identifies all the literal comprehension and interpretation skills. The student uses learning-connected discourse for all these skills.

The main skills important for handicapped students are those they can use in identifying ideas in selections. Blake (1974) identified these skills to include:

Finding main ideas in paragraphs
Finding supporting ideas in paragraphs
Finding main and supporting ideas in longer selections
Skimming and scanning (p. 73)

Finding the main ideas in paragraphs is considered below as an illustrative skill.

Finding Main Ideas in Paragraphs   The main idea is the keynote of the paragraph. It is the topic the writer carries out with supporting ideas. The main idea may be either directly stated or implied in the paragraph. The writer ties his or her main ideas and supporting ideas together with guides to coherence.

Table 11-6   Common Guides to Coherence

---

1 Transitional words and phrases (conjunctions). Writers use many conjunctions. For example:
   a Joint relations: *and, also, in addition, furthermore, moreover, in other words.*
   b Cause-effect relations: *therefore, because, consequently, and so, thus, accordingly, as a result.*
   c Similarities: *similarly, in the same way, in a like manner, likewise.*
   d Differences: *however, nevertheless, on the contrary, or, nor, on the other hand, still, yet, rather.*
   e Time relations: *afterward, meanwhile, subsequently, then, now, soon.*

2 Repetition of content (direct repetition, pronouns, or synonyms). Some writers repeat an idea throughout the selection. They may use three forms of repetition: restating certain content (a word, phrase, or sentence); making pronouns stand for content; and having synonyms stand for content.
3 Parallel structures. Some writers use parallel words, phrases, clauses, or sentences to show ideas of similar importance.
4 Enumeration. Some writers show connections by marking their ideas. They may use letters (*a, b, c, . . .*), or numerals (*one, two three, . . . ; first, second, third, . . .*)
5 Writers' descriptions or notes. Sometimes, in longer selections, writers tell you what ideas they present and how they arrange them.
6 Heading and subheadings. Writers may use headings and subheadings to show relations among parts. Different orders of headings and subheadings go with different levels of complexity. The different orders of headings and subheadings are shown by the different sizes and styles of type.

Source: Blake (1974, p. 73).

The students should be taught to use guides to coherence to find main (and supporting) ideas. Guides to coherence are focal points in the relations between main ideas and supporting ideas. Students should look for guides to coherence like *for example*, *namely*, etc. By locating the guides to coherence, the students can find the ideas in the paragraph more easily. Table 11-6 has some frequently used guides to coherence.

Sometimes the writer directly states his main ideas in paragraph headings or topic sentences. Blake (1974) outlined the following information for students to check as they read to identify main ideas.

   1 Paragraph headings. Paragraph headings are titles telling what the paragraph is about. They may be statements or questions. Headings, of course, are easy to find. They are put in different type or print from the rest of the paragraph. They usually are in a different position from the rest of the paragraph.
   2 Topic sentences. Writers sometimes put a main idea in one or more sentences called topic sentences. Here are ways the pupil uses to find topic sentences.
      a He looks at the relations among the sentences. The topic sentence is the most general statement. The other sentences are about *it* more than they are about *each other*.
      b He uses guides to coherence. The topic sentence may be linked to the

supporting sentences by phrases like *for example*, *namely*, *because*, and so on.

c He uses position clues. Writers may put topic sentences anywhere in the paragraph: at the beginning, within the selection, or at the end. However, in any one selection, a writer may adopt a certain style and stick to it. (p. 74)

If the main idea is implied, it is more difficult to figure out. Implied ideas are suggested by the sentences of the paragraph taken together. Students must go beyond the different words to find the common idea to which the sentences refer. They must state this implied idea in their own words. They must check out their statements against each of the writer's sentences to see if they support each other. If yes, then the students have found the implied idea. If no, then they reformulate their statements to support the writer's sentences.

SAMPLE READING LESSON PLAN

This lesson plan is designed to teach the phonic principle explaining the sound change of the letter *c* when it is followed by the vowels *e*, *i*, or *y*. It is based on some information described by Banes and Wills (1971). The general and specific learning principles used in this lesson plan are identified in the left margin. Note that the type of learning required by the objective is concept learning; therefore, the specific principles influencing concept learning were used to plan the lesson.

Contiguity	*Scope:* This lesson plan is limited to the soft *c* rule. The students have already learned the hard *c* rule, i.e., when the letter *c* makes the sound /k/. The initial presentation of this lesson is described below.
	A. Initial presentation
Instructions and intent **Reinforcement**	Get the students' attention for the reading lesson by drawing the body and head of a cat on the board. Use verbal praise to reinforce appropriate behavior. Praise each individual student by name.
Verbal instructions	Tell the students that they are going to learn what sound the letter *c* makes when it is followed by the vowels *e*, *i*, or *y*.
Oral and visual presentations	Write the letter *c* and the three vowels on the board.
Structure	Tell the students you have a story that will help them figure out the correct sound of the letter *c*. Direct their
Oral and visual presentations **Orientation and attention** **Preview question** **Amount of practice**	attention to the drawing of the cat. Tell the students that the cat is mad. (Draw a frown on the cat's face as you talk.) Ask the students what sound a cat makes when it is mad? Give the group a chance to respond with the sound, Sss. Go around the group and ask each student to make the sound of the mad cat. Enthusiastically respond to each student. Prompt the correct response as necessary.

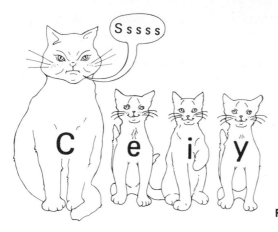

Figure 11-1 Mediating picture clue.

Write Sss in the balloon coming from the cat's mouth and label the name of the cat as *c* (see Figure 11-1). Explain to the students that the cat gets mad every time his little brothers and sisters follow him around (add the small cats to the drawing). Ask the students if they can guess the names of the baby cats. If necessary, prompt *e, i,* and *y.* (Finish the drawing by adding the appropriate names.)

Simultaneous presentation

Nature of rules

Relevant and irrelevant dimensions

Positive and negative instances

Positive and negative instances

Following the above activity, have the students draw Figure 11-1 on their own index cards. They can use these cards on future practice activities to help prompt correct responses. Write and explain the rule for the sound change of the letter *c* when it is followed by the vowels *e, i,* or *y* on the board. Emphasize that the baby cats (the vowels) must immediately follow the cat (*c*) to make it sound mad (Sss). Write some sample words on the board; the list should include words containing both sounds of the letter *c*. Draw the appropriate cats and review the correct sounds of the letter *c*. Provide the students with a list of words containing both sounds of the letter *c* (see Table 11-7). Ask the students to draw all the appropriate cats into each word. For each word, ask individual students if the cat named *c* is mad? Ask them to tell you the sound that each letter *c* makes. Let the students use their index cards to prompt the correct

Simultaneous presentation

Table 11-7   List of Words with the Letter C Sounds

cat
city
come
peace
cent

response. Also write the exercise on the board and leave the correct answers on the board.

Recitation
Relevant and ir-
relevant dimen-
sions

Ask students to tell you the rule. Also review that the vowels *e, i,* or *y* must come immediately after the letter *c.*

B. Instruction and practice

Plan appropriate activities. Be sure to use multiple-practice activities and provide knowledge of results. Keep using simultaneous presentations until the students do not need the help.

ARITHMETIC

Arithmetic deals with quantities and a variety of operations. Handicapped students need to learn a wide range of arithmetic skills. More importantly, handicapped students need to participate in arithmetic as a problem-solving activity. Teachers should not teach mechanistic computation. The goal of a functional arithmetic program should be for the students to learn the concepts involved and then become skillful in dealing with the skills quickly and accurately. The key question is whether the students can use the skill in their adult personal and vocational tasks.

Skills appropriate for handicapped students include aspects of number, numeration, relations, operations with whole numbers, operations with rational numbers, measurement, problem solving, and geometry. Table 11-8 shows the array of broad and specific arithmetic skills. The approximate mental age associated with the normal development of each specific skill is included in the table.

The major broad skills of arithmetic are briefly described below. A sample lesson plan illustrates how to apply the principles of learning to arithmetic instruction. You will need to consult other resources, e.g., Fuys and Tischler (1979) and Reisman (1978, 1980), for detailed information on the broad and specific skills of arithmetic. In addition, there are several excellent commercial materials available to help you teach arithmetic. Project MATH (Cawley et al., 1976) is one example.

Number

Handicapped students should learn to deal with cardinal numbers, ordinal numbers, and rational numbers. Concept learning is required to learn about these numbers. The students learn a label to designate a set of elements. This process requires the students to learn defining rules pertaining to concepts like oneness, twoness, etc. (Blake, 1974). Table 11-9 defines the specific number skills. The following objectives illustrate specific skills within the broad skill of number.

Given a set containing one to nine members, the student will name the number associated with the set with 100 percent accuracy.

Table 11-8 Arithmetic Skills

Skill	Approximate mental age: 5-6 years	7 years	8 years	9 years	10 years	11 years	12 years	13 years
Number								
Cardinals	1 to 5	0 to 9	10 to 300	400 to 1000		Set of primes Set of composites		
Ordinals		First to fifth	Sixth to tenth	Tenth up				
Rationals	½ of object	¼ of object	⅓ of object ½ of set ¼ of set ⅓ of set	¾ of set ⅔ of object	Set of fractions Identifies numerator and denominator	Set of decimals	Set of negatives	Set of rationals
Numeration								
Number words		One to ten	Ten to hundred	Centimeter, meter Hundred to thousand Kilogram, liter				Compares any two rationals
Arabic numerals		0 to 99	100 to 1000	1000 to 100,000	100,000 to 1,000,000	100,000,000		Converts measures
Roman numerals				I to X	X to C C to M Convert units	M		
Decimals, fractions		Write ½ Writes ¼	Write ⅓	Money notation		Writes tenths, hundredths	Writes any rational number Percent notation	
Place value		Ones Tens	Hundreds	Thousands	Hundred thousands	Tenths Hundredths	Thousandths Hundred thousandths	
Relations								
Equality, inequality	One to one correspondence As many as, less and more than	Equality symbol	Greater and less than symbols		Fraction more than, less than	Decimals—more than, less than		
Location	Inside, outside, on							
Ratio					Simple forms 3 for 10¢	Simplifies ratios	Computes missing term Converts ratio to decimal	

Measurement

Liquid	Full and empty	Recognizes cup, tablespoon. Recognizes teaspoon	Uses cup, pint, quart, gallon	Uses liter	Converts units		Compares liter and quart. Milliliter
Weight	Light and heavy	Nearest pound		Nearest ounce. Nearest kilogram	Peck, bushel. Ton		Kilograms. Compares kilogram and pound
Linear	Long and short	Nearest inch	Nearest ½ inch. Nearest centimeter	Nearest ¼ inch. Converts units. Uses meter	Maps distances	⅛th in. Reads odometer. Uses map scale. Latitude, longitude	¹/₁₆th inch. Light year. Millimeter. Finds height in centimeters. 2.5 cm = 1 inch. Compares kilometer and mile
Time		Hour. Half-hour. Days of week	Quarter hour. 5 minutes. Months of year	Minute. Uses notation	Second. Decade. Century	Time zones A M P M	
Money	Recognizes penny. Recognizes nickel	Value of penny. Value of nickel. Value of dime. Value of set with above coins	Change to 25¢	Value of quarter. Value of set with quarters. Change to $1			
Temperature			Degree of Fahrenheit scale	Uses Celsius thermometer	Freezing, boiling		Body temperature 37°C

Operations with whole numbers

Counting		0 to 99. By 1s, 10s to 100. By 5s to 100. By 2s to 40	Even and odd. By 10s to 1000. By 100s to 1000	Estimates to tens	Estimates to hundreds	Estimates to thousands	
Addition		Sums to 5 or less. Vertical, 3 addends. 2 digits + 1 digit. Sums to 12	Basic facts. 2 digits, renaming. Vertical, 4 addends. Communicative property	Associative property. 4-digit numbers. 5-digit numbers	6-digit numbers		

Approximate mental age

Skill	5-6 years	7 years	8 years	9 years	10 years	11 years	12 years	13 years
Operations with whole numbers								
Subtraction		Differences to 5 2 digits; Differences to 12	Basic facts 2 digits, regrouping; Borrowing from 0s	Any 3-digit number; 4-digit numbers; 5-digit numbers	6-digit numbers			4-digit divisors; Finds mode; Finds median
Multiplication			Products to 10; Commutative property	Basic facts; Powers of 10; Zero property; One property	2 digits × 1 digit; 2 digits × 2 digits	3 digits × 3 digits; 4 digits × 4 digits; Greatest common factor of 2 numbers; Lowest common multiple of 2 numbers		Writes percent as fraction; Percentage increase; Percentage decrease
Division				Basic facts; 2 digits, no remainders; 2 digits, remainders		2-digit divisor	3-digit divisor; Average set	Changes percent to decimal
Operations with rational numbers								
Counting				Orders two fractions; Orders set: ½s, ¼s; Orders set: ⅓s		Reduces fractions; Equivalent fractions	Estimates to tenths; Estimates to hundredths	
Addition					Fractions, same denominator	Fractions, unlike denominator; 2 decimals; 2 mixed numbers	2 negative integers; Negative and positive numbers	

	Level 1	Level 2	Level 3	Level 4	Level 5	Level 6
Subtraction				Fractions same denominator	Fractions, unlike denominator 2 decimals	2 negative integers Negative + positive numbers
Multiplication					Lowest common multiplier 2 fractions Whole numbers and decimal	2 mixed numbers Reciprocal
Division		½ of even numbers to 10	½ of even numbers to 20			2 decimals 2 fractions Mean
Problem solving	Chooses addition sentence to fit picture Chooses subtraction sentence to fit picture	Solves addition problems with money—cents only Solves subtraction problems with money—cents only	Solves addition problems with money—dollars and cents Solves subtraction problems with money—dollars, cents Solves problems using multiplication facts	Solves problems using division facts	Chooses correct operation to solve one-step problems	Recognizes pertinent information Solves two-step problems
Geometry	Sorts by shapes: ball, box, can Recognizes square, circle, rectangle, and triangle	Sorts by shapes: egg, cone Names square circle rectangle, and triangle	Recognizes open and closed curves Knows terms: round, square, opposite sides, point Differentiates two objects: same size and same shape (congruency)			

Table 11-9 Specific Number Skills

Cardinal numbers
A cardinal number designates how many elements there are in a set. For example, five pencils, three girls, and so on.

Ordinal numbers
An ordinal number designates an ordered relation among the elements of a set, i.e., it shows place or position. For example, the first boy, the second car, etc.

Rational numbers
A rational number is any number which can be expressed as the quotient of two integers where the divisor does not equal zero. For example, ½, .5, or 50%.

Given an object divided into thirds, the students will identify one-third of the object with 100 percent accuracy.

Numeration

Numeration is the process of expressing numbers in order of their magnitude. Numeration includes number words, arabic numerals, roman numerals, decimals/fractions, and place value. Students use paired-associate verbal learning to learn numeration. That is, they learn associations between names and symbols. Students also use concept learning to learn place value. Table 11-10 defines the specific numeration skills. The following objectives illustrate specific skills within the broad skill of numeration.

Given the task, the student will write the numerals 0 to 9 with 100 percent accuracy.

Given an amount of money, the student will write the amount using decimal notation with 100 percent accuracy.

Given a decimal, the student will identify the place value of any number to the thousandths place with 100 percent accuracy.

Table 11-10 Specific Numeration Skills

Number words
Number words include one to ten, ten to hundred, centimeter to meter, and so on.

Arabic numerals
There are ten digits which represent precise quantities: 0, 1, 2, 3, 4, 5, 6, 7, 8, 9. These digits are combined in various ways to form any whole number or fraction, including decimals and percents. Roman numerals can also be used to represent some number.

Place value
Place value is the value assigned to a digit with respect to the place it occupies relative to the units place. Place values are shown by positions in multiple-digit numerals. That is, starting with the one's place, we have tens, hundreds, etc., to the left and tenths, hundredths, etc., to the right.

. . . . 1,000s	100s	10s	.10s	.100s	.1000s . . . .

Relations

Relations involve the correspondence of two or more sets. Specific skills include equality and inequality, location, and ratio. All these skills require concept learning. The specific relations skills are illustrated by the following instructional objectives.

> Given a box, the student will point to a location inside the box with 100 percent accuracy.

> Given two numbers, the student will compare them using greater-than and less-than symbols with 100 percent accuracy.

> Given two equivalent ratios, the student will fill in the missing term with 90 percent accuracy.

Equality and Inequality   Equality and inequality refer to relative amounts and sizes, that is, the concepts same or different. Blake (1974) specifies one to one correspondence and comparisons as the crucial ideas. One to one correspondence refers to the matching of elements, that is, a pairing of set elements in which every element of a set is matched with an element in another set (Blake, 1974). Comparisons are the judgments about equality and inequality. For example, sets are equal when every element in a set is matched by an element in another set and unequal when such matching does not occur. Table 11-11 has some common terms referring to comparison.

Location   Location is the relative position of elements in space. Some typical concepts handicapped students should learn are shown in Table 11-12.

Ratio   Ratio is the relationship between two quantities. A ratio shows relative size and rates of change. For example, a 3:1 ratio in inches means that there are 3 inches in 1 unit for every inch in another unit. It also means that for every 3-inch change in 1 unit there is a 1-inch change in another.

Measurement

Measurement involves using numbers to describe objects and relations. Time, money, temperature, liquid, weight, and linear units are all types of measurement. Table 11-8 lists all the specific skills within each of these measurement units. Concept learning is required to learn the different units of measurement.

The students have two tasks to learn when dealing with measurement. First,

Table 11-11   Common Comparison Terms

more—less	big—little	long—short
large—small	many—few	heavy—light
high—low	tall—short	all—some
young—old	enough	double—triple

Source: Blake (1974, p. 116).

Table 11-12   Typical Location Concepts

around	first—last	far—near—beside
edge	above—below	bottom—top—middle
center	beginning—end	in front of—behind
middle	left—right	
	high—low	
	under—over	

Source: Blake (1974, p. 117).

the students should learn the units and their synonyms and abbreviations, e.g., penny, cent, 1¢; 1 inch, 1″; and so on (Blake, 1974). Second, the students should learn the relations between units, (Blake, 1974) e.g., 60 seconds equal a minute, 12 inches equal a foot, and so on. Listed below are several objectives that illustrate the students' tasks in measurement.

Given two objects, the student will compare them using the terms light and heavy with 100 percent accuracy.

Given a set of coins, the student will compute their value with 100 percent accuracy.

Given a line segment, the student will measure it to the nearest $\frac{1}{16}$th of an inch with 100 percent accuracy.

Operations with Whole Numbers

Operations deal with the manipulation of numbers. Counting, addition, subtraction, multiplication, and division are operations performed with whole numbers. All these operations involve concept learning. The following objectives illustrate several operations with whole numbers.

Given the task, the student will count to 100 by tens with 100 percent accuracy in 15 seconds.

Given any two 4-digit numbers, the student will subtract the numbers with 100 percent accuracy.

Given a whole number, the student will round it off to the nearest tenth with 100 percent accuracy.

Counting   Counting is finding the number of elements in a set or subset. Students should learn to count single elements by one and by groups or subsets of two, five, and ten. Blake (1974) cautions teachers to make a careful distinction between rote counting and rational counting. In rote counting, the student says the numerals without attaching them to elements. In rational counting, the student attaches the numerals to the elements.

Addition   Addition is an operation for combining quantities. The addition terms, properties, and combinations are shown in Table 11-13.

Table 11-13 Addition Terms, Properties, and Combinations

Terms

Four important terms are addends, sum, plus, carry. Pupils should learn these so they can follow directions.

addends	the numbers added
sum (n)	the result of adding
sum (v)	synonym for add
plus (n)	name of the addition symbol
plus (v)	synonym for add
carry	regroup 10s, 100s, etc.

Properties

The commutative principle indicates that the direction of the summing does not affect the outcome.

$$a + b = b + a$$
$$3 + 2 = 2 + 3$$

The associative principle indicates that the sum is the same regardless of how the numbers are grouped.

$$a + (b + c) = (a + b) + c$$
$$3 + (2 + 4) = (3 + 2) + 4$$

Among other values, these properties make for greater flexibility in adding.

Basic Combination

The basic addition combinations are the combinations involving the ten numbers 0 to 9. The pupil can calculate any sum when he uses these combinations with bridging and regrouping or, in some cases, without bridging and regrouping. Below are the combinations and their inverses; e.g., the inverse of 0 + 1 is 1 + 0.

0 +0	0 +1	0 +2	0 +3	0 +4	0 +5	0 +6	0 +7	0 +8	0 +9
1 +0	1 +1	1 +2	1 +3	1 +4	1 +5	1 +6	1 +7	1 +8	1 +9
2 +0	2 +1	2 +2	2 +3	2 +4	2 +5	2 +6	2 +7	2 +8	2 +9
3 +0	3 +1	3 +2	3 +3	3 +4	3 +5	3 +6	3 +7	3 +8	3 +9
4 +0	4 +1	4 +2	4 +3	4 +4	4 +5	4 +6	4 +7	4 +8	4 +9
5 +0	5 +1	5 +2	5 +3	5 +4	5 +5	5 +6	5 +7	5 +8	5 +9
6 +0	6 +1	6 +2	6 +3	6 +4	6 +5	6 +6	6 +7	6 +8	6 +9
7 +0	7 +1	7 +2	7 +3	7 +4	7 +5	7 +6	7 +7	7 +8	7 +9
8 +0	8 +1	8 +2	8 +3	8 +4	8 +5	8 +6	8 +7	8 +8	8 +9
9 +0	9 +1	9 +2	9 +3	9 +4	9 +5	9 +6	9 +7	9 +8	9 +9

Table 11-13 (Continued)

Higher-Decade Addition
Higher decade addition involves the basic combinations in the one's place and 10's, 20's, etc., in the tens place.

$$
\begin{array}{ccc}
12 & 34 & 61 \\
+\ 5 & +\ 4 & +\ 6 \\
\end{array}
$$

Bridging is necessary when the sum in the one's place is 10 or higher and requires carrying to take the number in the tens place to a higher decade.

$$
\begin{array}{ccc}
16 & 42 & 78 \\
+\ 5 & +\ 9 & +\ 6 \\
\end{array}
$$

Multiple-Digit Addition
Numbers of various sizes are added: e.g., 1-digit, 2-digit, 3-digit, and so on. Some algorithms and problems involve regrouping, or carrying 10's, 100's, and so on.

53	5 tens	3 ones	1 /
+68	6 tens	8 ones	53
121	11 tens	11 ones	+68
	12 tens	1 one	121
1 hundred	2 tens	1 one	

Some do not involve grouping.

53	5 tens	3 ones
+34	3 tens	4 ones
87	8 tens	7 ones

Column Addition
Column addition involves more than two addends. Single-column addition usually involves the basic combinations, higher decade addition, and bridging. For example:

$$
\begin{array}{l}
2 \\
7 \\
5 \\
4 \\
\underline{5} \\
23 \\
\end{array}
$$

$2 + 7 = 9$	basic combination
$9 + 5 = 14$	basic combination
$14 + 4 = 18$	higher decade addition
$18 + 5 = 23$	higher decade addition with bridging

Multiple-column addition usually involves these things and carrying. For example:

1 /	2 /	2 /	
22	7	8	7
65	6	9	9
88	4	6	8
175	19	5	4

Source: Blake (1974, pp. 119–121).

Subtraction Subtraction is the operation for finding the difference between quantities. It is the inverse of addition. Table 11-14 shows the subtraction terms and combinations.

Table 11-14 Subtraction Terms and Combinations

Terms

Minus, remainder, and borrow are important terms related to subtraction problems.

minus	synonym for subtract
remainder	result of subtraction
borrow	regroup 10s, 100s, etc.

Basic Combinations

The subtraction combinations are the combinations involving the ten numbers 0 to 9. Again, the pupil can deal with any subtraction problem when he used these combinations with or without regrouping. The combinations are below.

0	1	2	3	4	5	6	7	8	9
−0	−0	−0	−0	−0	−0	−0	−0	−0	−0

1	2	3	4	5	6	7	8	9	10
−1	−1	−1	−1	−1	−1	−1	−1	−1	−1

2	3	4	5	6	7	8	9	10	11
−2	−2	−2	−2	−2	−2	−2	−2	−2	−2

3	4	5	6	7	8	9	10	11	12
−3	−3	−3	−3	−3	−3	−3	−3	−3	−3

4	5	6	7	8	9	10	11	12	13
−4	−4	−4	−4	−4	−4	−4	−4	−4	−4

5	6	7	8	9	10	11	12	13	14
−5	−5	−5	−5	−5	5	−5	−5	−5	−5

6	7	8	9	10	11	12	13	14	15
−6	−6	−6	−6	−6	6	−6	−6	−6	−6

7	8	9	10	11	12	13	14	15	16
−7	−7	−7	−7	−7	−7	−7	−7	−7	−7

8	9	10	11	12	13	14	15	16	17
−8	−8	−8	−8	−8	−8	−8	−8	−8	−8

9	10	11	12	13	14	15	16	17	18
−9	−9	−9	−9	−9	−9	−9	9	−9	−9

Multiple-Digit Subtraction

As with addition, we have multiple-digit subtraction. Some algorithms and problems involve regrouping (borrowing):

	5 hundreds	14 tens	16 ones
656	~~6~~ hundreds	~~5~~ tens	~~6~~ ones
−167	−1 hundreds	6 tens	7 ones
489	4 hundreds	8 tens	9 ones

	5	14	16
	~~6~~	~~5~~	~~6~~
	−1	6	7
	4	8	9

Some do not.

656	6 hundreds	5 tens	6 ones
−143	−1 hundreds	4 tens	3 ones
513	5 hundreds	1 ten	3 ones

Source: Blake (1974, pp. 121–122).

Multiplication   Multiplication is the operation for combining equal-sized quantities. The multiplication terms, properties, and combinations are shown in Table 11-15.

Table 11-15   Multiplication Terms, Properties, and Combinations

Terms

Factors, times, product, and carry are important terms relating to multiplication.

factors	the numbers multiplied
times	a synonym for multiply
product	result of multiplying
carry	regroup 10's, 100's, etc.

Properties

As with addition, the commutative and associative properties apply to multiplication.

Associative Principle	Commutative Principle
$a \times b = b \times a$	$(a \times b) \times c = a \times (b \times c)$
$4 \times 3 = 3 \times 4$	$(4 \times 3) \times 2 = 4 \times (3 \times 2)$

Further the distributive property relates addition and multiplication.

$$a \times (b + c) = (a \times b) + (a \times c)$$
$$5 \times (5 + 2) = (5 \times 5) + (5 \times 2)$$

Basic Combinations

Again the basic combinations involve the ten numbers 0 to 9. With or without regrouping, they enable the pupil to calculate any product. Below are the combinations and their inverses.

0	1	2	3	4	5	6	7	8	9
×0	×0	×0	×0	×0	×0	×0	×0	×0	×0

0	1	2	3	4	5	6	7	8	9
×1	×1	×1	×1	×1	×1	×1	×1	×1	×1

0	1	2	3	4	5	6	7	8	9
×2	×2	×2	×2	×2	×2	×2	×2	×2	×2

0	1	2	3	4	5	6	7	8	9
×3	×3	×3	×3	×3	×3	×3	×3	×3	×3

0	1	2	3	4	5	6	7	8	9
×4	×4	×4	×4	×4	×4	×4	×4	×4	×4

0	1	2	3	4	5	6	7	8	9
×5	×5	×5	×5	×5	×5	×5	×5	×5	×5

0	1	2	3	4	5	6	7	8	9
×6	×6	×6	×6	×6	×6	×6	×6	×6	×6

0	1	2	3	4	5	6	7	8	9
×7	×7	×7	×7	×7	×7	×7	×7	×7	×7

Table 11-15 (Continued)

0	1	2	3	4	5	6	7	8	9
×8	×8	×8	×8	×8	×8	×8	×8	×8	×8

0	1	2	3	4	5	6	7	8	9
×9	×9	×9	×9	×9	×9	×9	×9	×9	×9

Multiple-Digit Multiplication
Again, numbers of various sizes are multiplied. There are two situations to teach about. Both involve the notion of place value. The first is the no carrying and carrying situations. The ideas are the same as those involved in addition. The second is the multiple-digit multiplicand and/or the multiple-digit multiplier. Here the crucial elements is to list and group products and partial products appropriately by their place values.

Source: Blake (1974, pp. 122–123).

Division Division is the operation for separating equal-sized quantities. It is the inverse of multiplication. Table 11-16 shows the division terms, properties, and combinations.

Table 11-16 Division Terms, Properties, and Combinations

Terms
Crucial terms for problem solving are divisor, dividend, quotient, and remainder.

divisor	the number of sets being formed, the number divided by.
dividend	the total, the number being divided.
quotient	the size of the sets which are formed, the result of dividing.
remainder	the partial set left when the number of sets in the total is uneven

Terms relating to multiplication and to subtraction are also pertinent.

Properties
Division is distributive over addition.

$$(a + b) \div c = (a \div c) + (b \div c)$$
$$(12 + 6) \div 3 = (12 \div 3) + (6 \div 3)$$

Basic Combinations
The basic combinations undergirding more complex division again involve the ten numbers from 0 to 9. Below are the combinations.

0	1	2	3	4	5	6	7	8	9
÷0	÷0	÷0	÷0	÷0	÷0	÷0	÷0	÷0	÷0

0	1	2	3	4	5	6	7	8	9
÷1	÷1	÷1	÷1	÷1	÷1	÷1	÷1	÷1	÷1

0	2	4	6	8	10	12	14	16	18
÷2	÷2	÷2	÷2	÷2	÷2	÷2	÷2	÷2	÷2

Table 11-16 (Continued)

0 ÷3	3 ÷3	6 ÷3	9 ÷3	12 ÷3	15 ÷3	18 ÷3	21 ÷3	24 ÷3	27 ÷3
0 ÷4	4 ÷4	8 ÷4	12 ÷4	16 ÷4	20 ÷4	24 ÷4	28 ÷4	32 ÷4	36 ÷4
0 ÷5	5 ÷5	10 ÷5	15 ÷5	20 ÷5	25 ÷5	30 ÷5	35 ÷5	40 ÷5	45 ÷5
0 ÷6	6 ÷6	12 ÷6	18 ÷6	24 ÷6	30 ÷6	36 ÷6	42 ÷6	48 ÷6	54 ÷6
0 ÷7	7 ÷7	14 ÷7	21 ÷7	28 ÷7	35 ÷7	42 ÷7	49 ÷7	56 ÷7	63 ÷7
0 ÷8	8 ÷8	16 ÷8	24 ÷8	32 ÷8	40 ÷8	48 ÷8	56 ÷8	64 ÷8	72 ÷8
0 ÷9	9 ÷9	18 ÷9	27 ÷9	36 ÷9	45 ÷9	54 ÷9	63 ÷9	72 ÷9	81 ÷9

Uneven Division

Uneven division is division involving a remainder.

$$\begin{array}{r} 8 \\ 3\overline{\smash{)}26} \\ \underline{24} \\ 2 \text{ left over} \end{array}$$

Division with Multiple-Digit Quotients

The basic combinations involve quotients which are in the ones place. Long division includes quotients containing tens, hundreds, and so on (i.e., a plural digit number), multiplication, subtraction, keeping the ones, tens, and other places in line, and "bringing down" or restating the dividend.

$$\begin{array}{r} 213 \\ 3\overline{\smash{)}639} \\ \underline{6} \\ 03 \\ \underline{3} \\ 09 \\ \underline{9} \end{array} \qquad \begin{array}{r} 246 \\ 3\overline{\smash{)}739} \\ \underline{6} \\ 13 \\ \underline{12} \\ 19 \\ \underline{18} \\ 1 \end{array}$$

Division with Multiple-Digit Divisors

Divisors may involve tens, hundreds, and so on.

$$16\overline{\smash{)}382} \qquad 165\overline{\smash{)}3825}$$

Such problems involve the long division steps named above. Also, they involve trial divisors and rounding divisors up or down.

Source: Blake (1974, pp. 124–125).

Operations with Rational Numbers

Operations with rational numbers is the extension of operations with whole numbers to fractions. The major operations are described in Table 11-17. All involve concept learning. Below are some illustrative instructional objectives.

Given two fractions with different denominators, the student will subtract with 80 percent accuracy.

Given a set of fractions, e.g., ½, ¼, and ⅛, the student will find the lowest common denominator with 100 percent accuracy.

Table 11-17   Operations with Rational Numbers

Counting

Counting involves dealing with how many elements; therefore, counting with fractions involves focusing on the numerator to determine how many elements are involved and focusing on the denominator to find the nature of the elements counted. Beyond this, dealing with fractions involves other concepts: reducing fractions to lowest terms, finding common denominators, and dealing with mixed numbers.

Addition

To be added, fractions must have common denominators, i.e., only like elements can be added. Beyond this, adding fractions involves adding numerators.

$$\frac{a}{c} + \frac{b}{c} = \frac{a+b}{c}$$

This rule, of course applies to any number of fractional parts.

$$\frac{a}{c} + \frac{b}{c} + \frac{c}{c} + \frac{d}{c} + \frac{e}{c} = \frac{a+b+c+d+e}{c}$$

Subtraction

Subtraction also requires common denominators. The basic rule is the inverse of the addition rule.

$$\frac{a}{c} - \frac{b}{c} = \frac{a}{c} - \frac{b}{c}$$

Multiplication

Multiplication does not require common denominators. Both the numerator and the denominator are multiplied.

$$\frac{a}{b} \times \frac{c}{d} \times \frac{e}{f} \times \frac{g}{h} = \frac{a \times d \times e \times g}{b \times d \times f \times h}$$

Division

Division does not require a common denominator. Quite directly, dividing *by* a fraction involves multiplying the dividend by the reciprocal of the divisor.

$$\frac{a}{b} \div \frac{c}{d} = \frac{a}{b} \times \frac{d}{c}$$

Source: Blake (1974, pp. 125–126).

Problem Solving

Practical situations involving arithmetic require problem solving. These problems may be described orally or in writing. The specific type of learning required depends on the problem. Two illustrative objectives are listed below.

Given a picture, the student will choose an addition sentence to fit the picture with 100 percent accuracy.

Given a word problem with extraneous information, the student will identify the pertinent facts with 100 percent accuracy.

Blake (1974) specified three major steps in solving practical arithmetic problems. The steps are specifying the problem, gathering the pertinent data, and determining and applying the operation. These steps are described in Table 11-18.

Table 11-18   Steps in Problem Solving

Step 1: The Question

The question is the focus of the problem. The data and the operation are determined by the question. Also, the question specified the unknown. Solving the problem involves finding the unknown—the answer to the question and thus the answer to the problem. Pupils must focus first on the question. The common practice in arithmetic teaching materials of stating the data before the question slows down the location of the question and necessitates a rereading of the data before the question can be answered.

Step 2: The Data

The data are the given information. They pertain to the question and the units to which the operations are applied. Pupils need to focus on identifying the data required to answer the question. Sometimes, the data are not given or are insufficient. For example:

How much will it cost to buy a ruler for each member of the class? Here, the pupil has to supply two bits of missing data: the cost per ruler and the number of class members.

Sometimes, too many data are supplied. For example:

How long will it take Joe to drive 150 miles? He is driving at the rate of 50 MPH.
His car is using gas at the rate of 20 miles per gallon.
The information about gasoline consumption is superfluous here. Pupils need to learn to rule out such extraneous data.

Step 3: The Operation

The operation is the way the data are manipulated to answer the question. The operation follows from the question. Among problems, the needed operation is indicated with various amounts of explicitness. For example, given these data: Susie weighs 52 pounds, Joe weighs 81 pounds, the question can be posed in different ways.

Use subtraction to find the difference in their weights.
What is the difference in their weights?
How much more than Susie does Joe weigh?

Table 11-18 (Continued)

Joe weighs how many more pounds than Susie?
How much must Susie gain to weigh as much as Joe?

Pupils should learn to look to the question to find the needed operation. More specifically, they need to learn the relation between certain operations and certain phrases, e.g., addition—how many in all, subtraction—how much more, and so on.

Source: Blake (1974, pp. 127–128).

SAMPLE ARITHMETIC LESSON PLAN

This is a measurement lesson plan. The unit of measurement being taught is time. The student uses concept learning to learn about time. As usual, the general and specific principles of learning used in this lesson plan are identified in the left margin.

Contiguity	*Scope:* This lesson plan is limited to counting the number of hours and minutes between two times.
	The initial presentation and one instruction and practice activity are described below.
	A. Initial presentation
Instructions and intent	Janet, during the past several days we have been working with time. Today we are going to use what you have learned and something new. Let me show you what I
Reinforcement	mean. Janet, how long is it from 10:30 to 12:30? That's right. It is 2 hours. If you worked from 10:30 to 12:30 you would get paid for 2 hours of work. Suppose you worked from 10:30 to 12:45. That is more than 2 hours, but not 3 hours. Today we will learn how to count those extra minutes because you will be paid for those minutes.
Structure	Let's use me as an example. School lasts from 8:45 to
Oral and visual presentations	3:30. I want to know how many hours and minutes I teach each day.
	8:45 − 3:30 = _____ ____ hours _____ minutes (on an index card).
Expository method	The first thing we do is count from 8:45, hour by hour, till we get to 3:30. I will write the hours as you count. (Janet should say these hours.)

9:45
10:45
11:45
12:45
1:45
2:45

Orientation and attention	Why did you stop at 2:45? That's right. We can't count to 3:45 because I don't work that long. Employers don't pay you for time you don't work.

Simultaneous presentation

We stopped at 2:45. Janet, how many hours did you count between 8:45 and 2:45. Look at the card on which I wrote them as you counted. (Point to card.) That's right. There were 6 hours. Write the 6 in the blank.

Relevant dimension

There are some extra minutes. I also worked from *2:45* to *3:30.*

Expository method

Look at this clock. Where is the *minute* hand at 2:45? It is on the 9. Put a line by the 9. Where's the *minute* hand at *3:30*? Put a line by the 6. Now count in the direction of the arrow from the 9 to the 6. How many minutes is it? Forty-five minutes is correct. Write the number of minutes in the blank. Great.

B.   Instruction and practice

Simultaneous presentation

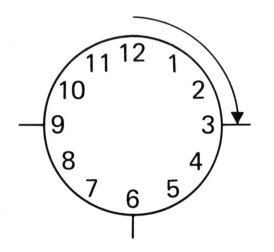

1. List hours.
2. Write number of hours in blank.
3. Mark minutes on clock of last hour you wrote.
4. Mark minutes on clock for 3:20.
5. Count minutes between the 2.
6. Write answer in blank.

List hours here.

11:30 − 3:20 = _____ hr. _____ min.

SUMMARY

Functional academics include the basic skills of reading and arithmetic. Some understanding of these skills is crucial to the handicapped student's goal of personal and vocational independence. This chapter discussed the organization of a functional academic program and presented an array of reading and arithmetic skills. The purpose was to describe curriculum options, ranging in difficulty from simple to complex, for developing a functional academic program.

Structuring and Managing a Functional Academic Program

Structuring and Managing a program requires decisions about the following topics.

Scope/Instructional Objectives   Handicapped students should have objectives corresponding to the reading and arithmetic skills needed for their adult personal and vocational tasks.

Sequences   Handicapped students should have the same sequence of instructional objectives as normal students. In brief, skills should be ordered on the basis of their complexity.

Placement Level   Reading and arithmetic instructional objectives should be set on the basis of handicapped students' mental ages. Instruction should begin at a level appropriate for the student's prerequisite skills.

Entering Behavior   Handicapped students often do not attain the appropriate prerequisite skills. Teachers must teach the necessary prerequisite skills or choose instructional objectives lower in the hierarchy of skills.

Scheduling   Handicapped students need more time to learn particular skills. The more severe the handicap, the more adjustment that needs to be made.

Allocating Personnel and Resources   Commonly used organizational patterns for teaching include regular-class and special-class placement. Regular-class placement should be accompanied by tutoring by a resource teacher, intraclass grouping, and individual tutoring. Handicapped students will need instruction in functional academics beyond the elementary school years.

Guiding Notions on a Functional Academic Program

The following notions should guide the characteristics of a functional academic program.

Intraindividual and Interindividual Variations   Across skills, any one student will progress at different rates in the several skills. Similarly, among students, each will progress at different rates through any one and all skills. The teacher should make provisions for assessing each student's status and progress, gearing his instruction to that assessment, and recording the results of the assessments and the nature of the instruction.

Need for Multiple Presentations   Handicapped students need a number of presentations of information. These presentations cannot be merely repetitions. Instead, they need to be multiple presentations in a variety of settings.

Variety of Procedures   Students and teachers need a variety of instructional procedures for each instructional objective.

Reading

Reading is the process of grasping the message conveyed in written symbols, determining the literal meaning of the message, and interpreting what the message means for a particular situation. The student's tasks are to grasp information presented visually and to interpret and apply that information. The students use word recognition, word analysis, literal comprehension, interpretation, and application skills to accomplish the reading tasks.

Word-Recognition Skills   The student uses word-recognition skills to identify a word's pronunciation. Once she or he can pronounce the word, the student can attach it to a meaning in her or his oral vocabulary. There are two broad word recognition skills: learning sight vocabulary and phonetic analysis. Students use discrimination learning and verbal learning to identify words by sight. Students use concept learning and discrimination learning when they learn phonetic analysis.

Word-Analysis Skills   Students use word-analysis skills to figure out the meaning of words not in their oral vocabulary. There are five broad word analysis skills: structural analysis, context analysis, denotative meanings, figurative language, and dictionary use. The student uses concept learning and verbal learning to learn structural analysis. The student uses discrimination learning and learning-connected discourse to become familiar with context analysis.

Literal Comprehension and Interpretation Skills   The student uses literal comprehension and interpretation skills to identify and respond to ideas presented in connected discourse. The main skills include finding main ideas in paragraphs; finding supporting ideas in paragraphs; finding main and supporting ideas in longer selections; and skimming and scanning. Learning-connected discourse is the specific type of learning required by all these skills.

Arithmetic

Arithmetic deals with quantities and a variety of operations. Handicapped students need to participate in arithmetic as a problem-solving activity. There is no justification for teaching mechanistic computation. As with reading, the key question is whether the students can use the skill quickly and accurately in their adult personal and vocational tasks. Handicapped students should learn the arithmetic skills of number, numeration, relations, measurement, operations with whole numbers, operations with rational numbers, and problem solving.

Number   Learning a number is learning a label to designate a set of elements. Handicapped students should learn to deal with cardinal numbers, ordinal numbers, and rational numbers. Concept learning is required to learn about these numbers.

Numeration   Numeration is the process of expressing numbers in order of their magnitude. Numeration includes number words, arabic numerals, roman numerals, decimals/fractions, and place value. Students use paired-associate verbal learning to learn numeration.

Relations   Relations involve the correspondence of two or more sets. Specific skills include equality and inequality, location, and ratio. All these skills require concept learning.

Measurement   Measurement involves using numbers to describe objects and relations. Time, money, temperature, liquid, weight, and linear units are all types of measurement. Concept learning is required to learn the different units of measurement.

Operations with Whole Numbers   Operations deal with the manipulation of numbers. Counting, addition, subtraction, multiplication, and division are operations performed on whole numbers. All these operations involve concept learning.

Operations with Rational Numbers   Operations with rational numbers are extensions of operations with whole numbers to fractions. All involve concept learning.

Problem Solving   Arithmetic problem solving involves using arithmetic to figure out unknowns in practical situations. The three major steps in problem solving are specifying the problem, gathering the pertinent data, and determining and applying the operation. The specific type of learning required depends on the type of problem.

REFERENCES

Alexander, J. E. (ed.). *Teaching reading*. Boston: Little, Brown, 1979.

Banes, N., & Willis, I. H. The associative memory link. *Teaching Exceptional Children*, 1971, *3*, 67–69.

Blake, K. A. *Teaching the retarded*. Englewood Cliffs, N.J.: Prentice-Hall, 1974.

Blake, K. A. The next step: Producing a reading program. *Journal of Research and Development in Education Monograph*, 1976, *9*, 60–63 (a)

Blake, K. A. Relationships among groups: Results and principles for program structure and management. *Journal of Research and Development in Education Monograph*, 1976, *9*, 49–59. (b)

Blake, K. A. Word meaning skills: Results and principles for instructional procedures. *Journal of Research and Development in Education Monograph*, 1976, *9*, 31–40. (c)

Blake, K. A. Word recognition skills: Results and principles for instructional procedures. *Journal of Research and Development in Education Monograph*, 1976, *9*, 26–30. (d)

Blake, K., Williams, C., Aaron, I., & Allen, J. *Special reading instructional procedures for mentally retarded and learning disabled children*. Project NIE 202340. Washington: Bureau of Education for the Handicapped and the National Institute for Education, 1971–1976.

Bond, G. L., & Wasson, B. *Reading difficulties: Their diagnosis and correction* (4th ed.). Englewood Cliffs, N.J.: Prentice-Hall, 1979.

Cawley, J., Goodstein, H., Lepore, A., Sedlak, R., & Alphaus, V. *Project MATH*, Tulsa, Okla.: Educational Progress, Inc., 1976.

Fuys, D. J., & Tischler, W. *Teaching mathematics in the elementary school*. Boston: Little, Brown, 1979.

Heilman, A. W. *Phonics in proper perspective* (3d ed.). Columbus, Ohio: Merrill, 1976.

Otto, W., & Chester, R. D. *Objective-based reading*. Reading, Pa.: Addison-Wesley, 1976.

McLaughlin, P. J. *Type of concept, type of problem, and type of presentation on retarded and normal pupils' concept learning*. Unpublished doctoral dissertation, University of Georgia, 1975.

Reisman, F. K. *A guide to diagnostic teaching of arithmetic* (2d ed.). Columbus, Ohio: Merrill, 1978.

Reisman, F. K. *Mathematics for exceptional children: Instructional adaptations suggested by developmental and learning theory research*. Columbus, Ohio: Merrill, 1980.

Chapter 12

Vocational Education
and Placement

Vocational education is currently a top priority in the U.S. Office of Education. With the continually high rate of unemployment in the country, job training and rehabilitation programs have taken on greater importance. Vocational and career education for handicapped students plays an important role in the success of these programs. Unless students receive systematic training and preparation in specific job competencies, it is unlikely they will be able to adapt to a viable job placement.

Learning Goals

You should be able to answer these questions in detail after reading this chapter:

- What are six types of vocational skills, i.e., vocational subdomains? Describe the skills in each.
- Write three short-term vocational objectives.
- What is the difference between skill acquistion and skill performance?

- Describe a four-pronged analysis of vocational problems typical of handicapped students.
- Explain how each of these techniques is used in vocational instruction: color coding, easy-to-hard presentation, reinforcement, positive practice.
- How can a changing-criterion technique be used to accelerate production rates?
- How can self-reinforcement be employed to accelerate production rates?
- How do parents' attitudes and individual levels of functioning influence employability?
- What is SSI and how does it affect employability?
- What guidelines should be followed in approaching employers for placement of handicapped individuals?

This chapter describes the types of jobs and occupations in which handicapped students can expect to be placed. Instructional objectives for several categories of these vocational skills are provided. The instructional strategies section of this chapter relies heavily on behavioral training techniques; this involves *acquiring* new skills and *performing* (producing) at competitive rates. A series of lesson plans highlighting learning strategies is provided as well. Next, considerations in competitive-employment job placement are discussed in detail. This is an important area for teachers to be aware of since vocational education programs must address the difficulties and issues involved in vocational placement.

VOCATIONAL SKILLS DOMAIN

To identify all possible jobs and occupations for handicapped workers would be an impossible task. Jobs are constantly being adopted, created, and expanded depending on the nature of the industry, geographical area, and characteristics of the worker. This section identifies several of the most-frequent categories of jobs in which handicapped students are placed and then lists representative skills of the subdomains. Figure 12–1 depicts the constellation of work skills which are discussed in this chapter. Below is a brief description of each category.

Domestic Skills Subdomain

This subdomain involves vocational skills which are required for light housework and clean-up. Domestic skills emphasize clothes cleaning and laundering and room cleaning. The work skills included in this subdomain are typically performed by maids in motels, hotels, convalescent centers, and hospitals. Becker's (1976) recent survey of job-training placement of retarded youth indicated that over 33 percent of the 1458 students sampled were in the hotel or restaurant occupation. These skills are also critical for independent living in group homes or boarding houses. It would appear that domestic skills should be included in the educational curriculum for most handicapped students.

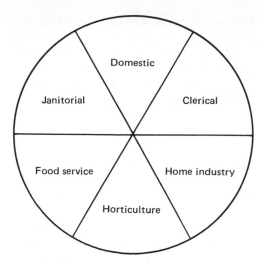

Figure 12-1 A constellation of work skills.

Food Service Skills Subdomain

Food service and preparation is an important skill area for vocational and independent living. Recent Department of Labor surveys indicate that food service is one of the primary sources of employment for mentally retarded workers. Furthermore, it is also critical to independent or semi-independent living in a group home. The number of skills outlined in Figure 12-1 are only a very small proportion of the many which a creative teacher could identify for instruction. This subdomain involves food preparation as well as food clean-up. It is important, however, to assess where the student will be placed. For example, in many restaurants dishwashing would be an automated task and the student would have to operate a machine. Previous training and familiarization with the machine would be very helpful to the student.

Office/Clerical Skills Subdomain

This subdomain provides a representative array of office and clerical skills which include folding, stapling, packaging, and filing. Clerical skills are required in most businesses and government organizations and vary in degree of complexity. It would appear that clerical skills are important vocational behaviors for students to acquire because of the availability of these jobs in many settings. Furthermore, many clerical jobs are not difficult and are entirely within the learning capacity of severely handicapped students. Since most clerical skills involve fine motor proficiency, this is also a good category of skills for training fine motor abilities. These skills are only a small fraction of the many office and clerical jobs which are available.

Janitorial Skills Subdomain

The janitorial skills subdomain consists of heavy cleaning work and usually involves physical or gross motor involvement. Mopping and buffing floors are one example of this subdomain. The skills portrayed in janitorial and domestic skills subdomains are closely related, yet provide an excellent source of employment for many handicapped individuals. There is a perpetual turnover of employees in these jobs. One advantage of these jobs is that frequently janitorial contracting companies send maintenance people out in teams for clean-up. Many handicapped individuals perform with more confidence if there are workers available for support.

Home Industry Skills Subdomain

Home industry skills represent another cluster of vocational behaviors in which the handicapped student should receive instruction. These include basic tool use and identification. For example, competency in use of a hammer, screwdriver, wrench, and saw will allow for the construction of different materials and objects. In addition to being useful in possible jobs such as helping on a farm or aiding a carpenter these skills will also facilitate independent living. The skills provided in this subdomain emphasize proficiency in the use of basic tools and are required before moving on to more complex tools.

Horticulture Skills Subdomain

In predominantly rural areas landscaping and horticulture skills are important vocational behaviors for students to learn. Working in a greenhouse, florist shop, or landscaping company are different placements for which handicapped students may be prepared. Horticulture skills can be taught ideally to the young child, with increasingly complex skills being presented as the student becomes older and more proficient. The development of horticulture skills is also excellent for helping the handicapped student acquire appropriate leisure skills, e.g., working with plants. With the continuing popularity of plants, it would appear that greenhouse operations will expand and develop, creating a demand for workers in this area. Handicapped individuals should be able to learn many of these skills.

Job Placements

Recently, Becker (1976) surveyed thirty-five school districts across twelve states serving 1438 educable mentally retarded youth. One hundred eighty-five jobs were reported. Although these are too numerous to mention here, Table 12-1 provides a summary of the categories Becker found. The percentages indicate what percent of the students were placed in jobs falling in that category. The later half of this chapter provides more detailed information on the job-placement progress.

SETTING VOCATIONAL SKILLS OBJECTIVES

In Figure 12-1 an effort was made to logically arrange from simple to complex the skills in each subdomain. In selecting objectives the teacher should carefully complete a task-analytic assessment of target skills in several subdomains. Selection of these skills should be made in conjunction with the parents and with

Table 12-1 Job Placements

Job category	Percentage of students placed
Hotel and restaurant	33.59%
Building maintenance	13.00%
Retail trade	7.86%
Auto service	6.75%
Construction	5.49%
Agriculture and horticulture	4.45%
Clerical	3.82%
Medical service	3.48%
Motor vehicle transportation	2.85%
Domestic service	2.50%
Personal service	2.43%
Laundry: cleaning and pressing	1.32%
Machine and woodworking	1.18%
Bakery products	1.11%

an eye to finding what type of job placement might be appropriate for the student.

Here are two vocational objectives for a mildy handicapped student. One skill involves stripping paint and the other working with plants or flowers.

1 Given a painted board, paint remover, scraper, rags, paint brush, newspapers, two cans, cleaning solution, and workshirt, S will remove all the paint from the board with 100 percent accuracy for 3 consecutive training days.

2 Given plants, work table, and flats filled with soil, S will take stem cuttings with 100 percent accuracy for 3 consecutive training days.

The following objectives might be selected for a more severely handicapped student:

1 Given a dirty ashtray, a cloth, and a trash can, S will clean the ashtray in 2 minutes with 100 percent accuracy for 3 consecutive training days.

2 Given an unopened can, manual can opener, and trash receptacle, S will open the can with 100 percent accuracy within 3 minutes for 3 consecutive training days.

Tables 12-2 and 12-3 are task analyses for the stripping-paint skill and the can-opening skill. The reader who is interested in more vocational task analyses is referred to Wehman and McLaughlin (1980). Over 100 task analyses have been developed and field-tested and are available in that text.

INSTRUCTIONAL STRATEGIES

Once assessment data have been collected; objectives established, and task analyses developed, it is necessary to analyze the student's work behavior and decide what type of problem, if any, is present. Handicapped students' vocational problems can be divided into learning a skill and then performing it

Table 12-2   Task Analysis of Stripping Paint

 1   *S* will put on workshirt to protect clothes.
 2   *S* will place several sheets of newspaper on the work surface.
 3   *S* will place a board and stripping materials on the newspaper.
 4   *S* will place a can of stripper in front of the work surface.
 5   *S* will open the can of stripper.
 6   *S* will pour a small amount of stripper into a can.
 7   *S* will put cap back on can.
 8   *S* will pick up the brush with one hand.
 9   *S* will touch tip of the brush in the stripper.
10   *S* will place wide surface of brush on one end of the top of board.
11   *S* will slowly spread the stripper along surface using short strokes.
12   *S* will completely cover top surface of the board.
13   *S* will place brush on a newspaper.
14   *S* will wait until paint "bubbles up."
15   *S* will pick up scraper.
16   *S* will move scraper to one side of the board.
17   *S* will place scraper flat-side-down on the board.
18   *S* will scrape softened paint in a short stroke.
19   *S* will use a rag to wipe removed varnish off scraper.
20   *S* will repeat Steps 16, 17, 18 until top surface is clean.
21   *S* will turn board so that a new side faces up.
22   *S* will repeat Steps 3–20 until all four sides are stripped.
23   *S* will wipe scraper of all residue.
24   *S* will wipe fill can one-third full with cleaning solution.
25   *S* will place brush in can and swish around.
26   *S* will wipe brush on side of can.
27   *S* will wipe brush on a rag.
28   *S* will repeat Steps 24–26 two more times.
29   *S* will lay brush out on a newspaper to dry.
30   *S* will empty contents of both cans outside.
31   *S* will throw away rags and newspapers.

Table 12-3   Task Analysis of Can Opening
(Using right hand; reverse hands if left-handed.)

 1   *S* places a can on the counter.
 2   *S* picks up can opener by grasping top handle of opener with right hand.
 3   *S* places cutting edge of opener over rim of can.
 4   *S* grasps both handles of opener with left hand and squeezes them together so that hole
     is punched in can.
 5   *S* grasps turning key with right hand so that thumb is on under side of the end closest to
     S and first 2 fingers are on top side of the end furthest away.
 6   *S* turns key 180° away from him.
 7   *S* repeats Steps 5 and 6 until can is opened.
 8   *S* drops left hand to hold only bottom handle and grasps top handle with right hand.
 9   *S* pulls handles apart and lifts.
10   *S* puts opener on counter.
11   *S* pushes down one side of lid.
12   *S* grasps opposite edge of lid with thumb and index finger of opposite hand.
13   *S* lifts lid from trash receptacle.
14   *S* throws lid from can into trash receptacle.
15   *S* replaces trash receptacle top.

accurately at a high-enough rate to meet competitive-employment standards. These problems are described below.

Analysis of Vocational Problems

Acquisition Problem: Discrimination Deficits A problem typical of handicapped workshop clients is failure to attend to the salient cues (size, color, form) of a task. The person ignores relevant variables and instead may try to assemble or sort materials without watching what he or she does or while attending to the wrong cue in the task. As Gold (1973) notes, this is the main obstacle for the mentally retarded in acquiring complex manual skills. Gold (1972) has found that retarded people can master a difficult job at a rate similar to that of nonretarded peers when they attend to relevant dimensions.

Acquisition can also be impeded by the students' failure to attend to verbal cues of the supervisor. A common characteristic of severely handicapped adults is noncompliant behavior and inability or unwillingess to follow simple instructions. Even though an individual may attend a learning task, failure to follow instructions can interfere with acquisition rates, particularly if job requirements or materials vary slightly from day to day.

Acquisition Problem: Sensory Motor Deficits Many handicapped students receiving vocational education also display sensory motor deficits. For instance, students with cerebral palsy, loss of limb, and spasticity or athetosis may require prostheses or specially arranged environmental support.

Certain students may be visually handicapped or hearing-impaired, thus prohibiting the use of standard training procedures. The rare combination of both aural and visual handicaps in some students is perhaps the most difficult disability to overcome for the acquisition of complex work skills. Yet some researchers have found that such disabilities need not impede learning progress on difficulty tasks such as bicycle brake assembly (Gold, 1976).

Low Production: Slow Motor Behavior Once a vocational task is mastered, high-rate performance becomes important. This is a serious problem with many severely and profoundly retarded students, particularly those with a long history of institutionalization. Slow motor behavior is one characteristic of handicapped students who have not previously been required to meet a work criterion for success. Students may be persistent and stay on task, but their actual motor movements are lethargic and at far too low a rate to be competitive (Hollis, 1967a, 1967b). Often such individuals are unresponsive to the commonly used workshop incentives such as praise or money.

Without objectively established work criteria, it is difficult for teachers to determine which students are performing competitively. Those who stay on task and do not disrupt workshop routine are often viewed as performing adequately. This view is based on a popular vocational training model of "work activity" or "keep busy" rather than on a developmental model which looks to expand the individual's work skills repertoire.

Low Production: Interfering Behaviors Equally problematic in accelerating production rates are interfering or competing behaviors, such as high levels of distractability and hyperactivity, out-of-seat behavior, excessive looking around, making bizarre noises, and playing with the task.

Similarly, the work performance of some students may be highly susceptible to changes in the work environment. Fairly commonplace alterations in setting or routine, e.g., furniture rearrangement, can upset work behavior, thus making continuity of programming extremely difficult. A student may display criterion-level work rates, but only for short periods of time. Interfering or competing behaviors interrupt the work level required for successful community placement.

Training Techniques

To meet these various vocational problems, a logically arranged sequence of training and behavior-management procedures is required. This section provides a hierarchy of techniques and guidelines for alleviating these vocational problems. Teachers may draw on the techniques which are the most effective, the least time consuming, and the most economical. The sequence is affected by traditional methods of alleviating problems within the world of competitive employment. The less-severe or more-typical training and management procedures are listed as most desirable for use.

For example, giving a verbal reprimand would be preferred (Schutz, Wehman, Renzaglia, & Karan, 1978) to using restraint if both procedures were equally effective in alleviating the problem. However, it may be necessary for a teacher to use his or her own discretion with each student in determining the most-appropriate procedure. If a teacher has had previous experience with a particular student and has found that a verbal reprimand increases inappropriate behaviors (e.g., Madsen, Becker, Thomas, Koser, & Plager, 1970), it would be beneficial to begin with the next technique in the hierarchy to ensure success.

Table 12-4 contains a summary of the proposed hierarchy of training and behavior-management procedures for ameliorating vocational problems. These are arranged for each problem area.

Acquisition Problem: Discrimination Deficits The most-frequently used training method in competitive employment is verbal instructions. Many times a

Table 12-4 Logically Arranged Hierarchy of Procedures for Alleviating Work Problems

---

I *Learning or acquisition problem: discrimination deficits*
   1 Verbal instructions
   2 Model and verbal instruction
   3 Verbal and physical guidance
   4 Task breakdown into simpler steps (easy to hard sequence) and repeat of Steps 1–3
   5 Cue redundancy or stimulus fading, depending on task
   6 Constant reinforcement for correct responding to Steps 1–5.
II *Learning or acquisition problems resulting from sensory motor deficits* (Assess handicap to be sure there is a physical problem.)
  A Poor motor coordination
   1 Verbal instructions
   2 Model and verbal instruction
   3 Physical and verbal guidance

Table 12-4 (Continued)

     4 Task breakdown into simpler steps (easy-to-hard sequence) and repeat of Steps 1–3
     5 Prosthetic device or physical arrangement of materials
     6 Cue redundancy or stimulus fading
     7 Same as for Step 6 above
  B Visually handicapped
     1 Verbal instructions (detailed)
     2 Physical guidance and verbal instructions
     3 Tactile cue redundancy and repeat of Steps 1 and 2
  C Acoustically handicapped
     1 Gestural instructions
     2 Physical guidance
     3 Task breakdown into simpler steps (easy-to-hard sequence) and repeat of Steps 1 and 2
     4 Cue redundancy or stimulus fading, depending on task
  D Deaf-blind
     1 Physical guidance
     2 Tactile cue redundancy
III *Low production: slow motor behavior*
  1 Verbal prompt (e.g., "Work faster.")
  2 Verbal prompt plus model
  3 Physical prompt (paired with verbal)
  4 Reinforcer proximity
     a Presence of pennies
     b Presence of backup
  5 Increased frequency of receiving pennies
  6 Increased amount of pennies and/or back-ups
  7 Increased frequency of redemption of pennies
  8 Verbal reprimand plus no reinforcement
  9 Response-cost
  10 Isolation-avoidance
  11 Positive practice
  12 Presentation of aversive stimuli
IV *Low production: interfering or excessive behavior*
  Representative classes include:
     a Nonfunctional competing behaviors
     b Bizarre noises
     c Out-of-seat behavior
     d Aggression vs. objects
     e Aggression vs. people
  1 Verbal reprimand and prompt
  2 Verbal reprimand and physical prompt
  3 Reinforcement proximity (pennies are then backup)
  4 Increased frequency of receiving reinforcement (pennies)
  5 Increased amount of pennies and/or backup
  6 Increased frequency of redemption
  7 Response-cost
  8 Time-out
  9 Restraint
  10 Overcorrection-positive practice
  11 Isolation-avoidance
  12 Presentation of aversive stimuli

new task will be presented with only a verbal explanation. Thus, this should logically be the initial method used to train a new task. If it is unsuccessful, the teacher must attempt to train a task through alternative methods.

Alternatives include verbal instructions paired with modeling of the correct movements (Bellamy et al., 1975; Clarke & Hermelin, 1955), or priming the response and physical guidance (Williams, 1967). Breaking down a task into small measurable components (task analysis) is also effective in aiding acquisition (Friedenberg & Martin, 1977; Gold, 1972), as is presenting learning material in an easy-to-hard sequence (Gold & Barclay, 1973; Irvin, 1976). For those who fail to attend to relevant cues or task dimensions, cue redundancy, e.g., color-coded parts, facilitates acquisition (Gold, 1974).

Acquisition Problem: Sensory Motor Deficits   In meeting the needs of students with sensory motor deficits, the teacher must first consider the individual's physical capacity. For those with poor motor coordination due to cerebral palsy or loss of limb, the first four suggested strategies in the hierarchy do not differ from those used with students whose acquisition problems are due to discrimination deficits. However, if the individual's physical limitations are extensive, the arrangement of materials or the use of prosthetic devices such as specially designed jigs, may be crucial in the acquisition of vocational skills (Hollis, 1967a). It may be necessary for the teacher to modify the task so that students can complete a task with the least effort and most speed.

Low Production: Slow Motor Behavior   As students become more proficient at performing a task, increasing the rate of production to competitive-employment standards becomes a focal point. The severely developmentally disabled must produce at a competitive level to obtain and maintain community-workshop employment. A verbal prompt to "work faster" appears to be the least time consuming and most-efficient technique, providing that it is effective (Bellamy et al., 1975). Peer modeling (Brown & Pearce, 1970; Kazdin, 1973b; Kliebhann, 1967) and trainer modeling have also increased production rate.

The manipulation of reinforcing events is another extensive area of possible techniques. Increasing reinforcer proximity, increasing the frequency or the amount of reinforcement, and increasing the number of redemptions of token reinforcers in a work period are all logical techniques for increasing production rates (e.g., Schroeder, 1972). Furthermore, our experience indicates that mixed schedules of reinforcement, such as continuous social reinforcement for each unit completed and penny or token reinforcement for every ten units completed, can be extremely effective in altering production rates with the severely handicapped (Wehman, Renzaglia, Schutz, & Karan, 1976). Intermittent schedules of reinforcement are a means of programming for response maintenance and approximating competitive-employment work situations.

However, if the problem of low production rates still persists, and the teacher has established a minimum criterion for production rate, the use of aversive consequences may be necessary. Implementing a verbal-reprimand procedure and no reinforcement (Schutz et al., 1978) or a response-cost procedure for low production may be effective if used in conjunction with positive consequences for acceptable work rates. With an established minimum criterion for performance, an isolation-avoidance procedure may also be used successfully (Zimmerman, Overpeck, Eisenberg, & Garlick, 1969). An isolation-avoidance procedure entails removing the student from the work area if a designated criterion is not met.

Because low production is often a result of slow motor behavior, implementing a positive-practice-overcorrection procedure with the intent of teaching fast motor behavior is a feasible alternative (e.g., Rusch & Close, 1976). This procedure requires guiding the student quickly through a task a number of times (so that it constitutes an extended duration), and therefore teaching a student to move with speed. If positive practice is implemented, the teacher must take care to make the physical guidance sufficiently unpleasant so that it is not socially reinforcing.

This procedure was recently applied to a profoundly handicapped adolescent who was performing at a very low production rate (Wehman, Schutz, Renzaglia, & Karan, 1977). When positive reinforcement for meeting criterion work levels was combined with positive practice, the student rapidly reached the target rate. In this situation, the individual increased the rate of on-task behavior to avoid positive-practice training.

Low Production: Interfering Behavior   Low production rate as a result of nonfunctional competing behavior poses a somewhat different problem. The teacher must not only increase a student's work rate, but also decrease or preferably eliminate the amount of time he or she engages in the interfering behavior. Manipulating different parameters of reinforcement may also be effective with this problem.

To decrease many interfering behaviors, it may be necessary to implement aversive consequences. The use of response-cost (Kazdin, 1973), time-out (MacDonough & Forehand, 1973), restraint, and positive-practice (Azrin, Gottlieb, Huqhart, Wesolowski, & Rahn, 1975; Wehman, Schutz, Renzaglia, & Karan, 1977) procedures as immediate consequences for engaging in interfering behaviors may successfully decrease stereotypic behavior, aggression, out-of-seat behavior, and making bizarre noises. These techniques have been effective with handicapped populations in different settings (Gardner, 1969), and should be seriously considered in vocational programs.

General Treatment Strategies

To facilitate specific sequences of training and management techniques, a number of general strategies for treatment may be employed. The general intervention strategies discussed in this section include changing-criterion methodology, isolated treatment programs, and self-control strategies.

Changing-Criterion Strategy   A changing-criterion design may be used when work behaviors are gradually shaped to a competitive level (Axelrod,

Hall, Weis, & Rohrer, 1974; Bates, Wehman, & Karan, 1976; Hartmann & Hall, 1976). Under this design, a student must meet a minimum criterion or level for production rate to earn reinforcement. As the individual's productivity consistently meets the criterion, the criterion is gradually increased or made more stringent. Thus, over time and with the use of effective behavior-shaping methods, productivity may greatly increase from the initial criterion.

This design may be used with specific operant techniques to alleviate low production due to slow motor behavior or competing behaviors. In the case of low-production behaviors, a changing time contingency may be introduced. This procedure requires setting a specific time limit for the completion of a task; it places the student under a time limit to receive reinforcement. A timing device, such as a kitchen timer or sports timeclock, may be used as a cue for the student and as an indicator when the time limit is not met. As the individual consistently meets the required time limit, the time allowed can be gradually decreased. This procedure has been successfully demonstrated and evaluated in a changing-criterion design in a recent study performed with an institutionalized profoundly handicapped adult (Renzaglia, Wehman, Schutz, & Karan, 1978).

Isolated Treatment

Low production rates resulting from student's excessive interfering behaviors pose a difficult remediation problem. Operant techniques employed within the work environment, such as manipulating different parameters of reinforcement, may not obtain successful results with particularly distractible or disruptive individuals. It may be advantageous to implement a treatment program in a relatively stimulus-free environment. Previously discussed training techniques may be enhanced by reducing the number of environmental cues to which a student might attend. As increased on-task behavior is demonstrated, the treatment program may be gradually faded back into the work environment.

A general strategy of behavior control which may be used in an isolated treatment program is differential reinforcement of other behavior. With this approach, the individual might be reinforced for instances of not being bad (Repp, Dietz, & Dietz, 1976; Wehman & Marchant, 1978), for instances where he was performing only the appropriate behavior, or for low rates of responding (Dietz & Repp, 1973). Differential reinforcement is used in most training efforts when the student is taught fine discriminations and also in the reinforcement of high work rates. It is certainly not limited to an isolated treatment program. However, in an isolated, relatively stimulus-free environment, it may be easier to use differential reinforcement of the target behavior.

Self-Management Strategies

The operant techniques and procedures discussed thus far pertain to external control on the part of the teacher. These techniques involve staff-administered contingencies; if relied on entirely, they present potential disadvantages to self-sufficient vocational behavior.

One major problem is that an external-control approach precludes the development of self-directed choice behaviors on the part of the student. Many rehabilitation professionals recognize this deficiency as a primary obstacle in the community-transition process for these students. Secondly, an external-control approach presents a number of inherent drawbacks. Since it is difficult to notice all instances of an appropriate response, a teacher usually misses many opportunities to reinforce a student. Furthermore, the change agent him- or herself may become a cue for a behavior rather than a natural environmental stimulus (Redd & Birnbrauer, 1969). This drawback relates also to the problem of transfer of training and durability of program progress. Thus, whenever possible, external control must be viewed not as an end itself, but as a means to train a student to control his or her own behavior and achieve self-selected goals.

Self-control has been defined in reference to "those behaviors an individual deliberately undertakes to achieve self-selected outcomes" (Kazdin, 1975, p. 192). Self-control training procedures which are applicable to handicapped students include self-observation, self-reinforcement, and stimulus control.

Self-observation has been successfully implemented with mentally retarded students through the use of behavioral graphs (Jens & Shores, 1969) and daily feedback of work performance from a videotape (DeRoo & Haralson, 1971). With this procedure, a student is trained to become aware of his or her work performance through immediate external feedback and through a visual record of work behavior. Gradually self-observation can be faded to pictures of improvement in work performance.

Self-reinforcement is another strategy which holds potential, particularly in classes that use a token economy as a motivational system. Two concepts of self-reinforcement are self-administered reinforcement and self-determined reinforcement. An important requirement for both self-administered reinforcement and self-determined reifforcement is that the individual is free to reward himself at any time, whether or not he performs a particular response (Skinner, 1953).

Self-administered reinforcement refers to the student's taking a reinforcer himself, but under an externally determined criterion. Once a student's self-administered reinforced response is shaped, it is possible to move toward self-determined reinforcement. This broader concept of self-reinforcement allows students to determine their own work criteria (e.g., Glynn, 1970). It may be possible for contingency contracts to be set up between students and workshop supervisors. Within such a contract would be a set rate of work and social skills which an individual agrees to perform. In return, he or she can self-select reinforcement preferences for performance of the contract.

How handicapped students can manage their own work behavior was illustrated recently (Wehman, Schutz, Bates, Renzaglia, & Karan, 1978). Production rates were assessed under no reinforcement, externally administered reinforcement, and self-administered reinforcement, with pennies used as reinforcers. Treatment conditions were presented in a latin square sequence to control for the effects of order. Results indicated that through modeling and physical priming initially the trainee was able to reinforce himself and maintain a high level of production. Other research in workshop settings also supports the development of self-management skills in the severely handicapped (Helland, Paluck, & Klein, 1976).

Another self-control strategy which may be employed is stimulus control. Stimulus control refers to specific behaviors performed in the presence of specific stimuli which serve as cues and increase the probability that the behavior will be performed. For example, self-observation may function as a reinforcing consequence initially, and may also function as a discriminative stimulus for subsequent task-related behaviors.

Possible applications of the stimulus-control strategy, in classes for handicapped students, include altering stimuli which consistently lead to frustration-aggression situations, modifying cues that presumably contribute to task failure, or pairing positive stimuli with low-preference tasks. Social behaviors such as eliciting social greetings, being on time, or appropriately using leisure time might also be developed through stimulus control.

SAMPLE VOCATIONAL PROGRAMS

Below are listed two programs which put together the different components discussed in systematic instruction. A clerical skill and home industry skill are presented, with an objective, a task analysis, and detailed teaching procedures for each.

Program One: Applying Pressure-Sensitive Labels

Instructional Objective   Given the materials and the command, "Label the envelope," *S* will correctly label the envelope ten out of ten times for 3 consecutive training days.

Prerequisite Skills   Pincer grasp and full use of both arms and hands.

Task Analysis

1   *S* will look at envelopes.
2   *S* will reach toward stack of envelopes.
3   *S* will touch stack of envelopes.
4   *S* will grasp one envelope.
5   *S* will pick up envelope.
6   *S* will place envelope in front of self, with front of envelope facing up.
7   *S* will pick up sheet of labels.
8   *S* will place sheet of labels in front of self.
9   *S* will position fingers on label in upper left-hand corner.
10   *S* will grasp one corner of label.
11   *S* will pull label off sheet.
12   *S* will move label over envelope.
13   *S* will position label in center of envelope.

14 *S* will place label on envelope.
15 *S* will rub hand back and forth across label.
16 *S* will place labeled envelope in box.

Pretest

1 Do not provide consequences or physical assistance during pretest.
2 Place *S* in the training area with the materials listed above.
3 Say to *S*, "Label the envelope." Give no further verbal cues.
4 Watch *S* to determine which steps of the program he completes correctly.
5 Record a plus (+) for each step *S* completes correctly. Record a minus (−) for each step he or she does incorrectly or omits.
6 *S* may be able to do some of the steps in the program before training begins. If this occurs, *do not* eliminate these steps from the training sequence.

Teaching Procedures

1 *T* will place a stack of envelopes in front of *S*. On the back of each envelope *T* will draw a happy face so that the envelope will be right-side-up.
2 *T* says, "Watch me. I will get this envelope ready for labeling."
3 *T* proceeds through Steps 1 to 6, giving special instructions to make sure the happy face on the back is not upside-down (which would result in the envelope being upside-down).
4 *T* instructs *S*, "Now you get these envelopes ready for labeling."
5 *T* guides *S* through Steps 1 to 6, giving verbal and tactile cues only as necessary.
6 Reinforce with praise or tangibles as appropriate. (When *S* can correctly position five envelopes for three consecutive attempts, proceed to next step.)
7 Using a magic marker *T* will mark off a rectangular area approximately 1½ times the size of the label on the front of the envelopes.
8 *T* says to *S*, "Watch me. I will label this envelope."
9 *T* proceeds through Steps 7 to 16, giving special instructions that the label is to go *inside* the marked rectangle.
10 *T* instructs *S*, "Now you label these envelopes."
11 *T* guides *S* through Steps 7 to 16, giving verbal and tactile cues only as necessary.
12 Reinforce with praise or tangibles as appropriate. (When *S* can correctly label five envelopes for three consecutive attempts proceed to next step.)
13 Repeat Steps 1 to 16 while gradually fading out all visual cues. To do this:
a Fade out the happy face on the back of the envelopes by penciling the faces lighter and lighter. Then remove the cue completely.
b Fade out the rectangle by switching from magic marker to pencil. As it becomes lighter, also make it smaller so that it approximates the size of the label. Then remove the cue completely.

14 This skill is considered learned when S completes all steps of the task correctly for 3 consecutive training days.

Program Two: Bolting Wood Together

Instructional Objective Given two pieces of wood and a nut and bolt, S will bolt the two pieces of wood together with 100 percent accuracy in 10 minutes for 3 consecutive days.

Prerequisite Skills Pincer grasp and eye-hand coordination to align holes and nut to bolt.

Task Analysis

1 S will place wood pieces, bolt, and nut on top of work station.
2 S will pick up one piece of wood with left hand.
3 S will pick up other piece of wood with right hand.
4 S will place two wood pieces together.
5 S will align drilled bolt holes on top of one another.
6 S will grasp both aligned pieces of wood in one hand.
7 S will pick up bolt with other hand.
8 S will align bolt with hole.
9 S will insert bolt through hole.
10 S will hold bolt in hole with one finger and will pick up nut with other hand.
11 S will align nut with bolt.
12 S will turn nut on bolt until finger is tight.
13 S will place assembled wood on table.

Pretest

1 Do not provide consequences or physical assistance during the pretest.
2 Place S in the training area with the appropriate materials on a flat surface.
3 Tell S, "Bolt together these two pieces of wood."
4 Watch S to determine which steps he or she completes correctly.
5 Record a plus (+) for each step completed correctly, and a minus (−) for each step done incorrectly or omitted.
6 S may be able to do some of the steps of the program before training begins. If this occurs, *do not* eliminate these steps from the training sequence.

Teaching Procedures

1 Teacher will model the skill, giving verbal explanation of each step (1 to 13).
2 Teacher will give S materials and the command, "Bolt together these two pieces of wood." She will give physical assistance and verbal cues throughout the completion of the task when she notes omissions, hesitations, or uncertain moves.

3 Teacher will have S repeat the task, gradually decreasing frequency of physical—then verbal—cues.

4 Teacher will give the command and S will complete the task without any physical or verbal cues on five out of five trials.

5 Teacher will acknowledge correct moves and give praise for appropriate behaviors throughout completion of the task on all levels.

6 To assist in showing how to align holes and hold wood in place, teacher can give S two pieces of paper with prepunched holes and have S place brads through each of the sets of holes and fasten; or S could be given two pieces of cardboard with prepunched holes and place pegs or pencils through each set of holes.

7 To practice the skill used in aligning the nut onto the bolt and turning, give S small jars and jar lids and have him or her place and tighten the lid onto the jar. For this skill, have S simply practice screwing and unscrewing the nut onto the bolt in isolation.

8 For practice in thumb and first finger movement used in screwing the nut, have S turn the bottom on back of a wind-up clock or the winding mechanism that sets the hands, or twist the dial on a combination lock.

9 For practice in eye-hand coordination required to place the nut onto the bolt, have S place a handful of washers, one by one, onto a stationary-stick, nail, pencil, etc., held tight in the wood.

ISSUES IN JOB PLACEMENT

The previous discussion of training studies suggests that handicapped individuals can succeed in a sheltered work environment. Although this is a positive development, it still falls considerably short of job placement into competitive employment (Mithaug & Haring, 1977; Usdane, 1976). There are several reasons for this. First, few sheltered workshops pay the minimum wage; rather, they compensate on a piece-rate basis. Subsequently, many workers earn only $80 to $100 a month, if that. Second, sheltered employment is primarily restrictive; that is, it includes only handicapped workers and therefore limited opportunities for interaction with nonhandicapped individuals. Sheltered employment unfortunately perpetuates segregated programming. Furthermore, in sheltered workshops there is rarely the full spectrum of fringe benefits, e.g., Blue Cross, which are available in many competitive employment situations. A final limitation of sheltered employment is that it is often needlessly a terminal placement for many individuals. It becomes terminal because the employee is a critical part of the production process and invariably is "carrying" several less-productive workers. Therefore, the workshop supervisor may be reluctant to move the worker into competitive employment from the shop.

Factors to Consider in Job Selection

There are numerous variables which must be evaluated before job placement occurs. Because potential job openings for handicapped individuals are often difficult to locate, program staff are frequently tempted to decide arbitrarily which trainee is most suited for placement in a rare job opening rather than search for job specifications which most suit a given individual. In this regard, Mithaug, Hagmeier, and Haring (1977) have noted:

> We can begin by focusing upon one job at a time, rather than trying to analyze the entire job market at once. Also, we should specify the most probable job placements for our client's immediate career. Finally, we can analyze the job situation of selected placements, noting and listing the work skills and habits necessary for entry. . . . Unfortunately, information on methods to use in this assessment is not available. All we can suggest is that the focus be on the job supervisor. (p. 91)

There are several other factors which must be considered and these are discussed below. They are essential in order to identify the most appropriate job for handicapped clients.

Client's Previous Work History

Systematic vocational instruction for severly handicapped individuals has been in practice only in recent years (e.g. Bellamy, Horner, & Inman, 1979). Therefore, examination of the previous work record of a handicapped client will frequently yield a history marked by successive failures. Many handicapped individuals have, in the past, been dismissed from public school vocational education programs, sheltered workshops, and even community-based activity centers under the rationale that progress was not possible. However, even a record of failure may provide important information when considering job placement. Through this record, specific breakdowns in programming can be identified. Examples of this might include client preference for certain rein-forcers, lack of seizure control, or volatile behavior problems, which occur under different conditions.

An investigation of previous work may be done by initially surveying the following sources:

1 Parents and family members
2 School personnel
3 Rehabilitation intake workers and counselors
4 Case managers or social workers assigned to the trainee
5 Written records from schools, activity centers, or workshops

These sources frequently document some aspect of the trainee's previously attained production rates, quality of work, length of work history, and level of independence in a work setting. The work attitude of the trainee as well as the family's attitude toward work and transportation needs may be available. An analysis of this information, which is admittedly not always a valid predictor of job success (Gold, 1973), can nevertheless help the job coordinator avoid the mistakes which may have been made earlier.

Level of Functioning and Physical Characteristics

Once previous job-history information has been gleaned, then a careful analysis of the client's level of functioning should be undertaken.

Mithaug and Hagmeier's (1978) Prevocational Assessment Checklist is one possible assessment tool which might be used. Though this tool was designed for sheltered workshops, it has numerous items which would be equally appropriate for those entering competitive employment. The interested reader might also consult the vocational behavior checklists listed by Wells and Warner (1977). From this screening, a list of job categories or types of jobs which most suit the trainee's competencies can be generated. The following client characteristics influence the type and length of job placement:

1 Frequency of on-task behavior
2 Degree of independent mobility
3 Communication skills
4 Degree of self-initiated work behavior
5 Appropriateness of social skills
6 Presence of concomitant handicaps, e.g., vision impairment

Clearly, certain jobs require more of the above-stated abilities than others. For example, picking up and bagging trash on a college campus requires independent walking and orienting skills. Well-developed social skills might not be necessary. On the other hand, for operating a utility elevator in a large hospital, ambulation skills could be impaired, but number identification and selection, fine motor skills, and social skills should be well-developed.

There are other more-subtle variables regarding the characteristics of the trainee which may be critical for the ultimate success of a placement. As with nonhandicapped workers, certain trainee personality and physical characteristics when mixed with personality traits of the immediate supervisor affect job success and ease of adjustment to a new work setting. The easiest way of analyzing the interaction of these factors is to have program staff spend time within the work setting before making the placement. It is usually necessary to examine the group dynamics, the flexibility or rigidity of the supervisor, the age and openness of co-workers, and whether other handicapped personnel are present in order to identify critical behaviors necessary for entry into that job site. If supervisors have had previous experiences with disabled employees, and these experiences were *positive*, there is usually a better opportunity for making the placement.

Supplemental Security Income (SSI)

One frequently cited obstacle to job placement of the handicapped is the threat of losing guaranteed financial aid payments from the government. Although these payments are relatively low ($189.40 per month, if there is no other earned income, as of July 1978), parents and sometimes clients themselves often prefer the arrival of a guaranteed check each month rather than risk job placement. In addition, if the SSI benefits are reduced to $0 per month according to local and federal deduction formulas, Medicaid benefits are also lost. The loss of Medicaid can be serious for those individuals who require much medication since Medicaid pays all but 50¢ on every prescription. However, other than in this area, a good medical insurance plan gained through employment provides equal or better medical coverage for the working individual.

Placement personnel must approach this aspect of the employment process as a serious concern to all involved, and reduction of financial aid due to employment must be fully explained to the family. If the client and family understand these procedures, they will find that during the first 12 months of employment there is little risk of losing all forms of monthly income. That is, if the job is terminated, SSI benefits can be readjusted to the pre-employment level within 10 to 20 days. If an individual clearly must retain Medicaid benefits, it would be wise to arrange for part-time employment rather than a full-time job. In this way, the part-time employee, depending upon his or her rate of pay, would probably retain some portion of SSI benefits and, therefore, remain eligible for Medicaid coverage.

Living Situation and Transportation Needs

The individual's living situation is another factor which can play an important role in job selection. For example, the distance from the job to the trainee's home must enter into the decision to seek employment with a given company. Transportation is usually a problem because most severely disabled individuals cannot drive and may not be able to use public transportation. Thus, transportation must be worked out by the work-experience coordinator, rehabilitation counselor, and parents. Below are listed some of the ways in which this potential obstacle to placement can be worked out:

1 Consider whether a placement is available which is close enough for the client to walk.

2 Have the parents take the individual to work.

3 Have the parents form a car pool with parents of other trainees, if possible.

4 Complete bus training if public transportation is available and feasible.

5 Have a co-worker pick up the trainee and take him or her home; work out an equitable pay situation.

6 Investigate whether the locality has a bus or van which is used to help disabled or senior citizens get around the community.

Unquestionably, the transportation problem can be a major stumbling block. The work coordinator must be diligent and initially may have to participate in the actual transporting of the trainee. Once the individual is formally hired and is being paid regularly, parents and co-workers may view him or her in a more credible light and, therefore, make a greater commitment toward transportation assistance.

Client and Parent Attitudes

As noted above, many handicapped individuals have experienced more than one disappointment because of unkept promises made through previous programs. Therefore, the objective of job placement is frequently met with much skepticism on the part of the parent or guardian. Indeed, the client's attitude may also reflect that of the parent. The "I-don't-want-a-job" philosophy often stems from the fact that the individual has learned from his or her parents that it is not necessary to work. If this is the case, job-placement personnel must provide assurance to the entire family that the objectives and techniques of the program are sound and that the prospective employee deserves the dignity of risk (Perske, 1972). Several factors may persuade reluctant families:

1   Assurance of continual daily on-the-job supervision and "inservicing" of nonhandicapped co-workers in the job setting.
2   Assurance that the trainee's placement spot in his or her current program will be kept open if the job placement does not work out.
3   Careful explanation of the rules and regulations governing the Supplemental Security Income which most severely disabled persons receive and which will be halted upon full-time employment.
4   Careful explanation of the amount of weekly wages and fringe benefits which will now be available to the individual.

Approaching the Employer

The initial personal contact is critical in terms of making a placement. It is during this stage that a full description of the program, clients' abilities, staff's training capabilities, as well as the generally positive aspects of hiring handicapped workers is related. This contact will also give the job coordinator an opportunity to find out what other job possibilities are available and what the prevailing sentiment is toward hiring disabled clients.

Some employers, unfortunately, have had disappointments in attempting to work with other programs for the handicapped. These disappointments may be expressed in terms of "The counselor came only the first day," or "No one else was here to teach us how to work or communicate with him," or "They came the first day with the teacher and we never heard from them again." During the initial contact, it is important to dispel these concerns and point out the differences between the present training program and others. *The sincerity demonstrated during this time must be proven true in order to establish a good future working relationship with the company or organization.* It is necessary to keep in mind that interacting with business is not the same as interacting with special education- and rehabilitation personnel. Handicapped clients' capabilities must be presented in general descriptive terms. Their potential benefit to the company must be presented in business terms, such as the predominantly positive track record which handicapped workers have after initial supervision. If the attitude toward the program and future placements appears positive, then a trial training period may be negotiated.

Establishing a Training Period

The establishment of a training period may take place during the initial personal contact or during future contacts. It is not unlikely that several more contacts may precede the agreement on the training period. This becomes more likely with larger businesses with extensive personnel division hierarchies. Approval needs to be given by the director of personnel as well as by the immediate foreman or supervisor. The length of the training period should be based on the client's abilities, prior training, the job surroundings, and the skills involved. The training period may be viewed as extended training from the classroom or workshop and hence be nonpaid for a short period of time. On the other hand, National Association for Retarded Citizens funds may be used for on-the-job training, or rehabilitation counselors may provide funds to reimburse employers. For rehabilitation funds to be used, however, the counselor must be convinced of the trainee's employment potential. This is usually quite difficult with severely retarded individuals, who have been previously excluded in most cases. *The training period should be presented to the potential employer and parents as a predictor of the client's ability to perform the job accurately and within the specified time frame.*

Ideally, the immediate supervisor will agree to directly observe the trainee at certain periods of time throughout training. In this way the company will be aware of the progress the trainee is making. Furthermore, the supervisor can advise the job coordinator in ways that the job may be completed more efficiently. The job coordinator must keep careful objective records of the trainee's progress. These may include:

1 Observing at different intervals of the day on-task versus off-task behavior.
2 Recording at different intervals of the day the frequency and type of trainer prompts required.
3 Recording at the end of each day the client's general work behaviors. These include absenteeism, tardiness, appearance, and social behavior with the supervisor and co-workers.

These data should also be collected after the hiring at selected follow-up intervals. This will document to the employer the success of the trainee and pave the way for other clients.

The training period is a time when the job coordinator and supervisor can work together in helping the client (Cooper, 1977). To a large extent, the rapport between the supervisor and trainee will facilitate the latter's hiring as well as the hiring of future trainees. The job coordinator's role in this process is twofold. One, there may be a demonstration of how to most effectively work with the trainee. The caution here is not to work with the client to the exclusion of the real supervisor; if this occurs, there may be difficulties in maintaining work performance once the job coordinator leaves. The second function of the job coordinator is to be an effective advocate for the trainee with other individuals in the environment. This may include getting media support, explaining the client's role in the work force to others in the work environment, or simply helping the trainee get adjusted to unfamiliar work surroundings.

Frequent communication will help families remain informed and avoid potentially embarrassing incidents with the employer concerning job require-ments imposed on the trainee. Even with daily communication, however, some parents may call the employer unnecessarily. As with most companies and government organizations, the employer is largely concerned that the employee is performing the job adequately; there is not usually time available to counsel worried or overprotective parents. Furthermore, this tends to cast a negative light on the trainee, who may subsequently be viewed as less independent.

In short, the work coordinator, teacher, or counselor, must not only function in a training placement capacity but also provide systematic supervision and follow-up once the placement is made. Furthermore, it is critical that the coordinator serve as a mediator between the employer's needs, client's capabilities, and parent's wishes.

Factors Involved in Identification of an Appropriate Employer

Once relevant factors which influence the job-selection process have been assessed, the selection of an appropriate employer is necessary. This includes selection of the company or organization to which the job coordinator and client will apply. It also involves knowing how to approach employers initially and overcoming the type of misconceptions and problems which many employers have with handicapped workers. Finally, an extended field-training period for purposes of evaluation may be established.

Community-Job Assessment

A survey of available community jobs must be initiated as the first step in locating a place of employment. This may be faciliated through screening newspaper want ads for low-skilled or nonskilled employment opportunities. Descriptions to look for within ads meeting the skill criteria are "Will train" or "No experience necessary." The types of jobs may vary from location to location. However, there will usually be those which fall under categories such as *food service, groundskeeping,* and *maintenance.* Although these are but a few of the types of jobs disabled individuals can perform, they have proven to be ones in which moderately and severely handicapped individuals can excel (Becker, 1977).

There are other means of screening the community for jobs as well. For example, reviewing the yellow pages in local phone books may yield major contractors in target occupational categories. Personal contacts within companies or organizations which have relevant jobs should also be used if appropriate. The National Alliance of Business usually has a local branch which may prove helpful, since it receives many job pledges from business and industry every year. Most states have an employment commission which receives a listing of job vacancies that may be appropriate.

Frequently universities, colleges, hospitals, and other large institutional settings are most fruitful in terms of job placement. These types of employers have several positive points. First, they typically have a high turnover of the types of jobs which handicapped persons can perform. Second, they frequently have a commitment to hire handicapped individuals. Third, the pay and benefits are often quite desirable. Finally, it may be most efficient to assign one teacher or job coordinator to the same job site and gradually increase the number of trainees. As a trainee becomes increasingly competent at the job, a second individual can be introduced to the employer. This process can continue until quite a few trainees have been hired.

Once several job leads have been identified, the next step is to follow through by making the initial telephone contact. This can be facilitated by a social contact or someone already working in the company who is willing to talk to the employer before the phone call. The director of personnel is the logical contact person in most cases. In our experience, an honest yet optimistic approach is best received. A brief explanation of the program in general terms should be followed by asking if the company would consider allowing a handicapped person to train for either the advertised position or a similar one. At times, employers may have jobs which are not advertised but which may be more appropriate for the client.

A general reaction will be generated by the employer through the telephone contact. This reaction may be positive, negative, or cautiously positive. In most cases it is best to eliminate the negative employers and concentrate on the positive employers. To a certain degree, this will be influenced by the type and number of appropriate job vacancies which an employer has. With the employer who appears to be receptive, an interview date should be set as soon as possible.

Job Interview

After the training period is established, a time for an interview between supervisor, trainee, and staff member must be set. The interview should take place after formal interview training has occured. The job coordinator should enter the interview only if the trainee's interview abilities break down, as in the case of some nonverbal individuals. The following job interview skills should be stressed in preplacement training:

1   Eye contact upon introductions
2   Good body posture when standing and sitting
3   Firm handshake and release after appropriate time span has passed
4   Ability to respond to small talk characteristic of an interview, e.g., "How are you?", "Have you worked before?"

Although lack of proficiency in each of these skills will not preclude placement, it will considerably enhance the trainee's being hired if there is evidence of good interview behavior and neat appearance.

SUMMARY

The purpose of this chapter is to discuss the role of education and job placement in the special education curriculum. The domains of vocational education are described. These include *domestic* skills, *food service* skills, *clerical* skills, *janitorial* skills, *home industry* skills and *horticulture* skills. A constellation of approximately 100 vocations are presented within the subdomains. Several sample short-term instructional objectives are then outlined.

In analyzing vocational problems of handicapped students, several categories can be identified. Learning or acquisition problems resulting from motor impairments or discrimination difficulties are two categories. Performance problems are classified according to slow work or high-rate of interfering behavior. Within each of these categories, intervention techniques are described. These interventions involve special prostheses, individualized reinforcement programs, task analysis, color coding parts in assembly tasks, and a variety of other methods based primarily on learning theory.

Self-reinforcement and self-observation are discussed as a means of stimulating independent work behavior. This involves teaching the student to take his or her own token at a predetermined payoff schedule. Staff benefits of a self-reinforcement program are optimal since it is not necessary for the teacher to always be present.

Most of the training techniques presented have their greatest utility in sheltered employment. Yet many handicapped individuals are capable of entering competitive employment. It is necessary, however, for adequate planning to take place before a job placement be made. For example, parental attitudes, student transportation needs, and previous work history are important variables in the placement process and should be assessed. Supplemental Security Income can affect employability as well; individuals who are employed cannot also receive SSI and may not be able to easily regain their allotments if the job is lost.

The importance of a positive approach to employers is also discussed. It may be necessary to make several visits to the potential job site before actually making the placements. For individuals who may have job difficulty an initial nonpaid training period may be advisable.

Vocational education and placement in the classroom is only the prerequisite for what is ahead in the world of work. Teachers and work coordinators must aggressively pursue job-training sites in the community and move toward eventual competitive-employment placements.

REFERENCES

Axelrod, S., Hall, R. V., Weis, L., & Rohrer, S. Use of self-imposed contingencies to reduce the frequency of smoking behavior. In M. J. Mahoney & C. E. Thoreson (eds.), *Self-control: Power to the person*. Belmont, Calif.: Brooks/Cole, 1974.

Azrin, N. H., Gottlieb, L., Hughart, L., Wesolowki, M. D., & Rahn, T. Eliminating self-injurious behavior by educative procedures. *Behavior Research and Therapy*, 1975, *13*, 101–111.

Becker, R. Job training placement for retarded youth: A survey. *Mental Retardation*, 1976, *14*(3), 7–9.

Bellamy, G. T., Horner, R., & Inman, D. *Vocational habilitation of severely retarded adults*. Baltimore: University Park Press, 1979.

Bellamy, G. T., Peterson, L., & Close, D. Habilitation of the severely and profoundly retarded: Illustrations of competence. *Education and Training of the Mentally Retarded*, 1975, *10*, 174–186.

Brown, L., & Pearce, E. Increasing the production rate of trainable retarded students in a public school simulated workshop. *Education and Training of the Mentally Retarded*, 1970, *5*, 15–22.

Clarke, A., & Hermelin, F. Adult imbeciles: Their abilities and trainability. *The Lancet*, 1956, *2*, 337–339.

Cooper, B. Occupational help for the severely disabled: A public school model. *Rehabilitation Literature*, 1977, *38*(3), 67–74.

DeRoo, W., & Haralson, H. Increasing workshop production through self-visualization on videotape. *Mental Retardation*, 1971, *9*, 22–25.

Dietz, S., & Repp, A. Decreasing classroom misbehavior through the use of DRL schedules of reinforcement. *Journal of Applied Behavior Analysis*, 1973, *6*, 457–464.

Gardner, W. I. Use of punishment procedures with the severely retarded: A review. *American Journal of Mental Deficiency*, 1969, *74*, 86–103.

Glynn, E. L. Classroom applications of self-determined reinforcement. *Journal of Applied Behavioral Analysis*, 1970, *3*, 123–132.

Gold, M. W. Stimulus factors in skill training of the retarded on a complex assembly task: Acquisition, transfer, and retention. *American Journal of Mental Deficiency*, 1972, *76*, 517–526.

Gold, M. W. Research on the vocational habilitation of the retarded: The present, the future. In N. Ellis (ed.), *International review of research in mental retardation* (Vol. VI). New York: Academic, 1973.

Gold, M. W. Redundant cue removal in skill training for the mildly and moderately retarded. *Education and Training of the Mentally Retarded*, 1974, *9*, 5–8.

Gold, M. W. Task analysis: A statement and an example using acquisition and production of a complex assembly task by the retarded blind. *Exceptional Children*, 1976, *43*(2), 78–87.

Gold, M. W., & Barclay, C. R. The learning of difficulty visual discriminations by the moderately and severely retarded. *Mental Retardation*, 1973, *11*, 9–11.

Hartmann, D., & Hall, R. V. The changing criterion design. *Journal of Applied Behavior Analysis*, 1976, *99*, 527–532.

Helland, C., Paluck, R., & Klein, M. A comparison of self and external reinforcement with the trainable mentally retarded. *Mental Retardation*, 1976, *14*, 22–23.

Hollis, J. H. Development of perceptual motor skills in a profoundly retarded child, Part I: Prosthesis. *American Journal of Mental Deficiency*, 1967, *71*, 941–952. (a)

Hollis, J. H. Developmental of perceptual motor skills in a profoundly retarded child, Part II: Consequence, change, and transfer. *American Journal of Mental Deficiency 1967, 71, 953-963.* (b)

Irvin, L. General utility of easy-to-hard discimination training procedures with the severely retarded. *Education and Training of the Mentally Retarded*, 1976, *11*(3) 247–250.

Jens, K., & Shores, R. Behavioral graphs as reinforcers for work behavior of mentally retarded adolescents. *Education and Training of the Mentally Retarded*, 1969, *4*, 21–26.

Kazdin, A. E. The effect of response cost and aversive stimulation in suppressing punished and nonpunished speech disfluencies. *Behavior Therapy* 1973, *4*, 73–82.

Kazdin, A. E. *Behavior modification in applied settings*. Homewood, Ill.: Dorsey, 1975.

Kliebhahn, J. Effects of goal setting and modeling on job performances of retarded adolescents, *American Journal of Mental Deficiency*, 1967, 72, 220-226.

Madsen, C., Becker, W., Thomas, D., Koser, L., & Plager, E. An analysis of the reinforcing function of "sit-down" commands. In R. K. Parker (ed.), *Readings in educational psychology*. Boston: Allyn and Bacon, 1970, 265–278.

MacDonough, T., & Forehand, R. Response-contingent time-out: Important parameters in behavior modification with children. *Journal of Behavior Therapy and Experimental Psychiatry*, 1973, *4*, 231–236.

Mithaugh, D., & Hagmeier, L. The development of procedures to assess prevocational competencies of severely handicapped young adults. *AAESPH* (American Association for the Education of the Severely/Profoundly Handicapped) *Review*, 1978, *3*(2), 94–115.

Mithaug, D., Hagmeier, L., & Haring, N. The relationship between training activities and job placement in vocational education of the severely and profoundly handicapped. *AAESPH* (American Association for the Education of the Severely/Profoundly Handicapped) *Review*, 1977, *2*, 89–109.

Perske, R. The dignity of risk and the mentally retarded. *Mental Retardation*, 1972, *10*(1), 24–26.

Redd, W. H., & Birnbrauer, J. S. Adults as discriminative stimuli for different reinforcement contingencies with retarded children. *Journal of Experimental Child Psychology*, 1969, *7*, 440–447.

Renzaglia, A., Wehman, P., Schutz, R., & Karan, O. Use of cue redundancy and positive reinforcement to accelerate production rates in two profoundly retarded workers. *British Journal of Social and Clinical Psychology*, 1978, *17*(2), 74–78.

Repp, A., Dietz, S., & Dietz, D. Reducing inappropriate behaviors in classrooms and in individual sessions through DRO schedules of reinforcement. *Mental Retardation*, 1976, *14*, 11–14.

Rusch, F., & Close, D. Overcorrection: A procedural evaluation. *AAESPH* (American Associaton for the Education of the Severely/Profoundly Handicapped) *Review*, 1976, *1*(5) 32–45.

Schroeder, S. Parametric effects of reinforcement frequency, amount of reinforcement, and required response force on sheltered workshop behavior. *Journal of Applied Behavior Analysis*, 1972, *5*, 431–441.

Schutz, R., Wehman, P., Renzaglia, A., & Karan, O. Efficacy of contingent social disapproval on inappropriate verbalizations of two severely retarded males. *Behavior Therapy*, in press.

Skinner, B. F. *Science and human behavior*. New York: Macmillan, 1953.

Usdane, W. The placement process in the rehabilitation of the severely handicapped. *Rehabilitation Literature*, 1976, *37*, 162–165.

Walls, R., & Werner, T. Vocational behavior checklists. *Mental Retardation*, 1977, *15*(4), 30–35.

Wehman, P., & Marchant, J. Reducing multiple problem bheaviors in a profoundly retarded child. *British Journal of Social and Clinical Psychology*, 1978, *17*, 149–152.

Wehman, P., & McLaughlin, P. *Vocational curriculum for developmentally disabled persons*. Baltimore: University Park Press, 1980.

Wehman, P., Renzaglia, A., Schutz, R., & Karan, O. Stimulatin productivity in two profoundly retarded workers through mixed reinforcement contingencies. In O. Karan, P. Wehman, A. Renzaglia, & R. Schutz (eds.), *Habilitation practices with the severely developmentally disabled*. Madison, Wis.: University of Wisconsin Rehabilitation Research and Training Center, 1976.

Wehman, P., Schutz, R., Bates, P., Renzaglia, A., & Karan, O. Self-management programs with mentally retarded workers: Implications for developing independent vocational behavior. *British Journal of Social and Clinical Psychology*, 1978, *17*(1), 58–68.

Wehman, P., Schutz, R., Renzaglia, A., & Karan, O. Use of positive practice to facilitate increased work productivity and instruction following in profoundly retarded adolescents. *Vocational Evaluation and Work Adjustment*, 1977, *10*(3), 14–19.

Williams, O. Industrial training and remunerative employment of the profoundly retarded. *Journal of Mental Subnormality*, 1967, *13*, 14–23.

Zimmerman, J., Overpeck, C., Eisenberg, H., & Garlick, B. Operant conditioning in a sheltered workshop. *Rehabilitation Literature*, 1969, *30*, 323–334.

Chapter 13

Recreation Skills

Educational programs which emphasize the development of recreation and leisure time skills in handicapped students are receiving increased attention by special educators (Wehman, 1977; 1979). Development of a leisure skills repertorie in students may facilitate increased proficiency in language, motor skills, cognition, and social interaction (Strain, Cooke, & Apolloni, 1976). Furthermore, games and related recreational activities which are integrated into other areas of instructional programming provide functional tasks which are conducive to establishing a positive learning environment.

There is a particularly strong need for recreation services to be provided for handicapped persons. Involvement in leisure activities, especially active involvement in community-based recreation facilities, may help handicapped children and adults become better accepted by peers. Perhaps the fundamental reason for leisure skills instruction, however, is that handicapped individuals usually have an abundance of free time. This is reflected in evenings, weekends, and holidays for children, a lack of adult services in many job prospects, as well as the extensive free time available to most residents of state institutions.

The questions below identifies representative areas of importance in the leisure-skills-curriculum domain.

Learning Goals

You should be able to answer these questions at the end of this chapter:

- Why is recreation an area which requires programming for handicapped students?
- What are the four major leisure skills subdomains in which recreation skills may be organized for instruction.
- Describe the basic differences between each of these subdomains.
- Discuss the five-step leisure skills assessment process.
- What are four types of leisure skills variables which a teacher should assess? Describe each briefly.
- How does leisure skills assessment relate to skill selection?
- Describe the leisure-skills selection model outlined.
- How does the individual's family life relate to selection of leisure skills for instruction?
- How does the availability of resources relate to selection of leisure skills for instruction?
- Identify and describe how at least four principles of learning relate to implementation of the detailed lesson plan.

This chapter is organized in the following way. First, a large number of leisure skills are identified and organized programmatically in the back of this chapter. These skills form the basis for recreation curriculum content, and a rationale for the organization of these skills is provided. Second, assessment and skills selection guidelines are then presented to guide the teacher in identifying lesson plans which illustrate leisure skills for instructions. Finally, several specific instructional techniques in different leisure skills areas are presented.

RATIONALE FOR RECREATION
CURRICULUM DEVELOPMENT

A logically planned scope and sequence of recreation skills provides the basis for three critically important instructional areas in programming: 1) skills assessment which will facilitate beginning a program; 2) sequencing and ordering the presentation of materials; and 3) evaluating student progress made in the curriculum. The implications of each of these points should be evident. Assessment instruments and data collection strategies may be determined by the format, precision, and sequence of the curriculum being used.

Second, careful sequencing of structured recreation programs leads to skills being acquired more rapidly and gives inexperienced teachers direction in training. Free play may be enhanced through different curriculum guidelines which provide the optimum antecedent events for different play situations.

A curriculum provides the "what" of an instructional program. It tells the teacher which skills can be taught to the student and in what order. In recreation, this is particularly important because of the necessity for a range of leisure skills choices to be presented to the student.

Evaluation of one individual may be conducted in the number of skills or games acquired or across the curriculum. The latter evaluation would be designed to tap different dimensions of cognitive or behavior development. The curriculum should be organized into a logical programmatic sequence. Evaluation of the individual's success through the curriculum sequence is facilitated by observation and recording procedures.

In short, a logical recreation curriculum sequence is the basis of a comprehensive recreation program. It should emphasize normalization and provide opportunities for self-initiated leisure-time skills.

There are few curriculum efforts in this area. The I CAN project is one curriculum which has been produced by a group from Michigan State University (Knowles, Vogel, & Wessel, 1975). In this physical-education-based curriculum, which was designed for trainable retarded children and youths, aquatics, body management, fundamental skills, and health-fitness are the four program content areas. Within each content area, an accountability system has been developed to evaluate whether performance objectives have been met.

TOWARD A RECREATION CURRICULUM

In an effort to expand earlier recreation-skill-curriculum work (Wehman, 1976), a large inventory of leisure skills for handicapped students is delineated in the back of this chapter. It has not as yet been thoroughly field-tested but has come through the brainstorming and logical analysis stage. It represents an attempt at a broad identification of leisure skills involving *object manipulation (toy play)*, *games, hobbies*, and *sports*. It is based largely on an analysis of what nonhandicapped children and adults do with their free time.

Activity Groupings: Description and Rationale

Most of us have a basic understanding of the differences between the skills falling into each activity category. However, this knowledge tends to be of a subjective nature, and the rationale is not based on a firm objective foundation of how one category may differ from another or why a given activity is classified under a specific category. The four major activity headings are not intended to bind the teacher, but, on the contrary, to provide leeway to utilize several kinds of recreation/leisure skills which fall into the different activity areas.

Depicted below are the criteria for inclusion of a leisure skill under a majority activity heading. General characteristics of activities falling under a specific heading are identified. Subsequent to familiarity with these characteristics, the teacher may wish to add to the curriculum by placing other activities that he or she finds or creates into the appropriate activity category.

Object Manipulation (Toy Play)

This activity grouping contains the most basic forms of leisure participation outside of self-stimulation. It involves the use of an inanimate object by the participant. The object (or toy) is the focus of the individual's attention and is not part of a larger game.

Usually no rules exist during object manipulation or toy play activity and, therefore, the individual may design his or her own activity for using the object. Objects (toys) are selected to stimulate solitary activity and to allow the individual to express him- or herself and exercise acquired abilities in each phase of development. The most practical toys tend to be those which have the widest possible range of application.

Games

Games are recreational activities which involve definite rules ranging from a simple to a high level of functioning for participation. They may or may not involve the manipulation of objects or toys. A game may involve competition and/or cooperation of participants and usually involves more than one person. The players must learn to take turns and abide by the rules. An intended outcome must be inherent in the game. As in the sports category, the concept of winning and losing is introduced. However, games are the purest form of recreation in that they are played because the participants enjoy playing that particular game, with sheer pleasure being the primary motivating factor. This activity category includes board and table games, social (get-acquainted) games, gross motor games, musical games, and card games.

Hobbies

Hobbies are recreational activities which have great potential to become lifelong leisure skills. An individual may pursue a hobby as a youngster and continue to excel in and utilize those skills with increasing degrees of sophistication throughout his or her lifetime. Pariticpation in hobbies tends to be less active than in either sports or physical games and may include activities such as stamp and coin collecting, playing a musical instrument, and a wide variety of arts and crafts activities. Participation in a hobby is usually of a solitary nature and, therefore, noncompetitive since the concepts of "win" and "lose" are nonexistent. While we would hope that an interest in many of the different leisure/recreation skills would continuously develop throughout a person's lifetime, it is typically the skills in the hobbies category that are most enduring for the individual.

Sports

The distinction between sports and games is characterized by a time line. Although activities in both categories employ a definite set of rules, sports tend to be more sophisticated in the rules and equipment used, with greater emphasis placed on the competitive aspects of the acitivty. Both individual and team sports are incorporated into the curriculum, requiring various ability levels of social and motor coordination. Developmentally disabled persons are becoming more active in sports nationwide as can be observed by the increased interest in Special Olympics and wheelchair sports and games for both children and adults.

In reviewing many leisure-skills- and recreation materials, it seems that activities cluster around one of these four areas. Clearly, a skill might belong in more than one category, but for ease of organization we have placed it in the category we consider to be most appropriate.

Within each major program area a number of program subcategories have been generated. For example, within Hobbies, pet care was identified. In Sports, winter sports was identified. Within the subcategories specific skills were then identified and sequenced from easy to more difficult. Obviously, all possible leisure skills could not be selected because of the large volume; however, an effort was made to be reasonably representative in selecting program subcategories in Hobbies, Sports, and Games. Within Object Manipulation, toys and other objects were selected on the basis of group discussions with parents and special education teachers at local schools and agencies serving handicapped students. It should be apparent that we have identified many skills which will be possible for severely handicapped students to learn.

ASSESSMENT PROCESS

Determining where to begin a leisure skills program for handicapped individuals is a five-part process. This process includes:

1 Assessment of general level of behavioral functioning, either formally through adaptive behavior instruments or anecdotally through behavior observation. Use of the Learning Accomplishment Profile, Adaptive Behavior Scale, or other screening devices is appropriate.

2 With this information, the individual may then be exposed to different levels of leisure activities for the purpose of gaining an approximate index of his or her recreational skills. The leisure skills in the appendix to this chapter may be used.

3 As it becomes clear at which level the person is functioning, target behaviors which may be realistically attained by the individual should be identified.

4 Target-behavior selection must be directly linked to general adaptive-behavior deficits. For the developmentally disabled a recreation program should rarely be instituted for fun alone. While fun is a necessary ingredient for program success, leisure activities must be selected with the purpose of facilitating adaptive behaviors such as language and motor skills. These must be functional and chronogically age-appropriate.

5 Target behaviors must be observable and easily measurable. Having "fun," becoming "better adjusted," or releasing "pent-up anxieties" is difficult to measure and is an inconclusive means of evaluating program progress. Several dependent variables which might be used to overcome this difficulty include frequency of physical action on objects, diversity of action on materials (i.e., number of different objects acted upon), length of time engaged in appropriate activity, and latency of response (time between presentation of objects and action on material). Measurement of task-analyzed games may be done in the following way: each component in the response chain is taught individually and a certain criterion of success must be met before the next response is taught.

Response measures may be coded by using a self-initiated (SI), verbal (V), gestural (G), or physical-prompt (P) system. Plus or minus may be recorded by the trainer according to the level of assistance required at each step in the task analysis. The section below provides a more detailed discussion of these specific leisure variables.

SPECIFIC LEISURE SKILLS VARIABLES FOR ASSESSMENT

Task-Analytic Assessment

Although there are a number of areas which can be assessed in a recreation environment, an initial consideration must be: *Does the individual know how to interact with the materials?* Stated another way, when given leisure skills materials, can the participant use them appropriately? If not, then systematic instruction is required.

What is required for evaluating leisure skills proficiency is task-analytic assessment. An instructional objective must be written for a given material. The objective should reflect the specific skill which the teacher wants the child to learn. An example of a task-analytic assessment for playing with a spinning top is provided in Table 13-1. This table contains a task analysis for playing with a top and the verbal cue provided during the assessment. The recording form indicates that for the first 5 days of assessment (baseline) the child performed a total of three, three, two, four, and four steps independently. This indicates that instruction should begin at Step 3 in the task analysis.

There are multiple advantages to this type of observational assessment. First, the information collected about the child on this particular play skill helps the teacher pinpoint precisely where instruction should begin. In this way, the child does not receive instruction on skills in which he is already proficient. Second, this facilitates step-by-step individualized instruction for children with complex learning problems. Evaluation of the child's proficiency with different

Table 13-1   Task Analytic Assessment for Playing with a Top

	M	T	W	Th	F
1. S approaches top	+	+	+	+	+
2. S places hands on top	+	+	+	+	+
3. S finds handle of top	+	+	−	+	+
4. S pushes handle down on top once	−	−	−	+	+
5. S brings handle up	−	−	−	−	−
6. S brings handle down on top twice	−	−	−	−	−
7. S brings handle up each time	−	−	−	−	−
8. S brings handle down on top three times	−	−	−	−	−
9. S brings handle up each time	−	−	−	−	−
10. S brings handle down on top four times	−	−	−	−	−
11. S brings handle up each time	−	−	−	−	−
12. S brings handle down on top five times	−	−	−	−	−
13. S brings handle up each time	−	−	−	−	−
14. S stops top from spinning	−	−	−	−	−
15. S puts top away	−	−	−	−	−

toys over an extended period of time will also be more objective and precise, and will be less subject to teacher bias.

Duration of Activity

If the individual has some degree of proficiency with leisure materials, then the instructional variable of interest may be the length of time the participant engages in activity. This is assessed by recording the amount of time he or she engages in different activities.

Since this may be an extremely time-consuming measure to use with several individuals, the teacher may elect to observe only half the participants one day and the other half the next. Another option would be to record activity involvement only twice a week instead of daily.

The length of independent leisure activity is particularly important to assess because of its relevance to most home situations where parents cannot constantly spend time with their handicapped child. A frequently heard request from many parents is to teach the child to play independently, thereby relieving the family of continual supervision. A careful assessment of the child's duration of leisure activity before instruction will help the teacher and parents set realistic independent leisure goals for the child. Table 13-2 presents a sample data collection sheet.

Discriminating between Appropriate versus Inappropriate Object Manipulation

Another assessment issue faced by teachers and researchers is differentiating between appropriate actions with objects versus actions which would not be

Table 13-2 Initial Object Assessment

Leisure Skill Object	Minutes/Seconds Engaged with Object	Type of Action
1. Waterpaints		
2. Record player		
3. Plants		
4. Goldfish		
5. Ball		
6. Magazine		
7. Box of Crackerjacks		
8. Lincoln Logs		
9. Viewfinder		
10. Pinball machine		

considered appropriate. Several play studies have failed to address this issue (Burney, Russell, & Shores, 1977; Favell & Cannon, 1977; Wehman, 1977a). Inappropriate play actions have typically been considered those behaviors which are harmful or destructive to the child, peers, or materials. However, many profoundly retarded and autistic children will exhibit high rates of repetitive self-stimulatory behavior with toys, i.e., banging, pounding, slamming, which are not necessarily harmful or destructive yet are still inappropriate. Furthermore, the problem is compounded since with certain objects banging or slamming actions may be appropriate. Many children will do unusual things with toys which *might* be considered appropriate by other observers.

Hence, teachers are faced with having to assess the qualitative nature of object manipulation. There are several ways of coping with this. The first involves using two to three observers periodically and having these observers rate the appropriateness of the action. Objective judging provides a checks and balances system for the teacher.

A second method of assessing appropriateness of object manipulation is to identify the principle actions which a nonhandicapped child of comparable mental age might use with each object. These actions may serve as guidelines.

Identifying a number of fine motor categories for object manipulation is yet another means of coding the qualitative nature of responses. This requires generating a fine motor classification system which observers can use as a basis for recording actions. Tilton and Ottinger (1964) provide nine categories, which are self-explanatory, and which were identified after extensive observational analysis of normal, trainable retarded and autistic children. They are listed below:

1   Repetitive manual manipulation
2   Oral contacts
3   Pounding
4   Throwing
5   Pushing or pulling
6   Personalized toy use
7   Manipulation of movable parts
8   Separation of parts of toys
9   Combination uses of toys

Leisure-Preference Evaluation

Assessing favorite leisure activities is an important step in initiating a recreation program. The goal in this process is to identify which, if any, activities are preferred by the participant. This is a fairly easy task. By employing duration assessment, the amount of minutes/seconds spent with each leisure material can be recorded. This observation and recording should take place for at least a week. It does not require that the client be verbal.

A second means of assessing leisure preference is through presenting a small number of different materials and determining the amount of time before the participant responds. This is referred to as a *latency* measure of behavior.

McCall (1974) used latency as a measure of the length of time which elapsed before infants acted on a variety of objects which were presented. Each of the objects possessed different stimulus attributes, such as configural complexity or sound potential. Through measuring passage of time until a response occurs, teachers may be able to evaluate the relative attractiveness of and preferences for certain materials with severely handicapped individuals.

Frequency of Interactions

For many severely handicapped children, an important instructional goal is to initiate and sustain interaction of each other during free play. One way of assessing such social interaction is a simple count of the number of times one child 1) initiates an interaction, 2) receives an interaction, and 3) terminates an interaction. Duration assessment may be used to measure the length of the interaction between peers and also between the child and adults in the room.

A second means of gathering more information on social interactions is the coding of specific types of interactions. Carney and her associates (1977) have detailed the following social-interaction skills:

A   Reccives interaction
   1   Receivcs hug
   2   Returns smile
   3   Gives object to the one who has requested it
   4   Returns a greeting
   5   "Receives" cooperative play
   6   Answers questions
   7   Recognizcs peers, teachers by name
   8   Shows approval
   9   Discriminates appropriate time, place, situation before receiving
B   Initiates interaction
   1   Greets another person
   2   Requests objects from another person
   3   Initiates cooperative play
   4   Seeks approval
   5   Seeks affiliation with familiar person
   6   Helps one who has difficulty manipulating environment
   7   Initiates conversation
C   Sustaining interactions
   1   Attends to ongoing cooperative activity
   2   Sustains conversation
D   Terminates interactions
   1   Terminates cooperative play activity
   2   Terminates conversation

This sequence provides an important step toward detailing the specific skills which teachers should be attempting to elicit in handicapped children. In addition to providing sequence, these skills may be task-analyzed and the child's proficiency on selected behaviors assessed. These four categories of interaction can be employed to code the qualitative nature of the interaction (Hamre-Nietupski & Williams, 1977).

Direction of Interaction

Analyzing toward whom interactions are directed may also be helpful in assessing which individuals in the play environment are reinforcing to the child. Child-teacher interactions occur more frequently than child-child interactions, especially with severely handicapped children. Structured training by an adult is usually required to increase child-child interactions.

When making home visits and observing the child playing at home with siblings or with neighborhood children, the teacher should assess the direction of interactions. This assessment should be done when the child interacts not only with handicapped children, but also with nonhandicapped peers. This type of behavioral analysis can be revealing, since most nonhandicapped children do not include handicapped children in play unless prompted and reinforced by adults.

In conducting a behavioral assessment of social interactions, the teacher might use the checklist below as a means of coding a number of interactions:

Student	Initiated interaction	Received interaction
Robert		
Wendy		
Martha		
James		

This form, however, would not allow for analyzing the *direction* of interactions. The checklist below would facilitate assessing which peers or adults the child interacted with:

Student	Initiator or recipient of interaction				
	Robert	Wendy	Martha	James	Teacher
Robert					
Wendy					
Martha					
James					

MODEL FOR SELECTION OF LEISURE SKILLS

While the leisure-skills variables discussed above are important in the program-development process, it is equally important to systematically review criteria for skill selection. These criteria include the participant's *leisure skills preference, level of functioning and physical characteristics, access to materials, the age-appropriateness of the skill,* and *the quality and support available in the home environment.* These criteria must be carefully assessed before beginning a program.

Leisure Skill Preference

The initial question to consider in determining which leisure skills to select for instruction is: *How does the individual presently spend his free time?* Stated another way, this refers to what leisure skills the individual currently engages in.

There are several reasons for using this as an indicator. One, it may provide the teacher with insights as to the category of leisure activity (e.g., games, sports, hobbies, toys) the participant enjoys. Second, the activity may be used as a reinforcer for other new leisure skills which are objectives of instruction. Third, and perhaps most important, it allows the teacher to determine what the participant can already do and at what level of proficiency. Through placement of a variety of leisure skills materials and task-analytic assessment, a determination can be made of object preferences and quality of performance with different materials.

As an illustration consider the placement of a variety of hobby-type materials, (i.e., goldfish, record player, waterpaints). The teacher could observe and record which materials were preferred by assessing those which were selected, how proficient the individual was with the material, and for what period of time he engaged in its use. Similar assessments might be made with toys, gross motor recreational equipment, such as playground equipment, and simple card or board games. This could also be done with several materials from each leisure category. The data-collection sheet presented earlier in Table 13-2 represents a means of assessing durations.

Although this type of assessment may be helpful in determing the participant's leisure skill preference, it does not tell the teacher *what* materials and/or activities to make available. With the large number of leisure skills available, this becomes a critical question.

Level of Functioning and Specific Educational Needs

The participant's present level of functioning will greatly affect the choice of materials and activities which should be provided for assessment. Consideration of the individual's abilities across major curriculum areas cannot be ignored. The factors in Table 13-3 must be evaluated in determining which leisure skills to target for instruction.

Although the questions asked in Table 13-3 are certainly not comprehensive, they do reflect the points which must be considered in determining which materials and activities are appropriate for assessment. Behavioral checklists

Table 13-3   Considerations in Assessing Participant's Level of Functioning in Certain Skills

Expressive and receptive language

How long does the participant attend to a task?

Is the participant able to focus attention on a simple task if other stimuli are at a minimum?

Does the participant express his- or herself verbally, gesturally, or not at all?

How does the participant interact with authority figures?

Does the participant have difficulty determining the important aspects of the task?

Does the participant understand one-step versus two-step instructions?

Physical/motor characteristics

Does the participant hold up his or her head?

Does the participant sit on the floor unsupported?

Does the participant turn his or her head to watch a moving object?

Does the participant have a functional pincer versus palmar grasp?

Does the participant have a full use of at least one arm?

Does the participant reach for an object when placed in front of the body? When placed under a barrier and out of sight?

Does the participant ambulate independently?

Does the participant use a prosthetic device in his daily living?

and guides such as the Learning Accomplishment Profile or the Minimum Objective System (Williams & Fox, 1977), provide considerably more detail. This is necessary for determining the approximate level at which the individual is functioning.

What will be determined from this type of screening assessment is:

1   What behaviors is this individual currently capable of?
2   What are the behaviors or component skills which make up the leisure activities that are targeted for instruction?

A general parity or agreement between these two questions must be made in order for the leisure skills selection to be not too hard.

Consider the following illustration of this process. Susan's individualized education program (IEP) indicates that at her present performance level she is unable to attend for a period longer than 3 seconds, yet she demonstrates competent fine motor behavior (e.g., ability to grasp and pick up objects, push and pull objects, squeeze, release, and transfer). She is usually withdrawn from others and stays in the corner engaging in high rates of self-stimulation, i.e., twisting string or picking up scraps of paper from the floor and putting them in her mouth. Susan's teacher has provided a variety of card and board games for Susan and the other students in the play area. However, Susan does not play appropriately with the games. Her approximate level of functioning is not at parity with the skills required in the board games. This is one example of how capricious material can interfere with the individual's leisure skills development.

If the IEP committee has done a good job of initial assessment and instructional objectives have been clearly specified, then selection of leisure skills may be facilitated through interrelating IEP objectives with leisure skills goals.

Physical Characteristics

In most cases, new behavior can be developed and maintained in individuals who are functioning at low developmental levels. This is done through behavioral training techniques which are discussed in a later section of this chapter. However, the participant's physical characteristics will directly affect selection of leisure skills for instruction. Individuals with severe motor impairments such as an inability to hold up the head, extreme spasticity, or uncontrollable seizures present additional problems in the identification of appropriate leisure skills for instruction.

What is important to remember is that even though such physical disabilities are rarely reversible, they need not interfere with leisure skills programming. For example, the child with spasticity in arms and hands might enter into a game of moving a Ping-Pong ball back and forth through the use of a head pointer. This same skill might also facilitiate scanning and head pointer control on a communication board. Another illustration might involve using oversized pieces in a table game initially for the spastic child who is unable to use standard-sized materials. The adaptions are endless and require only a teacher's creativity and the occupational/physical therapist's knowledge of motor development.

Age-Appropriate Level of Skill

Another variable which must be considered in the assessment and skills-selection process is how age-appropriate the skill is. The principal question to consider is: *Would a nonhandicapped individual of comparable chronological age engage in this activity in his or her free time?* Severely handicapped adults on the floor pushing a toy truck around or playing with a dollhouse are examples of inappropriate skill selection.

This is, admittedly, a difficult area, especially with adolescents and adults. Very little leisure skills research has been reported with this age population. The answer to this problem is usually found in a detailed breakdown of the skill into very small behaviors. For example, the prospect of teaching plant care to a severely or profoundly handicapped individual may appear remote. However, if this hobby is divided into several skills (e.g., putting dirt in the plant, the flower in dirt, the holder on the plant, watering the plant), and each skill is task-analyzed, then learning problems will be reduced. This is especially true for those teachers who understand how to implement shaping and chaining instructional procedures.

Because of the difficulty in identifying age-appropriate skills, we have provided Table 13-4. This table presents representative skills in categories of

Table 13-4 Representative Objects, Games, Hobbies and Sports Appropriate for Severely Handicapped Adolescent and Adult Leisure Skills Instruction

Major program category	Representative items
Object manipulation—Bubble Gum, Camera, Dice, Flashlight, Frisbee, Guitar, Handgripper, Hammer, Medicine Ball, Scissors, Telephone, Vending Machine.	
Games—Board and table games—Bingo, Checkers, Crossword Puzzles, Darts, Foosball, Ping-Pong, Pinball, Pool, Scrabble, Tic-Tac-Toe.	
Motor games—Arm Wrestle, Charades, Finger (Thumb) Wrestling, Jump Rope, Tetherball, Tug of War.	
Musical/Rhythmic games—Hokey Pokey, Limbo, Name That Tune.	
Card games—Concentration, I Doubt It, Old Maid, Slap Jack, War.	
Hobbies—Camping, Cooking, Decorating for Social Events, Leatherwork, Pet Care, Plant Care, Spectator Leisure, Community Events, String Art, Sunbathing, Woodwork.	
Sports—Badminton, Bowling, Fishing, Horseshoes, Shuffleboard, Jogging, Weight Training, Winter Sports.	

object manipulation, hobbies, sports, and games for adolescents and adults which may be appropriate for instruction.

Access to Materials and Events

The most capable individual will have difficulty engaging in a variety of leisure activities without access to materials or events. At the least, this involves transportation and some degree of financial resources. This leads to the question: *Can the participant get to community events, and if unemployed, does he or she have the money to make necessary purchases?* Although leisure activities can be engaged in without money (i.e., building a snowman), usually some funds are necessary for new materials and replenishing old materials.

There are other factors to consider as well. For example, initiating a social encounter may be difficult without knowledge of how to use a telephone. Interaction with toys or other play objects at home will be difficult if they are stored away in a closet or have been destroyed with no funds to purchase new ones. Similarly, many residents in state facilities have difficulty operating the television or stereo which is placed 8 to 10 feet above the floor.

In short, a careful assessment of what to teach must include a look at the amount and types of materials available, the proximity and physical design of local recreational facilities, the ease of transportation, and the availability of skilled recreational personnel to provide training. An analysis of these variables will, at a minimum, facilitate a decision concerning how broad a program to establish. It will also help identify what areas need more adaption and planning. Table 13-5 provides a summary of the variables which must be considered.

Home Environment

Perhaps the most critical factor in leisure-skills selection is evaluation of the home and neighborhood environment. The age of the individual's parents, the

Table 13-5   Participants Access to Materials and Resources

Amount and types of materials available

What toys, games, or other recreational materials/equipment are available to the participant at home, school, or work environment?

Can recreation materials/equipment be borrowed by community agencies (e.g., public library, university curriculum center)?

Are funds available in the home, school, or work environment to purchase additional recreation equipment?

Does the participant have access to a record player, radio, or other equipment for musical enjoyment?

Proximity and physical design of community recreation opportunities and ease of transportation

Are leisure service agencies offering recreation opportunities to special populations?

Is the participant making use of the recreation services that are readily available in the community?

Can the participant utilize nonadapted playground equipment?

How close is the local park and playground to the participant's home?

Is activity for the participant in the community recreation program significantly hampered because of architectural or attitudinal barriers, or lack of appropriate programming?

Is adequate transportation available for the participant to get to utilize community recreation facilities?

Availability of skilled recreational personnel

Are the community recreation personnel working within the community to facilitate participation of persons with special needs?

Is there a trained recreation consultant/staff available to help develop programs for special populations?

presence of siblings or other relatives in the home, the type of home, and the attitude of other home members will greatly influence the variety and independence of leisure activities engaged in.

Location of the home will also affect the selection process. Urban living presents different problems from those in sparsely populated rural areas. Sensitivity of local communities and neighborhood members to handicapped persons will also be reflected in the amount of funds which are appropriated for therapeutic recreation programming. Table 13-6 is a checklist of factors to consider in evaluating the home environment for leisure-skills selection.

The willingness of parents and other family members to follow through on the school training programs is important as well. Marchant and Wehman (in press) found that demonstration and behavior rehearsal with a foster mother of a severely retarded child was instrumental in generalizing table game skills from the classroom to the home. This example of parent-professional partnership is vital to maintenance of a leisure-activities repertoire in severely handicapped individuals.

Table 13-6 Participant's Home Environment

The participant lives with _____

Relationships and ages of other persons in home _____

_____

_____

How does the participant utilize his free time at home?

Does the participant utilize his leisure time independently or with assistance in the home?

What leisure activities and interests are enjoyed by others in the home?

How many hours per day do housemates/siblings spend with the participant?

Do housemates have any natural talents (e.g., athletics, musical ability) or learned talents (e.g., cooking, tools)?

How is the participant perceived by him- or herself and by family members?

What are the present attitudes toward recreation and leisure held by the participant's family members?

Does the participant reside in an urban or rural area?

What is the general attitude of the neighborhood toward integration of handicapped persons into community programs?

Does the participant interact with others in the neighborhood?

INSTRUCTIONAL STRATEGIES AND LESSON PLANS

Toy Play

One part of the recreational inventory outlined in the back of this chapter involves toy play. This is an area which reflects cognitive, motor, and social development in children (Piaget, 1951), and may provide an effective medium for assessing the general level of functioning of handicapped children. The way in which children interact with toys and other peers in a free-play situation may provide a gross profile of the child's skill level. For example, in clinical situations a number of behavioral indices may be evaluated, thereby providing observational data on the child's exploratory behavior, relationship to parents and peers, language, cognitive development, and persistence. Preferred toys can also be evaluated as potential reinforcers.

Toy Play Objectives

Selection of relevant toy play objectives is important because it may be possible to accelerate collateral skills in the child's repertoire, such as fine motor skills (Bradtke, Rosenblatt, & Kirpatrick, 1972). Three objectives are provided below.

1   Given a set of different-sized blocks, the child will identify and arrange at least 10 different formations within a 30-day period.

2   Given a dollhouse, the child will demonstrate how to open and close the doors of the house and how to place different dolls in the rooms of the dollhouse for 4 out of 5 consecutive days.

3 Given a Jack-in-the-Box, the child will wind it frequently enough so that the Jack pops up for 4 out 5 consecutive days.

It is usually optimal to identify toy play objectives which allow the child several different correct responses. Objectives 1 and 2 allow for some creativity by the child; the third objective does not.

Sample Lesson Plan for Object Manipulation

In order to further illustrate how learning conditions affect acquisition of toy play skills, we have provided a sample lesson plan. This plan is directed toward helping young severely multiply handicapped children improve exploratory play skills. Unfortunately many multiply handicapped children fail to explore their environment through simple motor movements such as reaching and grasping. Therefore, selection of a skill for instruction, such as shaking a rattle, is an important first step in developing greater sensory awareness.

Skill: Shakes rattle

Objective: Given rattle, placed within an arm's length from student, and the verbal cue "Shake the rattle," S will grasp the rattle and move it rapidly from side to side, producing a rattling sound for a minimum of 5 seconds, three out of four trials on 3 consecutive days.

INSTRUCTIONAL PROCEDURES

Task Analysis

Student Behavior:	*Teacher Behavior:*
1 S looks at rattle	**1** "Look at the rattle."
2 S extends arm and hand in direction of rattle	**2** "Touch the rattle."
3 S places fingers around it	**3,4** "Hold the rattle."
4 S grasps rattle in fist	
5 S lifts rattle	**5** "Pick up the rattle."
6 S shakes rattle for 1 second	**6–10** Shake the rattle."
7 S shakes rattle for 2 seconds	
8 S shakes rattle for 3 seconds	
9 S shakes rattle for 4 seconds	
10 S shakes rattle for 5 seconds	

Acquisition

Initially, the teacher should establish Ss baseline performance. T gives the initial cue, "Shake the rattle." T gives no further assistance and no feedback, but records S's performance on a data sheet, with = for the correct response and − for an incorrect response by each step in the task analysis. Baseline data should be collected for three sessions.

After establishing a student's baseline performance, T should begin the instructional phase of the program. The rattle should be visually stimulating (colorful) as well as aurally stimulating (producing the loud rattling sound).

Orientation and Attention

Parts Learning

Amount of Material

The task should be analyzed in its component parts. One step at a time from the task analysis is specified as the target skill. *T* gives the verbal cue for the target step. If *S* responds correctly, he or she is immediately reinforced and told *why* the reinforcement is being given. If *S* does not respond appropriately, *T* repeats the cue and models the desired response. If *S* still does not respond, *T* physically assists him or her in making the response, then reinforces.

Knowledge of Results

Incidential Learning

Shaping

Initially, any approximation of the desired response should be reinforced. Gradually *T* requires responses which more closely resemble the stated target skill.

Chaining

After *S* has learned each step separately, the steps must be chained together. *T* gives the initial cue, "Shake and rattle." If *S* responds correctly, he or she is reinforced and given appropriate feedback ("Good shaking the rattle"). If *S* does not respond, *T* should give the verbal cues for each step, separately and sequentially, to guide *S* through the response. *T* must gradually fade the cues and prompts until *S* responds to the initial cue alone.

Amount and Distribution of Practice

S should practice the skill daily. Instructional sessions should consist of four 15-minute sessions per day. The first 10 minutes should be used for instruction, and the last 5 for data collection. *T* records *S*'s performance on data sheets.

Reinforcement for this task should include edibles paired with social praise. *Each time S exhibits the desired response, T reinforces it.* *T* gradually fades the edible component, reinforcing with social praise only.

Retention

After the student has attained mastery on the stated objective (shakes rattle 5 seconds, three out of four trials on 3 consecutive days), he or must continue to practice the skill for half the number of trials it took to achieve initial mastery. This will provide for 50 percent overlearning.

Degree of Original Learning

Transfer

Degree of Original Learning

The *S* should continue to practice for the same number of trials it took to achieve initial mastery. This provides for 100 percent overlearning. *S* should perform the stated task in a variety of settings and with a variety of instructors. An attempt should be made to include the family and home setting in the instructional planning.

Items other than the original rattle should be substituted during the practice sessions. For instance, *T* should provide different types, colors, and sizes of rattling objects.

The reinforcement schedule should also be varied. The edible reinforcers should be faded, leaving social praise as the main reinforcement. The social praise should be given intermittently and with a normal degree of enthusiasm.

Game Activities

Games represent a major aspect of any leisure-skills program. In the recreation-skills scope and sequence, game activities have been subdivided into simple imitative group games, card games, complex table games, and table-game sports. The subdivisions, although not totally arbitrary, represent one effort at sequencing clusters of skills.

Group games have been divided into the very simplistic types of games which young children play (e.g., Peek-a-Boo) and the more-advanced games such as Hide-and-Seek and Charades. Group games are an excellent medium for children to learn preacademic skills and to take turns cooperatively.

Card games and simple table games are also identified as clusters of skills which children and adults play for fun. Simple table games follow a general start to finish sequence. Once an indvidual has acquired this sequence in several games, other table games will be acquired more rapidly (Wehman, Renzaglia, Berry, Schutz, & Karan, 1978). Complex table games are those which do not follow the simple start to finish sequence and may involve backward moves (e.g., Checkers), or moves characterized by a typical direction (e.g., Chinese checkers). Table-game sports are a cluster of skills which represent a miniature-sized illustration of the real sport. Air hockey, pinball, and foosball are examples of table-game sports which individuals can be exposed to and taught how to play.

Game Objectives

Because games are an excellent means of teaching preacademic and social skills in children, the selection of objectives must be carefully planned. Below are listed objectives for three different types of games.

1 Given the table game, Picture Lotto, the child will play it with at least one peer and with no errors for 4 out of 5 consecutive days.
2 Given the group game, Follow-the-leader, the child will play it correctly for 4 out of 5 days consecutively.
3 Given an electric bowling game, the individual will take turns and follow the rules correctly for four out of five sessions consecutively.

Marchant (1979) has developed a sequence of table games to use with early childhood handicapped and trainable severely retarded children. This sequence portrays that a progressively more-advanced sequence can be used with nonverbal children through use of signing communication.

Adapting and Designing Games

Handicapped children often have physical or perceptual problems which inhibit them from using commercially made game materials successfully. Teachers have the option of either securing the commercial materials and adapting them to meet the needs of the students or designing and making table games for the students. As with eating and other self-help devices, the teacher must remember that adapted game materials should be used only when it is absolutely necessary because of the tendency for persons to become dependent on such adaptations.

It is also important to remember that one goal of game instruction is normalization, so whenever possible, game materials should be identical to those used by nonhandicapped persons.

When adaptations are necessary, they should be done to meet the individual needs of the student, and whenever possible auxiliary staff, such as physical, occupational, or speech therapists, should participate in the planning of such adaptations.

Students with poor fine motor skills may need to have game cards or playing pieces built-up on heavy cardboard to make them easier to grasp. For the same students, it may be necessary to tape down the game board down or use a piece of Dycem to hold it in place on the table. If pictures on the game board are too close together, it may be necessary to cut the pictures and separate them on a larger board so the pieces are easier to place. Positioning a student in a prone position over a roll or wedge instead of at a table may facilitate manipulation of the playing pieces if the student needs better extension of the upper extremities.

For a student with perceptual problems, many game boards are too cluttered with fancy designs so that the student cannot determine where the track begins or goes. Such figure-ground difficulties can be reduced by covering all unnecessary designs on the board with solid-colored contact paper and by using prompts such as big stars to indicate where to begin and arrows to point to the correct pathway. Such prompts can be faded as game skills are acquired.

The above examples represent ways the materials themselves might be adapted. In addition to adapting materials, it may also be necessary to adapt the rules of commercial games to meet the needs of disabled persons. This may be done to reduce the length or complexity of a commercial game, and should be done to meet the individual needs of students with whom the games will be used. Rules may also be adapted to permit nonverbal students to use manual language or to point out their replies on an answer sheet.

Endless adaptations of games are possible for the determined teacher, but in some instances no commercial games are available or can be adapted for a particular objective. Teacher-made games can fill this void if care is taken in planning and making them.

Such games should be made with large, clear pictures which are uncluttered and usually contain only one item. Items in the game should be spaced appropriately for the students with whom the game will be used. Game materials should be realistic and colorful when possible and made of durable materials. Lamination, clear contact paper, or dry mounting should be used on the games, particularly if the students exhibit drooling problems. Colorful tape borders should be put around boards to discourage students from pulling off the coverings, and rubber cement rather than glue is suggested as an adhesive for paper pictures to ensure proper placement and sticking. When carefully made, the laminated or covered games can be wiped clean and used for several years.

Playing pieces should be large enough to be easily grasped and released by the students. Blocks or other small toys can be utilized as can poker chips if the students can handle these easily.

The rules for teacher-made games should be written down sequentially and should include the objectives and materials for the games. They must be clear and easily understood so that the game can be played the same way by all players. The game should be implemented initially with another adult so that necessary changes can be made prior to instructing students to use the game. All materials and the rules should be kept together in a box, and lost or destroyed pieces should be replaced immediately.

Sample Lesson Plan for Games

As an illustration of instructional techniques applied to teaching a table game, the lesson plan below has been developed. Playing checkers is a common table-game leisure skill which can be taught to most handicapped individuals given systematic instruction.

<u>Skill</u>: Playing Checkers
<u>Objective</u>: Given checkers, checkerboard, and rules of the game, S will play the game independently with no errors nine out of ten times.

INSTRUCTIONAL PROCEDURES

Task Analysis (From: Wehman, 1977)

Student Behavior:	*Teacher Behavior:*
1 S identifies black from red	1 "Point to the black." "Point to the red."
2 S identifies one color as being his men	2 "Point to your men."
3 S places pieces correctly for game	3 "Show me how you set your side of the board."
4 (a) S moves piece diagonally (b) S moves piece on same color (c) S moves piece forward	4 "Show me how you move your man."
5 S single-jumps opposition	5 "Show me how you jump the other man."
6 S takes the other man after jumping him.	6 "Show me what you do when you jump the other man.
7 S avoids being jumped	7 "Show me what happens if you get jumped."
8 S double-jumps opposition	8 "Show me how you jump two men."
9 S takes both men after double-jumps	9 "Show me what you do."
10 S moves his piece to other side of board to receive king.	10 "Show me what happens when you get to the other side of the board."

11 S crowns opposition by placing checker on top of opposition checker after reaching other side of board

11 "Show me what happens when the other man gets to the other side of the board."

12 S identifies physical difference between king and single checkers

12 "Point to the king."

13 S moves king in forward and backward directions

13 "Show me how the king moves."

14 S plays games with no procedural mistakes

14 "Let's play checkers."

Initial Presentation

Today I'm going to show you how to play checkers. This is a game you can enjoy playing with your friends here at school and at home.

Distinctive Features

This is the checkerboard, and these are the checkers. Look at the checkers. All of them are either red or black. I want you to sort the checkers for me. Put all the red ones here, and all the black ones here.

Redundancy

Good. Now watch while I set up the board. This is the way you always start the game. All the red checkers are yours, and all the black ones are mine.

I'm going to teach you how to move your checkers on the board. The way you win the game is to take all my checkers off the board by jumping them, before I jump all yours.

Acquisition

**Parts Learning
Amount of
Material
Nature of
Rules
Chaining**

The task-analysis presentation of the skill provides for parts learning and reduces the amount of material a student must deal with at a given time. It also reduces the complexity of the rules, in that they are presented one at a time, before being chained together.

Prior to beginning instruction, T must establish S's baseline performance. T gives initial instruction only and no further assistance or feedback. T records student responses on a data sheet. Baseline data should be recorded for three sessions.

T specifies one step at a time as the target step. S must meet criterion on one step before he or she moves on to others.

High Contiguity of Instances

Breaking the skill down into smaller increments also facilitates concept learning. S practices one concept over and over until he masters it, before going on to new concepts involved in the game.

**Knowledge of Results
Incidental Learning**

T gives the verbal cue for the target step. If S responds correctly he or she is immediately reinforced, and told *why* reinforcement is given. If S does not respond appropriately, T repeats the cue and models the desired response. If S still does not respond, T physically assists him or her in making the response, then reinforces.

Fading	After S has learned all steps and they have been chained together, T must gradually fade the cues for each step. T gives the initial cue, "Let's play checkers." If S plays the game correctly, T reinforces him or her by saying, "Great! You played the game exactly right." If S does not play the game correctly, T cues him or her as necessary and gradually fades those cues.
Amount and Distribution of Practice	S should practice the game four times daily, two times per session. S has attained mastery when he or she plays the game nine out of ten times with no procedural errors. At the end of each session, T should record data for one game.

Reinforcement for this skill shall be strong social praise. It should be given immediately and consistently, following the target skill.

Retention

Degree of Original Learning	S must continue to practice the skill for half again as long as it took him to achieve initial mastery. This provides for 50 percent overlearning.

Transfer

Degree of Original Learning	S should continue to practice for the same number of trials it took to achieve initial mastery. This provides for 100 percent over-learning.

S should play the game with a variety of partners and in a diversity of settings. The student's family should be encouraged to play the game at home.

A variety of reinforcement should be used. Tangibles should be faded out (if used at all), and social praise only should be used. A diversity of phrases can be used to reward S for a properly played game. These include: "Great game"; "You didn't make any mistakes!"; "That was really fun"; etc.

Hobby Activities

Hobbies include scrapbook and collection activities, arts and crafts, and life science activities. Hobbies are defined as those activities with which an individual spends an extended period of time and which allow for personal development and growth. Typically, hobbies require some degree of fine motor coordination and are rather passive in nature.

Hobbies can be a valuable outlet for handicapped individuals who live alone or who have limited social contact. Unlike many leisure activities, a hobby frequently results in a finished product in which an individual can take pride.

Hobby Objectives

The following objectives represent different skills within the hobby sequence.

1 Given materials for weaving, the individual will weave a shawl and/or scarf for personal use with no errors.

    2 Given a variety of beer cans, the individual will arrange a collection of beer cans over a 6-month period.

    3 Given a pet dog, the individual will care for and spend time with the animal.

Sample Lesson Plan for Hobbies

The lesson plan described below represents a sewing skill. This skill requires considerable fine motor skill. Sewing and embroidery skills are frequently taught at local high schools or community colleges as creative leisure skills.

Skill: Sewing an A-line skirt

Objective: Given a pattern (consisting of two main pattern pieces and waistband; no darts; zipper and snap closure), necessary materials, and verbal directions, S will independently cut a pattern out of fabric and sew the pieces together to form the specified item. S must perform each step independently on three consecutive sessions. S will produce two specified items within 2 weeks.

INSTRUCTIONAL PROCEDURES

Task Analysis

Student Behavior:		T's Verbal Directions:	
1	S places pattern of fabric so there is no over-lapping	**1–3**	"Cut out the pattern."
2	S pins pattern pieces in place		
3	S cuts out each pattern piece		
4	S places front and back pieces with right side of fabric together	**4,5**	"Sew the right side seam."
5	S sews right side seam on machine		
6	S sews left side seam on machine, up to 6 inches from waistline	**6**	"Sew the left side seam. Leave room for the zipper."
7	S turns skirt right-side-out	**7–10**	"Turn the skirt right-side-out. Sew on the waistband and sew the ends.
8	S pins waistband in place, so right side of waistband fabric touches right side of skirt fabric, and top edges are even		
9	S sews waistband in place on machine		
10	S sews closed each end of waistband on machine		

11	*S* turns waistband right-side-out	**11,12**	"Hem the inside of the waistband."
12	*S* hems under inside raw edge of waistband, by hand		
13	*S* pins zipper in place at left side seam	**13,14**	"Sew in the zipper."
14	*S* sews around zipper, on machine		
15	*S* sews snap at left side opening, by hand	**15**	"Sew on the snap."
16	*S* pins hem in place	**16,17**	"Hem it."
17	*S* hems skirt, by hand.		

Initial Presentation

Today I'm going to teach you how to sew a skirt. You will be able to wear the skirts we make together, and make more in the future.

Organization You always use a pattern when you sew. You place it on the material and use it to cut out the pieces for the skirt. Then you sew the pieces together—I will show you how. After that, you sew in the zipper, a snap, and hem the skirt. That's all you have to do!

High Contiguity of Instances We'll work on one step at a time, until you learn it. Then we'll work on the next step.

Acquisition

Prior to instructions, *T* should establish *S*'s baseline performance, over three sessions. *S* provides the materials and verbal instructions but no assistance or feedback. *T* records *S*'s performance on a data sheet.

Parts Learning Amount of Material The task-analysis presentation provides for parts learning, and reduces the amount of material *S* must deal with at a given time.

S should practice one step at a time repeatedly for the entire training session. *S* must perform each step independently on three consecutive sessions before moving on to the next step.

Chaining After *S* has learned all steps separately, the steps are chained together.

Incidental Learning Fading *T* should provide modeling and prompting as necessary. *T* should gradually fade this assistance, and give only the verbal instructions.

Simultaneous Exposure During instruction, present *S* with examples of skirts sewn correctly and incorrectly (simultaneously). Have *S* point out one that is correct.

Knowledge of Results *T* should use strong social praise to reinforce this skill. *T* delivers the reinforcement immediately following a correct response on the target step.

Amount and Distribution of Practice *S* should practice the skill daily, for 30 minutes each day. After the 30-minute session, *T* should record data on *S*'s performance. During data collection, *T* should give no assistance or reinforcement.

Retention

Degree of Original Learning   *S* should produce one more skirt, in a 1-week period. This provides 50 percent overlearning.

Transfer

Degree of Original Learning   *S* should produce two more skirts, within a 2-week period. This provides 100 percent overlearning.

    S should use a variety of fabrics and sewing machines. Verbal instructions should be varied slightly each session.

Sports

Since competition is a facet of life to which all individuals must become accustomed, competitive individual and team sports are an important aspect to leisure-skills training. The concept of win and lose characterizes many relationships and life situations and the developmentally disabled person must learn how to win graciously and also how to accept defeat. Sports are an excellent medium for this development. Furthermore, there is probably no other level in this skill chart which provides the opportunity to work cooperatively with a team. The give and take required in a team relationship may also facilitate acceptance of handicapped persons by nonhandicapped peers.

Sports Objectives

    1 Given the availability of playground bars, the child will swing down the bars (by way of ladder rungs) eight out of ten times for 4 out of 5 consecutive days.

    2 Given a softball team, the individual will play the games according to all the rules with no errors for four out of five consecutive games.

    3 Given a set of different barbell weights, the individual will lift 50-, pound 75-, pound and 100-pound weights by the end of a 6-month period of training.

Sample Lesson Plan for Sports

This lesson plan is designed for the young handicapped child. Ball skills clearly involve gross motor actions but may be designed into game and social activities as well.

Skill: Rolling a ball
Objective: Given a large rubber ball, *S* will independently roll the ball 6 feet with two peers in a group. *S* will perform the skill four out of five times on 3 consecutive days.

INSTRUCTIONAL PROCEDURES

Task Analysis
    1 *S* sits on floor with legs spread open
    2 *S* sits facing *T*

  3 *S* holds ball on floor in front of body
  4 *S* extends arms, pushing ball forward with palms
  5 *S* releases ball as arms are fully extended
  6 *S* rolls ball 1 foot
  7 *S* rolls ball 2 feet
  8 *S* rolls ball 3 feet
  9 *S* rolls ball 4 feet
 10 *S* rolls ball 5 feet
 11 *S* rolls ball 6 feet
 12 *S* rolls ball to peer
 13 *S* rolls ball to second peer in group.

Initial Presentation

Modeling

Today I'm going to teach you how to roll a ball. Once you've learned how, you can have fun playing ball with your friends and your family. Watch while I show you how.

Acquisition

Before beginning instruction, *T* should establish *S*'s baseline performance. *T* sits on the floor facing *S* 6 feet away. *T* rolls ball to *S* and encourages him or her to roll it back. *T* gives no additional assistance or feedback. *T* records data on *S*'s performance for three sessions.

T then begins instruction (unless *S* meets criteria during baseline).

Parts Learning
Amount of
Material
Incidental
Learning
Knowledge of
Results
Chaining
Amount and
Distribution
of Practice
Fading in
Peers

The task-analysis format provides for parts learning and reduces the amount of material *S* must deal with one skill at a given time.

One step at a time is specified as the target skill. *T* models and prompts the target step as necessary, and reinforces correct student responses.

After *S* has learned all the steps, *T* chains them together. *S* should practice the skill daily for 15 minutes. After the 15-minute session, *T* should record data on one ball-rolling sequence.

Once *S* has reached criterion on the distance, another child can be added to the group. If this works out appropriately, a third child can enter the ball play.

Reinforcement should be edible, paired with social. *T* should gradually reduce the edible, providing only social praise.

Retention

Degree of
Original
Learning

S must continue to practice the skill for half again as long as it took him or her to achieve initial mastery. This provides for 50 percent overlearning.

Transfer

Degree of
Original
Learning

S should continue practicing for the same number of trials it took to achieve initial mastery. This provides 100 percent overlearning.

S should perform skill with a variety of partners, using different balls in different settings.

SUMMARY

The purpose of this chapter is to provide information pertinent to leisure-skills curricula and programs for handicapped individuals. The chapter is developed so that it presents a large inventory of leisure skills in the subdomains of toy play, games, sports, and hobbies. Following this inventory, located in the back of the chapter, is a discussion of assessment- and skill-selection guidelines, as applied to leisure-skills program development. Detailed lesson plans which illustrated principles of learning described in Chapters 4, 5, and 6 are then presented across each of the four subdomains.

There are several leisure skill competency areas which can be assessed in handicapped individuals. These include task-analytic assessment, or the *proficiency* with which materials are engaged, the *duration* of actions, the *materials preference* of each individual, and the frequency and direction of social interactions. *Appropriateness* of object actions is also discussed as a factor which affects the reliability of the teacher's observation and recording system. These specific variables are only assessed after a five-step process of general screening and evaluation are undertaken.

From leisure-assessment data, skill selection must be made. The guidelines in this chapter will help the teacher decide which skills to select for instruction. The individual's level of functioning and educational needs are considered as important as the physical characteristics. Parental attitude and financial resources for materials also play a factor in deciding what type of leisure skills to emphasize. The teacher should be prepared to justify the skills which are selected. In each of the subdomains, several sample instructional objectives are provided. Following these objectives, a detailed lesson plan highlighting specific instructional techniques is presented. The skills identified for instruction involve shaking a rattle, knitting, playing checkers, and rolling a ball. These skills are appropriate for individuals with different levels of functioning. For example, interacting with a rattle might be appropriate for a multiply handicapped preschooler; on the other hand, knitting is a better skill for a mildly handicapped child or adolescent.

The leisure-skill curriculum area must continue to develop and be taught in settings outside classrooms. Local parks and recreation departments need to be involved as consultants to educators in helping modify activities for handicapped students. It is necessary for recreation specialists and teachers to work closer if handicapped individuals are to acquire a repertoire of appropiated leisure skills.

REFERENCES

Bradtke, L., Rosenblatt K., & Kirpatrick W. Intensive play—A technique for building affective behaviors in profoundly mentally retarded children. *Education and Training of the Mentally Retarded*, 1972, 7, 8–13.

Burney, J., Russell, B., & Shores, R. Developing social responses in two profoundly retarded children. *AAESPH* (American Association for the Education of the Severely/Profoundly Handicapped) *Review*, 1977, 2(2), 53–64.

Favell, J., & Cannon, P. An evaluation of entertainment meterials for severely retarded persons. *American Journal of Mental Deficiency,* 1977, *81*, 357–362.

Hamre-Nietupski, S., & Williams, W. W. Implementation of selected sex education and social skills programs with severely handicapped students. *Education and Training of the Mentally Retarded*, 1977, *12*(1), 364–372.

Knowles, C., Vogel, P., & Wessel, J. Project I CAN: Individualized curriculum designed for mentally retarded children and youth. *Education and Training of the Mentally Retarded*, 1975, *10*, 155–160.

Marchant, J., Teaching games and hobbies. In P. Wehman (ed.), *Recreation programming for developmentally disabled persons*, Baltimore: Univ. Park Press, 1979.

Marchant J., and Wehman P. Teaching table games to severely retarded children, *Mental Retardation,* in press.

McCall, R. Exploratory manipulation and play in the human infant. *Monograph of the Society for Research in Child Development.* Chicago: University of Chicago Press, 1974.

Piaget, J. *Play, dreams and imitation in childhood.* New York: Norton, 1951.

Strain, P., Cooke, T., & Appolloni, T. *Teaching exceptional children: Assessment and modification of social behavior*. New York: Academic, 1976.

Tilton, J., & Ottinger, D. Comparison of toy play behavior of austistic, retarded, and normal children. *Psychological Reports,* 1964, *15*, 967–975.

Wehman, P. Selection of play materials for the severely handicapped: A continued dilemma. *Education and Training of the Mentally Retarded* 1976, *11*(1), 46–51.

Wehman, P. *Helping the mentally retarded acquire play skills: A behavioral approach.* Springfield, Ill.: Charles C. Thomas, 1977. (a)

Wehman, P. Research on leisure time and the severely developmentally disabled. *Rehabiltation Literature*, 1977, *38*(4), 98–105. (b)

Wehman, P. (ed.) *Recreation programming for developmentally disabled persons.* Baltimore: University Park Press, 1979.

Wehman P., Renzaglia A., Berry A., Schutz R., & Karan O. C. Developing a leisure skill repertoire in severely and profoundly handicapped adolescents and adults. *AAESPH Review*, 1978, *3*(2), 55–62.

Williams W., & Fox T. Minimum objectives curriculum. Burlington, Vt.: Center for Developmental Disabilities, 1977.

Appendix for Chapter 13

Leisure Skills Inventory for Developmentally Disabled Persons

Participant's Name _____

Participant's Age _____

Participant's Behavioral and Physical Characteristics _____

_____

_____

Date of Evaluation _____

Evaluator _____

Method(s) of Evaluation (check one):

    Direct Observation   _____

    Parent/Guardian Interview with Evaluator   _____

    Participant Interview with Evaluator   _____

    Combination Observation and Interview   _____

Age level*	Leisure skills category	Level of trainer assistance required (check one)			
		Self-initiates	Verbal cue	Verbal cue and model	Verbal cue and physical assistance
	I Object manipulation				
	1 *Balloon*				
C	1 Stretch balloon	_____	_____	_____	_____
C	2 Blow up balloon	_____	_____	_____	_____
C	3 Tie knot in balloon	_____	_____	_____	_____
C	4 Hit balloon	_____	_____	_____	_____
C	5 Catch balloon	_____	_____	_____	_____
C	6 Create static and stick balloon on wall	_____	_____	_____	_____
C	7 Hold helium balloon	_____	_____	_____	_____
C	8 Fill balloon with water	_____	_____	_____	_____
C	9 Pop balloon	_____	_____	_____	_____
	2 *Baton*				
C	10 Wave baton	_____	_____	_____	_____
C	11 Balance baton	_____	_____	_____	_____
C	12 Twirl baton	_____	_____	_____	_____

*C indicates chronologically age-appropriate skill for child.
 A indicates chronologically age-appropriate skill for adolescent and adult.
 C/A indicates chronologically age-appropriate skill for child, adolescent, or adult.

Age level*	Leisure skill category	Level of trainer assistance required (check one)			
		Self-initiates	Verbal cue	Verbal cue and model	Verbal cue and physical assistance
C	13 Throw baton in air	_____	_____	_____	_____
C	14 Catch baton	_____	_____	_____	_____
	3 *Beanbag*				
C	15 Stack beanbags	_____	_____	_____	_____
C	16 Underhand beanbag throw	_____	_____	_____	_____
C	17 Overhand beanbag throw	_____	_____	_____	_____
C	18 Toss beanbag from hand to hand	_____	_____	_____	_____
C	19 Balance beanbag on head	_____	_____	_____	_____
	4 *Bell*				
C	20 Hit bell off shelf	_____	_____	_____	_____
C	21 Ring bell and listen	_____	_____	_____	_____
C	22 Wear bell around neck/wrist	_____	_____	_____	_____
	5 *Blocks*				
C	23 Arrange blocks horizontally	_____	_____	_____	_____
C	24 Stack blocks vertically	_____	_____	_____	_____
C	25 Build block tower	_____	_____	_____	_____
C	26 Hit block tower over	_____	_____	_____	_____
C	27 Load blocks into toy truck	_____	_____	_____	_____
	6 *Bubble gum*				
C/A	28 Open bubble gum wrapper	_____	_____	_____	_____
C/A	29 Chew bubble gum	_____	_____	_____	_____
C/A	30 Blow bubble	_____	_____	_____	_____
C/A	31 Dispose of bubble gum	_____	_____	_____	_____
	7 *Bucket and shovel*				
C	32 Dig with shovel	_____	_____	_____	_____
C	33 Scoop sand into bucket	_____	_____	_____	_____
C	34 Fill bucket using shovel	_____	_____	_____	_____
C	35 Empty bucket	_____	_____	_____	_____
C	36 Build sand castle	_____	_____	_____	_____
	8 *Busy Box*				
C	37 Push in beeper of Busy Box	_____	_____	_____	_____
C	38 Pull handle of Busy Box	_____	_____	_____	_____
C	39 Slide door of Busy Box	_____	_____	_____	_____
C	40 Turn dial of Busy Box	_____	_____	_____	_____

Age level*		Leisure skills category	Level of trainer assistance required (check one)			
			Self-initiates	Verbal cue	Verbal cue and model	Verbal cue and physical assistance
	9	*Camera*				
C/A	41	Look through camera	_____	_____	_____	_____
C/A	42	Press button on camera	_____	_____	_____	_____
C/A	43	Wind camera	_____	_____	_____	_____
	10	*Cracker Jack*				
C	44	Open Cracker Jack box	_____	_____	_____	_____
C	45	Eat Cracker Jack	_____	_____	_____	_____
C	46	Find prize in Cracker Jack box	_____	_____	_____	_____
C	47	Close Cracker Jack box	_____	_____	_____	_____
C	48	Shake Cracker Jack box	_____	_____	_____	_____
	11	*Crayons*				
C	49	Pick up crayon and put in coloring position	_____	_____	_____	_____
C	50	Scribble with crayon	_____	_____	_____	_____
C	51	Trace line with crayon	_____	_____	_____	_____
C	52	Connect dots with crayon	_____	_____	_____	_____
C	53	Color picture within lines	_____	_____	_____	_____
	12	*Dice*				
C/A	54	Shake dice	_____	_____	_____	_____
C/A	55	Roll dice	_____	_____	_____	_____
C/A	56	Match dice numbers	_____	_____	_____	_____
C/A	57	Match die numbers to movement on game board	_____	_____	_____	_____
	13	*Etch A Sketch*				
C	58	Turn Etch A Sketch dials	_____	_____	_____	_____
C	59	Trace line on Etch A Sketch	_____	_____	_____	_____
C	60	Draw square on Etch A Sketch	_____	_____	_____	_____
C	61	Shake Etch A Sketch to erase design	_____	_____	_____	_____
	14	*Flashlight*				
C/A	62	Turn flashlight on/off	_____	_____	_____	_____
C/A	63	Focus flashlight on object	_____	_____	_____	_____
C/A	64	Scan ceiling with flashlight	_____	_____	_____	_____
C/A	65	Follow light on wall with flashlight	_____	_____	_____	_____
C/A	66	Touch illuminated spot on wall	_____	_____	_____	_____

Age level*	Leisure skill category	Level of trainer assistance required (check one)			
		Self-initiates	Verbal cue	Verbal cue and model	Verbal cue and physical assistance
	15 *Frisbee*				
C/A	67 Hold Frisbee	_____	_____	_____	_____
C/A	68 Roll Frisbee	_____	_____	_____	_____
C/A	69 Throw Frisbee	_____	_____	_____	_____
C/A	70 Catch Frisbee	_____	_____	_____	_____
C/A	71 Throw Frisbee through target	_____	_____	_____	_____
	16 *Glider plane*				
C	72 Assemble glider plane	_____	_____	_____	_____
C	73 Color glider plane	_____	_____	_____	_____
C	74 Throw glider plane	_____	_____	_____	_____
C	75 Throw glider plane through target	_____	_____	_____	_____
C	76 Catch glider plane	_____	_____	_____	_____
	17 *Guitar*				
C/A	77 Hold guitar	_____	_____	_____	_____
C/A	78 Strum guitar	_____	_____	_____	_____
C/A	79 Pluck guitar	_____	_____	_____	_____
C/A	80 Strum guitar to record	_____	_____	_____	_____
C/A	81 Strum guitar and sing to record	_____	_____	_____	_____
	18 *Hammer*				
C/A	82 Hit object with hammer	_____	_____	_____	_____
C	83 Drive toy bolt into Playskool Cobbler's Bench with hammer	_____	_____	_____	_____
C	84 Remove bolt from Playskool Cobbler's Bench	_____	_____	_____	_____
A	85 Drive nail into wood with hammer	_____	_____	_____	_____
A	86 Remove nail from wood with hammer	_____	_____	_____	_____
	19 *Handgrippers*				
C/A	87 Squeeze handgripper with one hand	_____	_____	_____	_____
C/A	88 Squeeze handgripper and feel forearm	_____	_____	_____	_____
C/A	89 Squeeze two handgrippers	_____	_____	_____	_____
	20 *Hula-Hoop*				
C	90 Walk through Hula-Hoop	_____	_____	_____	_____

Age level*	Leisure skills category	Level of trainer assistance required (check one)			
		Self-initiates	Verbal cue	Verbal cue and model	Verbal cue and physical assistance
C	91 Roll Hula-Hoop	_____	_____	_____	_____
C	92 Spin Hula-Hoop on floor	_____	_____	_____	_____
C	93 Swing Hula-Hoop on arm	_____	_____	_____	_____
C	94 Twirl Hula-Hoop around waist	_____	_____	_____	_____
	21 *Jack-in-the-Box*				
C	95 Stuff Jack-in-the-Box	_____	_____	_____	_____
C	96 Close Jack-in-the-Box	_____	_____	_____	_____
C	97 Wind Jack-in-the-Box	_____	_____	_____	_____
	22 *Lincoln Logs*				
C	98 Dump Lincoln Logs	_____	_____	_____	_____
C	99 Roll Lincoln Logs	_____	_____	_____	_____
C	100 Stack Lincoln Logs	_____	_____	_____	_____
C	101 Build with Lincoln Logs	_____	_____	_____	_____
	23 *Marbles*				
C	102 Pick up marble	_____	_____	_____	_____
C	103 Roll marble	_____	_____	_____	_____
C	104 Shoot marble with thumb	_____	_____	_____	_____
C	105 Pick up marble with toes	_____	_____	_____	_____
C	106 Arrange marbles in groups	_____	_____	_____	_____
C	107 Place marbles in container	_____	_____	_____	_____
	24 *Matchbox car*				
C	108 Push Matchbox car	_____	_____	_____	_____
C	109 Release Matchbox car down incline	_____	_____	_____	_____
C	110 Race Matchbox cars	_____	_____	_____	_____
C	111 Paint Matchbox car	_____	_____	_____	_____
C	112 Collect Matchbox cars and trade them	_____	_____	_____	_____
	25 *Medicine ball*				
C/A	113 Roll medicine ball	_____	_____	_____	_____
C/A	114 Pick up medicine ball	_____	_____	_____	_____
C/A	115 Throw medicine ball	_____	_____	_____	_____
C/A	116 Catch medicine ball	_____	_____	_____	_____
C	117 Lie on medicine ball and roll on floor	_____	_____	_____	_____
	26 *Mr. Bubble*				
C	118 Open bottle	_____	_____	_____	_____

Age level*	Leisure skill category		Level of trainer assistance required (check one)			
			Self-initiates	Verbal cue	Verbal cue and model	Verbal cue and physical assistance
C	119	Wave wand	___	___	___	___
C	120	Blow bubble	___	___	___	___
C	121	Catch bubble	___	___	___	___
C	122	Pop bubble	___	___	___	___
	27	*Multipurpose ball*				
C	123	Roll ball	___	___	___	___
C	124	Kick ball	___	___	___	___
C	125	Throw ball	___	___	___	___
C	126	Catch ball	___	___	___	___
C	127	Bounce ball	___	___	___	___
	28	*Music box*				
C	128	Open music box	___	___	___	___
C	129	Wind music box	___	___	___	___
C	130	Close music box	___	___	___	___
	29	*Popcorn popper lawnmower*				
C	131	Push popcorn popper lawnmower	___	___	___	___
C	132	Pull popcorn popper lawnmower	___	___	___	___
C	133	Push popcorn popper lawnmower down steps	___	___	___	___
C	134	Pull popcorn popper lawnmower up steps	___	___	___	___
	30	*Pound-A-Round*				
C	135	Push lever (bar) down	___	___	___	___
C	136	Attend to moving balls	___	___	___	___
	31	*Puppet*				
C	137	Draw puppet face	___	___	___	___
C	138	Hold puppet	___	___	___	___
C	139	Make puppet move	___	___	___	___
C	140	Make puppet talk	___	___	___	___
	32	*Rattle*				
C	141	Roll rattle	___	___	___	___
C	142	Shake rattle	___	___	___	___
C	143	Shake rattle to musical beat	___	___	___	___
C	144	Hit object with rattle	___	___	___	___
	33	*Rings and pole*				
C	145	Take rings off pole	___	___	___	___

Age level*	Leisure skills category	Level of trainer assistance required (check one)			
		Self-initiates	Verbal cue	Verbal cue and model	Verbal cue and physical assistance
C	146 Identify ring sizes (largest, next largest, etc.)	_____	_____	_____	_____
C	147 Identify ring colors	_____	_____	_____	_____
C	148 Pick up rings	_____	_____	_____	_____
C	149 Stack rings on pole	_____	_____	_____	_____
	34 *Rocking horse*				
C	150 Pet rocking horse	_____	_____	_____	_____
C	151 Mount rocking horse	_____	_____	_____	_____
C	152 Ride rocking horse	_____	_____	_____	_____
C	153 Dismount rocking horse	_____	_____	_____	_____
	35 *Scissors*				
C/A	154 Open and close scissors (cutting movement)	_____	_____	_____	_____
C/A	155 Cut paper on straight line	_____	_____	_____	_____
C/A	156 Cut out shape	_____	_____	_____	_____
C/A	157 Cut out picture	_____	_____	_____	_____
C/A	158 Cut shape out of folded paper	_____	_____	_____	_____
C/A	159 Hand scissors to other person	_____	_____	_____	_____
	36 *Silly Putty*				
C	160 Remove Silly Putty from plastic egg	_____	_____	_____	_____
C	161 Stretch Silly Putty	_____	_____	_____	_____
C	162 Roll Silly Putty	_____	_____	_____	_____
C	163 Make ball with Silly Putty	_____	_____	_____	_____
C	164 Make Silly Putty snake	_____	_____	_____	_____
C	165 Put imprint onto Silly Putty	_____	_____	_____	_____
	37 *Slinky*				
C	166 Stretch Slinky	_____	_____	_____	_____
C	167 Bounce Slinky	_____	_____	_____	_____
C	168 Walk Slinky down steps	_____	_____	_____	_____
C	169 Pull animal Slinky	_____	_____	_____	_____
	38 *Space Candy*				
C	170 Open Space Candy wrapper	_____	_____	_____	_____
C	171 Place Space Candy in mouth	_____	_____	_____	_____
C	172 Listen to Space Candy	_____	_____	_____	_____
C	173 Dispose of Space Candy wrapper	_____	_____	_____	_____

Age level*	Leisure skill category	Level of trainer assistance required (check one)			
		Self-initiates	Verbal cue	Verbal cue and model	Verbal cue and physical assistance
	39 *Talking doll (string toy)*				
C	174 Pull string on talking doll	_____	_____	_____	_____
C	175 Comb doll's hair	_____	_____	_____	_____
C	176 Feed doll	_____	_____	_____	_____
C	177 Put dress on doll	_____	_____	_____	_____
C	178 Take dress off doll	_____	_____	_____	_____
	40 *Telephone*				
C/A	179 Answer telephone	_____	_____	_____	_____
A	180 Deposit money in pay telephone	_____	_____	_____	_____
C/A	181 Dial phone number	_____	_____	_____	_____
C/A	182 Talk on telephone	_____	_____	_____	_____
	41 *Toy boat*				
C	183 Float toy boat	_____	_____	_____	_____
C	184 Hold toy boat under water	_____	_____	_____	_____
C	185 Pull toy boat around water on string	_____	_____	_____	_____
C	186 Make waves around toy boat	_____	_____	_____	_____
	42 *Toy box*				
C	187 Open toy box	_____	_____	_____	_____
C	188 Pull toy out of toy box	_____	_____	_____	_____
C	189 Place toy into toy box	_____	_____	_____	_____
C	190 Shut toy box	_____	_____	_____	_____
	43 *Vending machine*				
A	191 Locate vending machine	_____	_____	_____	_____
A	192 Select Item	_____	_____	_____	_____
A	193 Place coin in machine and pull lever	_____	_____	_____	_____
A	194 Consume item	_____	_____	_____	_____
	44 *Wagon*				
C	195 Pull wagon	_____	_____	_____	_____
C	196 Push wagon	_____	_____	_____	_____
C	197 Sit in wagon	_____	_____	_____	_____
C	198 Get out of wagon	_____	_____	_____	_____
	45 *Xylophone*				
C	199 Hold mallet	_____	_____	_____	_____
C	200 Play xylophone with mallet	_____	_____	_____	_____
C	201 Play xylophone to beat	_____	_____	_____	_____
C	202 Hit designated colored key with mallet	_____	_____	_____	_____

Age level*		Leisure skill category	Level of trainer assistance required (check one)			
			Self-initiates	Verbal cue	Verbal cue and model	Verbal cue and physical assistance
	46	*Yo yo*				
C		203 Put yo yo string on finger	_____	_____	_____	_____
C		204 Flick yo yo down	_____	_____	_____	_____
C		205 Pull up yo yo and catch it	_____	_____	_____	_____
C		206 Wind yo yo	_____	_____	_____	_____
C		207 Tie string onto yo yo	_____	_____	_____	_____
	II	*GAMES*				
	1	*Board and Table*				
C/A		1 Bingo	_____	_____	_____	_____
C		2 Blockhead	_____	_____	_____	_____
C		3 Break the Camel's Back	_____	_____	_____	_____
C		4 Candyland	_____	_____	_____	_____
C/A		5 Checkers	_____	_____	_____	_____
C/A		6 Chinese Checkers	_____	_____	_____	_____
C		7 Color Forms	_____	_____	_____	_____
C		8 Cootey Bug	_____	_____	_____	_____
C/A		9 Crossword puzzle	_____	_____	_____	_____
C/A		10 Darts	_____	_____	_____	_____
C/A		11 Dominoes	_____	_____	_____	_____
C/A		12 Foosball	_____	_____	_____	_____
C		13 Gingerbread Man	_____	_____	_____	_____
C		14 Goldilocks and the Three Bears	_____	_____	_____	_____
C		15 Hi-Ho Cherry-O	_____	_____	_____	_____
C		16 Jacks	_____	_____	_____	_____
C		17 Jigsaw puzzle	_____	_____	_____	_____
C		18 Lotto	_____	_____	_____	_____
C		19 Marbles	_____	_____	_____	_____
C		20 Pegboard and pegs	_____	_____	_____	_____
C/A		21 Pick-Up Sticks	_____	_____	_____	_____
C/A		22 Ping-Pong	_____	_____	_____	_____
C/A		23 Pinball	_____	_____	_____	_____
C/A		24 Pool	_____	_____	_____	_____
C/A		25 Scrabble	_____	_____	_____	_____
C/A		26 Spill and Spell	_____	_____	_____	_____
C/A		27 Tic-Tac-Toe	_____	_____	_____	_____
C		28 Tidley Winks	_____	_____	_____	_____
	2	*Motor*				
C/A		29 Arm wrestle	_____	_____	_____	_____
C		30 Boob Tube	_____	_____	_____	_____
C		31 British Bulldog	_____	_____	_____	_____
C		32 Capture the Flag	_____	_____	_____	_____

Age level*		Leisure skill category	Level of trainer assistance required (check one)			
			Self-initiates	Verbal cue	Verbal cue and model	Verbal cue and physical assistance
C/A	33	Charades	_____	_____	_____	_____
C	34	Church/Steeple/People Game	_____	_____	_____	_____
C	35	Dodge Ball	_____	_____	_____	_____
C	36	Duck Duck Goose	_____	_____	_____	_____
C/A	37	Finger (thumb) wrestling	_____	_____	_____	_____
C	38	Follow the Leader	_____	_____	_____	_____
C	39	Hand Slap	_____	_____	_____	_____
C	40	Hopscotch	_____	_____	_____	_____
C/A	41	Jump rope	_____	_____	_____	_____
C	42	Kickball	_____	_____	_____	_____
C	43	Monkey in the Middle	_____	_____	_____	_____
C	44	Mother, May I	_____	_____	_____	_____
C	45	Paper, Stone, Scissors	_____	_____	_____	_____
C	46	Parachute Play	_____	_____	_____	_____
C	47	Red Light/Green Light	_____	_____	_____	_____
C	48	Red Rover	_____	_____	_____	_____
C/A	49	Relay race	_____	_____	_____	_____
C/A	50	Sack race	_____	_____	_____	_____
C	51	Scavenger hunt	_____	_____	_____	_____
C	52	Simon Says	_____	_____	_____	_____
C	53	Spud	_____	_____	_____	_____
C	54	Steal the Bacon	_____	_____	_____	_____
C	55	Tag	_____	_____	_____	_____
C/A	56	Tetherball	_____	_____	_____	_____
C	57	Three-legged race	_____	_____	_____	_____
C/A	58	Tug-of-war	_____	_____	_____	_____
C	59	Twister	_____	_____	_____	_____
	2	*Musical/Rhythmical*				
C	60	Bamboo Sticks	_____	_____	_____	_____
C	61	Bear Hunt	_____	_____	_____	_____
C	62	Bingo Was His Name, Sir	_____	_____	_____	_____
C	63	Did You Ever See A Lassie?	_____	_____	_____	_____
C	64	Farmer in the Dell	_____	_____	_____	_____
C/A	65	Hokey Pokey	_____	_____	_____	_____
C/A	66	Home Rhythm Band	_____	_____	_____	_____
C	67	Hot Potato	_____	_____	_____	_____
C	68	I'm a Little Teapot	_____	_____	_____	_____
C	69	Itsy Bitsy Spider	_____	_____	_____	_____
C/A	70	Limbo	_____	_____	_____	_____
C	71	Little Sally Ann	_____	_____	_____	_____
C	72	London Bridge	_____	_____	_____	_____
C	73	Mulberry Bush	_____	_____	_____	_____
C	74	Musical Chairs	_____	_____	_____	_____

Age level*		Leisure skill category	Level of trainer assistance required (check one)			
			Self-initiates	Verbal cue	Verbal cue and model	Verbal cue and physical assistance
C	75	Musical Statues	____	____	____	____
C	76	My Mother was a Baker	____	____	____	____
C/A	77	Name that Tune	____	____	____	____
C	78	One-Two-Three O-Leary	____	____	____	____
C	79	Patty Cake	____	____	____	____
C	80	Ring Around the Rosie	____	____	____	____
C	81	Row, Row, Row Your Boat	____	____	____	____
C	82	She'll Be Coming Around the Mountain	____	____	____	____
C	83	Three Sailors	____	____	____	____
	4	*Card*				
C/A	84	Mix cards	____	____	____	____
C/A	85	Deal cards	____	____	____	____
C/A	86	Hold cards in hand	____	____	____	____
C/A	87	Arrange cards in hand	____	____	____	____
C/A	88	Taking turns	____	____	____	____
C/A	89	Draw a card	____	____	____	____
C/A	90	Play a card	____	____	____	____
C/A	91	Identify colors	____	____	____	____
C/A	92	Identify suits	____	____	____	____
C/A	93	Identify numbers	____	____	____	____
C/A	94	Identify winning hand	____	____	____	____
C/A	95	Concentration	____	____	____	____
C/A	96	I Doubt It	____	____	____	____
C/A	97	Old Maid	____	____	____	____
C/A	98	Slap Jack	____	____	____	____
C/A	99	War	____	____	____	____
	III	**HOBBIES**				
	1	*Books and magazines*				
C/A	1	Take book/magazine off shelf	____	____	____	____
C/A	2	Turn pages in magazine	____	____	____	____
C/A	3	Find seat in library	____	____	____	____
C/A	4	Check out book/ magazine	____	____	____	____
C/A	5	Acquire library card	____	____	____	____
	7	*Leatherwork*				
C/A	46	Cut leather	____	____	____	____
C/A	47	Lace leather	____	____	____	____
C/A	48	Stamp leather	____	____	____	____

Age level*		Leisure skill category	Self-initiates	Verbal cue	Verbal cue and model	Verbal cue and physical assistance
C/A	49	Punch holes in leather	___	___	___	___
C/A	50	Stain leather	___	___	___	___
C/A	51	Wax leather	___	___	___	___
	8	*Leisure walking*				
C/A	52	Wave to neighbor	___	___	___	___
C/A	53	Cross the street	___	___	___	___
C/A	54	Walk simple route	___	___	___	___
C/A	55	Use umbrella	___	___	___	___
C/A	56	Put on walking shoes	___	___	___	___
C/A	57	Buy ice cream from ice cream truck	___	___	___	___
	9	*Musical/rhythmical instruments*				
C/A	58	Hold guitar	___	___	___	___
C/A	59	Strum guitar	___	___	___	___
C/A	60	Pluck guitar	___	___	___	___
C/A	61	Strum guitar to beat	___	___	___	___
C/A	62	Play simple chord on guitar	___	___	___	___
C/A	63	Combine two simple chords to play guitar	___	___	___	___
C/A	64	Shake maraca (rattle) to beat	___	___	___	___
C/A	65	Hit metal object (cow bell, can) with stick	___	___	___	___
C/A	66	Shake bell to beat	___	___	___	___
C/A	67	Use tamborine	___	___	___	___
	10	*Nature*				
C/A	68	Walk through woods	___	___	___	___
C/A	69	Collect rocks	___	___	___	___
C/A	70	Collect leaves/flowers	___	___	___	___
C/A	71	Press leaves/flowers	___	___	___	___
C/A	72	Look through binoculars	___	___	___	___
C/A	73	Catch butterfly	___	___	___	___
C/A	74	Rake leaves	___	___	___	___
C/A	75	Collect seashells	___	___	___	___
C/A	76	Skip stone into water	___	___	___	___
C/A	77	Identify plant/tree (smell, touch)	___	___	___	___
	11	*Needlework*				
C/A	78	Hold needle	___	___	___	___
C/A	79	Thread needle	___	___	___	___
C/A	80	Cut thread	___	___	___	___

Level of trainer assistance required (check one)

Age level*		Leisure skill category	Self-initiates	Verbal cue	Verbal cue and model	Verbal cue and physical assistance
		Level of trainer assistance required (check one)				
C/A	81	Tie knot at end of thread	___	___	___	___
C/A	82	Push and pull needle through material	___	___	___	___
C/A	83	Weave thread over and under yarn	___	___	___	___
C/A	83	Make hook rug	___	___	___	___
C/A	85	Connect dots, needle, and yarn pattern	___	___	___	___
C/A	86	Make pot holder	___	___	___	___
C/A	87	Operate sewing machine	___	___	___	___
	12	*Painting*				
C/A	88	Prepare paint area	___	___	___	___
C/A	89	Finger-paint	___	___	___	___
C/A	90	Use waterpaint	___	___	___	___
C/A	91	Paint by number	___	___	___	___
C/A	92	Paint egg/rock	___	___	___	___
C/A	93	Tie-dye sheet	___	___	___	___
C/A	94	Paint fence	___	___	___	___
C/A	95	Wash and clean brush	___	___	___	___
C/A	96	Clean paint area	___	___	___	___
	13	*Paper art*				
C/A	97	Fold and cut paper	___	___	___	___
C/A	98	Color paper	___	___	___	___
C/A	99	Rub paper over object	___	___	___	___
C/A	100	Cut paper	___	___	___	___
C/A	101	Make paper airplane	___	___	___	___
C/A	102	Glue paper together	___	___	___	___
C/A	103	Do decoupage (tissue paper bottle)	___	___	___	___
C/A	104	Make mask	___	___	___	___
	14	*Pet care*				
C/A	105	Walk dog on leash	___	___	___	___
C/A	106	Put collar and leash on dog	___	___	___	___
C/A	107	Pet dog	___	___	___	___
C/A	108	Brush dog	___	___	___	___
C/A	109	Feed dog	___	___	___	___
C/A	110	Use of "pooper-scooper"	___	___	___	___
C/A	111	Feed goldfish/turtle	___	___	___	___
C/A	112	Feed hamster	___	___	___	___
C/A	113	Clean hamster cage	___	___	___	___
C/A	114	Take hamster out of cage	___	___	___	___
C/A	115	Pet hamster	___	___	___	___

Age level*		Leisure skill category	Level of trainer assistance required (check one)			
			Self-initiates	Verbal cue	Verbal cue and model	Verbal cue and physical assistance
	15	*Photography*				
C/A		116 Load film in camera				
C/A		117 Look through camera				
C/A		118 Press button on camera				
C/A		119 Wind camera				
C/A		120 Position object/person to take picture				
C/A		121 Use pinhole camera				
C/A		122 Make photograph album				
C/A		123 Use viewmaster				
	16	*Plant care*				
C/A		124 Put dirt in pot				
C/A		125 Plant seed				
C/A		126 Water and mist plant				
C/A		127 Position plant in sun				
C/A		128 Root plant				
C/A		129 Trim plant				
C/A		130 Put plant hanger on and hang plant				
C/A		131 Pick flowers				
C/A		132 Arrange flowers in vase				
	17	*Sculpture: clay work*				
C/A		133 Pound (wedge) clay				
C/A		134 Roll clay into ball				
C/A		135 Roll clay into cylindrical shape				
C/A		136 Stretch clay				
C/A		137 Paint clay				
C/A		138 Combine clay shapes to make figure				
C/A		139 Make clay ashtray				
	18	*Sculpture: paper-mache*				
C/A		140 Make paper-mache				
C/A		141 Make paper-mache hand print				
C/A		142 Make paper-mache boat				
C/A		143 Make paper-mache mask				
C/A		144 Paint paper-mache				
	19	*Sculpture: pipe cleaners*				
C/A		145 Bend pipe cleaner				
C/A		146 Join two pipe cleaners together				

Age level*		Leisure skill category	Level of trainer assistance required (check one)			
			Self-initiates	Verbal cue	Verbal cue and model	Verbal cue and physical assistance
C/A	147	Make pipe cleaner square	_____	_____	_____	_____
C/A	148	Make animal shape	_____	_____	_____	_____
C/A	149	Make pipe cleaner hanging mobile	_____	_____	_____	_____
C/A	150	Make three-dimensional box	_____	_____	_____	_____
C/A	151	Outline picture	_____	_____	_____	_____
C/A	152	Make pipe cleaner picture	_____	_____	_____	_____
C/A	153	Make pipe cleaner necklace	_____	_____	_____	_____
20		*Skateboarding*				
C/A	154	Sit backwards on board and skate	_____	_____	_____	_____
C/A	155	Lie on backside on board and skate	_____	_____	_____	_____
C/A	156	Lie on stomach on board and pull with hands	_____	_____	_____	_____
C/A	157	Stand on board and skate	_____	_____	_____	_____
21		*Spectator leisure/community events*				
C/A	158	Purchase ticket	_____	_____	_____	_____
C/A	159	Hand ticket to doorman	_____	_____	_____	_____
C/A	160	Locate seat	_____	_____	_____	_____
C/A	161	Buy refreshment from vendor	_____	_____	_____	_____
C/A	162	Use vending machine	_____	_____	_____	_____
C/A	163	Go to restroom	_____	_____	_____	_____
C/A	164	Attend event	_____	_____	_____	_____
C/A	165	Leave facility	_____	_____	_____	_____
C/A	166	Attend church	_____	_____	_____	_____
C/A	167	Go to movie theatre	_____	_____	_____	_____
C/A	168	Attend social dance	_____	_____	_____	_____
C/A	169	Go to ball park	_____	_____	_____	_____
22		*Spectator leisure/home*				
C/A	170	Use radio	_____	_____	_____	_____
C/A	171	Use record player	_____	_____	_____	_____
C/A	172	Use headphones	_____	_____	_____	_____
C/A	173	Select record	_____	_____	_____	_____
C/A	174	Use television	_____	_____	_____	_____
C/A	175	Use viewfinder	_____	_____	_____	_____
23		*String art*				
C/A	176	Tie knot in string	_____	_____	_____	_____

Age level*		Leisure skill category	Level of trainer assistance required (check one)			
			Self-initiates	Verbal cue	Verbal cue and model	Verbal cue and physical assistance
C/A	177	Braid string	_____	_____	_____	_____
C/A	178	Cut string	_____	_____	_____	_____
C/A	179	Hook string	_____	_____	_____	_____
C/A	180	Glue string onto object	_____	_____	_____	_____
C/A	181	Wrap string around box	_____	_____	_____	_____
C/A	182	Make string design on cardboard	_____	_____	_____	_____
	24	*Sunbathing*				
C/A	183	Put on bathing suit	_____	_____	_____	_____
C/A	184	Put on suntan lotion	_____	_____	_____	_____
C/A	185	Put on sunglasses	_____	_____	_____	_____
C/A	186	Lie on beach blanket	_____	_____	_____	_____
C/A	187	Lie on lounge chair	_____	_____	_____	_____
	25	*Table game hobbies*				
C/A	188	Place coin in machine	_____	_____	_____	_____
C/A	189	Operate machine	_____	_____	_____	_____
C/A	190	Take turns during game	_____	_____	_____	_____
C/A	191	Demonstrate knowledge of game completion	_____	_____	_____	_____
C/A	192	Play Foosball game	_____	_____	_____	_____
C/A	193	Play pinball	_____	_____	_____	_____
C/A	194	Play electric bowling game	_____	_____	_____	_____
C/A	195	Play pool	_____	_____	_____	_____
	26	*Woodwork*				
A	196	Chop wood	_____	_____	_____	_____
C/A	197	Sand wood	_____	_____	_____	_____
C/A	198	Measure wood	_____	_____	_____	_____
A	199	Saw wood	_____	_____	_____	_____
C/A	200	Whittle wood	_____	_____	_____	_____
C/A	201	Soap carving	_____	_____	_____	_____
A	202	Nail two pieces of wood together	_____	_____	_____	_____
A	203	Build five-sided cube	_____	_____	_____	_____
C/A	204	Make Popsicle stick building	_____	_____	_____	_____
	IV	Sports				
	1	*Badminton*				
C/A	1	Hold racket	_____	_____	_____	_____
C/A	2	Underhand shot	_____	_____	_____	_____

Age level*	Leisure skill category	Level of trainer assistance required (check one)			
		Self-initiates	Verbal cue	Verbal cue and model	Verbal cue and physical assistance
C/A	3 Overhand shot	_____	_____	_____	_____
C/A	4 Backhand shot	_____	_____	_____	_____
C/A	5 Serve	_____	_____	_____	_____
	2 Basketball				
C/A	6 Pass basketball	_____	_____	_____	_____
C/A	7 Catch basketball	_____	_____	_____	_____
C/A	8 Shoot basketball	_____	_____	_____	_____
C/A	9 Dribble basketball	_____	_____	_____	_____
C/A	10 Rebound basketball	_____	_____	_____	_____
	3 Bowling				
C/A	11 Select bowling ball	_____	_____	_____	_____
C/A	12 Pick up ball from ball return	_____	_____	_____	_____
C/A	13 Approach foul line	_____	_____	_____	_____
C/A	14 Roll ball down alley	_____	_____	_____	_____
C	15 Reposition pins (if toy set is used)	_____	_____	_____	_____
	4 Croquet				
C/A	16 Remove ball and mallet from rack	_____	_____	_____	_____
C/A	17 Place croquet ball in starting position	_____	_____	_____	_____
C/A	18 Serve ball	_____	_____	_____	_____
C/A	19 Hit ball to next wicket	_____	_____	_____	_____
C/A	20 Drive other player's ball	_____	_____	_____	_____
	5 Field hockey				
C/A	21 Hold hockey stick	_____	_____	_____	_____
C/A	22 Hit ball into goal	_____	_____	_____	_____
C/A	23 Pass ball to teammate	_____	_____	_____	_____
C/A	24 Stop ball	_____	_____	_____	_____
C/A	25 Run with hockey stick	_____	_____	_____	_____
C/A	26 Dribble ball with hockey stick	_____	_____	_____	_____
	6 Fishing				
C/A	27 Dig for earthworms	_____	_____	_____	_____
C/A	28 Pull worm out of pile of dirt	_____	_____	_____	_____
C/A	29 Bait hook	_____	_____	_____	_____
C/A	30 Cast baited fishing line	_____	_____	_____	_____
C/A	31 Wait for fish to bite	_____	_____	_____	_____

Age level*	Leisure skill category	Level of trainer assistance required (check one)			
		Self-initiates	Verbal cue	Verbal cue and model	Verbal cue and physical assistance
C/A	32 Pull in fish	_____	_____	_____	_____
C/A	33 Take fish off hook	_____	_____	_____	_____
	7 *Football*				
C/A	34 Underhand pass	_____	_____	_____	_____
C/A	35 Overhand pass	_____	_____	_____	_____
C/A	36 Catch football	_____	_____	_____	_____
C/A	37 Run with football	_____	_____	_____	_____
C/A	38 Tag opponent	_____	_____	_____	_____
C/A	39 Kick football	_____	_____	_____	_____
	8 *Golf*				
C/A	40 Place ball on ground	_____	_____	_____	_____
C/A	41 Hold golf club	_____	_____	_____	_____
C/A	42 Swing golf club	_____	_____	_____	_____
C/A	43 Putt golf ball	_____	_____	_____	_____
C/A	44 Drive golf ball	_____	_____	_____	_____
C/A	45 Follow through	_____	_____	_____	_____
	9 *Gymnastics: balancing*				
C/A	46 Balance on balance board	_____	_____	_____	_____
C/A	47 Walk balance beam	_____	_____	_____	_____
C/A	48 Walk sideways on balance beam	_____	_____	_____	_____
C/A	49 Walk backwards on balance beam	_____	_____	_____	_____
C/A	50 Form pyramid	_____	_____	_____	_____
	10 *Gymnastics: tumbling*				
C/A	51 Forward roll	_____	_____	_____	_____
C/A	52 Backward roll	_____	_____	_____	_____
C/A	53 Cartwheel	_____	_____	_____	_____
C/A	54 Tripod	_____	_____	_____	_____
C/A	55 Head stand	_____	_____	_____	_____
	11 *Handball*				
C/A	56 Put on glove	_____	_____	_____	_____
C/A	57 Bounce ball	_____	_____	_____	_____
C/A	58 Serve ball	_____	_____	_____	_____
C/A	59 Run toward ball	_____	_____	_____	_____
C/A	60 Hit ball against wall	_____	_____	_____	_____
	12 *Horseshoes*				
C/A	61 Select horseshoes and walk to stake	_____	_____	_____	_____

Age level*	Leisure skill category	Level of trainer assistance required (check one)			
		Self-initiates	Verbal cue	Verbal cue and model	Verbal cue and physical assistance
C/A	62 Grasp horseshoe	_____	_____	_____	_____
C/A	63 Throw horseshoes	_____	_____	_____	_____
C/A	64 Pick up horseshoes surrounding stake	_____	_____	_____	_____
	13 *Playground equipment*				
C/A	65 Seesaw play	_____	_____	_____	_____
C/A	66 Sliding board play	_____	_____	_____	_____
C/A	67 Swing play	_____	_____	_____	_____
C/A	68 Twirl-a-round play	_____	_____	_____	_____
C/A	69 Monkey bars play	_____	_____	_____	_____
	14 *Shuffleboard*				
C/A	70 Hold shuffleboard stick	_____	_____	_____	_____
C/A	71 Line up discs	_____	_____	_____	_____
C/A	72 Shoot discs	_____	_____	_____	_____
C/A	73 Shoot four discs alternating with opponent	_____	_____	_____	_____
	15 *Soccer*				
C/A	74 Pass soccer ball	_____	_____	_____	_____
C/A	75 Stop soccer ball	_____	_____	_____	_____
C/A	76 Dribble soccer ball	_____	_____	_____	_____
C/A	77 Kick soccer ball into goal	_____	_____	_____	_____
C/A	78 Goal keeper makes save	_____	_____	_____	_____
C/A	79 Make overhead throw	_____	_____	_____	_____
	16 *Softball*				
C/A	80 Throw underhand	_____	_____	_____	_____
C/A	81 Throw overhand	_____	_____	_____	_____
C/A	82 Catch ball	_____	_____	_____	_____
C/A	83 Swing bat	_____	_____	_____	_____
C/A	84 Hit ball	_____	_____	_____	_____
C/A	85 Run to base	_____	_____	_____	_____
	17 *Swimming*				
C/A	86 Enter swimming pool	_____	_____	_____	_____
C/A	87 Adjust to water	_____	_____	_____	_____
C/A	88 Walk through water	_____	_____	_____	_____
C/A	89 Breath control	_____	_____	_____	_____
C/A	90 Back float	_____	_____	_____	_____
C/A	91 Back float with kick	_____	_____	_____	_____
C/A	92 Backstroke	_____	_____	_____	_____
C/A	93 Prone float	_____	_____	_____	_____
C/A	94 Prone glide with kick	_____	_____	_____	_____
C/A	95 Rotary breathing	_____	_____	_____	_____

Age level*	Leisure skill category	Level of trainer assistance required (check one)			
		Self-initiates	Verbal cue	Verbal cue and model	Verbal cue and physical assistance
C/A	96 Crawl stroke	_____	_____	_____	_____
	18 *Tennis*				
C/A	97 Hold racket	_____	_____	_____	_____
C/A	98 Dribble ball with racket	_____	_____	_____	_____
C/A	99 Forehand shot	_____	_____	_____	_____
C/A	100 Backhand shot	_____	_____	_____	_____
C/A	101 Serve	_____	_____	_____	_____
	19 *Track and field: jogging*				
C/A	102 Bend leg	_____	_____	_____	_____
C/A	103 Foot placement	_____	_____	_____	_____
C/A	104 Heel-toe placement	_____	_____	_____	_____
C/A	105 Arm-leg rotation	_____	_____	_____	_____
C/A	106 Stop running	_____	_____	_____	_____
	20 *Track and field: softball throw*				
C/A	107 Hold softball	_____	_____	_____	_____
C/A	108 Overhand arm motion	_____	_____	_____	_____
C/A	109 Weight transfer	_____	_____	_____	_____
C/A	110 Hip rotation	_____	_____	_____	_____
C/A	111 Follow through	_____	_____	_____	_____
	21 *Volleyball*				
C/A	112 Underhand serve	_____	_____	_____	_____
C/A	113 Return ball over net	_____	_____	_____	_____
C/A	114 Pass ball to teammate	_____	_____	_____	_____
C/A	115 Rotation	_____	_____	_____	_____
C/A	116 Overhead spike	_____	_____	_____	_____
	22 *Weight training*				
C/A	117 Put weights on dumbell	_____	_____	_____	_____
C/A	118 Identify amount of weight	_____	_____	_____	_____
C/A	119 Underhand grip and lift	_____	_____	_____	_____
C/A	120 Curl	_____	_____	_____	_____
C/A	121 Lift weight over head	_____	_____	_____	_____
C/A	122 Benchpress	_____	_____	_____	_____
	23 *Winter sports*				
C/A	123 Put on gloves	_____	_____	_____	_____
C/A	124 Make snowball	_____	_____	_____	_____
C/A	125 Throw snowball	_____	_____	_____	_____
C	126 Build snowman	_____	_____	_____	_____
C	127 Decorate snowman	_____	_____	_____	_____
C/A	128 Sledding	_____	_____	_____	_____
C/A	129 Pull sled up hill	_____	_____	_____	_____

Acknowledgments

Permission to reprint the following copyrighted materials in this book is gratefully acknowledged:

Quotes on page 6 are reprinted from pp. 122, 125, 126 of "The End of the Quiet Revolution: The Education for All Handicapped Children Act of 1975." *Exceptional Children,* 1977, *44*(5), by A. Abeson and J. Zettel, with the permission of the Council for Exceptional Children. Copyright 1977 by the Council for Exceptional Children, Reston,Virginia.

Quotes on page 7 are reprinted from pp. 290, 291 of *Mental Retardation in School and Society,* by D. L. MacMillan. Copyright 1977 by Little, Brown, Inc. Used with permission of Little, Brown, Inc.

Figure 1-1 on page 9 is adapted from "Special Education as a Developmental Capital." *Exceptional Children,* 1970, 37, 229–237, by E. Deno, with permission from the Council for Exceptional Children. Copyright 1974 by the Council for Exceptional Children, Reston, Virginia.

Figure 1-2 on page 11, Table 1-1 on page 12, Table 2-1 on page 28, Table 2-2 on pages 29 and 30, and Table 2-3 on page 31 are reprinted from *Educating Exceptional Pupils: An Introduction to Contemporary Practices,* by K. A. Blake. In press by Addison-Wesley. Used with the permission of Addison-Wesley.

Table 2-6 on page 37 is reprinted from p. 7 of *Assessment in Special and Remedial Education,* by J. Salvia and J. Ysseldyke. Copyright 1978 by Houghton, Mifflin, Inc. Used with the permission of Houghton, Mifflin, Inc.

Quote on page 55 is reprinted from p. 8 of *Hey Don't Forget about Me: Education's investment in the Severely, Profoundly, and Multiply Handicapped,* by L. Brown, J. Nietupski and S. Hamre-Nietupski with the permission of the Council for Exceptional Children. Copyright 1977 by Council for Exceptional Children, Reston, Virginia.

Quote on page 58 is reprinted from pp. 174–177 of *Teaching the Retarded*, by K. A. Blake. Copyright 1974 by Prentice-Hall, Inc. Used with the permission of Prentice-Hall, Inc.

Quote on page 60 is reprinted from p. 221 of "Selected Considerations in Developing Curriculum for Severely Handicapped Students," by W. W. Williams and E. Gotts. In *Educational Programming for the Severely and Profoundly Handicapped.* Copyright 1977 in the Council for Exceptional Children. Reprinted by permission of the Council for Exceptional Children.

Table 3-3 on pages 64, 65, and 66 is abbreviated from pp. 124–126 of "Teaching Severely Handicapped Students to Ride a Bus," by N. Certo, R. Schwartz, and L. Brown. In N. Haring and L. Brown (eds.), *Teaching the Severely Handicapped* (vol. II). Copyright 1976 by Grune and Stratton, Inc. Used with the permission of Grune and Stratton, Inc.

Figure 3-2 on page 67 is reprinted from p. 46 of "Evaluation of Training Procedures Used in a Parent-Implemented Intervention Program for Down's Syndrome Infants." *AAESPH American Association for the Education of Severely Profoundly Handicapped.* Review, 1976, *1*(4), by M. Hanson, with the permission of AAESPH. Copyright 1976 by AAESPH, Seattle, Washington.

Quote on page 70 is reprinted from p. 34 of "Procedures of Task Analysis As Related to Developing Instructional Programs for Severely Handicapped Students," by W. W. Williams. In L. Brown, T. Crowner, W. Williams, and R. York (eds.), *Madison's Alternative for Zero Exclusion* (vol. V). Copyright 1975 by Madison Public Schools. Used with the permission of Madison Public Schools, Madison, Wisconsin.

Quote on page 79 is reprinted from *Vocational Curriculum for Developmentally Disabled Persons,* by P. Wehman and P. J. McLaughlin. Copyright 1980 by University Park Press. Used with the permission of University Park Pess.

Figure 4-1 on page 87 is reprinted from p. 253 of *Teaching the Retarded*, by K. A. Blake. Copyright 1974 by Prentice-Hall, Inc. Used with the permission of Prentice-Hall, Inc.

Quote on page 89 and 90 is reprinted from p. 377 of *The Mentally Retarded: An Educational Psychology,* by K. A. Blake. Copyright 1976 by Prentice-Hall, Inc. Used with the permission of Prentice-Hall, Inc.

Quote on page 91 is reprinted from p. 254 of *Teaching the Retarded*, by K. A. Blake. Copyright 1974 by Prentice-Hall, Inc. Used with the permission of Prentice-Hall, Inc.

Quotes on page 94 are reprinted from *The Mentally Retarded: An Educational Psychology,* by K. A. Blake. Copyrighted 1976 by Prentice-Hall, Inc. Used with the permission of Prentice-Hall, Inc.

Figure 4-3 on page 95, quote on page 103, and Table 5-1 on page 105 are reprinted from *Teaching the Retarded*, by K. A. Blake. Copyright 1974 by Prentice-Hall, Inc. Used with the permission of Prentice-Hall, Inc.

Table 5-2 on page 105–106 is reprinted from pp. 198–199 of "Cognitive Development," by P. J. McLaughlin, R. Eaves, and N. Fallen. In N. Fallen (ed.), *Young Children with Special Needs.* Copyright 1978 by Charles Merrill, Inc. Reprinted by permission from Charles Merrill, Inc.

Table 5-3 on page 107 is reprinted from *Teaching the Retarded*, K. A. Blake. Copyright 1974 by Prentice-Hall, Inc. Used with the permission of Prentice-Hall, Inc.

Figure 5-1 on page 109 and Figure 5-2 on page 110 is reprinted from pp. 201–202 of "Cognitive Development," by P. J. McLaughlin, R. Eaves, and N. Fallen. In N. Fallen (ed.), *Young Children with Special Needs.* Copyright 1978 by Charles Merrill, Inc. Reprinted by permission from Charles Merrill, Inc.

Figure 5-3 on page 112 and Figure 5-4 on page 113 is reprinted from pp 218–220 of *Teaching the Retarded*, by K. A. Blake. Copyright 1974 by Prentice-Hall, Inc. Reprinted by permission from Prentice-Hall, Inc.

Figure 5-5 on page 114, Figure 5-6 on page 116, and Figure 5-7 on page 117 are reprinted from pages 208–210 of "Cognitive Development," by P. J. McLaughlin, R. Eaves, and N. Fallen. In N. Fallen (ed.), *Young Children with Special Needs.* Copyright 1978 by Charles Merrill, Inc. Reprinted by permission from Charles Merrill, Inc.

Table 5-4 on page 118, Table 5-5 on page 119, quotes on pages 120 and 122, Figure 5-8 on page 123, Table 5-6 quote on page 124, Table 5-7 on page 125, quote on page 126, Table 5-8 on page 127, quote on pages 127, 128, 129, and 130 are reprinted from *Teaching the Retarded,* by K. A. Blake. Copyright 1974 by Prentice-Hall, Inc. Used with the permission of Prentice-Hall, Inc.

Quote on page 139 is reprinted from *Behavior Modification in Applied Settings,* by A. E. Kazdin. Copyright 1975 by Dorsey, Inc. Used with the permission of Dorsey, Inc.

Table 7-1 on page 168 is reprinted from pp. 449–464 of "An Analysis of Daily Report Cards and Parent-managed Privileges in the Improvement of Adolescents' Classroom Performance." *Journal of Applied Behavior Analysis,* 1977, *10,* by J. Schumaker, M. Hovell, and J. Sherman. Copyright 1977 and used with the permission of JOBA.

Quote on page 179 is reprinted from pp. 531–537 of "The Changing Criterion Design." *Journal of Applied Behavior Analysis,* 1977, *9*(4) by D. Hartman and R. V. Hall. Copyright 1977 by and used with the permission of JOBA.

Figure 9-1 on page 224 is reprinted from *The Neuromuscular Maturation of the Human Infant,* by M. B. McGraw. Copyright 1945 by Hafner. Used with the permission of Hafner.

Table 9-2 on page 222 is reprinted from p. 52 of "Cerebral Palsy," by E. E. Bobath and B. Bobath. In P. H. Pearson and C. E. Williams (eds.), *Physical Therapy Services in the Developmental Disabilities.* Copyright 1972 by Charles C Thomas, Publisher. Used with the permission of Charles C Thomas, Publisher.

Figure 9-2 on page 223, Figure 9-3 on page 224, Figure 9-4 on page 225, and Figure 9-5a on page 226 are reprinted from *The Neuromuscular Maturation of the Human Infant,* by M. B. McGraw. Copyright 1945 by Hafner. Used with the permission of Hafner.

Figure 9-5b on page 226 is reprinted from *Handling the Young Cerebral Palsy Child at Home,* by N. Finnie. Copyright 1975 by Dutton, Inc. Used with the permission of Dutton, Inc.

Figure 9-6 on page 226, Figure 9-7 on page 227, Figure 9-8 on page 228, Figure 9-9 on page 230, Figure 9-10, Figure 9-11, Figure 9-12, and Figure 9-13 are reprinted from *The Neuromuscular Maturation of the Human Infant,* by M. B. McGraw. Copyright 1945 by Hafner. Used with the permission of Hafner.

Figures 9-14 and 9-15 on page 236 and Figure 9-16 on page 243 are reprinted from "Physiological Analysis of Basic Motor Skills, 1. Growth and Development of Jumping. *American Journal of Physical Medicine, 40,* by F. A. Hellebrandt, G. L. Rarick, R. Glasson, and M. L. Carns. Copyright 1961 by and used with the permission of Williams and Wilkins.

Figure 9-17 on page 245 is reprinted from "Sequential Levels in Development of Prehension." *American Journal of Occupational Therapy, 28*(10), by R. I. Erhardt. Copyright 1974 by and used with the permission of AJOT.

Figure 9-19 on page 254 is adopted from *Handling the Young Cerebral Palsied Child at Home,* by N. Finnie. Copyright 1975 by Dutton, Inc. Used with the permission of Dutton, Inc.

Quote on page 257 is reprinted from p. 41 of *Sensorimotor Evaluation and Treatment Procedures for Allied Health Personnel,* by S. D. Facker and A. J. Huss. Copyright 1974 by Indiana University Foundation. Used with the permission of Indiana University Foundation, Inc.

Table 9-9 on page 267 is reprinted from "Cerebral Palsy," by E. E. Bobath and B. Bobath. In P. H. Pearson and C. E. Williams (eds.), *Physical Therapy Services in the Developmental Disabilities.* Copyright 1972 by Charles C Thomas, Publisher. Used with the permission of Charles C Thomas, Publisher.

Quote on page 280 and quote on page 282 from *Child Language and Education,* by C. B. Cayden. Copyright 1972 by Holt. Used with the permission of Holt.

Quote on page 283 is reprinted from p. 22 of *Language Handbook,* by J. R. Muma. Copyright 1978 by Prentice-Hall, Inc. Used with the permission of Prentice-Hall, Inc.

Quote on page 284 is reprinted from *Voice Problems of Children,* by K. S. Wilson. Copyright 1972 by Williams and Wilkins. Used with the permission of Williams and Wilkins.

Quote on page 285 is reprinted from *Terminology of Communication Disorders,* by L. Nicolosi, E. Harryman, and J. Kresheck. Copyright 1978 by Williams and Wilkins. Used with the permission of Williams and Wilkins.

Figure 10-1 on page 286 is reprinted from "When are Speech Sounds Learned?" *Journal of Speech and Hearing Disorders, 37,* by E. K. Sanders. Copyright 1972 by and used with permission of ASHA.

Quote on page 287 and quote on page 290 are reprinted from p. 316 of *Speech Correction: Principles and Methods* (6th ed.), by C. Van Riper. Copyright 1978 by Prentice-Hall, Inc. Used with the permission of Prentice-Hall, Inc.

Quote on page 295 is reprinted from p. 170 of "Semantic and Syntactic Development," by M. Bowerman. In R. L. Schiefelbusch, *Bases of Language Intervention.* Copyright 1978 by Little, Brown, Inc. Used with the permission of Little, Brown, Inc.

Quote on page 297 is reprinted from p. 1 of *Sourcebook of Language Learning Activities,* by W. J. Worthley. Copyright 1978 by Little Brown, Inc. Used with the permission of Little, Brown, Inc.

Quote on page 297 is reprinted from p. 13 of "Language Training for the Severely Retarded: Five years of Behavior Analysis." *Exceptional Children, 42*(1), by L. K. Snyder, T. C. Lovitt, and J. O. Smith. Copyright 1975 by and used with the permission of the Council for Exceptional Children, Reston, Virginia.

Quote on page 308 is reprinted from p. 85 of "Cognitive Factors in Early Linguistic Development," by L. B. Leonard. In R. L. Schiefelbusch, *Bases of Language Intervention.* Copyright 1978 by University Park Press. Used with the permission of University Park Press.

List on page 313 is modified from *Language and Learning Disorders of the Pre-academic Child,* by T. E. Bangs. Copyright 1968 by Prentice-Hall. Used with the permission of Prentice-Hall.

Table 11-2 on page 332 and Table 11-3 on page 333 and Table 11-4 on page 334 are reprinted from *Teaching the Retarded,* by K. A. Blake. Copyright 1974 by Prentice-Hall, Inc. Used with the permission of Prentice-Hall, Inc.

Table 11-5 on page 335, quote on page 335, Table 11-6 on page 336, and quote on page 336 are reprinted from *Teaching the Retarded,* by K. A. Blake. Copyright 1974 by Prentice-Hall, Inc. Used with permission of Prentice-Hall, Inc.

Table 11-11 on page 345, Table 11-12 on page 346, Table 11-13 on page 347-348, Table 11-14 on page 349, Table 11-15 on page 350, Table 11-16 on page 351-352, Table 11-17 on page 353, Table 11-18 on page 354-355 are reprinted from *Teaching the Retarded,* by K. A. Blake. Copyright 1974 by Prentice-Hall, Inc. Used with permission of Prentice-Hall, Inc.

Quote on page 378 is reprinted from "The Relationship between Training Activities and Job Placement in Vocational Education of the Severely and Profoundly Handicapped." *AAESPH Review, 2,* by D. Mithaug, L. Hagmeier, and N. Haring. Copyright 1977 by and used with the permission of American Association for the Education of the Severely/Profoundly Handicapped.

Index